ALSO BY TED C. FISHMAN

China, Inc.: How the Rise of the Next Superpower
Challenges America and the World

SHOCK
OF GRAY

THE AGING OF THE WORLD'S POPULATION
AND HOW IT PITS YOUNG AGAINST OLD,
CHILD AGAINST PARENT, WORKER AGAINST BOSS,
COMPANY AGAINST RIVAL,
AND NATION AGAINST NATION

Ted C. Fishman

SCRIBNER
New York   London   Toronto   Sydney   New Delhi

SCRIBNER
A Division of Simon & Schuster, Inc.
1230 Avenue of the Americas
New York, NY 10020

First Scribner trade paperback edition October 2012

SCRIBNER and design are registered trademarks of The Gale Group, Inc., used under
license by Simon & Schuster, Inc., the publisher of this work.

For information about special discounts for bulk purchases, please contact Simon &
Schuster Special Sales at 1-866-506-1949 or business@simonandschuster.com.

The Simon & Schuster Speakers Bureau can bring authors to your live event.
For more information or to book an event contact the Simon & Schuster Speakers Bureau
at 1-866-248-3049 or visit our website at www.simonspeakers.com.

Manufactured in the United States of America

3   5   7   9   10   8   6   4   2

Library of Congress Control Number: 2010029522

ISBN 978-1-4165-5102-7
ISBN 978-1-4165-5103-4 (pbk)
ISBN 978-1-4391-9113-2 (ebook)

To Sara, luminous and illuminating

You Are Old, Father William

"You are old, Father William," the young man said,
"And your hair has become very white;
And yet you incessantly stand on your head—
Do you think, at your age, it is right?"

"In my youth," Father William replied to his son,
"I feared it might injure the brain;
But now that I'm perfectly sure I have none,
Why, I do it again and again."

"You are old," said the youth, "as I mentioned before,
And have grown most uncommonly fat;
Yet you turned a back-somersault in at the door—
Pray, what is the reason of that?"

"In my youth," said the sage, as he shook his grey locks,
"I kept all my limbs very supple
By the use of this ointment—one shilling the box—
Allow me to sell you a couple?"

"You are old," said the youth, "and your jaws are too weak
For anything tougher than suet;
Yet you finished the goose, with the bones and the beak—
Pray, how did you manage to do it?"

"In my youth," said his father, "I took to the law,
And argued each case with my wife;
And the muscular strength, which it gave to my jaw,
Has lasted the rest of my life."

"You are old," said the youth, "one would hardly suppose
That your eye was as steady as ever;
Yet you balanced an eel on the end of your nose—
What made you so awfully clever?"

"I have answered three questions, and that is enough,"
Said his father, "don't give yourself airs!
Do you think I can listen all day to such stuff?
Be off, or I'll kick you down stairs!"

—Lewis Carroll, from *Alice in Wonderland*

CONTENTS

SHOCK OF GRAY

GRAY NEW WORLD

NOW IN HER EIGHTIES, MY MOTHER STILL DANCES AT HER GRAND-
sons' Led Zeppelin tribute concerts, swims Lake Michigan when the
water is brisk, hikes among penguins in Patagonia, and dons cross-
country skis as soon as the snow is deep enough. My late father, in
contrast, was at the peak of his professional and creative success in
his early sixties, but a barrage of ailments hit him hard at sixty-three.
He began a cruel fifteen-year decline that left him blind, immobile,
slow of speech, and utterly dependent. That he never lost his wit or
kindness or his ability to hold on to the joys of life was, to me, heroic.

My parents' different experiences neatly represent what is happening to millions of Americans and to vast portions of the globe's
population. The world is going gray. Getting not just older but *old*.
Sometime after sixty, it seems to happen to everyone: life-altering
events cascade one after another. In some combination, family nests
are emptied; jobs end or change; spouses, friends, and kin grow
gravely ill or die; bodies and minds decline; one's status and power
in the family and in social circles inverts; money draws down; and,
as remaining years grow fewer, relationships with time and eternity
shift.

And yet new worlds can open up, too. Time can expand, social
circles grow bigger, new passions take root. Freed from the relentless
demands of family and work, older people may experience a sweet
rejuvenation. People whom one might expect to be decrepit and
infirm are, well, dancing at Led Zeppelin tribute concerts. Or even
performing in them.

Meanwhile, although the world well understands how young people shape social life and business, it is just now beginning to see how the arrival of a historically enormous older population will affect all of us. Many old people, like my mother, will be healthy and vibrant, but many others, like my father, will need extraordinary resources to make it from one day to the next. The aging of the globe is having profound economic, political, cultural, and familial effects that are only going to intensify. Some of these changes will be welcome and others will not. Certain people will benefit and others will be harmed. Money and power are at stake, of course, as well as the well-being of millions of older people who have worked and loved and given themselves to all that life offers. But the well-being of the globe's young is also at stake, because it is they who need resources also required by the old, and because in the end, it is largely the young who, as family members, friends, and citizens traveling the continuum of an aging world, will eventually care for the old. And in time their older selves.

The signs of the shift, large and small, are everywhere, if we only will see them. Consider:

- In a room full of telephones and flat-panel displays, where staff is on hand twenty-four hours a day, calls begin to pick up around 9:00 a.m. That's when the more than 6 million elderly customers of Philips Lifeline tend to begin their daily routines. The service allows its clients to alert the company if anything threatens them. The morning is rife with dangers. The average age of a customer is eighty-two, but thousands of centenarians use the service, too. The large majority are women, a predictable reality in an older group. The mornings see millions of Lifeline clients head to the showers, step out on slippery tiles, and then make their way to the kitchen, where fire, knives, tall cabinets, area rugs, and wood flooring are mortal threats. If customers slip and fall, or a sleeve catches fire, or if they are overcome with anxiety and fear as the day begins, devices around their necks or on their wrists let them send signals, sometimes automatically, to the Lifeline call center. By mid-morning on a beautiful fall day, Lifeline has handled nearly seven hundred thousand calls.

A ticker on the wall keeps count. As often happens, some of the callers have died while on the line. An operator takes a call from a Mrs. Jones in Columbia, Missouri. "You fell? How far? Were you standing or in bed? So you're not hurt, but you need help getting up? I'll work on that right away." A few years ago, a Lifeline operator named Lisa had a flash of fame on the evening news after an eighty-year-old woman named Ana tumbled in her bathroom, broke the glass shower door, and lay on the floor beneath a potential guillotine of glass suspended precariously above her. Ana pressed the button on her pendant; it signaled a neighbor and Lifeline and an emergency team arrived to pull her to safety. But just as battle coverage does not tell much about a protracted war, news clips from the aging world do not give the whole picture. The busy command center with telephones and big LCD displays at Lifeline gives a broader view.

Like a situation room for elder angst, in its command center in Framingham, Massachusetts, Lifeline tracks the minute-by-minute flow of incidents and concerns through the day. News stations and the Weather Channel fill the walls. When alarm spreads on the screens with news of storms, blackouts, local shootings, and terrorist attacks, the phones at Lifeline start flashing madly in a widespread plea for help and comfort. Lifeline's employees are schooled in how to listen and decipher the cryptic messages of clients who are too distressed, too polite, or too proud to give clear indications about what has actually happened to them. They can discern whether there is a pattern of falling, a slur of speech that betrays a missed dose of a needed medicine, or a stroke. Callers who dial in more than usual signal the grave dangers of despair and loneliness. Operators reassure clients that all is fine or help is on the way, somehow managing to wrap calm, efficiency, good cheer, and solemn concern into one tone of voice. No one wants to cut a client short, or discourage one from calling again, but this is a business. Lifeline pays above the market rate for its operators, and time, which is plentiful to clients, is money to the company. And, after all, the operators may have other people to contact. They might have to call for paramedics to send them to a house, and perhaps pass on where the client hides the key and pass that information on, too. They have some clients they must call to remind to take their pills. The right number and the right color. And then, they have birthday calls to make. Every client gets one, and that's important. The company gives bonuses to operators based on the number of calls they handle and on the care they deliver. "It's a tricky balance," says Ron Feinstein, Philips Lifeline's longtime CEO, "but our people figure it out."

The business of Lifeline, according to Feinstein, is combating the hazards of isolation. The world, he believes, is largely in denial of the risks facing seniors in their stages of independence. Feinstein, who cares for people all over the country, seems to have every city map in his head. He talks about an eighty-five-year-old woman who lives on the forty-fifth floor of a high-rise on Chicago's Lake Shore Drive that is now filled almost entirely with elderly residents. He mentions another woman in Des Moines who lives alone in a house, and French Canadians in Montreal and Greeks in Toronto. He says the company must be sensitive to the different ways they all are likely to regard life alone in their eighties and nineties. Lifeline, however, prospers from the fact that all the clients crave their independence. One reason families are ill-prepared when crises overtake an old loved one, Feinstein says, is that "our society has an embedded 'gerontophobia,' in which people think they are younger than they are." This carries on throughout life, he believes, because society stigmatizes aging and leads the elderly to deny they are old. All the young-looking beautiful people on the covers of magazines for seniors, he complains, are part of a pervasive marketing mentality, not the real world in which quality of life declines and people struggle to live on their own and maintain their independence despite their fragility. "Mom will deny she's vulnerable, until there's an incident, then all hell breaks loose," he says. "Kids worry that Mom can't live alone if she'll break a hip or if the house nearly burns down, or if someone breaks in, or if a house cleaner notices that there is an unhygienic stain on the carpet and says she can only clean it so many times." For the price of a low-end cable television package, a family can sign onto Lifeline and buy a little more independence. "We're at the point where the children of our clients just hand over their credit cards."

In 2006, Philips, the giant Dutch technology company, paid $750 million for Lifeline. The purchase is part of the company's big bet on health-care services for the growing population of elderly. It is hardly the only company tying its future to an aging world. Home care alone is a $140 billion business that is growing ever larger. Philips Lifeline cannot grow the way mainstream businesses do, however. Nurturing long-term relationships with customers is challenging, Feinstein notes, when a large percentage of your clients die every year. But the potential population of clients, and the need for the service, is rising as the older populations of the United States and the world grow. Lifeline expects to thrive.

- Two motorcyclists pull up to the old-fashioned Fullerton Inn Bed and Breakfast in Chester, Vermont. They are covered neck to toe in riding leathers. One helmet comes off to reveal a red-faced man with white mustache and white hair pulled back into a greasy ponytail. The other rider is a woman with abundant white hair that she shakes out and ties back with an outlaw bandanna. They climb heavily off their bikes, and the leather around their midsections reveals the ample girth beneath. Soon they are followed by ten or twelve other bikers rumbling into the parking lot. Off come the helmets. Every Easy Rider is gray or balding or both and, since the movie *Wild Hogs,* a Hollywood cliché. All appear to have invested their retirement savings in Harley-Davidson motorcycles. And on their rebel looks as well.

  Harley-Davidson motorcycles are the centerpiece of a loose gang of retirees who find the bikes let them embrace a safe counterculture and conspicuously consume at the same time. What is surprising is how late-life riders purchase remarkably similar rebel personae. Indeed, Harley-Davidson's vast popularity creates a problem for the company. Motorcycles were once a youth product, but now they signify a rite of passage transpiring well beyond middle age. The median age of a Harley rider in 2009 was seven years older than it was in 2004. The big Harleys do not sell well to twenty- and thirtysomethings because younger riders think the big, heavy bikes are for old fogies. As its riders get older, Harley is selling fewer bikes, and is searching for an effective strategy to lure the younger riders it will need to thrive in the future. In 2009 the company cut production, closed two plants, and exacted concessions on pay and benefits from its workers. The company also urged older employees to take early retirement. For those that succumbed, the prospect of spending free time and scarce money on a Harley "retirement vehicle" may be bittersweet.

- A pretty woman sits in a convention center in Orlando, Florida, the site of a large annual event for companies and charities that build and run multiunit housing specially designed for older people. On her lap sits a toy baby seal. Its name is "Paro," and it has snow-white synthetic fur over its sleek body, two coal black eyes, a black nose, and a fixed wee smile. The woman, modeling the animal in an exhibit set up to look like a room in a nursing home, is stroking the fur lethargically while smiling blankly. Her job is to simulate a potential user of the toy seal, which is actually an interactive robot designed to calm the nerves of aging dementia sufferers in institutional settings. When petted, Paro emits sounds of a real baby seal. Studies show that dementia patients get attached to the fuzzy little robot, which was designed and manufactured in Japan. The seal has become a star not just at senior housing conventions, but at marketing events around the world where consultants teach others "how to turn silver into gold," and capture the market demands of an aging population. An administrator from a nursing home offers a testimonial, saying that residents get quite emotionally attached to the robot seals and are thrilled by their cute sounds.

- The German state of North Rhine–Westphalia offers a program that turns local sex workers into nursing home caregivers. In a report on the effort, the *British Medical Journal* cites concerns in Germany over that aging country's thousands of unfilled caregiver jobs, despite high general unemployment. One nursing home official is quoted as saying that the retraining of prostitutes is "an obvious move [since prostitutes possess] good people skills, aren't easily disgusted, and have zero fear of physical contact." One former prostitute already employed as a caregiver reflects, "Prostitution taught me to listen and to convey a feeling of safety. . . . Isn't that exactly what's missing so much in care for elderly people?"

- The year is 2006. An industrial engineer at a surgical instruments company shows off the pristine shop floor in his company's fifty-year-old factory building. The company has manufacturing facilities in Germany and the United States. He's proud of the company's skilled workforce, which makes intricate, custom-designed tools that its customers demand be the world's very best. He picks up a scalpel, balancing it on his finger tips. "The weight and feel is one of the hallmarks of our tools," he says proudly. "Surgeons train with them when they are in medical school and use them throughout their own careers." He says that the company's workers are the most prized part of the production process. Many have been there for years and have tens of thousands of hours in experience that cannot be replaced. In this setting, older workers are extremely valuable. Recently, though, the company has been experimenting with lower-cost lines for the market emerging in Asia, particularly China. "We would never sell what we make there to our premium clients at home," he says, "but there are customers there who can't afford our best, so we're making a different line for them."

  In 2007, the same engineer shows off his company's nascent effort outside Shenzhen, China. There are a handful of newly hired workers, all young women in their early twenties, turning out surgical tools that look just like the company's products made in Germany and the United States but that glisten a little less brightly. The company has moved a couple of its expensive tool-making machines from Switzerland to the Chinese site to try them out with the new employees. A sixty-year-old Swiss engineer who helps run the U.S. operations has moved to China to help get things up and running. "It's a small operation for the local market," says the first engineer. "We're keeping all the production for Europe and the U.S. going. It would be too expensive to move everything here, to buy new machines like these, and we have the best workforce in the world in our other plants."

It is 2008. The Chinese factory is filled with more than a hundred new hires, most of them young women and all working at brand-new machines. When asked how the company recreated the workplace and highly skilled workforce so quickly, the engineer says, "Remember those Swiss machines you saw back home? We took them to some smart young engineers at a company in China and they built copies for us, at one-fifth the price. We're now thinking of moving nearly all our production here." What goes unsaid is that the once-invaluable older American and German workers are destined to lose their jobs.

- One hundred and twenty bright young students enroll in Stanford University's new undergraduate class "Longevity." The semester-long interdisciplinary class explores what longer lives mean for society and the students themselves. Topics include death and dying, aging and engineering (Stanford is in the heart of Silicon Valley), and the economic implications of health care. It is team-taught by a psychologist and neurologist and features guest lectures by activists and experts on financial markets, families, and labor economics, and by the former CEO of one of the world's largest insurance companies. The key lesson: longer life spans touch nearly everything humans do. The students, who are among America's very best and brightest, are thrilled by the class, not only because the material is fascinating but because unlike most people their age, they see the gray new world that is coming.

- Jurga, a woman in her sixties, once taught Russian literature in a Lithuanian high school before the fall of the Soviet bloc. She lived and breathed the Russian classics. "The literature is so beautiful, so rich," she says. "You could escape from life into Russian literature." Life under the Soviets was good to her. She traveled frequently to Russia on state-sponsored vacations and seminars where she met others steeped in Pushkin, Tolstoy, and Dostoyevsky. When Russian Soviet dignitaries came to Vilnius, she was their tour guide. The collapse of the Soviet Union ended that. Lithuanians lost all interest in Russian culture as they both reasserted their own and turned to English as their global tongue.

"Young Lithuanians all wanted to leave the country and get better jobs in Germany, England, and the U.S.," Jurga says. "The schools all dropped Russian language studies." Unemployable in her own country, Jurga found her way to America in the late 1990s at age fifty-five, on a tourist's visa. Her only work since arriving has been caring for single Alzheimer's patients in their homes. She moves in, offers them care and home-cooked Lithuanian meals, and over time watches them decline and die. Now she takes care of a man whose only other family is an aged sister. Jurga works ninety-one hours a week. The days are mostly silent, except for the baby talk she exchanges with her charges. She keeps her favorite books nearby, but finds that reruns of *Seinfeld* and old movie comedies and musicals soothe her agitated patients. "We get up and dance and laugh and try to be happy," she says. With her current charge, Jurga has watched Tony Curtis, Jack Lemmon, and Marilyn Monroe frolic and vamp through *Some Like It Hot* more than fifty times.

- In the town square of a small village in Wales, near ancient stone churches, a table of Polish workers sip coffee and read the latest sports news in *Dziennik Polski,* the daily paper from London that serves Great Britain's half-million Polish immigrants. A local high school history teacher at the next table leans over to the closest Pole to inquire how long the men have been in Wales. "More than two years," one answers. "We are all in construction. I am the boss. Today we are sightseeing from Llanelli, to see something new." Since the European Union allowed Poles free immigration to Britain, the Welsh city of Llanelli has attracted a community of forty thousand Poles. Though some have returned home as jobs have grown scarce, most see dimmer prospects in Poland and try to stay. Wages in Poland can be one-tenth the comparable wages in the United Kingdom, so even a couple of months of work abroad pay off. The teacher asks the man if he will stay in Wales. "No. I buy property in my country to fix and rent. But now there is no one in Poland to work on it. All the plumbers, electricians, and carpenters are in Western Europe or America. There are no more young people left anywhere. In Poland you must hire persons from Belarus or Ukraine. And if you go to Kiev in Ukraine, you cannot find Ukraine people. They are in Poland. You must hire workers from Kazakhstan or Georgia."

- Sitting in the audience at Tokyo's Kabuki-za, the large theater that is the center of Japan's most famous dramatic art, a young American conductor, Will C. White, watches a 220-year-old routine called *The Girl Returning from School* (*Tenaraiko*). The girl is played by a small actor with a bright, expressive face, who is dressed in a long kimono in colors and symbols that signify her youth, and wears a traditional black wig adorned with flowers.

    "The girl," explains White, "is on her way home from school. She has her papers and an umbrella and is walking along, carefree, until she is distracted by butterflies. She begins to chase them, caught up in the delight of the moment. Then she writes love poems on scraps of paper that she lets float in the breeze, and she dances. The girl is a playful child but utterly balanced and graceful at the same time. You know in the back of your head that all the Kabuki actors are men, but this guy was the perfect preteen girl, and, my God, so completely convincing."

    White's Japanese companion leans over to him midway through the performance and whispers, "That's an eighty-one-year-old man." The role is being played by a living Japanese national treasure, Nakamura Shikan VII, one of a long line of legendary Kabuki performers. He began on the Kabuki stage in 1933 at age five.

- In March 2010, Ida Ruth Hayes Greene, of New Jersey, earned her high school diploma, one month shy of her ninety-ninth birthday, making her the oldest citizen of the state ever to complete the degree. Jay Leno noted Greene's achievement on his nighttime talk show, adding, "On the advice of her guidance counselor, she will attend a two-year college."

Hey, Where Are the Kids?

These are just a few examples of the many ways the world is changing as a result of mankind's greatest gift to itself, the engineering of longer lives. But the other part of the dynamic is that people are having smaller families. The evidence goes mostly unseen, hidden in plain sight. For people who live in North America, east Asia, and nearly all of Europe, the most immediate evidence is probably sitting right at the dinner table. Take a count. If you have a large, extended family, you might wait until a big group of you gather. Look first at the oldest generation at the table. Maybe they are the grandparents, or the great-grandparents, or some great-aunts and great-uncles. Chances are they have lived a good while longer than their parents did. Count how many children belong to each adult; the numbers almost inevitably grow smaller with each successive generation.

If you are a working adult, then your immediate family is almost certainly smaller than the family you were raised in, particularly if you spent a number of years working your way toward an advanced degree. If your immediate family is half as large as the one you grew up in, you are in the mainstream of families over much of the planet. Survey your friends. Their story is bound to be similar.

I took a poll of my family, then polled friends, too. The stories were mostly the same. My father was one of five children, my mother one of two. They meant to have three children, but had four because my brother and I are twins. I grew up with sixteen cousins. My wife and I have a son and daughter, and just one niece and one nephew on my side. Our big, loud family gatherings over birthdays and holidays once required carloads of borrowed folding chairs and multiple tables. Now we're down to one table, and my middle-aged and elderly relatives outnumber the kids. Talk about doctors and money, once hush-hush so the kids wouldn't hear, is all in the open.

As a white, middle-aged American, I am one of a big group of Americans whose families are shrinking. My family's story is well-told in the pages of the national census. I do not yet know how long I will live. I am told my great-grandfather died at 104, but his son, my paternal grandfather, lived to sixty-two. I do know that between my wife and me there is a good chance one of us will survive past ninety. Actuarially, if we make it to sixty-three together, there's a fifty-fifty chance one of us, probably my wife, will last another thirty years. Women are sturdier late in life.

As it happens, my wife would turn ninety-one in 2050. That's a big year in demographics. Predictions made today often aim to describe the world at midcentury. The U.S. National Institute on Aging is one group peering into the future. In 2010, America's population of people between the ages of seventy-five and eighty-five hit 17 million, but it will reach 30 million in 2050. While American centenarians are a statistical blip today, the institute predicts there will be 2.5 million people over one hundred in 2050. Every age group over sixty-five will grow much faster than the general population, but the numbers of the oldest-old, people over eighty-five, will proportionately grow most.[1]

The same is true the world over. In rapidly aging Japan, the population as a whole will count 25 million fewer people in 2050 than today, but the elderly population will grow so rapidly that it will make up nearly *40 percent* of Japan's population by then. Europe, too, while still growing in size today, will likely have begun to shrink by 2050. In any case, the proportion of elderly—pick any group over sixty-five—will rise faster than the young or middle aged. Nearly three in ten Europeans will be over sixty-five, one in six over seventy-five, and *one in ten over eighty*, which is more than triple the current proportion.[2]

What about the developing world? The UN estimates that between 2005 and 2050, the population of the developing world will have grown by 2.3 billion, but that the percentage of children under fifteen will drop. The group of people ages fifteen to fifty-nine will grow by 1.2 billion, and the group over sixty by 1.1 billion. In Latin America, the proportion of people over sixty-five will rise to 18.5 percent, three times higher than today. Brazil, Chile, and Mexico may have older populations than the United States by then. Today, half of Latin America is under fifteen years old. In 2050 half will be over forty years old.

Want to see how fast developing countries are becoming aging developed ones? East Asia leads the way, showing industrialized Europe and America what is in store in the near future and showing poorer countries full of striving youth how fast they will grow old.

The numbers are pretty shocking. Fewer kids, more old people—nearly everywhere in the world.

Two Hundred Billion More Years in a Single Generation

The Romans are said to have had a life expectancy of about twenty-five years. By 1900, the average life expectancy across the globe had improved only to thirty. The number was so low mostly because infant and childhood mortality were high. For people who made it past those dangerous periods, reaching middle age was common. Still, for most of human history, a life that passed age forty-five beat the odds.[3] Today life expectancy at birth worldwide averages about sixty-four years.

If one adds up all the extra years of human life that result from this great expansion of life spans and multiplies it by the current world population, the magnitude of the miracle becomes apparent. Today's 6.7 billion people will enjoy more than *250 billion extra years of life* on earth over what would have transpired had we been born a century ago. Today's world population will live more than 280 billion extra years than if we all had been born under the Caesars.

13

The future of baby boomers in the United States shows some of what is to come. Beginning around 2026, when boomers begin to hit their eighties and nineties, they will constitute the largest group of the oldest-old in the country's history. This group will reach its size not just because there are so many boomers but because they live so much longer than their parents and ancestors. In the United States, in the year 1900, average life expectancy at birth was forty-nine years and three months, but in the year 2000 life expectancy was seventy-six years and ten months. Over the twentieth century, life expectancy lengthened between 1.5 and 2.7 years per decade. The drop in infant mortality accounts for much, but not all of the gain. Take just about any age in a normal life span, and the chance of a person living longer into the future from that age has also gone up. Today's twenty-year-olds and eighty-year-olds can both expect to live longer than twenty-year-olds and eighty-year-olds ever have before.

The U.S. government tabulates not just overall life expectancy, but also life expectancy at different ages. The results show the amazing progress made in extending life. In 1880, only about one in sixteen people then sixty-five would make it to eighty-five in 1900. Fast forward to 1980. Of Americans who turned sixty-five that year, more than one in three survived to see age eighty-five in the year 2000. The chances of living from sixty-five to eighty-five years old have gone up more than fivefold.

When the world's population passes 9.1 billion in 2050, people will likely be living even longer. If life expectancy grows at the same rate in this century as the last, the world's population at midcentury will have lived about 500 billion more years than they would have had they been born in 1900. Our collective human experience, having already changed, will change again.

The future will refine the math. But even if these counts are off by half, there will still be hundreds of billions of added years for people on the planet in the coming century or two. That bears repeating: *an aging world adds hundreds of billions of years of collective human life to the burdens of the planet.*

And while we will likely engineer ever-longer lives, can we figure out how to fill the extra years with vitality and joy? Will we learn how to keep older people active, not idle? Rework the world so that older people can act longer as participants, and less as dependents? Who will pay for the care of the old? Who will perform it? Billions of extra human-years would seem to virtually require a second planet.

Global Aging Accelerates Globalization

The faster that countries age, the more strident the demand that goods, jobs, and people move seamlessly across borders. Younger countries that are rich in youth but short in funds reshape themselves to suit the needs of older countries rich in funds and short on youth. Older nations have, and will, spread their wealth, lifting hundreds of millions of young people in faraway places out of poverty, productively investing in the young people and their nations.

The demands of a society where an older population grows more rapidly than any other group will give rise to a society that extracts the powers of youth where they abound. And in a seeming contradiction, aging societies that press employees to pay today for the welfare of workers tomorrow will find their young workers passed over in the job market, as businesses shop for youth elsewhere in the world where the public expense of an aging society is not wrapped up in a current paycheck. The health and welfare of the young and old will be bound together in ways that push far beyond our current fiscal, social, and ethical boundaries. Our world, which until recently was a place where young people died in far greater numbers than old people, has changed into a world where far greater numbers of older people will need the financial, emotional, intellectual, and physical support of younger people. At the same time, younger people will vie for the treasure controlled by their elders: money, power, status, even land. Will a world that is increasingly old be one ever more driven by family loyalty? By adaptive commerce? Or, by governmental control? The answers will depend on the decisions we make in our families, workplaces, and communities. Nobody knows yet.

A Book of Stories

The best way to see how global aging will inform life in the future is through the insights of people engaged in that change today. What follows draws on my conversations with hundreds of people around the world who are thinking about and struggling with demographic change. Few of us lead lives untouched by global aging, but some of the most important ways we are affected by it are often hidden in plain sight. Today, we are in the first ten minutes of a demographic dénouement that is centuries in the making but is already altering nearly every important relationship we have, from the family table to the workplace, from our neighborhoods and cities, to the domains of national politics, international trade, and geopolitics.

The aging world is diverse, complex, and often paradoxical. But once we look for it, we see it, because it involves people. And so the pages that follow do not examine the minutia of government budget deficits or offer lists of policy recommendations. (References to many excellent more specifically policy-oriented treatises can be found in the book and its notes.) Neither do I lay out a tightly prescriptive universal set of "solutions" for individuals, as desirable as that might be. Why? Because the goal of this book is to see individuals and connect their lives to the dynamics of our changing world. Only in that way will we figure out, at the top of our intelligence, how to make the most of an inevitably older world. I hope I have captured the desires and aversions, the courage and fear, the creativity and despair of everyday people concerned for themselves, their children, and their parents—which is to say that I hope we all see ourselves in these pages. Population aging is personal, it is local and it is global, and we all must adapt in ways that are also personal, local, and global. As the light shines from womb to tomb and around the world, here are some of the themes that emerge:

- Global aging is the result of mankind's greatest triumphs, and we are unlikely to make the trade-offs that would reverse it.
- Our successes force us to reconsider how to maintain every benefit that delivered us to an aging world.
- One's own aging is a surprisingly global affair.

- The spheres of active, healthy, engaged older adults will grow. Nevertheless, employers and customers in the marketplace will ruthlessly winnow out economically valuable older people from those who are merely able.
- An aging world is an increasingly dependent world. It will demand that a growing portion of the population devote their lives to the growing share of the people who need care.
- Global aging dramatically transforms the relationships between men and women, and visa versa.
- Age discrimination pays and the world is ingenious at figuring out ways to marginalize and exploit older people.
- The aging world moves people around the globe, and their movement propels global aging.
- Young people today will live in a far older world tomorrow, and it is the present that, for better or worse, will prepare them.

The American writer Kathleen Thompson Norris once observed that "in spite of the high cost of living, it's still popular." And in an aging world, it's more popular than ever. Let us see.

CHAPTER 1

GREETINGS FROM FLORIDA, GOD'S WAITING ROOM

Estimated number of Americans over age 65 in the year 2025:
66 million

Percentage of Americans who currently live in Florida: 6

Percentage of Americans aged 75 to 84
who currently live in Florida: 8.3

Percentage of residents of Sarasota, Florida, over age 65: 33

Average age of residents of Pines of Sarasota,
a nursing home: 87

Expected length of stay: 3 years

THE FUTURE OF THE UNITED STATES, AND INDEED, MUCH OF THE developed world, has already arrived in Florida. You can see that future in many places, and one of them is a huge mobile-home community south of Tampa, where three thousand "manufactured homes" sit side by side on quiet narrow lanes. The homes are solidly built, not the long, flimsy trailers that still provide down-market housing in older trailer parks. The ones here are true houses, with front porches and architectural details that suggest suburban living. Everyone knows purchasing a mobile home in a retirement community is a lousy investment, but it is nonetheless a low-cost way to buy the Florida retiree lifestyle, which is to say a life of sun, ease, and maybe even a longer life.

So the people come, every day from all over the United States and even Canada. In the Florida trailer park, three busy, happy, often boozy, clubhouses with swimming pools and spas begin filling up with men and women when the midday sun abates and happy hour begins. The men and women come in every version of old—skinny-sickly, fat but fit, tanned, sunburned, stooped, wheezing, strutting, low-energy, and enthusiastic. Many still smoke. Some of the men have scars from heart operations or skin cancers that have been removed. The hats come in great variety and the footwear is all about comfort. The shuffleboard deck, anathema in Florida's posher "adult" communities, but still highly popular in middle-class retirement enclaves, pulls in a good crowd. There's liquor on deck, too, which helps the newcomers meet the long-timers.

There are, naturally, Americans from all over. But a respectable number of Brits and Germans have arrived to enjoy the laid-back American-ness of the place. Then there are the Canadians. Americans may send to Toronto for cheap prescription drugs, but Canadians descend on Florida for a drug they desperately need, but can't get through the mail: the Florida sun. They soak it up like a long-craved vitamin, which it is. If global warming were only about heat and added sunshine, it would be a fine tonic for the aging world that Florida portends. (About nineteen out of twenty older people are deficient in vitamin D, which the sun amply provides. They are at high risk of diabetes, heart disease, and immune deficiency; people from cold climes are especially vulnerable.) Suffering longer winters, the Canadians arrive before everyone else and blend seamlessly into the state's winter havens of resort homes, condos, and mobile-home communities.

One reason that Florida telegraphs the future is that it has the oldest population of the fifty states. More than 3.3 million people over age sixty-five—nine out of every fifty residents—lived in the Sunshine State in 2010. A University of Florida study estimates the number will climb by about 115,000 every year until at least 2030. And that's not even including the nearly one million older "snow-birds" from the United States and Canada who travel to Florida for a few winter months, but are not counted as residents. In fact, about half of all North American snowbirds come to Florida.

Measured against the rest of North America, and nearly all the world, Florida's population is older in almost every way, because it is pulling old people to itself. The arriving sun-worshipers drive their cars south down through Canada, the northern Plains states, the Midwest, and the Northeast, all homing in on Florida. They generally are leaving cities and towns that are themselves rapidly aging, but are still, on the whole, quite a bit younger than Florida.

The (C)old North Heading South

The ones coming from farthest away are the Canadians, who live to 80.4 years, more than two years longer than their southern neighbors.* Canada is also aging because Canadian women have been having, on average, fewer than two children since the 1970s. Their fertility rate today is about 1.5. The aging of Canada is treated in politics and the press as an urgent concern. In 2001, nearly one in eight Canadians was sixty-five or older, a portion that will almost double by 2026.

Leaving their country, Canadians pass through American communities that are aging much like Canada's mostly white population. Florida-bound Canadians from Ontario or Nova Scotia might first pass through Maine, a state already nearly as old as Florida and even more alarmed at the prospect of aging. Small Maine towns share the fate of small towns nearly everywhere in aging North America, Europe, and east Asia. Once overwhelmingly young places are now quite old, because the big families of yesteryear are now big families of older relatives. The few young people growing up in the towns often leave and never return. In aging, depopulated Maine, just about any job is prized by older workers. Snowbirds pass homemade

* The Population Reference Bureau in Washington chalks up much of the difference to the fact that Americans are more often dangerously overweight than Canadians. Compared to Canadians, more than twice the percentage of American men and three times the percentage of American women are obese. Half a century ago, Americans lived longer than Canadians.

road signs that announce the many jobs that Mainers are willing to do. One at the end of a long driveway says "Used Books and Pool Cleaning"; another two miles down the road says "Hair Stylist and Firewood." The old, large employers are mostly gone. Shoe factories and paper mills that once employed whole towns packed it in long ago. So Maine has become a place where older workers need two or more jobs to get by. More than one in twelve working-age Mainers hold more than one job, about 50 percent higher than the national average.[1] As the state's elderly population swells ever larger, the number of people over sixty-five will more than double from the year 2000 to 2030.

Far to the west, snowbirds traveling through North Dakota also see a state with a shrinking and rapidly aging population. Stop for coffee in a small-town restaurant or truck stop and one might wonder whether the locals have hidden all the children in cellars. Talk at the counter is likely to be about grade schools closing for lack of students, or the availability of jobs in the local, small nursing homes, which in North Dakota are often a community's largest employer. The average age of a farmer in the wheat- and sugar-beet-growing state is about fifty-eight. And that's just the average. The farmer in his or her seventies and eighties is a commonplace in North Dakota. The size of the state's population of people age seventy-five to eighty-four has tripled since 1980 while the size of the state's population has barely budged.

The Golden Years State

As odd as it seems, Canadians traveling south might even meet Californians on their way to Florida, where some communities have become attractive to refugees from the Golden State. California is warm, but not home to the tropical heat some retirees crave. California is also deeply, frighteningly in debt, in part because of pension obligations to a large and rapidly aging group of retired and nearly retired public sector employees who have helped create a $500 billion unfunded hole in the state's finances. California is expected to grow by 172 percent by 2040. The biggest percentage boost will be among those eighty-five and older, whose numbers will *triple* by then. Because California has long had a strong pull on immigrants, both from abroad and from other states, the Golden State is relatively young. But Californians live about one year longer than the U.S. average.

Californians exiting the state also carry with them word of change that may not always sit well with an aging white population.* California today has the diverse population that foreshadows change in the rest of the nation. The number of elderly Hispanics in California will grow 300 percent in the next twenty years. Contrast that to non-Hispanic white elderly whose number will grow by "only" 50 percent. Meanwhile, the number of nursing home residents in California will likely double to 170,000 by 2050. That's a lot of new beds for a state that already struggles to pay what it owes to older citizens.

Continuing toward Florida, one sees a patchwork of demographic change. The Midwest is aging, and some southern states are bustling, but their older populations are growing rapidly, too. Kentucky, for example, is one of America's most rapidly aging states. In 1995 Kentucky's proportion of people over sixty ranked twenty-eighth among the fifty U.S. states; by 2025 it will rank twelfth.

Stretched Lives, Stretched States

Travelers to Florida who drive through state capitals and see the glistening domes and historic sites might pause to wonder whether an aging continent could even build glistening capitals today. To listen to the worried governors who work in those state capitals, the answer is an emphatic no. The high cost of pensions and services for an aging society would not allow for all that brick and mortar optimism. Because state governments are brilliant at creative accounting, no one really knows how much U.S. states owe to their aging populations, except that the debt burden is huge. Reputable estimates of the gap between money owed to state and local pension plans and the money

* Since the 1990s, more Californians have been leaving the state to live elsewhere than out-of-staters arriving. One favorite spot to move is Utah, one of America's least diverse states.

on hand range as high as $3.23 trillion. That's only for government pensions, not any of the other services an aging population needs.

The numbers on aging populations in U.S. states have been crunched in a frightening volume called *Measuring the Years*,[2] published by the National Governors Association, the nonpartisan, collective voice of the state leaders. American states, like a man whom the gods grant eternal life but deny eternal youth, must somehow persevere as they are ever-weakened, blow by blow, by aging populations that sap resources from every other local government function: education, infrastructure, cultural programs, health care for younger groups, policing. Once the slide begins—as it most certainly has—the states fear it will accelerate their decline. Places that triage resources to serve older populations can lose their young or leave them ill-prepared for the wealth-creating jobs that require investment in children from early childhood through their university graduations.

One reason Florida is so attractive to retirees is that compared to other states, Florida underspends on services for its younger citizens.* Some whole communities are designed so that they need not support local programs or schools for the young. Sun City Center in Florida is a large non-city of nearly twenty thousand retirees whose median age exceeds seventy-five. Children account for only four of every one thousand residents. The community's small school requires relatively little public money.

The governors also know and worry about the fact that more resources in their states will be needed to manage and treat chronic disease. Currently, half of all people aged sixty-five and over have two chronic health conditions, and the proportion of those with chronic conditions is expected to rise.

These are just a few challenges facing state governments. The truth is that nearly every aspect of people's lives will be affected by demographic changes, and that means rethinking how every state service and level of government operates.

Best to point the car to where sunshine is what matters, and where the old can be young again. Welcome to Florida!

---

* Florida, for example, ranks near the bottom in per capita education spending for children.

The Dream Begins

Florida certainly faces the challenges the rest of aging America is struggling with, but it is facing them by design. The state may have done more than any other place in the world to attract older migrants. How did it get to be so old?

"Florida, like the rest of the world, was, until fairly recently, very young," observes Gary Mormino, professor at the University of South Florida in Tampa and one of the leading historians of the state. "On the eve of World War II the median age of the population of Florida was younger than that of the United States as a whole. Florida was certainly not a good place for seniors to come. It was hot, humid and, above all, hard to get to. Still Florida had long been promoted as a place for cures. Ponce de León planted the idea, but even long after the Fountain of Youth was discredited, the state was full of places offering to cure whatever problems you had. The cure—hot springs, salt water, sunshine, and others depending on the site and the huckster—created a view of Florida as a place for rejuvenation."

Mormino recounts how it wasn't until the 1920s and the construction of the first highways into the state that travelers from the northern states started coming in large numbers. For the next thirty years, until the outbreak of World War II, the state catered to "Tin Can Tourists," motorists who traveled through the state in jaunty cars strapped with gas cans, tents, and canned foods. Soon they pulled trailers, too. Cities cleared fields for trailer parks, some of them vast expanses for hundreds of vehicles, where the Tin Can Tourists could stay in their traveling accommodations. Trailer parks for travelers morphed into residential trailer parks and trailer courts for people who used mobile homes as low-cost housing in what Mormino calls "The Florida Dream."

The Long Gray Line

"Greetings from Florida, God's waiting room," reads a popular T-shirt. It's a riff on an old Bob Hope line. There is lots of waiting to do in the communities where the elderly congregate in Florida.

At a grocery store that has a progressive policy for hiring older workers, you wait out a traffic jam in the condiment aisle. A delay has resulted from a dropped jar of sweet gherkins, and an efficient seventy-one-year-old lanky shop boy with a mop striding purpose-fully—not hurriedly—toward the spill, worried that the tremulous woman who dropped the jar might tumble into the slipslop of glass and vinegar. No rush. He'll get there. An aisle over, there's a backup behind an overtanned woman whose pudgy, blue-veined legs burst out of knee-length pastel yellow shorts. She's studying the numbers for sodium, fiber, and fat content on the labels of every brand of baked beans like a forensic accountant, shaking her head crossly at the first few she picks up—Campbell's Pork and Beans, Van Camp's Original. The etiquette of the store is to wait, freezing time until she's done. Just as at the cash register one waits while the purchasers ahead methodically count out their money and just as methodically count their change, and when they get muddled, begin again.

The younger immigrants—students and Rust Belt refugees who work the cash registers—learn not to roll their eyes when the older customers pinch pennies and dimes from their coin purses, adjust their glasses to read the long, faintly printed receipts, and count the items listed against those in the bag, or complain, usually needlessly, that a sale price was overlooked.

One must learn patience, too, at the lurching sound of cars in the parking lot and the sight of them nearly missing other cars pulling in and out. Everyone knows older drivers can be time bombs; stories about fatalities involving older drivers over seventy are frequent front-page news in Florida.* There is the story about the eighty-seven-year-

---

* Nationally, deaths involving drivers over seventy were up by 27 percent from 1991 to 2001. The National Highway Traffic Safety Administration, which collects figures of crash rates among drivers of different ages, notes that "the crash rate per mile increases slowly at 65; then, at 85, it soars to a rate nine times higher than that for all drivers between 25 and 69. The only age with a worse crash rate per mile are 16-year-olds." By 2025, one in four drivers in Florida will be over sixty-five. Drivers over seventy-five make up 4 percent of drivers, but 10 percent of deaths. A 2007 Rand Corporation study found that older drivers and their passengers are seven times more likely to be killed in a car accident than other drivers. But there's another side of the mortality equation with the elderly and cars. Taking away their licenses can be deadly, too, keeping people from the food stores, pharmacies, and other services they need.

old who drove his car into Madeira Beach near St. Petersburg, which calls to mind the demented ninety-three-year-old who killed a pedestrian nearby and then continued on the highway with the corpse on the windshield. The accident rate of elderly drivers is similar to that of teenagers, but the older ones are far more likely to end up dead.

And then there is the waiting that goes on in the state's many waiting rooms attached to the doctors' offices, clinics, and hospitals that fill long boulevards on the edges of the cities the elderly prefer. Eventually, there's the waiting that's visible all around: resigned and heroic, terrifying and welcomed, denied and embraced—the wait for death. In Florida's more elderly confines, reminders of this wait are everywhere, seen in the gait of men who walk with nurses to catch their falls, in the clusters of card-playing widows and near-widows who are scrupulous in their bridge game but have already cheated at the actuarial tables. Hands and heads shake and wobble, and talk obeys the essential rule that keeps complaints about cancer, joint problems, and husbands dead or in decline to a minimum. In God's Waiting Room, the message is clear: don't wait at all. Instead, rush toward life, embrace it, make the most of the time left. An hour lived, they tell you, is one less hour to live, so fill the remaining time richly. This is the miracle of Florida's impressive elderly. What they wait for urges them to wait as little as possible for life's pleasures—some selfish, some giving. And amid the waiting everywhere there occurs a flurry of activity embracing ever-shortening life.

One place to see such hurry is Sarasota, the former circus town.

Here Come the Sunbirds

Sarasota is but one of a long stretch of retirement destinations that run along the midsection of Florida's western edge on the Gulf of Mexico. Islands, keys, bays, coves, inlets, and white sand beaches stretch for hundreds of miles along the twisting watercolor coast.

Sarasota proper has some 53,000 residents, but the greater Sarasota area is home to 800,000 people. Among communities with a quarter of a million people or more, greater Sarasota, where the median age is variously calculated, depending on how one maps the area, between forty-one and fifty-five, is credibly labeled the oldest in the United States. Nearly a third of the population in Sarasota County is over sixty-five years old, and one household in two is home to someone over sixty-five.[3]

Sarasota at its best may be the finest place in the world for older people to make new homes. The community encourages physical activity and social life, pushes people outdoors, and, despite its smallish size, stands as a capital of culture. That Sarasota attracts the well-educated and the rich informs the quality of life, too.

"People who move to Sarasota are the cream of the older crop," says Dr. Bruce Robinson, chief of geriatrics at Sarasota Memorial Hospital. "They have resources, mobility, and a good perspective." Robinson, who grew up in the Missouri Ozarks, contrasts the Sarasota retirees to the people over fifty he knew in his hometown. "People like my grandparents stayed there because they were poor and could not think of being anywhere else. They had family and kinship, so communities took care of people. That's not the case in Sarasota. If you come here to retire, you'd better have money when you get into trouble because you're far from your family and you'll need to pay to be taken care of."

For the northerners who settle today in Sarasota, verdant trees, lapping waves, and warm skies, flush with birds, affirm life. Birds are in fact one of the area's spectacular draws. The Gulf Coast has around 240 species. Eagles and hawks glide in the thermals over woodsy flatlands. Brown pelicans, silhouetted before the orange, vaporous sun, hang low over the tranquil waters, eye the deep, dive to scoop fish into their gullets, and then heave themselves back into the air. Pert speckled and snowy plovers, needle-nosed sandpipers, curious terns, and black skimmers patrol the salty shores or tuck into their beach nests. Sarasota has perhaps the most resplendent bird life of any metropolis in the United States. Yet somehow, despite decades of breakneck construction on the waterfront and wetlands, spilled Gulf oil, the dense profusion of hotels, upscale retirement homes, and gargantuan concrete condo complexes, plus the spread of immaculately groomed golf courses and sprawling malls, Sarasota remains so lush and clear that millions of birds still color the landscape and sky.

The bird life adds more than beauty to the landscape. It engages the residents in the natural environment. Research at Cornell University shows how much more personally and mentally engaging a life amid beautiful flora and fauna can be. People walk more, bend more, study the changes around them with happy interest, and feel more connected. That's all healthy.

Migrants who come to Sarasota in the second half of life, or its final third, quarter, or tenth, do not come to grow old and fade. They come for rejuvenation. They come to spread their wings.

"Eighty-five here is not the same as in an aging town in the Midwest. The eighty-five-year-olds here look sixty-five in comparison. The expectations that go with chronological age are so different here. A lot of it has to do with the opportunities here and also the presence of the sun," says Pam Baron, who moved to Sarasota from Denver and is now director of senior services at Jewish Family & Children's Service of Sarasota-Manatee. Baron is one of the leading voices in the community for senior services and helped steer an initiative to catalog the resources in Sarasota that are important to its older residents and the businesses and organizations that serve them. Older migrants often report that they chose the community for the level of activity it offers over others.* Eighty-three percent of the older migrants to Florida say they moved to the state for the sunshine and warm weather, and for what they can do under the sun.

The Beat Generation

"In the North you don't see the sun and you're susceptible to SAD, seasonal affective disorder," Baron says.** "People here wear pink

* "Active Aging" is a hot topic, promoted heavily in public health literature, in self-help books for older people, and by companies that sell "active aging communities." While the benefits to staying active are legion, most older Americans either do not want to be active or cannot be active. The Centers for Disease Control reports that only one-fifth of the population over sixty-five stays active on a regular basis.

** Seasonal affective disorder, also known as Winter Depression, does afflict older people, though vulnerability seems to drop with age. Victims of SAD are likely to feel its effects most in the winter when the days grow shortest. They may also succumb at any time of year if they do not get outside enough. Office workers, who are cooped up all day, are susceptible. Bright, artificial light is part of a battery of therapies that have helped people.

and lime green clothes. The women go out dressed in coral, bright pink, and powder blue. The older guys are in wild shirts they'd never wear at home in Rockford, Illinois. Put all that stuff together and it does extend life."

Along wide beaches that rim the local keys, drum circles gather to greet the sun, and to say thank you as the sun says good-bye. The groups at daybreak are small, but loud. The rituals at dusk can attract hundreds of people. White-haired, pink-domed guys in sarongs, or with beards down to their belly buttons beat drums and whoop and chant to the god they've come for. Some are lithe with impressive physiques; others let their bellies drape over their loin-cloths.

All ages come for these rituals, and the older guys hand tambou-rines to frat boys and grandkids and pretty girls and point to the sun. Relatively younger women in eensy-weensy bikinis or dresses of tas-seled gossamer straight out of the *Arabian Nights* spin and wiggle in an approximate beat to the drums, while onlookers of all ages create an impromptu amphitheater. A group of three top-heavy ladies and one rail-thin, deeply tanned friend, all in their seventies and eighties, join them. The women, who have similarly teased white hair, dark glasses the size of training bras, and pastel shirts and shorts, push their way into the front ranks, to set up a bulwark of aluminum fold-ing chairs and sit low in the sand. The four women, hailing from a small town in Ontario, shake in their chairs, snake their arms in the air, bobble their heads, roll their eyes, and smirk. A minute later they have choreographed an animated, in-sync, impromptu beach-chair Bollywood routine.

The drum circles that claim Sarasota beaches cast off pretense and embrace the elements of sun, sky, and air. They also offer therapy for free. Ask a drummer during a brief lull in the action what keeps him coming to the beach with his big zebra-skinned African djembe, and he extols the mind-clearing, joint-moving, social medicine the circle provides. "Read Oliver Sacks!" he shouts as he begins again to slap the top and sides of his drum.

Sacks, the well-known neurologist and bestselling author, writes in *Musicophilia: Tales of Music and the Brain* that music, in this case drumming, has the power "to reconfigure brain activity, and

30

bring calm and focus to people who were sometimes distracted or preoccupied by incessant tics and impulses. . . ." Sacks also argues that the drum circle promotes "musical and social bonding with others." What begins as a miscellany of isolated and self-conscious individuals, he says, almost instantly grows into a cohesive group. Drum circles, Sacks says, are also therapeutic for people with dementia, because drumming "calls upon very fundamental, subcortical levels of the brain." In other words, drumming penetrates below conscious thought and inhibition, to the purely physical level: "Rhythm can restore our sense of embodiment and a primal sense of movement in life."[5]

Once, at a Senate hearing, Sacks testified together with Grateful Dead drummer Mickey Hart on the virtues of music and rhythm for older people. Hart is also a widely published musicologist and director at the Institute for Music and Neurologic Function. He told the senators, "As modern technology takes us further from our natural rhythms, the use of percussion for healing has greater potential than ever. . . . It is a practice widely acknowledged to help focus attention and help people break free of the boredom and stress of daily life. When we speak of this type of drumming, we are speaking of a deeper realm in which there is no better or worse, no modern or primitive, no distinctions at all, but an almost organic compulsion to translate the emotional fact of being alive into . . . something you can dance to." Drumming and dancing together allay loneliness and alienation, Hart said, and combat the tendency of older people to spend long hours in front of the television. It lets them have direct contact with young people, benefiting even those whose health may hinder them in other ways. "In a drum circle nonverbal communication is the means of relating." It boosts self-esteem, makes people feel creative, and helps focus their minds.

What the Widow Knew

Sarasota has served as a portal for such passionate, highly personal reinvention for over a century. The city's ties to the more staid northern Midwestern states date back to its beginnings as a resort.

In 1910, Sarasota had fewer than nine hundred residents, but advertisements extolling its charms filled pages in Chicago newspapers. One ad caught the eye of Chicago's most celebrated society woman, Bertha Palmer, widow of merchant, developer, and hotelier Potter Palmer, who died in 1902 and reportedly left a fortune worth $25 million (more than $1.5 billion in 2010 dollars). On seeing it, Mrs. Palmer saw a chance to get away.

Palmer made the trip in her own private railcar with her son and father. Over the next year she began to acquire land and in the end held ninety thousand acres, about six times the landmass of Manhattan.[6] Soon after the Palmers arrived, they were followed to town by other magnates and their families. By the early 1920s, Sarasota's first frenzied building boom was under way. Out of all the towns born during the early Florida land booms, says one early history of the city, Sarasota "was the only one founded upon an aesthetic ideal."[7]

The city's developers stuccoed-over wooden-frame houses, added Spanish and Moorish arches, and painted them salmon and white, all to create an aura of permanence in a state already getting a reputation for fly-by-night deal making.[8] Americans in the 1920s had been steeped in Mediterranean schmaltz. Hollywood blockbusters with Rudolph Valentino and Douglas Fairbanks showed these heroes sword-fighting, swinging from balconies, and making love in arabesque tents and palaces. Architects were hired to create an Old World look that distinguished it from the New England and Midwestern styles that the likely new residents knew from home. A former set designer for D. W. Griffith was brought in to help the effort. In 1924, the Sarasota phone book listed fifteen real estate firms. By 1926 there were two hundred.

Another Midwesterner helped push the Mediterranean fantasy into overdrive: circus impresario John Ringling, who, in the mid-1920s, was one of the world's richest men. By 1926, Ringling had acquired tens of thousands of acres in the growing city's downtown and along the keys. He built two hotels, and carved out a thirty-seven-acre tract on Sarasota Bay for a Venetian-style mansion for himself and his wife. The grounds also housed a museum for Old World master paintings, including several large canvases by Rubens, and other European treasures. "It was the seat of [the Ringlings'] Sarasota empire," writes former curator at the Ringling Museum Michael McDonough, "and one of the city's greatest pieces of architectural propaganda."[9]

Sarasota's real estate boom crashed in 1926. Development stopped cold and when the Great Depression hit, the city went into deep freeze, reverting to its leaner agricultural economy. "The city looked almost exactly the same from 1926 until the next boom began in the 1950s, except that a lot of the infrastructure went to hell," says Sarasota author and local historian Jeff LaHurd. Ringling struggled after the bust. To perk up the city, he made Sarasota the winter headquarters of his circus. Nevertheless, John Ringling died at age seventy, in financial ruin. His art holdings were the sum of his wealth in the end, and he left the museum and its collections to the State of Florida.

Memory's Big Top

The Ringling estate remains one of the psychological anchors of Sarasota. It houses a small circus and circus museum. The galleries show off an enormous, intricately detailed model of the full Ringling Brothers Circus that took a volunteer fifty years to make. There is an ornate auditorium for concerts and shows, a café, and the neighboring art galleries. On any given day the Ringling complex is filled with grandparents with grandchildren in tow. But it is more than a tourist attraction. It is a near-perfect intergenerational bridge in a community where the retired transplants are often separated from their families at home.

Here is a place that gives an older generation a window through which they can travel with young visitors to their own youth—a borderless, multimedia, exotic, erotic, strange, and dangerous entertainment that existed before color television or the Internet. There are no camel dung sweepers on the Web, but Grandma saw them and smelled them, or can say she did. The circus museum allows older Sarasotans the chance to fill in their lives, and describe the characters they once were before they were retired grandmas and grandpas, back when they were immigrants, romantics, daredevils. A frail man with a walking cane painted in festive Mexican pink and green stands in front of a poster of a family of aerialists. He lifts his cane to the poster and tells two young girls with him about the Wallendas, the twentieth century's most famous aerialists. "They are from near my hometown, close to Potsdam," he says, "and they came to America just after the family. They came to Ohio a couple times. I wanted to be a Wallenda. I tied some rope between two trees about ten feet off the ground and tried to walk on it. I fell a lot. But so did the Wallendas.* Some of them fell to their deaths." At a portrait of Emmett Kelly, the famous tramp clown, grandparents offer lessons on clowns, hobos, and the Great Depression.

Older volunteers, nearly 650 of them, fill roles everywhere in the complex. They mind the ticket booths and stores, naturally. But they also lead tours peppered with their own reminiscences. It takes up to two years of training to be a docent in the museums, less for the volunteers who maintain the extensive gardens or drive the trams. The volunteers include a cluster of veteran wood carvers. "It's a highly skilled group. They get together every week and get out their tools," says Hollie Corbitt, the volunteer coordinator at the museum complex. "I have to say that, given the age of some of them, it's a little scary when they pull out the power tools." The men carve replacement pieces for the gilded antique wagons. They also create new wooden circus animals. "There's a dentist in the group. When they were carving a tiger, he wouldn't let anyone else near the teeth," says Corbitt.

While there are a small number of students and younger volunteers, it is older people who donate the vast bulk of the work. The average age of an older volunteer is seventy-two, says Corbitt. Together the hours put in by the 650 volunteers equals the work of thirty-one full-time employees. They save the institution millions. "The bulk of them are in pretty key positions," says Corbitt, "and

* While the older man reminiscing at the museum may still recall his youthful fantasies to be a Wallenda, the Wallenda family exemplifies active aging. In 1970, Karl Wallenda, age sixty-five, walked 750 feet on a high wire across Tallulah Gorge to promote tourism in the State of Georgia. Eight years later, at age seventy-three, he made a similarly daring walk in Puerto Rico, but fell to his death due to faulty connections in the wire's rigging.

we could not open the doors without the volunteers." The docents who guide the tours of the collections are most often former teachers and professors. A tram driver is a former army general. "Many of the volunteers might live in age-restricted communities and this is where they can see and meet people of all ages."

Corbitt adds that once volunteers are accepted, they hold on to their jobs as long as they possibly can. The tenacity of the volunteers is causing some institutional anguish. "We are entering a phase," says Corbitt, "where health is becoming a challenge for the staff, especially relating to some of our longtime volunteers who have been here maybe twenty years. They have deep relationships with the curators and all of us. This is their second home. But we're at the point now where some of the volunteers need us more than we need them."

Corbitt says that for the volunteers who have a hard time with their duties, the challenges are physical, not cognitive or behavioral. "Their limitations can be severe, perhaps requiring the services of a caregiver or nurse. It is a difficult problem because they are also important to us in other ways. They might be generous donors, for example. We need to find ways to help them transition out of their current role, but also find ways to keep them engaged. It is a difficult conversation to have, and we are not good at it yet."

When a volunteer quits, moves away for health reasons, or dies, there is a strong sense of loss among the group. Corbitt makes it a policy to attend any memorial service she is invited to. "I've been going to a lot of them lately," she says.

The Last Place to Be

Walking through Plymouth Harbor with Harry Hobson, the executive in charge of Sarasota's oldest continuing care retirement community (CCRC), is a bit like hopping tables at a charity ball. During the high season, from January through April, the city's civic organizations and philanthropies host about one hundred galas. Plymouth Harbor is one of more than two thousand CCRCs in the United States, which together are home to some six hundred thousand residents. Many are modest. Plymouth Harbor sits at the very top of the market. The Plymouth Harbor complex has a range of living arrangements that allows residents to move in when they are in good health and have their own apartments. As they grow frailer, they can stay at Plymouth Harbor, choosing care in their rooms, or a move to another apartment where they can get help with daily activities, such as bathing and eating. Should they need rehabilitation following a health setback or surgery, there is a section for full nursing care, too. For most residents, Plymouth Harbor, like other CCRCs, is the last place they will ever live. It is, in effect, a super-premium long-term care insurance policy in the physical shape of a luxury high-rise.

The average age of residents is the mideighties, and their average net worth is at the upper reaches of the wealth pyramid. Buying into the place is expensive and the monthly payments are high. Doctors, high-priced attorneys, Wall Streeters, patent holders, professors with lots of savings and good pensions, corporate chiefs, wealthy widows, people who sold expensive houses elsewhere, and other fortunates call it home. Casual conversation draws on the sum of thousands of years of collective memory stretching back over a century. Hobson is endearingly starstruck by his residents. He has a gift for eliciting their life stories and walks around the lobbies with an ear out for snippets of living history. He stops by the table of a tall, thin, regal-looking man in a wheelchair. The man is a former church official with a military past. A Chinese speaker, he served in the U.S. Army during the Second World War as part of the American officer corps dispatched by President Franklin D. Roosevelt to serve directly under Chiang Kai-shek. He is talking to a fellow resident about China today, and Hobson makes introductions. It comes out that the man was present when Mao Zedong and Chiang Kai-shek toasted each other once the Japanese withdrew from China. He tells how he watched them both lift their glasses, and saw them, soon to be at war against each other, stop short of sipping from their glasses. It's an astonishing story and Hobson says that one hears amazing things all the time. The tall man in the wheelchair, Hobson lets on, is battling late-stage cancer and his presence will be deeply missed.

Farther on, Hobson comes to a former bigwig at one of the world's largest consumer products companies, a couple of industrialists, former surgeons, and the aging parents of a top executive at a Fortune 500 company. They are, in short, a plum roster of the class of folks who cannot escape the fat envelopes that carry invitations to black-tie money raisers.

Plymouth Harbor is just one of many senior residences in the area. The *Yellow Book of Senior Living Options* has 178 pages jam-packed with ads for communities for active and not-so-active older adults nearby. Most have comfortably banal interchangeable pictures of smiling white-haired women dressed in crisp blouses, big earrings, and brooches. Most have interchangeable names, too. "Oak" this, "Pines" that, "Sunset" or "Palm" something or other. Many ads show rooms with comfortable chairs that are not so comfortable; but they defeat frail people trying to stand up. Flowers and white linens adorn the tabletops; Oriental carpets dress the floors; and fussy drapes and chandeliers complete the decorative style that senior housing architects call "Grandma's Williamsburg." Competition for residents is fierce in West Florida, and communities tend to get high marks from their clients, who are happy to be in the South, and are indispensable, unavoidable sources of information for potential customers shopping around.

The arrangements residents make to live in the different developments come in a dizzying variety depending on when the developments were built, the regulations and market forces in place at the time, and the age and needs of the customers they serve. Some operations are strictly for-profit, others are charitable organizations governed by boards and donors. Still others are ingeniously concocted hybrids of profit and charity. The senior housing industry has created vast fortunes for those who have puzzled out how to cobble together the profit and not-for-profit sector. One scheme, for example, might involve a developer who builds a senior residency and sells it to a not-for-profit philanthropy that he set up himself, and then, through still other business shells under his control, signs up the "charity" for exclusive service contracts that tie the residents to dining plans, health care, and other essentials from the developer's own for-profit organization. Should anything go terribly wrong that urges residents to sue, they may find only empty corporate shells and no one legally responsible for anything. The legal boxes-within-boxes can grow so complex that residents themselves have a hard time penetrating them.

White-Haired Lab Rabbits

In addition, Sarasota is rich in hundreds of companies that help older people live in their own homes outside of a more formal senior living development. The region has become a kind of Silicon Valley for aging services, with a cluster of businesses, social services, and academic centers that create ever-new ways to serve older clients. The critical mass of firms means there is also a steady stream of innovation in business models, services, and technology to serve the older market.

Plymouth Harbor, which opened in 1996, was the brainchild of a minister in the United Church of Christ. It remains affiliated with the church, but is not exclusive to its congregants. Churches argue that even high-end senior residences are part of their religious and charitable mission. Tax officials in the United States have wondered what charitable purpose is fulfilled by selling million-dollar apartments to the very rich. So far, the churches (and other religious organizations) have preserved their coveted tax-free status, claiming that their mission is also to minister to the wealthy and that extra monies earned go to support programs for the less fortunate.

"People made their initial move to Sarasota when they were in their midfifties or sixties, and they enjoyed the winter home lifestyle. As they age they move on in their life planning, and look at the CCRCs. They discover it isn't just a nursing home. It's a whole new life."

Or at least a reengagement with the life they want, perhaps most of all because it is social. Activities, which include academic lectures and art classes taught by working artists, are not condescending, and emphasize physical activity. At the edge of the property is a small island with a boat launch, from which residents—average age eighty-five—pick from Plymouth Harbor's twenty kayaks, then paddle their way along the shore in hope of getting up close to local sea turtles and manatees.

Hobson waves to a couple coming through the lobby in tennis clothes and whispers that the gentleman carrying a bag of rackets is near ninety and on his second artificial hip. The people who run CCRCs often offer statistics to show that their residents live, on average, a good deal longer than the general population, up to eight years longer. That would place them among the longest-lived communities in the world. The numbers are not perfect. Some research shows that people who move into senior communities shorten their lives; the stress of change is the killer.[10] But most places are not at the high end of the market. CCRCs such as Plymouth Harbor already cater to a wealthier population that has a better chance at extreme longevity than the hoi polloi. They often enter when they are already near or past their average life expectancy, and before they face serious health complications. They will likely stay active for some years before they move along the continuum of care. And when they do fall ill, or simply fall, help is always just down the hall.

Farther on in the lobby at Plymouth Harbor is a resident of another ilk. One of the city's art doyens, she wears a short black dress and is draped with a chunky free-form necklace with bits of silver, crystal, and stone. Hobson says she's been involved in the arts in Sarasota for more than thirty years. There are twenty volunteer committees based in Plymouth Harbor, but much of the activity happens out in the city. It is a part of the social currency in town, and the residents at Plymouth Harbor know the charity beat intimately.

Emmett Kelly Meets Pagliacci

"Because the arts community here dates back to the 1920s, the city has the quality that big-city Northerners are used to," says Susan Danis, the petite, rapid-fire executive director of the Sarasota Opera, which is arguably the mothership in the city's cultural sea. "And there's a whole service industry that's grown up around it. People come for the arts, but they also want good restaurants, first-class health care, and tools to take better care of themselves." Elsewhere around the country, opera attracts younger audiences, but the bulk of the audience in Sarasota is over sixty. Danis says the older demographic goes well with the vision of the house's maestro, who is committed to performing works as faithfully as possible to how their composers intended them. This conservative approach sells out nearly every performance and forges a fierce loyalty among older donors and volunteers keen on seeing works done well and as they know them. The commitment runs so deep that local donors have stepped up to endow a young artists program, where promising singers in their twenties come for a season to be steeped in the classics. "Young singers are exciting for our audience," Danis says, adding that they want to hear the great voices that will be filling other major houses in the future. "So, we are very committed to young talent and our maestro is one of the last at an important house to give younger singers big roles." The opera uses the young casts to educate and socialize with audiences and to reinforce the patrons' ties to the company.

Older Sarasotans make up an indispensable foundation to the opera's operations. There are thousands of donors in town, and hundreds who give at the top levels. One Sarasota transplant, William Schmitt, donated $4 million to kick off the recent renovation of the main auditorium in the 1926 Mediterranean Revival former vaudeville theater (where Will Rogers and Elvis Presley once performed). The board and committees are top-heavy with people who tend to be older than those on boards and committees at other houses. "One good thing about Sarasota is that there is always someone older than you," Danis observes. "I just had a board member turn seventy and it feels like he's a baby. We had another board member who retired at a hundred. He came to every meeting perfectly groomed and seemed so vital, but his memory started to slip. We have another ex-board member who is 103 and who makes references to Tammany Hall corruption in New York [in the 1920s]. Our assistant house manager is ninety-six and he could kick your ass."

In all, the opera has three hundred older volunteers. There is, for instance, a large group of women volunteers in the company's costume shop. "They're a great big sewing circle," says Danis. "They can embroider and smock anything and their finishing is great. It is very social for them."

The renovation of the opera house was meticulous in making

sure that the company met the needs and expectations of its older clientele. "It was totally about audience amenities, and way beyond what's needed for handicap access," says Danis. "If you build everything for wheelchair access, they will come." The company put in extra public bathrooms and made them extrawide for people with walkers and wheelchairs. Toilet stalls are big enough to accommodate the help of a caregiver and the sinks allow for extra space for wheelchairs to roll under. Special soap dispensers were designed to automatically lather people's hands. Towel dispensers were put next to every sink so no one has to take extra steps. "We had to make sure that even with our audience, people could get to the bathrooms and back to their seats in a reasonable amount of time, and we designed everything to make it easy and to speed the flow."

Older audiences do have patterns and preferences that no renovation can oblige. "Last night we had someone with a heart attack and the EMTs had to come," Danis says about the *L'amico Fritz* opening. "We had an older woman who dropped her glasses from the balcony and hit another one in the head. We have patrons who knock others down. One of the biggest things we have to deal with is patrons who don't want to miss a performance no matter what has happened to them . . . they won't let you call for help. I have to go up to them and say, 'Ma'am, you're blue, let's call the EMTs.' They arrive in less than two minutes and can get people out so we don't have to stop the performance. We tell the performers to just sing on. Our audiences have a lot of oxygen tanks and adaptive chairs," Danis notes, "especially during the matinees."

The New You

Sarasota has more not-for-profit service organizations per capita than any American city its size or larger. And almost certainly, more than any its size in the world. Every year a new spate of well-heeled and well-to-do residents move there, newly disconnected from the business and social lives they led in the places they have left. The informal rule at Plymouth Harbor that discourages people from rambling on about what muckety-mucks they were when they came to Sarasota applies nearly everywhere that former muckety-mucks gather in town.

"No matter how successful you were in your old job, the minute you walk into town, you're starting out at ground zero, to reinvent yourself and prove yourself all over again," says Roberta Schaumleffel, who came to Sarasota after working twenty-eight years in Columbus, Ohio, in business and in education. "You just can't expect people to know who you are."

Schaumleffel began volunteering at the Ringling Museums after she arrived. To have something to talk about at dinner, it helps to have a new affiliation that places one in the class of active Sarasotans. Those who come to town with the means and energy to spearhead new organizations of their own design are the über-active, seeing the latter stages of life as a time of summing up and giving back, a time to figure out how to leave the world a better place. Call it intervention as a mode of personal reinvention.

Writing about the retirees from Great Britain to the Sun Coast of Spain, British anthropologist Caroline Oliver observed that the act of moving "is employed cognitively by migrants to rethink and rewrite the common scripts of dehumanization, invisibility, and marginality associated with old age. . . . [M]igrants creatively engage with ideas and images associated with place, travel, culture, and age to realize certain aspirations about time—use of the body and aging, sociability and cultural identity." Oliver saw how the retirees she studied willfully overcame reservations about moving to an unfamiliar spot on the map, and focused intently on the positive aspects of a lifestyle for their age group in their new homes.[11]

Sarasota's bigheartedness centers largely on efforts to boost the arts, promote the environment, and provide services to area children. The impulse to help children carries with it some contradictions in a community as old and wealthy as Sarasota. Bob Carter, the president and CEO of Sarasota's Senior Friendship Centers, Inc., a full-service senior center in the middle of town, notes the irony that so few of the charitable dollars awash in Sarasota go for programs for seniors. There is money galore for kids' programs, but it is older people who make up the disproportionate bulge in the community. Older donors, Carter says, do not get the good feeling giving to needy people their age or older. It reminds them too much of what's in store for them later. But everyone likes to help children.

Playing Santa to Kids and Scrooge to Their Parents

The money and time given to children's programs can be generous indeed. Stephania Feltz leads Girls Inc., an organization in town that runs summer and after-school programs for young girls, many of them minority grade-schoolers from low-income families. Despite the relatively low cost of the programs, around $115 a month per child, nearly half of the girls in the programs get financial assistance. Sarasota's service-oriented workforce is among the lowest paid of any metropolitan area in the United States, and the needy families who use Girls Inc. are so sensitive to the cost that when the prices were raised by $40 a month, so many girls dropped out that Feltz had to do a special round of fund-raising to lower the price back to an affordable level and offer more aid.

"Only 30 percent of our girls live with their biological moms or dads," Feltz says, "and many are with their grandparents or foster parents. Many live with a single mom employed in a low-level job in health-related fields, or who works two jobs, cleaning houses, working in restaurants or hotels to make ends meet. Some are undocumented immigrants."

Feltz describes Sarasota as a Tale of Two Cities. Poor workers are attracted to low-pay service jobs for local employers who will go to any lengths to keep the wages low. "At the same time, Sarasota is one of the most philanthropic communities you could ever find." A population that is wary of paying living wages to adults nevertheless lavishes services on poor and working-class children. Helping children gives donors a psychological stake in the future; paying their parents low wages protects donors' own futures. Another civic leader in town likens Sarasota to a Third World economy. "There's a Club Med economy with the retirees on really long vacations, existing on top of a predominantly low-wage service economy. The cost of housing is very high, so the workers commute long distances from the lower-rent communities at the fringe."

The low cost of service workers can help stretch the nest eggs of Sarasota's retirees, but for some, life, and death, in the community can be pauperizing. The community's age mix is also reflected in the gender mix. Women make up a greater proportion of the adult population at every age, but in the age brackets above seventy the gap begins to widen markedly. For Sarasota that means that a large proportion of the residents are women who live for longer periods dependent on retirement income. If it lasts. The uncertainty of money lasting is usually worse for women, particularly if they are married to men who fall prey to lengthy or otherwise expensive illnesses. Not only do women often spend their time taking care of their sick partners, they often spend down their bank accounts on medicines and professional care. At the local YMCA, morning exercise classes are filled with women in their seventies and older, doing step aerobics, lifting weights, and exercising in the swimming pool. It is not just that the women see the benefits of good health for themselves, says the Y's director. Many are working out to be strong enough to care for their invalid husbands.

Staying Well by Doing Good

So far, mainstream volunteerism in the United States is at odds with the practice of Sarasota. Though research repeatedly shows that volunteerism among older people decreases the incidence of disease and prolongs life, it is still surprising how few people do it. Formal, structured programs that make it easy for people to sign up make a big difference.

Nancy Morrow-Howell, professor of social work at Washington University in St. Louis, notes that the great bulk of volunteer programs in the United States, especially the kind that enlist unpaid workers for defined work over regular periods of time, are centered around younger volunteers. For those of high school age through their twenties, there are innumerable opportunities for so-called service-learning projects and philanthropic internships. In the country's bigger, better-known volunteer organizations, older volunteers are scarce relative to their portion of the national population. In the Peace Corps, which sends Americans overseas, mostly to work in low-income countries, volunteers over fifty make up just 7 percent of the ranks. In AmeriCorps, where volunteers usually live and work in needy American communities, volunteers over sixty make up just 3 percent of the corps.[12]

Morrow-Howell also points out that the aims of younger and older volunteers are usually fundamentally different. Younger volunteers seek roads into the world of adults; they want personal growth, training and experience, adventure and social networks that may help them professionally. In large part, volunteer programs that engage young volunteers are intended at least as much for the development of the volunteers as for the targets of their work. Seen more broadly, the programs are often intended to develop the human capital of the volunteers, to make them more suited to mature roles in society.

In contrast, programs that enlist older volunteers are often designed chiefly to benefit those whom the volunteers help. These programs, too, are often focused on the development of youth, and enlist older volunteers to act, for example, as mentors or tutors. The success of the programs is measured by the progress of the young people helped, not by the benefits to the older volunteers. If younger volunteers gain experience and skills, the older volunteers deploy their experience and skills in what they do. And yet, Morrow-Howell notes, even older volunteers, particularly low-income elders, will use volunteering as a way to build up their skills and transition into a paying job, though the jobs they move into are often less demanding government-subsidized jobs in the not-for-profit sector. The number of opportunities is small. Meanwhile, the level of volunteering drops off with age, with the sharpest drop coming after age sixty-five when people tend to develop chronic diseases.

As the Money Runs Out

Pines of Sarasota is a nursing home that used to be called the Sarasota Welfare Home before "welfare" became a dirty word in America. It was founded in 1948 to serve six elderly indigent men in Sarasota who had no place to live. Today, Pines serves three hundred elderly Sarasotans who have nowhere else to go. Their average age is eighty-seven and they typically stay for three years. Compared to nursing-home patients in the 1970s, they are much older and sicker. Younger, less infirm people have more options today, which means that homes such as Pines carry the heaviest burden for residential care. Most of its residents need twenty-four-hour care. The vast majority are women, many of whom spent their last dimes caring for husbands now gone.

"We've experienced older parents living here at the same time as their children," says John Overton, president and CEO of Pines. Overton moved to Sarasota from Canada, where he ran an assisted-living residence. When he and his wife first arrived, they took over a large family home and created a small assisted-living facility for residents who paid with their own money. That is a far cry from the institutional Pines, which though clean and well attended, is filled with inhabitants who offer a sobering picture of a final stop, despite an earnest attempt by the staff to brighten the environment. On one visit, nurses and patients are draped with leis, and the dining room features hula girl and pineapple decorations assembled by some of the residents. But it does not look as if anyone is particularly cheered up.

One common strategy for children whose parents need care is to move and hide their mother's or father's assets so that they appear pauperized to government auditors. Patients who are penniless are eligible for government assistance under the Medicaid program. Pines does not turn people away if they cannot pay, and even well-to-do families use this largess to preserve their own wealth, perhaps for their own care needs later on.

"We take people in on a 'Medicaid pending' basis," says Overton, "and sometimes we are conned by adult children who hollow-out their moms' estates. But even if there's a con, we can't put people on the street. Our dementia residents have no upside potential, and increasingly other institutions in town won't take them."

What Overton describes as a con is in fact a legal strategy that a small but thriving industry in Sarasota helps to put into action. Lawyers and investment advisors actively and aggressively market ways to protect assets. Some of the strategies are laid out in complex trust documents passed between high-fee law firms and private bankers. Others come on with ads on Florida highways that have all the subtlety of billboards for personal injury attorneys and bail bondsmen.

Yet real poverty is also an issue for the region's oldest-old, and serving the poor is the primary mission of Pines. Sarasotans age eighty-five and older, seven in ten of whom are women, are more likely to live in poverty than any other group over sixty-five.

The local assumption about Pines is that it serves people off the street, but the majority of the patients, Overton explains, arrive after having planned carefully for their retirement, only to see their own illness or a spouse's deplete their savings. In fact, one of the only groups of people excluded from Pines is homeless people from the streets. Sarasota is a land of elderly caregivers and recipients. More than one in five people over sixty in the area describe themselves as caregivers. Nearly as many are caring for parents as they are for spouses.

Overton shakes his head when asked about the willingness of well-off Sarasotans to support Pines. "We talk about it a lot in our strategic meetings," he complains. "It just isn't a sexy topic for the people here, and we cannot get the wealthy to give money. Even though the need is greater than ever, it is harder than ever to get people to give. People want to hear about what their money is doing for the future. Some donors want to give to organizations that helped them. When you serve people with dementia, you don't have a big alumni group. The fear factor in this business is the reality of the aging process. People may like to know that there is an institution in town that takes care of the elderly in the worst situations, but they don't want to get too close to it. Even people in my position and professional care providers have a hard time facing that they could end up in a place like this."

Boomers Booming Along, or Not

One of the mixed blessings in creating an older community that is enviably active is that inactivity is unenviable. If social currency accrues to those who remain youthful, it is debited from those who are less so. There is pressure in town to be counted among the young elderly, and that means staying active, fit, and attractive. The plentiful mix of age-defying medical and cosmetic services in town attests to the pressure.

"Although it's natural and beneficial to view active engagement in life positively, there is a danger in idealizing old age as a time of high activity," says John A. Krout, director of the Ithaca College Gerontology Institute in New York State. "Not all people do or will have the resources, opportunity, physical or psychological ability, or inclination to be highly engaged. Some older people are too ill, too financially challenged, or too heavily involved in caregiving to meet the emerging definition of the active elder."

Krout argues that the idealized older people who regularly appear in ads raise the possibility that mass culture will expect elders to conform to a new active picture of them as "bungee jumping, parachuting, volunteering, painting and . . . [doing] tai chi." He wonders whether society will label those less active as failures and create a two-class system. The view would be just as unrealistic, he asserts, as the picture of frail, inactive, poor elders it replaces, because elders are as diverse in activity levels as they are in other ways. Boomers, Krout fears, may be particularly defenseless against the pervasive pop view of active elders, both because boomers are widely predicted to be more active at later ages than their parents and because they are more resistant to old-age stereotyping.

Many boomers seem driven to deny aging and defy past age-linked behavior, Krout says. "They do not identify with those older than themselves, preferring instead to think that they can remain youthful—or at least not become old—by stretching their conception of midlife well into their seventies or even eighties. The current mantra is sixty is the new forty."[13]

In Sarasota, the whirl of the migrants who have come before the boomers already presages the split Krout predicts. It shows in their age-defying activities and philanthropy. Defying stereotypes about aging is itself empowering. But denying the needs of the less active elderly may end up as a collateral price society pays for its new image of later life.

Redefining Oneself Redefines One's Group

The pervasive culture of volunteerism among older adults in Sarasota puts the city at the vanguard of an active aging movement. In places where active aging finds support and mutual reinforcement from within the community, as it does in Sarasota, older adults see their lives after their formal careers as opportunities to redraw and broaden their identities rather than narrow them. Hope Jensen Schau, a sociologist and professor in marketing at the University of Arizona, describes retirement not as a winding down and freezing of the self, but a life transition as ripe with opportunities for reinvention as other turning points, such as adolescence, college, marriage, parenthood, a new job. Jensen Schau surveyed hundreds of active but retired older Americans from across the country, all over sixty-five, and shadowed many of them in their activities.

"They were doing amazing things," she says. "One man rode a bicycle from Houston to the Pacific and up the coast, and then across the northern border of the U.S. and down to New York City. Older women, who in their youth were discouraged from doing anything that made them sweaty, were now competing in tennis tournaments for the first time, or playing basketball for the first time, in their seventies." Jensen Schau sees behavior through the lens of a market researcher and describes the trend toward reinvention as a form of collaborative consumption, in which a group of older people can redefine how an even larger group may behave and make choices with time and money. Because Sarasota has a critical mass of people reinventing themselves, reinvention becomes a normal and desirable activity. Reinvention is the fashion. In some ways, Jensen Schau observes, their self-reinvention can be more assertive than that of their juniors. "The active older people we studied try hard to keep their cultural capital—their knowledge of current news, movies, exhibits and so on—very high. It is part of their identity development."

Although most of the people in Jensen Schau's study were active reinventors, she says "it is unrealistic to think that they could still do their former jobs. They retired for good reasons. They were either cognitively or emotionally unable to be back at what they were doing."

"We Help People Hit the Wall High"

In Sarasota, the philosophy of activity spreads so deep it has become part of the institutional drive in the town's CCRCs. The Glenridge on Palmer Ranch competes with Plymouth Harbor and the small group of other local high-end CCRC complexes. It sits on ninety flat acres of what was formerly part of Bertha Palmer's vast estate. The sprawling complex, described in sales material as having "all the grandeur of a resort hotel," consists of four-story apartment buildings with some single-floor villas. Neat rows of tall palms divide the quiet grounds. Signs around small ponds warn wanderers that alligators may lurk in the water. It's no joke: no one sits near the ponds. From midday until sunset not many walk under the hot sun on the paved paths, either. A few attendants in cheerfully printed scrubs walk small, coifed dogs. The animals belong to residents no longer able to make the rounds.

Big common areas make up the core—restaurants, an ice cream parlor, a pocket café, gift store, and a canteen. A reading room reminiscent of a quiet corner in an old college library stocks several thousand volumes, including current bestsellers. The grand staircase in the lobby spirals around a fifteen-foot-tall cylindrical glass aquarium teeming with iridescent fish. The sight of fish gliding through clear waters has proven benefits for dementia sufferers. It makes them more alert and calm and heightens their appetites. The unwritten rules of senior communal living practically mandate aquariums (and in colder climes, aviaries), but few match the encased coral reef at Glenridge, stocked and maintained by a nearby marine research institute. Opposite the aquarium another attitude adjustment zone beckons—the Glenridge cocktail lounge, the Thistle Stop—a hub of late afternoon activity. Busy bartenders in vests and bow ties knowingly pour their regulars' favorites and shine up the glasses and bottles with the eye and efficiency of steak-house pros.

"I can't imagine a lifestyle that would exceed this unless you're [an aged] Bill Gates or Donald Trump," says Howard G. Crowell, Jr., a former U.S. Army three-star general who is the CEO of Glenridge. Crowell is in his midseventies. He's tall and fit, and keeps his full head of brown hair in a neat executive clip. Even in the heat of summer, Crowell wears dark, conservative suits. Though he speaks with the authority of a man who could command an army over a continent, which he did as chief of staff of the U.S. forces in Europe, he laughs loudly and can be disconcertingly frank about his job, his residents, and the state of the very old in America. He's a tough old softie. "There are those with $10 million or more who find managing their own health care is extremely difficult even if they can afford it. If the goal of society is to provide something like we have to a general public that's aging," which Crowell thinks it ought to be, "you have to provide the right mix of feeding, nursing, and maintaining where older people live."

For that, he says, you need to see younger people engaged in the process. Crowell is not sanguine about the prospects. Glenridge points to the difficulties. The residents there have already been separated geographically from their families, most of them for a decade or more, by the time they get to Glenridge. "We get them in their second retirement," Crowell says. "They moved to Sarasota long ago to have their own lives, and like it here." Even if their children don't. "I see moving into the Glenridge as the greatest gift older people can give to their children." No one will have to worry about their care, he says. Neither the residents nor their families need to be constantly hunting for people who can come in and replace caregivers on the move. "It's not an easy job for families. You have to provide constant distraction for the people here. . . . Some are like children who can find themselves unhappy with their immediate circumstances, as if they didn't get a toy or didn't get what they wanted. In a social sense they can become like kindergarteners."

The answer, says Crowell, is a full plate of activities. He recalls a single week during which three men at Glenridge lost their wives to cancer. "One man was a former chaplain schooled in loss. Another was a politician who was very well connected. And the third was a very wealthy individual. Every one of them was deeply involved in something here. They played tennis, volunteered, and held meetings. The more involved they became, the shorter their bereavement periods." Crowell throws up his hands. "The bereavement period vanished."

What is the goal of the Glenridge? Crowell asks rhetorically.

"We help people hit 'the wall' high," he says, invoking a customary metaphor for both dementia and death. "The higher you are on The Wall when you meet it, the better your life has been and the better your children's lives have been. Now, how do you stay high on the wall when [age conspires to] push you down? Our mechanism is to put people into as much activity as they can possibly deal with at their level."

Practically speaking, Crowell sees keeping residents active as a massive logistics operation, where the theater, classes, transportation, dining options, fitness and rehab, health care and grounds-keeping, security and spiritual resources of his institution must all be kept humming. His description of the needs of the Glenridge could double as a description of communities where any aging population can "hit the wall high." In Sarasota, 72.1 percent of the people over eighty-five years old report needing assistance with basic care activities, and because the city has one of the largest populations of eighty-five-year-olds in the nation, it offers a view of what the rest of the country will need to provide as the number of oldest-old grows dramatically.

Society, he says, "doesn't want to deal with old people. If you're living at home and you are the oldest person on the block, you can feel you're a pain in the ass. But if you're in an environment where there's always someone your age who shares your experiences, where people have losses together, and there are clubs and activities, you can deal with it." The Thistle Stop is the most popular place "in town" for dinner and socializing, Crowell says, because people in their seventies and eighties feel very comfortable and safe socializing there. Crowell cites internal research data that he says show communal setting and socializing add three to four years to the lives of Glenridge residents.

Conversations with Glenridge residents prove Crowell is right to think residents move in part to spare their children. They do not want to take their children away from their lives at home. It is often true of the oldest parents, those in their mideighties and older, who have educated, professional children who are themselves pressured by the expenses and time demands of their lives. And they do not want their children caring for them. As much as they value the people in service at Glenridge or wherever they may be, caregiving is seen as stoop work and they are loath to engage their children in it.

Independent Days

On a visit with one nonagenarian couple in their suburban house-sized two-bedroom apartment (call them Gordon and Maggie Bitler), coffee and cake are shared with their sixty-two-year-old daughter visiting from the West Coast. Gordon, a retired professor, and Maggie, a former schoolteacher, both possess a percolating intelligence that comes out in questions and observations that are up to date on politics and science. They are well-known and well-liked at Glenridge, in part because they have a strong circle of friends in Sarasota built over twenty years. Crippling pain in Maggie's hips now keeps her in a wheelchair and most nights she takes her dinner in their apartment, carried to her by Gordon, who dines with friends downstairs. Often they join him back at the room to visit while Maggie eats her supper, and share coffee and a drink. None of the Bitler children lives anywhere near. One daughter lives with her husband in South America where they promote environmental awareness. Another child, a son, with his own joint problems, lives in Chicago as a stay-at-home dad. The daughter now visiting comes once or twice a year. She herself is in her early sixties and like her parents is talkative and engaged.

But she also goes a bit stir-crazy on her visit. She speaks a little manically to visitors, interrupts her parents when they offer an idea, and lets her eyes dart around while she squirms in her chair. Even at the Glenridge, with "the grandeur of a resort hotel," small doses of doting wear on dutiful, well-meaning adult children. One of the mantras about kids and grandkids visiting in Sarasota's higher-end CCRCs is: "It's good when they come. It's better when they go."

The well-to-do have the luxury to recite it, but the sentiment is a common one among people in old age. If they have an alternative to relying on their children, they often leap for it. More than nine in ten older Americans say independence is among their foremost objectives.[14] Getting help at the Glenridge may count for the residents as a version of self-sufficience, freeing them from the fear of burdening family and friends.

Hide the Wheelchairs!

The main dining room at the Glenridge is bright if a bit fussy. A maitre d' greets residents as they come in. If they enter by wheelchair or with the aid of a walker, their equipment is removed by a staff member as soon as they sit down. It goes to a holding area out of sight at the back of the restaurant. Crowell does not want any evidence around the public areas that suggests the place is a home for invalids. It gives too sobering a picture to the residents, but just as importantly, it is not a welcome sight for prospective residents shopping for the right atmosphere for their final home. It is much better for them to see the three-hundred-seat theater, the schedule of lectures, shows, and cabarets. To see the committees in action and the buses taking residents off the grounds to keep their cultural and social lives in Sarasota as current as they can.

Prospects grew scarcer in the aftermath of the global credit crisis and the collapse of the American real estate market. Retirees who depend on income thrown off by real estate, dividends, or stock earnings saw their circumstances sharply reduced. The fear that ensued was reflected in a March 2009 survey that showed Americans at or near retirement expected it to take seven years for their investments to return to their precrisis levels,[15] not counting the money they would have to draw out of their diminished accounts in the meantime.*

Florida was especially hard hit. Sarasota, which in 2005 was a forest of building cranes, sank into a real estate depression. Owners in older condominium developments abandoned their units to banks. Some condos were forsaken by speculators and landlords who could not attract buyers or renters. Others were vacated by people who moved

---

* According to data tracked by CareerBuilder.com, older workers grew even more pessimistic as the U.S. economy improved from 2009 to 2010. The service found that nearly 70 percent of older workers hoped to delay their retirement, largely because they were financially unfit to stop working. That reflected an increase of 10 percent over the year before.

back to wherever they came from. What new buyers were attracted to town refused to consider the vacated buildings, fearing they would be trapped in deteriorating money holes with few other residents to share the costs of upkeep. Older buyers do not generally move into places that *might* recover their value in a few years. In 2008 and 2009, Sarasota slipped so far out of growth mode it lost population for the first time in decades. The senior housing industry was also thrown into crisis in Florida and nationwide. Older Americans could no longer easily sell their homes to free up money for new retirement residences.

One fear is that if a new population of elderly is hindered from moving into existing institutions, the business models in the senior housing universe could collapse, leaving people who thought they had bought insurance for housing and care for the rest of their lives at the mercy of a collapsed marketplace. Big national developers of adult communities teetered on bankruptcy, creating a wave of fear among residents in developments all over the country. In Sarasota, many of the residences and developments that cater to retirees offered their current dwellers strong incentives for referrals. Not only might they earn some extra money, or perhaps a television or golf cart, but they could help fill the financial holes that threaten to swallow them up.

"The effects that the economic crisis had on the lives of the elderly in Sarasota rippled through the community in ways that surprised a lot of people," says Pam Baron. "Many of the elderly who hoped to move into residences with higher levels of care cannot now make the move. They also can't afford as much home care as they used to. That has cut out a lot of the low-wage jobs. At the same time, the home health agencies we work with began attracting a better educated, more qualified worker, even at $8.50 an hour. They get a lot of applications from better-qualified people, like retired teachers, who come in because they need the income."

Con Men and Thieves, Swindlers and Touts

In good times and bad, much of the economy that caters to older adults has a house-of-cards flimsiness to it. The Glenridge and Plymouth Harbor at the top end may serve the rich who will always be with us, but their residents are not safe from predation. In the midst of one conversation at the Glenridge, Crowell was interrupted by a well-dressed gray-haired woman in silvery pearls.

"Howard," she said urgently, "I have to talk to you."

Not now, he told her, he was in a meeting.

"Howard, it's urgent, I really do have to talk to you."

Crowell is accustomed to demands for a chat over matters posed as urgent that end up being routine. Problems with air-conditioning, or with a perceived inattention by the staff, perhaps. He has become used to telling people to wait just a bit. But Crowell saw the gray-haired woman was more insistent and scared looking than he would have expected. He stepped to the side to see what the matter was and told her he would meet her in his office in three minutes. The woman informed him that her financial advisor had skipped town under a cloud of suspicion and that she could not get any information about her accounts with him. Sarasota was deeply affected by the Ponzi schemes that came to light in 2009. Bernard Madoff's network, which soaked clients of $65 billion, plucked a large circle of Sarasota investors clean. And another "mini-Madoff," Art Nadel, was a Sarasota advisor who was also a prominent donor to local service organizations and cultural institutions, such as the opera company. He bilked locals, including many residents at the higher-end CCRCs, of $350 million. When Crowell was stopped in the hall, word was that Nadel had left a suicide note but could not be found. He was later arrested.

Not surprisingly, in a community with a surfeit of older people who are sick and frail, but have money, there are grifters who make a specialty of preying on them. In 2006, in an effort to lure disabled victims in their eighties and nineties, a pair of shady insurance agents set up a company that promised long-term care insurance that would provide clients with caregivers and medical attention at home. The fine print on the policies sold, however, said only that the company would provide the names of caregivers and medical contacts, but no actual service. For that service, they charged annual premiums up to $5,040.

In 2008, a Sarasota dermatologist, Michael A. Rosin, earned a twenty-two-year prison sentence and was ordered to pay $11 million to the government in restitution. Three years before, Rosin was one of the only doctors in the area who performed Mohs surgery, a procedure that removes cancerous sections of skin with minimal scarring. The demand for his services in a tropical haven for retirees was high, but not high enough for him. His arrest stemmed from his practice of testing his own patients and finding that in nearly every case their biopsies were positive, though in fact some patients didn't have cancer. He operated on people whether they had cancer or not. On some patients he operated often. One patient was operated on seven times for nonexistent cancer. Some who may or may not have had cancer went under the knife more. Thirteen patients had the procedure twenty or more times, and one patient had it 122 times. Rosin's own staff grew suspicious, and, sickened by the practice, submitted a chewed-up piece of gum to the lab. It came back positive for cancer. They turned him in.

The area's storms regularly blow in contractors who are chiselers in more ways than one. A typical scheme inflates the estimates of damage on a house, then confuses and defrauds older residents as shoddy repairs make matters worse. A pet ploy among contractors is to gouge seniors after storms leave their homes easily breached by strangers or vulnerable to water damage. Another common swindle entails slathering a house with paint that runs off in a matter of days, ruining the exterior, then charging more to fix the problem. The schemes repeat ad infinitum because too few of those duped report them. Victims who do step forward often provide details too scant to offer solid leads for police.

The Gray Area of the Law

The pickings are so rich that Florida's attorney general opened a "Seniors vs. Crime" office in town in order to flush out the bad actors and encourage older victims to overcome embarrassment and report the crimes. It is part of a statewide program that employs older volunteer sleuths as investigators. In the year before the program arrived in Sarasota, Seniors vs. Crime handled thirty-five hundred cases in Florida. The program fills many gaps. It is staffed by retired law enforcement professionals. "I was a sergeant in the Orlando police department," says David Blacklock, a cheerful man with red cheeks, unkempt hair, and a voluminous white beard who now looks like he belongs more in a woodland castle than a police station. At Seniors vs. Crime, Blacklock coordinates a group of volunteers who take up cases the police will not touch. "We only do civil cases, nothing criminal. And most are small cases, which for law enforcement are the lowest of low priorities."

The work, he says, could not be more satisfying. The teams Blacklock works with, all but a few of them volunteers, include a retired homicide detective, a onetime postal inspector, an ex–New York City transit cop, and "many former middle managers from business and government who know how to get things done." Volunteers staff storefront offices in dozens of communities. Most offices open for four hours, two days a week. One office, in Delray Beach, in southeast Florida, opens five days a week. "There are a lot of elderly Jewish ladies down there. They have lots of money and they get ripped off all the time. The office is very busy."

So far, the program has recovered millions of dollars for older victims. The effort comes at no cost to taxpayers. Expenses are covered by earnings from cases settled with the state. When one of Florida's largest pharmacy chains was accused of routinely under-filling the prescriptions of older customers—giving them fewer pills than were on the prescription label—the firm offered a large sum to the program as part of its settlement with the state attorney general. Because older volunteers work directly with state law enforcement officers and attorneys, they can leverage their work in a way that gives them real power over wrongdoers. "We give them the chance to be Superman and Superwoman," says Blacklock.

Counting Pennies, Day by Day

The economic reverberations of the 2008–9 market reversals reordered the lifestyles and plans of every class of retiree in Western Florida. Restaurants along the main strips posted "Closed For Season" signs in the spring, but never opened again. The attrition of stores left big gaps in formerly thriving strip malls. Local schools were losing hundreds of students a month, and the taxpayers that supported them. Sarasota is one of the most open communities in America when it comes to hiring older workers. They are everywhere. The sandwich counter at a Subway sandwich shop on the road out to the Glenridge employs a phalanx of younger workers with lilting Indian accents and older women. One, gaunt and sun-beaten, another plump with a cotton ball of white hair, work side by side to ready sandwiches. Elsewhere in America one might assume that the darker-complexioned immigrants were the employees for the older white bosses, but here one assumes the reverse. It is the older women who are the minimum wage workers and the others part of the family that owns the franchise. At the lunchtime rush, the line at Subway stretches to the door, and it, too, is a line of mostly older diners, nearly all of whom are ordering the double-long sandwiches for five dollars and wrapping up the second half to bring home. "It's something, isn't it?" says a woman in line who appears to be in her midseventies waiting with her middle-aged daughter. "I don't think it would have been this crowded a year ago."

Publix, the local supermarket chain, has earned goodwill for years for its willingness to hire older workers. Following the economic downturn, every job opening was met by hundreds of applications from people past the usual retirement age. One conundrum for local employers is how to make room for younger workers when the older ones do not leave the job as often as they once did. A local paper reported that even the number of sick days older workers typically took off dropped dramatically.

Hair Transplants, Vein Reductions, and Injections of Cash

Sarasota Memorial Health Care System ranks as both the region's second largest employer and the second largest hospital in Florida. Seven hundred and fifty doctors and a staff of four thousand work at the not-for-profit hospital and its handful of satellite facilities.

Only the county school system has more employees. Wal-Mart, the nation's largest private employer, has several giant stores around the area but employs less than half the people the hospital system does. Publix, the big supermarket chain, employs a thousand fewer employees locally than the hospital. The nearby headquarters of Tropicana Products company, a division of Pepsi and the world's top-selling brand-name fruit juice, has half as many local employees as Sarasota Memorial. The hospital system is well-regarded. Its big payroll does not exist because it is the only choice for patients in town, or because patients always view it as the best. A for-profit hospital is the preferred home to hundreds of doctors and their patients and there are several other community hospitals in the area, too. Around thirteen hundred doctors work in the area, with more than two out of three of them specialists, paid above the national average.[16]

The large main campus of Sarasota Memorial is anchored by bright white towers that look more like resort hotels than a city medical center. Palm trees circle the property. The modern halls on the inside are lit for calm, some in tropical colors. From Highway 41, the main street that runs in front, the hospital looks eerily quiet, devoid of pedestrian traffic and screaming ambulances. That is by design. Though the hospital receives nearly eighty thousand emergency cases a year, most of the traffic comes unobtrusively into the center of the campus, keeping the appearance of alarm low.

The outward calm also masks Sarasota Memorial's role at the center of the most important segment of the local economy, health care. If Sarasota could not provide the care its older residents demanded, it could not attract them. With the implosion of the construction market, the medical sector has become the second largest niche in the local economy. Add in the service firms such as advertising agencies, lawyers, and accountants that cater to the sector as well as medical-equipment manufacturers and laboratories, and health care may be the primary economic driver of Sarasota. It is certainly a potent force in bringing outside money into the community, what economists call "export" revenue, which comes mainly in the form of federal Medicare money spent on the care of the area's residents age sixty-five and older. Medicare accounted for about 55 percent of the hospital's revenue in 2008.[17] Medicaid, the other big government health program, made up 7 percent. The federal money counts as "export" revenue because it is disbursed in Sarasota, but was raised largely by taxes collected outside of the area. Aging communities often turn to their hospitals and other medical services for economic growth, hoping the incoming money will make up for what they lack in other sectors, such as manufacturing, that once were more powerful engines in local economies. Sarasota is doubly blessed as a medical "exporter." It attracts older, federally funded patients from outside to settle there at the very age they become magnets for Medicare money. That helps to account for why Sarasota has a disproportionately high number of specialists. Ironically, in Sarasota, one of the oldest communities in the world, geriatricians, who are on the low end of the government's reimbursement schedule, are in short supply.

Federal money is just part of the story in Sarasota's medical economy. Specialties that rely on customers who pay with their own money also flourish in Sarasota. The city has seventy-six dermatology clinics in its phone listings. By contrast, Pittsburgh proper, which has six times Sarasota's population, has eighty-two. Rockford, Illinois, three times Sarasota's size, has twenty-two dermatology clinics listed. Bismarck, North Dakota, an important regional medical center, has five. Sarasota has ninety cosmetic dentistry clinics. Bismarck has seventeen. Rockford has twenty-two.

The section of Highway 41 that runs from downtown Sarasota past the hospital is the kind of wide, loosely zoned business thoroughfare that in other cities might be filled on each side with long rows of car dealerships. In Sarasota the highway is lined with pharmacies, banks and, most prominently, medical and other quasi-medical white-coat practices. Walgreen's, the big drug store chain, has some branches just a few hundred yards apart. Orthopedic surgeons have a whole building big enough to house a small school. A large, multistoried "Eye Center" competes with a similarly big "Sight Center" and the Strom Eye Center and a couple of other ophthalmologists a little ways down. "Clinic" must sound too clinical; nearly every big practice calls itself a "center." An angioplasty center advertises six doctors on its signboard. Down the street stand a medical center for women, the "Lipo

Reshape Center," a LASIK center, an angioplasty center, an orthopedic surgeons' center, an integrative medical center, and the Sarasota
Plastic Surgery Center. Looking for a chiropractor, an acupuncturist,
or a mesotherapy weight loss center (which targets fatty areas of the
body with "microinjections of conventional or homeopathic medicines")? In search of prolotherapy (which purports to heal painful
parts of the body by injecting solutions that encourage inflammation),
or nearly any variety of Asian folk medicine? Or still more cosmetic
dentists? It is all a short distance apart.

Dr. Bruce Robinson, the geriatrician at Sarasota Memorial, has
served as medical director at both Plymouth Harbor and Pines. Robinson believes that the abundance of health-care options in Sarasota
is due directly to the consumer preferences of retirees with extra
money. They want the very best health they can buy. Even when
their money cannot actually buy the health they want, they spend it
anyway.

"The challenge in health care in Sarasota," he says, "is that well-
heeled old people find all their money is no good in a doctor's office.
Most doctors work according to what the government pays for different procedures and treatment, and the doctors are not allowed to offer
two times the treatment or to take extra money from the patients. It
is the same with health insurance plans; they give the same care to
everyone. I have done a lot of different kinds of care. I have worked
in nursing homes, CCRCs, and hospitals, and I can never give people
with money all they want, which is more time and more care."

In Sarasota, however, people with money find ways to spend more
on health. Some doctor groups have set up "boutique care" where
for a large yearly retainer, the doctors make themselves available for
nearly anything a patient could want from them. Their phones are
always on, office hours are long, and families can call with endless
questions about their older parents.

"People with money can pay to abuse the system, but if you gave
that care to every older person, you'd have to put the whole military
budget into health care and still hold bake sales to pay for it." Robinson notes that people who demand high levels of care also demand
a lot of service. In a strange turn, it is the demand for service that
spawns Sarasota's low-wage economy. "Service jobs are low paid,

and that makes for a lot of uninsured workers." Sarasota, he says, is filled with young workers who have no health-care coverage at all. "There's a tension between the people with so much money that they always feel underserved in health care, and the people who cannot get served at all because they don't make enough money."

The people who can spend are also willing to try the wide variety of alternative medicines and treatments that can only be purchased for cash. Some are offered by conventionally trained doctors now willing to push beyond the mainstream. Many are offered in a parallel universe of nontraditional healers.

"A lot of the antiaging stuff," says Robinson, "is pure retail medicine: hair transplants, vein reduction, a lot of kinds of dermatology. . . . Dermatology is a golden specialty. . . . Sarasota is a good spot for antiaging doctors. A lot of well-heeled people are unhappy with their internists, who can spend only ten minutes with them, but an antiaging doctor who is paid directly will spend a lot of time with them."

In this way, as in so many others, moving to Sarasota is all about rejuvenation. As America moves closer to Sarasota in age, communities across the country will have to decide whether to embrace their older populations as Sarasota has, or whether they will either more, or less, smooth, or thwart, their transitions. For individuals everywhere in an aging world, the Sarasotans' relish for engagement in late life is a sunny vision for the gift of extra years.

CHAPTER 2

A BRIEF HISTORY OF
LIVING MUCH LONGER

Centenarians alive worldwide in the year 2000: 180,000

Number of centenarians alive in 2010: 450,000

Expected number in the year 2050: 3.2 million

A MAN I'LL CALL DOUGLAS SITS ACROSS THE TABLE OVER A PLATE of grilled vegetables at a Greek restaurant in a large southwestern American city. He orders broiled fish, with nothing on it but lemon. Douglas says he does not care to reveal his real name with his story, but he is excited to tell it. The danger, he says, is that people would dismiss him if they learned his age.

"I never could do what I'm doing now," Douglas says. "If my age got out, it would kill everything, in my personal life and business." Douglas goes to heroic lengths to conceal the number. He's compactly muscular, with bulky shoulders and a muscular neck that supports his shaved head. The isometrics of his ever-tight brow have bulked up the muscles around his strawberry blond eyebrows. When Douglas makes a point—many of which seem rehearsed—his gestures are emphatic and animated, but his movements are slightly out of sync with his words. They make Douglas come across as a hammy granddad who tears up the dance floor at a family wedding but is way off the beat. Yet a listener willing to adjust to Douglas's rhythm finds that slowly, but surely, his passion for life proves catchy.

Although vigorous now, Douglas fought a frightening battle with gastroparesis, or "paralyzed stomach," ten years ago. A virus, or bad food, or maybe a reaction to a drug (his doctors never learned), left him hospitalized and tormented by pain for half a year. He could barely eat then. Time and bland food brought Douglas back. He has worked hard to erase the episode, reasserting his youth and strength with an alternative, highly restrictive diet of his own design, tai chi, and a work schedule that usually keeps him busy sixty hours a week. Nevertheless, he ages as all people do and there are some signs he simply cannot hide.

For example, the clatter and jibber jabber of a busy Greek restaurant at lunch hour whip up a sonic bombardment for Douglas. Hearing loss is hard to disguise, but nearly inevitable as people age. The problem lies beyond the physical condition of the inner ear; changes in the brain make it harder to separate sounds so that ambient noise collides with the sounds that were once easier to zero in on.

Douglas also has the light, freckled, vulnerable skin of a former redhead. Pale scars on his face and neck hint at skin cancers carefully removed. He doesn't mention the scars. If Douglas utters his age at all, he first makes the hearer swear to keep his secret, then leans forward and silently, conspiratorially, mouths "Seventy-two." It may be true. He reveals his age sotto voce because he's proud of the man he is still, at whatever age he really is, and proud to have beaten back death when he was in crisis. He's fit, but doesn't look wildly younger than seventy-two, or wildly younger than seventy-five either. Douglas's secret is barely a secret at all.

A Girlfriend or Two

Douglas is aware he remains hearty at a stage when he needs to be steeled, or resigned, to the fact that biology conspires with age, not against it. He knows in his bones that older age is a time of tumult, and he means to drive his own change as long as he can, in the hope that he can thwart for a while what nature has in store. He is right to think so. Diet, exercise—particularly activities that promote strength and balance—and engagement are still the basics for lasting physical, cognitive, and emotional health. They do not, however, reverse how the body ages. Douglas knows, too, from his past episode, that his stomach is a time bomb that can shut him down again at any time.

Douglas is about to take off on his sixteenth trip in two years to developing Asia. He hands over a sheet of paper detailing his breakneck itinerary: six cities in Vietnam, China, and Mongolia in seventeen days. He is a lifelong serial entrepreneur, but until recently stuck to the U.S. market, where he built and sold four businesses and grew rich. These days, though, Douglas is down on America. Part of the problem, he says, is that the country is so youth obsessed it doesn't see the value in guys like him who are older and can still create jobs and wealth, and actually be sexy and powerful.

"America isn't a country that values new ideas anymore," he says. He's bitter about it. He perks up when he turns to his new ventures in Asia. That's a place where his maturity is a virtue, he says, where older people can interact with the young.

"The kids there are hungry. They listen to what I can teach them. They think I've got something. And I do."

One thing Douglas has is a younger girlfriend. Or two. Or more. He doesn't announce this outright. It also comes out in code, about how he is feeling virile, how he is strong and energetic. One of Douglas's two businesses in Asia helps local fire departments keep records. That, he says, is his bread and butter. The other business is his passion. Douglas's prior illness left him little faith in Western-style medicine. "It focuses too little on keeping people well and too often makes people sicker," he says. Modern medicine, he believes, is all mobbed up, filled with ruthless drug companies, corrupt doctors with deep conflicts of interest, overspecialization, overreliance on machines, and impersonal care. He is drawn to traditional Eastern medicine, which he praises for promoting lifelong health, and for keeping people in balance spiritually and physically, connected to their inner selves and the greater cosmos. The meditative Chinese exercise form he practices emphasizes harmony. Douglas's other new business in Asia is an herbal supplements business. It sells the kind of products that make men search for ways to talk in transparent codes about their energy and strength.

The Great Light Switch Becomes a Dimmer

One thing the spirited, endearingly ornery Douglas does not fully grasp is why, as a septuagenarian in the twenty-first century, he even has the luxury to lie about his age. Or why he is alive at all. Or why the Chinese are healthier now than they ever have been before, though they rely less on traditional medicine than in the past. Or—most anathema to his beliefs—why his efforts to live longer through diet modification, Chinese medicine, and exercise may help him live better, but have little chance of actually adding many years to his life.

What longevity Douglas enjoys results from myriad other factors that, in combination, have changed the world from one where people most often died suddenly from a relatively small set of killers, to one where they live far longer and manage their dangers. Advances in education, public health, urban living, human rights, and the vanquishing of infectious disease are, taken together, the main ingredients in the modern potion that foils early death and gives us the joys and sorrows of longer lives. Death still inevitably comes, of course, but only recently has it moved aside to make room for so many billions of people to age into their fifties and well beyond.

Guy Brown, a biochemist at the University of Cambridge whose research explores how cells fail during disease, traces the history of death through the ages in his philosophically smart and scientifically lucid book *The Living End*.[1] Brown describes aging throughout most of human history as practically indistinguishable from death. Before civilization dedicated itself to public sanitation, and before modern medicine's assault on infectious disease, a life of good health was most often snuffed out in quick death. Existence, Brown says, was binary. Like a light switch, people were bright one moment and out the next. "The very shortness of life tended to mean that death too was short. People either died as children or in their prime, so aging and aged individuals were rare," Brown writes. "The most common causes of death were infections, violence, and childbirth. . . . On the whole, [the end] was rapid [with] relatively little gray area between life and death."

The literary and historical vision of death's moment, Brown points out, is either a "fevered soul wracked by delirium . . . and expiring with a final, faint breath" or a violent end. "Death" was regarded as an ominous presence that traversed the world snatching life. The dark, cowled specter that called on the doomed carried a scythe to slash his victims and instantly separate their souls from their bodies.

Nowadays, Death would be more accurately depicted toting a vial of slow-acting poison that afflicts victims with congestive heart failure or late-onset diabetes for years.* Modernity has made the former vision quaint, though it rears up vividly when epidemics, such as AIDS, SARS, and swine and avian flu, threaten otherwise healthy people in Old World ways. Violence—war, homicide, and suicide—is still one of the world's potent killers, taking about five thousand lives a day. (Suicides make up about four in ten of violent deaths, with older men the most common victims.)

We all know the list of past killers. We breeze through them whenever we fill out a standard health questionnaire. Measles, mumps, hepatitis, pneumonia, tuberculosis, tetanus, asthma, diabetes, epilepsy. Some of the diseases can still kill, and do, but not with the certainty they once did. In any place where public health regimes function reasonably well, the litany of disease is no longer the song of the Grim Reaper.

Many past killers no longer even show up on doctors' forms. The historian William H. McNeill details what often killed humans prior to the twentieth century. They included innumerable bacterial and viral threats from mice, rats, and bugs; also fungi, bacteria, and protozoa. (Doctors, pediatricians especially, used to want to know whether a family lived near bears, snakes, big cats, or killer reptiles.) Septic sores, gastroenteritis and other diarrheal ailments, complications from broken bones and teeth, and even muscle strains sped death.[2] Even places people once went to for healthful retreats could

---

* In the ancient worlds of Greece and Rome, the force of death was tied closely to the gods and spirit world. The prevalence of sickness and death often had a political dimension. To ancient Greeks the health of the political order was measured by the health of the people. In China, where emperors were charged with keeping harmony under heaven, plagues signaled a disruption in the celestial connections and challenged the legitimacy of the court. The traditional Chinese view lives on in contemporary politics where the leadership of the Communist Party fears that its legitimacy hangs in the balance with every potential outbreak of disease. That accounts both for the tendency toward secrecy when new health threats first rear up and for the determination to act once a health scare is public.

kill them. Public baths in Rome, for instance, attracted, at one hour of day, the sick, who were in search of water's curative powers, and at another time, the well, who sought the water's recreational calm.[3] But the baths were rarely flushed, and taking the waters was like wallowing in a giant petri dish.

How long did people used to live, compared to today? Brown notes that in sixteenth-century London one-fifth of children died before their first birthday, another fifth died by age five, and death rates stayed relatively high until children reached the age of ten.[4] From ten to forty, people were relatively hearty, but death knocked again thereafter. From late childhood to middle age people were a relatively heartier bunch, but still far more likely to die than their modern cousins, who are indestructible by comparison.

In sixteenth-century London, some men and women did live into their sixties and beyond, but not very often. Then, as now, making it to a later age improved one's chances of growing older still. Seventeenth-century Englishmen who reached twenty-five—only about half of Englishmen lived that long—had about a 6 percent chance of reaching eighty,[5] an age pretty close to the upper limit of the day. People saw eighty-five about as often as they saw unicorns.[6] Back then, the mortal fragility of children and adults over forty shaped everyday life with the same force as catastrophic weather or erratic rulers. Life constantly adjusted to death.

A Lucky Birth

Like Douglas, with his tai chi and picky diet, we like to think that the most important decisions we make affect how long and how well we live. By deciding the way we eat, exercise, and relax, by choosing or ignoring doctors, by identifying the places we live and work, by fixing the way we save, invest, or spend, and by choosing how we love and how we are loved, we believe we can strongly influence our longevity. Individual choices *are* important, but the choices themselves take place in a global system that influences the way we age far more than most of the steps we take as individuals. Aging is a global product and a global act.

Regrettably, beyond showing us we should make obvious changes to our bad habits, science still cannot point definitively to any meaningful and manageable life-extending changes that individuals might make that would add significantly to their years.* Yes, smokers, alcoholics, drug abusers, people who gorge their way to poor health, motorcycle riders who shun helmets, and people who have unprotected sex with mysterious strangers are likely to live longer if they change these habits. Yet many unhealthful behaviors hardly affect longevity at all. Overweight meat eaters, for instance, may, in general, live only a few months less than lithe vegetarians. Their quality of life may not match up to the people who stay fit, but their time on the planet is likely to be nearly equal.

In general the things that keep healthy people alive into their seventies and beyond keep most everyone alive into their seventies and beyond. If you look across history, at every culture that ever existed, reviewing all the scientific literature and self-help books, you find only one crack-sure mode of maximum life extension: it is best to be born sometime after the turn of the twentieth century, preferably, though not necessarily, in an affluent, developed country. Nothing else even comes close.

Only in the last hundred years has the world's ability to supply abundant and reliable food been overlaid atop societies that have complex and capable systems to keep people healthy. Public systems that dispose of waste and deliver clean water and safe food began to take shape in earnest during the nineteenth century. As public infrastructure spread, the scientific understanding of the causes of disease took hold and people took control over their personal hygiene. Modern medical science, especially breakthroughs from the mid-twentieth century onward, subdued the infectious diseases that once commonly killed people before they reached old age. In advanced industrial countries, public health efforts have such a broad reach that their citizenry can hardly keep track of them, but the efforts work miracles in the background all the same. Vaccination pro-

---

* One possible exception is going on a diet that drastically reduces, to near-starvation levels, how many calories one eats in a day. Sticking to an extremely low-calorie diet requires either rare self-discipline or forced restrictions. But who wants to do that?

grams hit us in the arm, but less visible networks that train people to design, administer, and monitor them make the programs work. Comprehensive public health systems have dozens of key functions.*

Read the Label

Better food, public infrastructure, and great science alone could not have doubled our life expectancy unless families adapted to the advances. For that, people needed the skills to teach themselves healthy practices, and in fact, one of the most potent life-extending phenomena in world history has been the rise of literacy over the last century.[7]

Why? In media-rich countries, health information fills the eyes and ears of consumers. Health news and health guidance pour ceaselessly from newspapers and magazines, television and the Web. In the United States, health is the eighth most frequently covered subject among stories carried by newspaper front pages, television news shows, and talk radio. An eighteen-month-long study of local and national news programs showed that one of every twelve minutes was devoted to health news, and that nearly every broadcast of the evening news included some health coverage.** It gets three times the coverage of education or transportation, but far less than politics or crime. Health information permeates popular entertainment. Teens cite their parents, friends, and favorite television shows as leading

---

* Life-extending public health systems are a hallmark of advanced industrial countries, but they are present in a handful of lower income countries, too. James C. Riley identifies fifteen less affluent countries, including China (even before its economy reached the world's top ranks), Sri Lanka, Costa Rica, and Jamaica, that have had great success prolonging life expectancy by developing local systems. Riley argues that what distinguishes the efforts in these countries is a commitment to provide basic public services in public health and education, services potentially available in any country, rich or not.

** The study, conducted from January 2007 to June 2008 by the Pew Research Center's Project for Excellence in Journalism, found "specific diseases such as cancer, diabetes, or heart disease received the most coverage at 41.7 percent. Public health issues such as food contamination, tainted vaccines, and binge drinking garnered the next most attention, accounting for nearly a third (30.9 percent) of all health coverage. News about health policy or the U.S. health-care system was not far behind, at 27.4 percent of the coverage."

sources of information about sexual health, but list school as first.[8] Grade-school health classes may be boring, but they are life-giving.

Then there are the uncountable sources of health information and safety instructions that come from every direction, but require an education to digest. Consider these sources: product labels and warnings; instructions handed out by pharmacies and doctors; directions and ingredient lists on foods—how to mix infant formula, how long to store a bottled sauce, how to read a label for allergens; plus warning signs, traffic signs, directions on how to safely use machines, and the notes on household chemicals that explain how to save someone after an accidental poisoning. The Internet now delivers whole medical libraries to users' desks, laps, and phones and is coming to equal physicians as a preferred source of health information. Recent studies show that patients with Internet access come to their doctor appointments far more informed than in the past, meaning they ask more informed questions and get better care.

Literacy, notes historian James C. Riley, gives people access to information from people they do not know. It endows people with a cosmopolitan view that helps people judge information from many sources and take responsibility for themselves and the people they care for, including their children. Literate societies can also be taught universal practices that promote public health. Thus is literacy possibly the world's greatest gift to life. Studies that compare the power of education to keep people well against other important factors, such as the level of economic development or the state of public health infrastructure, consistently put education ahead. Education allows people to put society's advances to work for themselves and their families. It is so central to good health and a long life that small amounts of education, doled out in the world's backwaters, save people in ways that, until this century, could only be prayed for. Looking over thirty years of research, Riley found a consistently strong relationship between schooling and the reduction of child mortality. Every additional year a young girl goes to school reduces the child mortality of the next generation by 7 to 9 percent. Extra years of education have the most pronounced effects in areas where families had little access to health services. Literacy linked families to the modern health practices even when doctors and clinics could not.

The Elixir of Urbanity

Another powerful booster of human longevity is the modern city. "Population aging and urbanization," notes the World Health Organization, "are the culmination of successful human development during the last century."[9] Cities, the WHO notes, are essential to the well-being of both urban and rural populations, because they are "the hothouse for new ideas, products, and services that influence the world."

In the past cities were hothouses of a different sort. For centuries, people were more likely to grow sick and die young in cities than in the countryside. Urbanites with means would seek cures under the country sun or in the mountain air. The fourteenth-century storytellers in Giovanni Boccaccio's *The Decameron* fled the mayhem and squalor of Florence during the Black Death for a country villa far from the city. Boccaccio's introduction to *The Decameron* details how the plague, which killed half of Italy, rapidly undermined urban life and forced the city's rich to organize their exit. European cities in his time were small. Florence, one of Europe's three largest cities, had around one hundred twenty thousand residents before the plague. The city was crowded and filthy enough to compound the ill effects of people's poor health practices and to speed epidemics.

In the nineteenth century, urban industrial centers sprang up before sanitary systems, refrigeration, or medical science could cope with the dual dangers of dense population and lethal industrial pollution. S. Jay Olshansky, professor of public health at the University of Illinois at Chicago, and his collaborator, the biodemographer Bruce Carnes, of the University of Oklahoma, note that in the early Industrial Revolution cholera, diphtheria, influenza, polio, smallpox, and tetanus ran rampant among new urbanites. Food turned rancid in leaky, moldy wooden iceboxes but was often eaten anyway. Urine and dung from humans, horses, and smaller animals made cities cesspits. Hospitals spread infections rather than contained them. The virulence of childhood disease regularly meant that children died before their parents. Those threats remained potent well into the twentieth century.

Today, in countries with even moderately good public health infrastructure, children rarely die before their moms or dads unless their moms or dads live past ninety.* Today, too, cities are the healthier places to live—sometimes far healthier places than the countryside is, or ever has been. Not just the big cities themselves, but their suburban and exurban orbits. The shift is a recent one.

Cities might not seem all that healthful, given what burdens them. They are homes to migrant populations from home and abroad. Migrants are often newly urbanized rural people who come in at the bottom of the economic pecking order. Many cities are places from which affluent people migrate, leaving for nearby suburbs or for other, more vibrant cities far away. Many formerly prosperous cities in the United States and Europe are bleeding industries and affluent citizens. In August 2008, *Forbes* enumerated America's dying cities; the list reads like a mass eulogy for second-tier industrial centers in the Midwest and Northeast. (*Forbes* dubbed Cleveland the "fastest dying city.") A 2007 report on Europe's cities commissioned by the European Commission[10] found populations decreasing in two-thirds of the 258 cities surveyed. Dozens of cities, in Central and Eastern Europe especially, are in deep decline. Modern plagues, such as HIV infection, drug abuse, and asthma caused by pollution, are rightly linked to city life.[11] Even the world's poorest cities attract people from the countryside. The poor rural areas feed the world's growing urban slums, now home to one-third of the world's population. In cities such as Jakarta, Mumbai, Rio de Janeiro, and Nairobi, the shanty towns offer more access to opportunity, meager as it is, than the countryside their residents left. Childhood mortality rates are often high in slums, and the exposure to infectious diseases endangers everyone.

---

* Large parts of the developing world remain dangerous to young children, of course. Children under five account for two of every five deaths in sub-Saharan Africa, while in the developed world ninety-nine of one hundred children under five survive. Deaths among people over sixty offer another stark comparison. In sub-Saharan Africa, fifteen of one hundred deaths beset people sixty or older, but in the developed world, eighty of one hundred deaths come to people over sixty. In the developing world overall, the percentage of deaths among children is shrinking while deaths suffered by older people is heading up. In developing countries in the Western Hemisphere, half of all deaths come to people over sixty, and in China the figure is up to 70 percent. The developing world's distribution of death across all ages will not spare it the challenges of an aging world. Population growth is so high in the developing world, including high-mortality regions such as sub-Saharan Africa, that older populations in poor countries will grow faster, in sheer numbers, than in richer countries.

But economic decline, population slides, and ill conditions in slums do not come close to negating the role of the modern city as a life-extender. Urban childhood mortality is so much lower and, relatedly, life expectancy so much higher, that cities have become the world centers for better health.[12] Urbanites report that they feel healthier than their rural cousins. All over the world, death rates among young people below age twenty-five are lower in cities than in the countryside. In the developing world, city children also tend to be taller, stronger, and better fed than country children; the disparity holds true even when poor city children are measured against similarly poor rural children.[13] In China, a government survey found that 30 percent of children born in the countryside were malnourished, compared to just 1 percent in the cities.[14] A rural school child in China is likely to be twenty-two pounds lighter and to stand four inches shorter* than a city child.[15]

Cities also give even poor people access to services they may well lack outside an urban center. Proximity to urban services, such as safe water, sanitation, and education. Being near health care may help, too, by raising the health consciousness of everyone. Cities also have the political clout to demand services from leaders and the resources to organize to address local needs.[16] A study of the relative healthfulness of Chinese cities compared to the Chinese countryside found that cities were better places by nearly every measure, including longer life spans.** The number of local hospitals in Chinese cities, however, had barely any bearing on how healthy or long-lived the local residents were.[17]

The differences are just as startling in New York City, where gains in life expectancy are trouncing the gains made in the United States as a whole. In 2004 alone, life expectancy of New Yorkers went up by five months. In the United States as a whole, life expectancy went

---

* Relatively low weight and short stature can signal a short life, too. A study of 5,654 men born in the twenty years after 1910 showed that the smaller among them had the highest rates of coronary heart disease and chronic obstructive lung disease. (D. J. Barker, et al., "Growth in Utero, Blood Pressure in Childhood and Adult Life, and Mortality from Cardiovascular Disease," *BMJ*, March 4, 1989)

** Surveys conducted by the Shanghai Academy of Social Sciences predict that Shanghai, where the average life span is nearly equal to that of Japan, will be home to the oldest population among large cities in the world.

up by two months. New Yorkers, on average, live nine months longer than the average American. Some of the gain is a statistical function of lower fertility rates; some of it comes from a drop in deaths among younger New Yorkers—AIDS is no longer the killer of young men it once was, and homicides are down—and some is from a real gain in the life spans of older adults.[18] Citizens in many large cities in Southern Europe and east Asia have an even greater advantage over their national populations.

Healthy Babies

There was a time, not so long ago, that a great frequency of death among infants and young children weighed on families in most of the world. But the poorest countries today have far lower infant mortality than did the richest countries in centuries past. The high infant mortality of the past plays into how people perceive life expectancy today. Statistics on the doubling and tripling of average life spans, when they are cited responsibly, come with the caveat that the averages have climbed so quickly because so many more children survive early childhood than in the past. In the United States, which does not have the world's lowest infant mortality rate, the twentieth-century decline in early childhood deaths has boosted the average life expectancy by thirty-three years. In other words, the decline in childhood deaths accounts for most, though not all, of the lengthening of the *average* life span.

So if the average life expectancy of Americans is to grow still decades longer, the great gains no longer come from lowering the already low death rate for the young but by engineering ways for the old to survive long past the ages they die at today.[19] The same is true in any country where people now live, on average, into their sixties, or older. There can be no big statistical jump in average life expectancy unless the great mass of people in their sixties and beyond find a way to hold on for decades more. Olshansky, for one, notes that gains are already slowing. He likens increasing life expectancy for the already long-lived to walking up a steep hill with a stone that gets progressively heavier.[20] Nevertheless, people who reach middle age are living longer than in the past, and the length of lives of adults keeps stretching out, between one and two and a half years every decade.

Centenarians Everywhere

Today, the world is abloom with new centenarians. The burgeoning of this oldest group may not make much of a dent in world demographic statistics, but the growth of the group, measured against itself, is still impressive. The United Nations Population Division estimates that in the year 2000 there were one hundred eighty thousand people in the world one hundred years old and older, but that by 2050 that number will have grown to 3.2 million. Boston University professors of medicine Thomas Perls and Dellara Terry codirect the *New England Centenarian Study*, a comprehensive look at the lives of forty-five centenarians in the Boston area. "[The] dramatic increase in the number of the centenarians is likely the result of relatively recent (over the last century) public health measures that have allowed people who would have otherwise succumbed to preventable or treatable causes of childhood or premature mortality to survive to a much older age," Perls and Terry write of their study on exceptional longevity. The doctors also note that the reductions of mortality at earlier, though still old, ages drive up the number of centenarians, because of both public health measures and medical interventions that allow people genetically prone to live long lives to survive to one hundred or beyond.

But as we will see in the next chapter, when a society has a large and growing number of old people, problems occur. Old people require the energies of young people, and when a society does not have enough young people, it is forced to change, often in surprising ways.

Douglas may bemoan how advanced medicine focuses too much on cures and too little on the whole self, but he is here in his eighth decade to say so because progress, though often maligned, has given humanity what it most craves—expanded time on earth—and created Douglas, a modern older man.

CHAPTER 3

SEÑOR MOMENT:
SPAIN'S DISCOVERY OF AGE

Life expectancy at birth of Spanish women: 84.4 years

Rank among the countries in the European Union: 1

*Expected percentage of Spaniards aged 65 or older
in the year 2050: 37*

*Percentage of Spain's people who were
foreign born in 2000: 2*

Percentage of foreign-born in Spain today: 12

MARCOS RUIZ, A STURDY SPANIARD, RESTS HIS SECOND CIGARETTE in the restaurant ashtray as he fills his wineglass with a plum-red Tinto Rioja. These few seconds will be the tobacco's only moment of rest. Marcos, an editor at one of Spain's premier publishers, is an ardent inhaler. When one cigarette flames out, he drums another out of his pack and lights up. Madrid restaurants have new rules on smoking but the laws lack force during the two p.m. lunch rush. The smoke and the wine add extra gravel and gravity to Marcos's voice and his laugh. Unkempt brown bangs, a poet's beard, and piercing dark eyes lend his erudite observations world-weary authority.

Though Marcos is in his early forties, the aging of his country already weighs on him. It weighs on all of Spain, where the current and impending age of the citizenry is a seemingly immutable feature in the landscape of Spain's public discourse—as recurrent as global warming, the end of peak oil, left and right political animosities, the relentless tide of immigrants and their reassertion of Islam, the country's eternal *fútbol* rivalries and the glory of the united Spanish team that won the 2010 World Cup. Yet common concern crosses more boundaries than the aging of the people.

"News about Spain can cover nearly any subject," Marcos observes, "and still work in the fact that its population is growing older." There is a long list of examples. One is the big real estate bust that began in 2007. It left 1.6 million homes still unsold by mid-2010, despite a steep drop in prices. That is about one-fifth fewer than the number of unsold homes in the deeply troubled U.S. market, which has nine times Spain's population.[1] One reason often given for the country's inability to dig itself out economically, or to manage its outsized public debt, is its aging and increasingly dependent population. Eighty percent of the wealth of Spanish households rests in real estate, so when prices skidded and the number of homes on the market climbed, the wealth of older Spaniards plummeted. During the Greek debt crisis, Spain's socialist ruling party tried to insulate the country with reforms, such as raising the retirement age from sixty-five to sixty-seven, freezing pensions, and an easing of what's allowable when companies fire workers. They met widespread protests, some of which nearly shut down Madrid.

Or, as another example, as newspapers and television roundtables wrestle with the issue of immigrants in Spain, they link the flood of newcomers to the needs of Spain's aging population for younger, lower-cost workers. The average age of natives in Spain is about forty three, but for immigrants coming into the country, the average age is thirty-two. Because of this age gap, there is a popular belief that a more generous immigration policy will increase the working-age population and help reduce the pension costs of the elderly beginning in 2030, which is when large cohorts born in the 1960s and 1970s in Spain will have retired.[2] A study by Banco de España, Spain's central bank, noted that in the near term the vast and sudden influx of foreign workers created a "huge labor supply shock" and significantly lowered the skill composition of the labor force. And, thus, brought the realities of the globalizing labor market into the domestic economy of Spain.

Foreigners Were Once Strange

Twelve percent of Spain's population is foreign born today. Yet foreigners in modern Spain are a new phenomenon. Historically, Spain sent large numbers of people into the rest of the world. Following World War II, Spaniards were recruited into other European countries for the low-wage agricultural, industrial, and domestic jobs similar to the jobs that large numbers of immigrants now fill in Spain. In the 1950s and 1960s, 1.2 million Spanish workers, young and old, male and female, mostly destitute, left to work elsewhere.* Foreign employers regularly recruited Spaniards out of poor rural villages. Thousands who pledged themselves to work in Germany were placed on chartered trains that delivered them directly to factories, or to city depots where families collected them to work in homes.

Through the 1960s and 1970s, the decades under the conservative, ardently pro-family dictator Francisco Franco, Spain had youth to spare. The government facilitated the export of workers in the hope they would send money home. One of the ironies of southern Europe today is that families have memories of relatives or countrymen who left home when their part of the world was deemed too poor and crowded to provide for them. For them, the new tides of people to their shores represent the same old story with an ironic twist ending: the once youngest, most fecund countries in Europe became the oldest and least willing to have children.

As with Florida, Spain's boom-and-bust economy had for decades relied heavily on tourism and retirees coming to the country. Spain began to draw foreign pensioners in earnest in the 1960s under Franco. The government turned the country's sunshine into a resource with which to lure tourists and retirees and inject Spain with foreign money. A frenzy of development followed Franco's death in 1975, and by the 1980s a boom in construction and services for retirees was well under way. Spain today is home to three hundred thousand pensioners from the United Kingdom and large contingents from Germany and Scandinavia. Now some of the older foreigners are needy themselves, and their residency makes Spain an ever-older place.

* In 1960, Spain's population was 30.5 million.

In the year 1953, only one of every five hundred residents of Spain was foreign born. By the early 1990s, the count had risen to one in every one hundred residents. Then, suddenly, immigration began in earnest. South Americans, Africans, and job seekers from the former Soviet bloc arrived by the hundreds of thousands every year. Nearly all of Spain's population growth was due to the arrival of foreigners, and so, too, was Spain's huge economic boom over the period. The arriving workers allowed Spain's own relatively older citizens to move up the economic food chain and leave low-productivity, low-wage jobs to the new kids. Immigrants provided Spain's work-around for its notoriously inflexible workforce, and Spaniards willingly accepted the bargain, so long as immigrants filled in lower-rank jobs that Spaniards could now abandon for better ones. Metropolitan Madrid, Europe's third largest urban agglomeration after London and Paris, suddenly became one of the most internationalized population centers in Europe. Immigrants from abroad now make up nearly one-third of its population. (According to a UNESCO tally, Los Angeles has the world's highest proportion of immigrants.) In all, close to one in eight people in Spain, better than 5.6 million individuals, is now a registered foreigner. Count the undocumented and naturalized immigrants and the number may climb by one million more.[3]

Off the Farm

Rural Spain is aging faster than any other region in Europe, and the migration of young people out of small towns has killed or decimated one village after another. In regions where agriculture remains labor intensive, such as Aragon, which needs fruit pickers in good times and bad, out-migration, aging, and urban prosperity made labor shortages seem permanent until the foreigners arrived in the country. But as unemployment hovered around 20 percent in 2008, 2009, and 2010, Spain's first generation of urbanites returned to the rural villages that recent generations had seemingly abandoned forever.* Tens of thousands of backbreaking, low-wage field jobs that

* Unemployment for the working-age population twenty-five and younger hovered around 44 percent, with young immigrants especially vulnerable to joblessness.

had recently required an army of foreign laborers were once again filled by native Spaniards.[4]

The ripple effects were great. Communities that had adjusted their social services around declining populations suddenly had influxes of Spanish families and were saddled with the needs of unemployed foreigners with their own families to support back in their home countries.

In good times, an aging society such as Spain needs new workers but in lean times struggles to keep them employed. Under economic stress, older people save more and spend less, stay in their careers longer if they can, and find jobs at low wages if they must. They tolerate foreigners less and grow reluctant to use tax money for social services for immigrants and their children, preferring that resources go to Spain's elderly who have their own, costly needs.

Shrinking Families, Bigger Choices

Year by year, Spain's numbers become more stark. Over the last quarter century the number of people over sixty-five in Spain has grown about 75 percent while the average birthrate, 1.35 children per woman of childbearing age, is near the bottom globally. Spanish women typically start having children at age thirty, as late as any other women in Europe.

Pick nearly any comparison of older people in Spain to younger ones, and the drift is the same. The country has more than one million more people over sixty-five than it does young people under fourteen, a disparity that continues to grow as the number of children withers and the population shrinks. Projections for Spain's population in the benchmark year of 2050 predict Spain will have 3 million fewer people than in 2009.[5] Every realm of society that needs a stream of young people is at risk. The percentage of Spaniards attending university has been going up but, after years of declining birthrates, Spain's pool of young people of university age is contracting.

The shrinking family size in Spain and in southern Europe generally has been the butt of jokes and complaints from critics who fear declining fecundity is reducing the region to what one Washington strategist calls "strategic irrelevance." And that's the kind view. Canadian conservative commentator Mark Steyn declared in his 2006 volume, *America Alone*, that Europe's "Gelded Age" would create a continent that will be "semi-Islamic in its politico-cultural character within a generation," and that by the end of the century "will be like a continent after a neutron bomb: the grand buildings will still be standing but the people who built them will be gone . . . Long before the Maldive Islands are submerged by 'rising sea levels' every Spaniard and Italian will be six feet under," wiped out by declining birthrates.

Spain's and Europe's demographic critics chalk up population change to indifference, laziness, and passivity. Yet nothing could be further from the truth. The changes in Spain result from determined choices that individuals and the nation have made, and continue to make. None of the trade-offs are taken lightly. The benefits of longer lives and smaller families are weighed against sacrifices and dangers every day. Demographic change in Spain, and much of Europe, is not capitulation. It is self-determination.

Where Have All the Soldiers Gone?

The thinning ranks of the young also shrink the ranks of Spaniards eligible for military service. In 2004, when the new Socialist government of José Luis Rodríguez Zapatero withdrew Spain's soldiers from the war in Iraq, Spain's shifting demographics were one of the underlying factors. For one thing, Spain's shrinking pool of youth and its smaller families make young Spaniards less, um, expendable than in the country's more bellicose past. For another, a growing percentage of young men in Spain are newly arrived Muslims. That complicates the home front if Spain allies in a war against Islamic nations. A glass tower now stands in Madrid's iconic Atocha Station to commemorate the 191 people who were killed and 1,800 who were injured by ten bombs set off in March 2004 in the city's train system. The government's investigation found that the main culprit, an ethnic Moroccan, was inspired by al Qaeda. Moroccans are Madrid's and Spain's largest immigrant group. More than six hundred fifty thousand Moroccans live in the country, and the vast majority of them have come to Spain sometime since 1999.

Amid the economic bust, anxiety about working-age immigrants stirred the rhetoric about the loss of jobs for Spaniards, the threats to Catholic Spain, and the rise of "Eurabia." The Spanish government began paying migrants to return to their home countries. Wherever in Spain there is talk of immigrants, the fertility choices of Spaniards and their exceptional longevity underscore the discussion. Certainly, goes a common view, if Spain were as fecund as it once was, it would not need immigrants.

Marcos Dines Out in a Nation of Foodies

With aging as the backdrop the news can sound glum, but look around the restaurant where Marcos dines. The zeitgeist of Spain that feeds the aging dynamic looks a lot cheerier. The room bustles and will stay lively for two hours over the midday *comida*. The mix of ages at the tables is impressive. Thin, dapper, gray-haired men in well-tailored suits hold court with juniors of descending ages. A stream of friends stops by with hugs and hearty handshakes for Marcos. He shares something with each of them, a bit of gossip, an observation on an upcoming election, news of a recently published poem by the dashing Chilean diplomat who sits three tables over. The visitors reciprocate, adding their stake to the social network. If the world's best hope for extended longevity is an austere low-calorie diet, the news has not hit Spain. Spain has the highest longevity of any country in the European Union. Life expectancy for men is 77.7 years and for women it is 84.4. In 2010, Spain had three times as many centenarians (ten thousand) as France, which is half again as populous, and twice as many as Italy, where the population is one-third larger. Life expectancy has been lengthening by nearly three years a decade even as Spaniards spend 40 percent more time at meals than Europeans overall. The habits around a typical Spanish diet of five to seven meals a day keep people well-fueled and socially connected.

In Marcos's Madrid, as in other Spanish cities, the tempo of work and life revolves around meals. Eating is so social in Spain that even bars offer breakfast. Two hundred thousand bars dot the country; that's one for every two hundred Spaniards. They lure people in all day long, beginning with breakfast. Spaniards, Italians, and Irish spend a larger proportion of their incomes on food and drink than any other Europeans. For men, eating out is the most important spare time activity in Spain; for women, it is only slightly less so.[6] Cafés fill up at midmorning when friends and coworkers meet to down a cup or two of strong coffee. Lunch follows in midafternoon, bringing out the wonders of Mediterranean fare. Fish and other seafoods are favorite proteins. Fresh vegetables, legumes, sheep and goat milk cheeses roll out slowly over a leisurely hour or two. Wine and coffee lubricate the lunch. A snack in the late afternoon might include a dish of cold seafood, a slice of *tortilla de patatas* made of egg and fried potatoes, or a sandwich, just enough to hold out until supper at nine or ten or later. Small plates with tapas offer a wide variation on the Mediterranean staples. Wine again, or maybe sherry, is a must.[7]*

At Marcos's table, a waiter delivers two airy baguettes and places them directly on the cloth. A series of small plates of starters follows. A ham sliced paper-thin hits the table. Marcos knows where in southwest Spain the ham comes from. This is just one of the hams he knows everything about. Ask him about the country's greens, its wine, its sherry, fish or cheese; his knowledge is encyclopedic and up to date.

The quality of Spain's food is a national point of pride. Its benefits, in the literature of diet and health, are exalted above the world's most potent, life-extending pharmaceuticals. The nation's fare all but promises long life, health, and pleasure, but its salubrity also bedevils Spain with a predicament. "It's our damn Mediterranean diet," Marcos grumbles, dipping a piece of bread into a dish of rich green olive oil, "it just won't let us die."

* At eleven p.m. or midnight, after supper, Madrileños walk. The city is filled with walkers. Spaniards spend more of their leisure time physically active than people in any other developed country. In 2008, the Organization for Economic Co-operation and Development (OECD) surveyed how people divided a typical day in eighteen developed countries. The French spent the most time at the table, nearly 140 minutes, while in Spain people spent less than 110 minutes. Watching television is the number one leisure activity in every developed country, however.

Eating to Live

The healthful virtues of what is generally extolled as a Mediterranean diet have become so well accepted in the last twenty years that the diet has entered the pharmacopeia of doctors treating the overweight and patients at risk for diabetes, heart disease, and cancer. Dozens of books in print rewrap classic Mediterranean dishes with prescription pads.

In 2005, the *British Medical Journal* published the results of a study of 74,607 healthy men and women sixty years old and older, from nine countries across Europe. Those surveyed were scored according to how closely their diet fit a version of the Mediterranean diet selected by the researchers. It was high in vegetables, legumes, fruits, and cereals, moderately high to very high in fish, and moderately low in dairy. It was also low in meat and low in saturated fats but high in unsaturated fats (mainly olive oil). Those who scored higher tended to live longer.[8]

Yet people who relish red meat and feast on cheese may not feel that the price in terms of shorter life span is inordinately high. Statistically, sixty-year-old men whose diets were the most unlike Mediterranean diets lived only one year less than sixty-year-old men whose diets neatly fit the study's definition. For some Mediterranean countries the differences in life span between nations where diets are generally considered dangerous were hardly meaningful at all.

The list of health risks Mediterranean diets seem to mitigate grows longer with every monthly cycle of medical journals. Pregnant mothers on Mediterranean diets lend their children extra defenses against asthma and allergies. Mediterranean diets help women maintain stronger bones as they age. They help ward off heart disease and many kinds of cancer. Versions of Mediterranean diets that are especially high in nuts seem to help people with metabolic syndrome manage their health problems better. It helps ward off Parkinson's disease and Alzheimer's disease. A four-year survey of ten thousand people published in 2009 found that people who stuck to a Mediterranean diet were less suicidal and depressed, though the study did not get to consider whether living in a highly social, sunny place where fresh fish and produce abound might also be mood balancing.[9] Death rates for all causes, age for age, are among the lowest in the Mediterranean regions.[10]

Still, the powers of the Mediterranean diet remain somewhat mysterious. There is wide, but recently weakening, consensus that its benefits accrue from its relative absence of processed food and saturated fats. It helps that the diet is high in fiber and complex carbohydrates and stocked with foods that deliver strong doses of antioxidants, vitamins, and minerals.[11] The correlations are strong, but when it comes to understanding the mechanisms that make the Mediterranean diet work, there are still some fat holes. The place of salamis and hams is one of them. The meaty version of the diet enjoyed widely in Spain, and evident on Marcos's table, would be widely scorned in most diet books.

The Carnivore's Dilemma

Sausage, with all its meat and fat, is more common in Spanish kitchens than the recipes in prescriptive Mediterranean diet books let on. Varieties of thick, paprika-reddened, fat-speckled chorizos hang in the open air in restaurants and taverns and are staples in Spanish home kitchens. They vie for pride of place with the white-cased *salchichón* with bloodred meat or overpacked *sobrasada* that puffs out like a flesh balloon. Sausages come delivered on small plates with cheese, olives, and toasts. Sausages go into soups, bean dishes, and little casseroles. Sausage is everywhere.

Spain's air-cured hams are even more evident than sausage. Where else but the Spanish capital does a popular restaurant chain advertise itself with hundreds of dried pig legs in the window, and call itself Museo del Jamón, the Museum of Ham? Spain cures about 40 million hams a year, nearly one per person. The people of Spain rank near the top of ham and pork eaters worldwide.*

To the prescribers of the ideal Mediterranean diet, the evils of fatty hams multiply when the curing process begins. It is then that

---

* Only the decidedly un-Mediterranean dieters in Denmark and the Czech Republic rely more on the pig.

the pig's back leg is bathed in nitrified salts. Too many nitrates, say critics, can damage the body's ability to absorb oxygen, and its use in curing is one reason proponents of the Mediterranean diet frown upon processed meats. The most publicized rebukes of processed meats tie consumption most directly to bowel cancer and less so to a variety of other ailments.

Demonized Flesh Part of a Faustian Bargain?

Nathan Bryan of the University of Texas at Houston has argued that some of the scientific community's view of the dangers of chemicals in processed meats has been out of sync with the latest science. "The public perception is that nitrite and nitrate are carcinogens, but they are not. Many studies implicating nitrites and nitrates in cancer are based on very weak epidemiological data. If nitrites and nitrates were harmful to us, then we would not be advised to eat green leafy vegetables or swallow our own saliva, which is enriched in nitrite and nitrate." A small glass of pomegranate juice, Bryan says, delivers one hundred times the level of nitrate as a hot dog. It may even be that there are unsung health benefits in hams, sausages, and even in hot dogs, which the idealized versions of Mediterranean diets leave out in the cold. "Nitric oxide [found in cured and processed meats and many fruits and vegetables] is an important signaling molecule in the human body to regulate numerous physiological functions, including blood flow to tissues and organs," says Bryan. His research suggests that foods high in nitrites and nitrates can help prevent and treat heart disease by increasing blood flow.

The science is far from settled, but new findings suggest that one reason for the longevity of people in Spain and Italy might be their fondness for the cured meats. A six-year-long study of Spaniards found that those who ate large amounts of cured Spanish ham had no greater likelihood of cardiovascular disease, hypertension, or weight gain than those who ate very little.[12] And research on diet and longevity, like sausage, is usually mixed and often overturned.

Social Eating

Spain's diet is distinct enough from others in the region that lumping it together with others does justice to none. The links between the longevity of Spain's people and its diet are complex. Spain's climate, agricultural possibilities, and proximity to the sea give its people access to fresh fruits, vegetables, and animal protein. Among the chief impediments to any Mediterranean-style diet outside the Mediterranean region are high cost and inconvenience. Even Spaniards pay a premium for the foods they prefer,[13] but they don't have to work hard when seeking them out.

If the Mediterranean diet promotes longer, healthier lives, it may do so in large part because of the lifestyles around the diet, not just the choice of foods. Xavier Medina, an anthropologist at Barcelona's European Institute of the Mediterranean, argues that the emotional needs for Spaniards to share food with family makes them the most social eaters in Europe. "It is unusual to see a person eating alone in a restaurant or drinking alone at a bar . . . such situations are avoided," he says. "In Spain, 'eating alone is like not eating at all.'"

Medical and social scientists will not go so far as to say that social networks reverse or retard aging, but they have long observed that people with strong social networks are heartier. People who have strong community ties, family relations, and good friendships will not lower their chances of getting sick or their likelihood of developing a chronic condition, but people with stronger social ties do have fewer accidents and are less likely to take their own lives than those with weaker ties. Moreover, among people who fall seriously ill, those with strong social networks recover faster and more fully than those who are more alone.* People who are more alone seem to

---

* There is evidence, for example, that people with strong social networks who are stricken with cardiac ischemia and cerebrovascular disease have better prognoses than those less integrated into a group. Matthew Daring, a geneticist at Ohio State University, found that laboratory mice with cancerous tumors who were placed in bigger groups with more toys often went into spontaneous remission. His research, published in *Cell* in July 2010, found that physical activity alone would not help mice improve as much. Interactions with others was the key. In more social environments, the tumors in the mice shrank an average of 77 percent.

have weaker immune responses, are less able to regulate the flow of hormones into their bloodstreams, and suffer from poorer cardio-vascular function.[14]

Carlotta Goes Home

You can talk about Spain's aging in a café in Madrid, but to really see it, you need to leave the capital for the countryside. Carlotta del Amo left the small hillside town of Sigüenza, in Spain's Guadalajara Province in the Region of Castilla–La Mancha,* to begin her university studies when she was eighteen. She never moved back, but still has strong ties to Sigüenza. Carlotta returns from Madrid nearly every weekend to visit her parents, a mother in her midsixties and a father close to seventy. The dynamics changing aging Spain strike her close to home.

"There are no young people left. Practically none at all," she says bemusedly, as if anyone would be surprised by the well-known facts of rural Spain. She offers a tour of Sigüenza's graying present. It begins with a ninety-minute drive northeast out of Madrid along Spain's arterial Highway A2.

Carlotta works as a publicist in Madrid. Slender, with a full head of thick, black curly hair, she confidently dons a dependable uniform of international urban cool: black slacks, a black blouse buttoned just enough, and a short, sporty black leather jacket. Her world revolves around television studios and magazine offices across Spain. Carlotta exudes a down-to-earth glamour her press contacts like. She's an urbane country girl who gets the job done.

Back in Sigüenza, among old friends and family, Carlotta loses her business edge. Blue jeans and a favorite loose, gray turtleneck replace her urban wear. Her posture relaxes; her hands tuck into her pockets. She flirts, she shrugs, she laughs, she pouts. She greets all she knows with two kisses. The social circle in the town is small enough that everyone is a local celebrity on return. Carlotta's family runs Sigüenza's most visible hotel and restaurant, just outside the

* Spain is divided into seventeen autonomous communities or regions and its regions into provinces.

center of town along the region's main thoroughfare. Her father, mother, and uncle built the place. The family claims it is a way station, not a destination. Nevertheless, people who stop to shop or order sandwiches at the profusely stocked deli counter, or sit in the lunchroom of the bigger dining hall enter as if they know the place. Liter jars filled with Sigüenza's deliciously floral sun-colored honey, a popular gift item, line the shelves. Every detail in the hotel has a homey touch. Carlotta's father, Angel del Amo, designed it in earth tones with a tile roof to fit in with local stucco houses. The resident cats perch outside in the window frames of guest rooms. After staying the night, Ricardo Bofill, the superstar architect from Barcelona, declared the Del Amo property "the perfect hotel."

Angel now spends his time in the hotel unofficially. Spain's pension rules offer strong incentives to retire at sixty-five. A short, strong man with gray hair and a boxer's nose, Angel still watches over the place and "consults" frequently with Carlotta's mother on how it is run.

"I am retired, but still meddle," says Angel, sitting at one of the tables in the hotel dining room. He has noticed, too, that much can go wrong after age sixty. "I worked, with my younger brother, but he had a partial liver transplant. Now he spends a lot of time in the hospital."

He grips a cigarette and leans back to peer with his narrow eyes over his crooked tough-guy's nose. Then, calling up the full range of storyteller expressions and gestures, he ushers a guest into his world.

Substituting a Whole Town

"In 1988, we brought the first immigrants into Sigüenza. My brother went to Santo Domingo in the Dominican Republic and he realized the waiters there were really good. He promised three of them he would bring them to Sigüenza. Back then, the highway was being built and we had a lot of business on account of the construction, but we couldn't get enough help from around here. Beginning in the 1970s, every young person went to Madrid, Barcelona, or Valencia. At first, not to go to school, but to work in the factories that were opening up. It was better to be a factory worker, they thought, than to be a peasant."

"At the beginning, people said, 'Oh, you have blacks working there,' but they saw that they were good workers. Now the 'black' population around here—I know they are not really black, but they are darker than the people from here—is bigger than the white population."

In the late 1990s, he says, the immigrants started bringing in their families, which was still easy to do back then. Immigration, as opposed to emigration, into Spain was so against the norm that the state had virtually no legal structures to deal with it. "As the people in Sigüenza got old, and their children were off working in the cities, the immigrants' wives and mothers started taking care of older people in their homes. The caregivers were usually around the same age as the people they were taking care of! It still goes on."

Angel recalls 1999 as the year of the biggest change. "We started getting people from all over. We've had Ecuadorians who sent most of their money home to their families in Ecuador. We once had a Romanian waitress who got drunk every night and went around showing her breasts to everyone. I don't hire Romanians anymore. If you or your friends have a bad experience with a group, you don't want them working for you. I had workers here from India and from Bangladesh, but then I realized that if I needed more people, the easiest thing for me was to ask the guys from Bangladesh and they could always come up with more."

Sigüenza's Bangladeshi immigrants are mostly men from the countryside. They come to Spain and land first in the low-wage textile and garment factories in Barcelona, only to find that the city makes them anxious. One Bangladeshi, picked up while hitchhiking into town said, in schoolbook English, that he is one of several Bangladeshi squatters living in an otherwise empty farmhouse several miles outside of Sigüenza. He works at the filling station across from the hotel. He said he grew up in a farm village, worked in Barcelona, and felt the city close in on him. He headed into the Spanish countryside to join friends in Sigüenza.

Immigrant groups in Spain, as elsewhere, have what amounts to brand identities, some based on prejudices and some on empirical experience and anecdotes shared among natives. Ecuadorians, Angel says, want to build houses in their own country and leave Spain after seven or eight years to catch up with the money they sent home. Dominicans and Peruvians prefer to stay in Spain and bring their families to live with them. Colombians, Angel says, sometimes stay and sometimes go. "It's hard to say because they can get involved with drugs. Africans from the former French colonies work extremely hard and they are great on the machines we have for washing dishes and pressing the laundry. And then there are the Spanish workers. I have one Spaniard who is a little racist, and I had to insist that he change."

As the immigrants have replaced the people in Sigüenza who have left or retired, Angel and the other employers in town have had to select which immigrant groups are best for them to network with. Angel's strongest connections are to the Bangladeshis and unsurprisingly he finds them the most simpatico, smart, and loyal. He is a good and steady employer. The stakes for the Bangladeshis are high. If they foul up, they risk destroying the reputation of their whole group, particularly the ones whose fates are intertwined with the network Angel is connected to.

Aging societies force people to globalize locally, in the workplace and in the home, while the bigger economic spheres around them globalize, well, globally. As some local factories move to low-cost countries, other local factories bring low-cost foreign workers to them. Foreign waitresses shack up with waiters from half a world away. A Dominican grandmother travels from Hispaniola to join her son or daughter, and finds herself holding the arm of a Spanish grandmother in Sigüenza who can no longer balance herself on the streets of the town she was born in. Strangers become intimates, show some cleavage, or they go to bat for you when you're in a jam; they do the jobs your sons and daughters will not or cannot do, while at the same time putting the more ambitious dreams of your kin within reach.

"Despite the changes," reflects Angel del Amo, "I feel I am unchanged. I tell my migrant workers they have to adapt. Usually after six to ten years working for me, when they have kids who are a little older, they move away to the city, but they still call me all the time and ask my advice. I give it and we talk. I now have friends from all over. I have a Bengali friend in Malaga. I have a good friend from Santo Domingo who I can call if I need someone beat up. He would do it."

The Quiet in Sigüenza

Sigüenza is now a quiet weekend retreat for lovers. Outsiders come to soak up Sigüenza's history and admire the twelfth-century castle that was maintained by the Catholic church as a bishop's palace. But what are charms to tourists are repellent to the young adult locals who seem more likely to live in Madrid and other big cities.

On Sunday at midday, some locals walk about the town center and circle a small park. The local bar Carlotta frequents is filled with people and talk. Many of the drinkers are weekend returnees. When Carlotta was a girl in the 1980s, she went to school with many of them. That world is gone. No one in the bar has brothers or sisters, nieces or nephews or children or grandchildren in the school these days. In less than a generation the town's school has gone from a bustling building filled with two thousand native Spanish children to a near-empty one filled with two hundred children from several nearby villages. About half are the children of immigrant workers, and others are foreign children, with no regular homes, who have been placed in Sigüenza's schools by church relief programs.

The mix of children in the school will no doubt change again but just how is hard to say. The schools, like schools in many smaller rural cities and towns the world over, may fill up with more non-native citizens. This may happen as Sigüenza accumulates a critical mass of foreign aunts, uncles, and family friends who can provide support for nieces, nephews, and others in their circles. Or the schools may empty out more, as even immigrant families work their way to Spain's and Europe's other cities.

The Provincialism of the Global Economy

The arrival of foreigners in Spain affects their home countries. Every worker in Angel's hotel has left a family and tilted the age balance at home. Ecuador, a country of around 14.5 million people, now counts seven hundred thousand of its citizens in the prime of life as residents of Spain. The Migration Policy Institute in Washington estimates that between 1982 and 2007, between 10 and 15 percent of all Ecuadorians moved abroad. In 2010, 1.5 million, or one in every ten Ecuadorians, was away. Their average age is thirty-three; most often they leave parents and children behind. Before 1998, Spain had virtually no Ecuadorians living in the country. They are the biggest part of a wave of people who left their native country and, in doing so, changed the economy of Ecuador significantly. Angel del Amo is correct about Ecuadorians' impulse to send money home. The Spanish government estimated in 2007 that the average monthly income for migrants in Spain was about $1,080. The average annual remittance home is about $360. For Ecuadorians, however, the figure is closer to $650. Money sent home is the second greatest contributor to Ecuador's GDP, exceeded only by the country's oil.[15]

Meanwhile, part of the vacuum left in Ecuador has been filled by migrants who enter Ecuador from Peru and Colombia. The absence of so many Ecuadorians, and the presence in the country of so many migrants has emerged as a central issue in Ecuadorian politics. Why was it, the country's president, Rafael Correa, a Ph.D. economist, wondered aloud during the country's 2009 elections, that Ecuador could not have a fuller benefit of a generation of its most able workers? Though Ecuador's fertility is comfortably above replacement rate, the sudden out-migration of such a large portion of its young adults is aging the country prematurely. Ecuador's age demographics now rival those of the oldest countries in Europe and east Asia.[16] After winning, Correa's administration inaugurated its Welcome Home Plan, a program to repatriate more than the usual number of returnees. The program gives tax breaks to returnees, lets them bring in furniture and equipment from abroad duty free, and offers seed money for them to start businesses in Ecuador.

"The idea is to recover . . . human capital, because even if you didn't go to school [abroad] or didn't get a formal education, you still learned how to do things in a different way," said a spokesman for Ecuador's Secretaría Nacional del Migrante (National Secretariat for Migrants). "We want to connect these people with opportunities in Ecuador so they can apply what they learned." The Ecuadorian government is making a bet that the country's economy can get more value out of the human, intellectual capital its citizens acquired abroad than it gets out of the remittances of money home. It can ill afford, the thinking goes, to let the needs of an aging European country accelerate Ecuador's economic and demographic decadence. After a year, eighty-six hundred Ecuadorian families returned[17] and took advantage of the program. The politics of age arbitrage now mix with economic nationalism and globalization.

As with Spaniards returning to small towns and rural villages, home is the ultimate insurance policy for economic migrants everywhere. Of the returnees to Ecuador from Spain, most were men caught without jobs after the collapse of the construction market. Ecuadorian women in caregiving jobs did not rush home. Aging Spain is keeping them employed. This poses a problem for the repatriation scheme. A disproportionate number of migrants from Latin America to Spain in the last decade have been Spanish-speaking women. The reasons might seem entirely obvious, given the needs of an aging population. The country needs caregivers and women from other Spanish-speaking countries who share the language, religion, and many of the cultural references of the Spaniards they care for. Elder care is everywhere the province of women, and when needs grow so do the roles for women. In 2005, during one of Spain's serial attempts to "regularize" immigrants, 220,000 foreigners filled out applications for domestic service jobs. The overwhelming majority of job seekers were from Latin America and 84.3 percent of them were women.

The demand for paid domestic help has also turned new immigration to Spain, especially Latin American immigration, into a largely female enterprise. Most of the women end up with jobs in Spain's cities. While the influx of native Spanish women into urban Spain may no longer tilt the gender balance of the cities—because today's rural population is too small to make much of a difference—the new addition of women from Latin America is helping, along with aging, to feminize the country's cities.

Is discrimination against women still prevalent in Spain? Of course it is. Spaniards prefer women as domestic help and caregivers. That's nothing new or unique. What is surprising, however, is that the women who come to Spain do not make the journey to be subservient, but rather to take charge of their economic fates, a path often barred to them if they stay in their home countries where men tend to be, still, very much in charge. Ecuadorians send more money home from Spain than other migrant groups because most of the Ecuadorian migrants are women, and they "invest" more in their role as family protagonist.[18]

The role of immigrants, even unskilled ones, in globalizing Spain's economy is valued within Spain, too. Aging, indebted Spain needs every mechanism it can find to create new business niches and jobs, and to shake up the labor market. Young migrants drawn to the aging nation can rejuvenate the most hidebound sectors. The cross-border financial needs of two hundred thousand Ecuadorians in Madrid has forged the city into a cutting-edge banking center for Latin America. Facilitating remittances is a highly profitable business, but was once overlooked by Spain's big financial institutions. Smaller players and money order companies milked the transactions, charging up to 15 percent to make an international transfer and then making more money still on trumped-up exchange rates that gouged another 3 to 5 percent from the money migrants sent home. When Spain's banks moved to capture a piece of the market, they changed the game, with new systems that relied on credit cards, electronic fund transfers, and links to branches or affiliates abroad. They charged low, flat fees. Recipients in the home country could now receive close to the full value of the money sent. According to a study conducted by Madrid's Center for Immigration, two-thirds of the migrants living in Madrid hope to remain in the city in the long run. Ecuador may not be able to lure the majority of its citizens home from Madrid as quickly as the government hopes, but in the meantime the city council of Madrid is working on what it calls "co-development programs" with cities in Ecuador to create businesses that serve the economies of both countries. What one country and global businesses call "cooperation," may be seen by another country, and economic and political nationalists, as co-option.

In the global movement of people and money in and out of

aging Spain, the big sweep of the changing economy and the intimate encounters between Spaniards and newcomers can also stir inane and grotesque public dramas. In the summer of 2009, Evelyn Dueñas, a twenty-eight-year-old Ecuadorian housekeeper in Valencia, made a stink in Spain and her home country when she placed a notice in two well-trafficked online auction sites. There, she announced that, on account of her aging, Alzheimer's-stricken mother's need for expensive care, her virginity was for sale for €15,000. "It's a great sacrifice, but I am doing it for my mother," Dueñas told television reporters. "I don't think it will solve all my problems, but it will give me some financial stability. Dueñas laid out more conditions for the bargain than a Hollywood prenup and ultimately demurred, but not before a torrent of comment in the media likened her to other, less publicized women who sell themselves every day, and to immigrants forced to sell their kidneys, lungs, and other body parts to raise money needed at home. Dueñas also got the attention of the Ecuadorian government, which was pushed to weigh in publicly on what the state could do for her mother. The politics of sex, immigration, the organ trade, colonialism, and the welfare state all conflate around the politics of age.

Off the Boat, by the Hundreds of Thousands

The shores of southern Europe—Spain, Italy, and Greece—have become the entry points that are more preferred, and most overburdened, by migrants to the continent. The desperate and hopeful from North, East, and West Africa continue to try their luck, but more recently new groups of Asians have been making their way, often with the help of human smugglers. Barbed-wire detention centers in Greece have been erected to hold and process, among others, new arrivals from Afghanistan who have paid smugglers up to thirty thousand dollars to handle the clandestine transport into the shadows of the immigrant economy. Southern European nations complain that it is unfair for them to absorb the brunt of in-migration; that it is only the circumstance of their geography that drives migrants to use the southern European entry points as a back door to the rest of Europe.

One common but harrowing strategy that smugglers and their clients try is to set off in a rickety boat (often after a long and difficult overland journey) and aim for one of the island territories of Greece, Spain, or Italy. At the height of the influx, Spain's Canary Islands, west of Morocco's southernmost coast, received boatloads of migrants from Ghana, Liberia, Senegal, and other countries. They arrived in thirty- to forty-foot-long *cayucos*, dilapidated, open wooden fishing boats long past their working lives. The migrants are their last haul. Elaborately painted in the green, yellow, and red of Senegal's flag, these boats are also adorned with symbols. Some have long-lashed eyes painted on the bows to help find their way. Not all the migrants are intercepted, and some drown at sea, but in 2006, a busy year, Spanish authorities intercepted thirty thousand people trying to reach the Canaries.[19] Resort beaches in the Canaries, where tourism is the dominant industry, piled up with dozens of abandoned arriving boats each day.

In 2004, Europe strongly considered, then rejected, a plan advanced by Germany and Italy to set up camps in North Africa to process migrants. The Spanish, who were then more enthusiastic recipients of undocumented foreigners than they were after the economic collapse, officially objected on humanitarian grounds. As unemployment rose, legislative revisions were pushed by Spain's Socialist government to tighten Spain's borders and give Spain's regions their own powers to control how many migrants traveled around the country in search of work.

Harvesting the Immigrants

In the complex regional and linguistic politics of Spain, different parts of the country and different constituencies have their own agendas. The influx of South Americans into the Basque Country and into Catalonia is commonly regarded as a threat to speakers of regional languages who fight against the incursion of the mainstream Spanish language. The effects on local languages of in-migration can be counterintuitive, however. In Basque Country, the influx of migrants has spurred some communities to redouble their commitment to the region's tongue, and in many locales enrollment in Basque language schools (as opposed to bilingual schools) has climbed.[20] Basques also run exchange programs for students from non-Spanish-speaking countries, such as Morocco, that allow young Moroccans to return on successive summers for a dose of Basque culture mixed with school, job training, and homestays with Basque families. The key for regionalists, of course, is to educate migrants in the region's tongue—not just Spanish. Under the laws Spain revamped in late 2009, the nation's regions can turn on and off services and restrictions to immigrants in order to suit their own economic and cultural agendas. New national laws also allow the regions to "cherry-pick" the immigrants that serve them.

For an aging population, the prospect of attracting and keeping foreign workers at the peak of their powers, while keeping them separated from their dependents, is hard-hearted, but economically wondrous. It spares the state from having to pay for the migrants' families' schooling and health care; from guarding their safety or subsidizing their housing or paying for their upkeep in hard times. What's more, should migrants remain separated from their families, they may be more likely to head home before they become dependent in their old age.[21] If they sicken or have an accident befall them, they may wish to join their families at home.

In all, keeping migrants from their children and their parents lets the host country both harness the migrants' ability to work and scrimp on the migrants' families' needs. In an aging country, the arrangement, if it can be pulled off, allows more of a nation's wealth to be spent on the needs of the growing proportion of older citizens.

The new laws also address a hard reality for aging countries: as populations decay, so does the base for their culture. Fears about the Islamization of Europe build on the specter of foreigners with alien beliefs and practices filling Europe's emptying house.

Meet the Hervas Family

Back at the bar, Carlotta introduces the Hervas family, including Mariano, the father, seventy-two, who Carlotta announces is the smartest businessman in Sigüenza. He is drinking with his two sons, Javier, forty-two, and Pedro, thirty-six.

Mariano holds a glass of beer in his thick-fingered, weathered hand. He owns and runs one of Sigüenza's largest private employers, a company that makes parquet flooring. During the building boom, the company had a tough time filling jobs with reliable workers willing to stay in Sigüenza. Mariano also owns the building that is home to the town's newest senior residence.

"I was born in Villacorza in the 1930s," he says, beginning his story in Spain's harsh civil war years. "It is a peasant village where the people had small farms. My parents had two mules to work the land. The town was too small for a school. I walked twelve kilometers through a path in the hills to get to my lessons. The path is now forested over, because no one walks it." Mariano was one of seven children, including two who died young. Families, he frowns, "had lots of things happen to them."

Spain's smallest towns, those with fewer than one thousand people, lost their populations faster than any others.[22] Officially, greater Sigüenza has twenty-seven smaller satellite communities, but some of them, such as Mariano's hometown, have no one left.

"I moved to Madrid in 1951 to study and work. I bought my parents an apartment in Madrid when I had enough money and moved them out of the village in 1965. That was a very typical thing to do. Then I decided to start a business, and thought I would do it in Sigüenza because the workers were cheaper and they were like me, from farms, and they worked very hard." Until around 1997, he says, his workforce was entirely Spanish to a man. "Now the workers I get are often refugees sent to me by the archdiocese because the local bishop is active in resettling people."

"It is incredible how many different places my workers have come from, thirty countries altogether." Mariano lists Iran, Morocco, Russia, Poland, Colombia, and the Dominican Republic. "They come to me and beg for a job. I pay for their training and when they break machines. I pay for the legal work to get them permits, and as soon as they can leave Sigüenza, they go off to the city."

To cities, that is, where the pay might be better and where the workers can commune with their countrymen who have also come to Spain. That game gets put on pause in tough economic times.

Mariano's floor business does not hum during construction busts, and immigrants become more willing to hold on to jobs if they have them. Despite the willingness of many Spaniards to leave the cities for assembly lines and menial work close to their ancestral homes, high unemployment sheds light on another aspect of aging Spain. More recent generations of educated Spaniards showed a strong willingness to refuse jobs they thought were beneath them and to stay unemployed. Smaller families enabled the choice. Parents with one or two children could support them while they waited for better jobs. Families can also offer a safety net for young, educated workers who risk taking less than secure jobs. Spain's so-called "contingent" workers, hired without long-term commitments, make up 30 percent of the workforce. Employers prefer contingent terms for younger employees because businesses do not want, or already bear, the high costs of older, long-term employees that they cannot easily shed. One reason youth unemployment skyrocketed in aging Spain during Europe's debt crisis is that younger contingent workers were easily let go, but entrenched older workers were not. Even so, older workers also faced pressures and incentives to leave jobs before age sixty-five.

When those of Mariano's generation left the villages for urban Spain or work abroad, they sent money back from their meager earnings to pay for housing for their parents. Today, older adults are at least as likely to spend money on adult children as the other way around. Spain's newly small families, the increasing prevalence of university education, and the rise in living standards all change the way money moves in families. Better-off parents are willing and able to pay to maintain their children's higher social status. The support may serve, in effect, as a down payment, or as insurance, for parents who expect to rely on their children for support, emotional and monetary, if their old age requires it.[23]

Doing Little, Getting Fat

Mariano refused to take his pension at sixty-five and says he plans to keep working "as long as I have my knees, hands, and head."

Friends near his age are puzzled. "I am the only one of my contemporaries officially working. The others all quit at sixty-five, and now they sit in a bar all day drinking, or they go to Madrid to take care of their grandchildren. Nearly everyone takes the pension, spends their time doing very little, and gets fat."

Mariano's assessment of his peers' desire to retire is confirmed by a study by one of Spain's big financial groups, la Caixa, which found that in general workers in Spain do not want to stay on the job past age sixty, and that only one-quarter of workers over age fifty would even consider working until age sixty-five.[24] Surprisingly, the study found that even despite deep fears about the future of Spain's economy, the reluctance of older Spaniards to prolong their work lives is resolute. Yet there are structural features built into Spain's retirement system that influence people's choices. These may well change in the face of Spain's economic bust and the rapidity of demographic change, but resistance has been fierce. Even people like Mariano and Angel, who own their own businesses, face pressure to retire in a system that penalizes their pension prospects if they hold on to their jobs. For employees at the whim of business owners, the pressures are even stronger: not just for retirement but for early retirement.

Though nearly every country in Europe has raised or is considering raising the official retirement age, employers often look for any means they can find to reduce their rolls of older workers, many of whom are not that old at all. Even in flush times when Spain's boom was gangbusters, Spain did not rate high among European and other developed countries in its ability to keep workers fifty-five and older on the job. In 2005, the OECD reported that just a little more than half of Spain's able population between the ages of fifty-five and sixty-five had jobs, which placed it thirteenth from the bottom and in a league with the Czech Republic, the Slovak Republic, France, and Greece. The rates were far worse in Hungary, Belgium, Austria, Poland, and Italy, where close to 65 percent of those between ages fifty-five and sixty-five do not work. In the United States, Japan, Switzerland, New Zealand, and all the Scandinavian countries except Finland, roughly two-thirds of the people in that age group are employed.

Workforce or Shirk Force?

For Mariano's and Angel's contemporaries, Spaniards over sixty-five, the employment numbers are far lower, and so is Spain's ranking, at fifth from the bottom, with only two or three of every hundred people working. In Korea and Mexico, by contrast, thirty in one hundred people over sixty-five work. The average workforce participation rate for people over sixty-five for the countries in the OECD survey was about 12 percent.[25]

The change in Europe's workforce participation is dramatic in itself. "In the early 1960s, the participation rate for [males] aged sixty and over was above 70 percent in each country, and 80 percent in several of them," observes Agar Brugiavini, an economist at the University of Venice. By the mid-1990s, that rate had fallen below 20 percent in Belgium, Italy, France, and the Netherlands, to about 35 percent in Germany, and to 40 percent in Spain.[26]

Undercutting the official retirement age is common in nearly every country in Europe. This age in Germany, the country that *invented* the official retirement age, was sixty-five in 2006, but the effective age for men is sixty-two and for women sixty-one. In France, men tend to retire at fifty-eight and women at fifty-nine. A mix of causes has driven the retirement age down. Some pension plans offer alluring payouts at earlier ages. Others have strong disincentives for people who work past official retirement ages.

Mariano is also right that retirees have plenty of time to sit around and get fat. In developed countries, the average retiree lives another eighteen to twenty years. That is one-third longer than retirees lived in retirement as recently as 1970.[27] In Spain, a longer retirement is likely because people tend both to retire younger and to live longer. This feeds the country's debt woes. For great numbers of the current crop of new retirees, two decades of postcareer sitting and eating will be a very real choice. Some may toy with reentering the workforce once they have retired, but, if the past is any guide, only a minuscule number of retirees will have regular employment again.*

* The OECD notes that among people age fifty to sixty-five who are not active in the workforce, only 5 percent have jobs one year after their initial exit. (*Live Longer, Work Longer*, OECD, 2006)

To Brugiavini, the spectacular drop in workforce participation in Europe is at least as momentous as the shift in the age demographics. The two trends, however, interact. When people stop working at younger ages, they both limit their time as producers and expand their time as unproductive consumers and dependents. (This leaves aside, for now, the great value of older people's unpaid work and contributions to their families and communities.) Each year lost off the effective retirement age has huge costs for the European economy. Most obviously, workers who stop working shrink the workforce, which in Europe is already predicted to lose one-seventh of its strength over the decade and a half ending in 2021. If the retirement age retreats, the workforce will wither more.

Of course, if people retire earlier and live longer, they expand the amount of time they need to live off someone's money. This could be their own savings, or money their states or former employers have put aside for them. It could be money other workers pay into the system. It could be some form of debt—again their own, their governments', or their former employers'. Or they could live on money from their families or especially generous friends. Maybe investments or business interests kick in a little, or a lot, too. In all likelihood, it will be some combination. And very likely, early retirees will outlive every calculation that went into planning how much money they would need to last all their days. People are resourceful, adaptable, and impressively generous to family members, so many will get by fine, but on reduced means for themselves and the families they will rely on.

Some countries have pension plans that do a great job of keeping older people out of the deepest depths of poverty. In 2009, amid the recession, Germany, France, and the Netherlands earned high marks. Others do far worse. Great Britain, where 30 percent of the population over sixty-five lives below the country's poverty level,[28] and Spain, where 28 percent fall into poverty, are among them. High poverty figures are a hallmark of economic downturns, but the short-term pain of recession is not what worries European Union policy watchers the most. They find the economic effects of the aging of the population scarier, in large part, because it has been so hard to engineer ways to get Europeans to once again work past sixty or sixty-five. Someone is going to have to pay for all of these people, and who that is, no one knows.

The Forsaken Elderly

Sigüenza has long had a residence for older citizens, though it runs on a decidedly older model from the one Mariano owns. On a hilly street not far from the cathedral a gate opens into an old gabled compound run by an order of nuns known as Las Hermanitas de los Ancianos Desamparados, the Sisters of the Forsaken Elderly. Established in Sigüenza in 1872 by a local priest, the residence allowed older people who had no family to trade their life savings for the promise of perpetual care and spiritual reflection. It was a private welfare home before welfare and state combined in Europe. The model shares one feature with some of the modern business plans of the elder care industry today, which also require a significant exchange of worldly goods to purchase an all but inviolable form of long-term-care insurance. But the terms the Sisters impose are very Old World. The disincentives for leaving the Sisters' compound once residents make the commitment to enter are exceedingly strong because residents have no worldly wealth at all from their first day forward. The Sisters require residents to surrender their social security payments. Healthy residents get 20 percent of their check back, about €80 a month, enough to buy beers or Cokes, snacks or cigarettes a few times a week in the shops outside. The home is also in charge of the care of the Sisters who run the residence. They, too, have bargained away their worldly lives for a livelihood in the home's wards.

By the look of the Sisters' home in Sigüenza, it has stayed true to its practices over many years. A knock on the door wakes a woman dozing at the front desk. She presses a buzzer and makes a call. Sister Carmen, the woman says, shows visitors around the home. In moments Sister Carmen appears, petite even in full habit: a large white coif and an ample black veil drop down her forehead to the top of her glasses. She is calm, in charge, and quietly cheerful.

Sister Carmen became a postulant to the order at age eighteen in 1943 following a youth marked by Spain's rebellion, war, and personal loss. "My father died when I was eleven and my youngest sister was one year old," Sister Carmen says with pain in her voice. "The violence upset me very much. I found peace with the Sisters of the Forsaken Elderly, but even within the order it hasn't always been tranquil." From 1955 to 1957 she worked in Cuba during the revolution that ultimately put Fidel Castro in power. After that came posts in Mexico and the Philippines. Sister Carmen's last thirty years have been in the home in Sigüenza. Now she is eighty-two. When asked if working in an elderly home, where so many people are frail and death visits regularly, makes her reflect on her own future, she says offhandedly, "I try not to think about it."

Pictures of Christ hang over the beds in every room, often the only decoration the residents have. Rooms are shared. Minimalism, Sister Carmen says, helps the older people focus and keeps tension down. Some have small televisions. Old tube sets perch in high places in some of the hallway lounges, too. A group of men so thin that their clothes hang on them as if they were children playing dress-up sit limply in vinyl chairs, their eyes directed weakly up at a game show.

"We have seventy-five men and seventy-five women," the Sister reports. "The women prefer to be separate from the men, so we don't put them together. The men seem to prefer it, too. There was one married couple, but one of them died and the spouse went back to the segregated ward. Men and women don't share much here, except their time in church and some public programs. We show movies in the chapel." The residence director picks the films; Sister Carmen offers reassurance that they are wholesome.

Within the wards, people are separated according to their health, and some live on inside the walls for decades. One of the shrunken men in the lounge says he has been with the Sisters for thirty years, which would put him at least in his midnineties. In the section for the severely infirm men, there is a line of wheelchairs occupied by shaking small bodies with big heads, each being spoon-fed by the staff.

The residence has a lush rose garden in a courtyard. "It's our meditation garden," says Sister Carmen, pointing to the blooms. Do the residents help tend the garden? "No," says the Sister, "they're not gardeners and they are old."

The Less Forsaken Elderly

Visitors to the Alameda Residencia para Mayores, the Alameda Residence for the Elderly, Sigüenza's new home for seniors, walk through big glass doors to a bright, open lobby. This is the residence Mariano built and owns, and it seems to suit his disdain for recumbent retirement. At a long, open workstation sits Beatriz Garcia Yusta, twenty-nine, a trained social worker who has moved back to Sigüenza to be with her family and boyfriend and work at the new residence. Until recently, the demand for homes for the elderly in Spain was negligible, especially when compared to other developed countries. Outside the biggest cities, modern elder care facilities were few and far between. Families were expected to care for their own. Spain's population shifts, which have reduced family sizes, pushed the workplaces of adult children farther afield from their parents, and extended life spans created the demand for new homes.

Most of the inhabitants of the Alameda Residencia would not describe themselves as forsaken. As much as the home run by the nuns seems shut off from the rest of the world, the Alameda Residence is designed to bring the outside in, and the inside world out. A parade of families comes through the big front doors on weekends to visit. Beatriz's first instinct when offering her tour is to bring visitors into the middle of the open lounge that spreads brightly over several thousand square feet just beyond her desk. A television in the corner tuned to a tense soccer game attracts grandchildren and adult sons, some dressed neatly in jackets, others in warm-up suits, who have set up a couple of rows of banquet chairs to watch the game. A few grandfathers watch, too, but grandmothers far outnumber grandfathers in the home and they prefer to chat and play cards with their daughters and granddaughters or their friends' daughters and granddaughters. Small crowds of well-dressed women sit and stand around the room. The older ones look like they have put on their Sunday best, but Beatriz reports that they are in their finery every day. Most of them come from small villages and towns, and it is their custom to put on tweeds and knits, necklaces and earrings, when they venture out. Meeting in the lounge is venturing out. The women greet Beatriz warmly as she works her way into their circles. Her rapport with them is evident. The staff is mostly female, too. Most are Spanish, but some hail from South America, or Africa.

Beatriz offers an introduction to Asunción, who looks like she's in her early seventies. The village where she grew up offered no work opportunities for her during the Franco years. Like her siblings and her friends, she went abroad. She served as maid to a family in Paris for twelve years. Asunción shared a small apartment with her brother and his wife, but her life there conspired against a marriage or children for her. Franco's pro-family goals notwithstanding, the proportion of Spanish women who marry has been dropping steadily since 1950.[29] The decline in the rate of marriage in Spain follows along with women's independence in the workforce and their rising levels of education. In Asunción's case, work but not education played a role. The decline of marriage in Spain has also contributed to the country's dearth of children.

Two generations separate Beatriz from Asunción, but as players in Spain's demographic change, they take similar roles. Asunción emigrated from her village to another country, and then spent time in Spain's larger cities before moving back to small-town Spain. (Moving back to her original village was out of the question. Asunción says only eleven people remain there.) She earned a living, saved, and now is a participant, as a consumer, in Sigüenza's best new job engine, the Alameda Residence. Beatriz left Sigüenza for an education, but brought back with her the advanced skills she acquired at her university and now deploys in Sigüenza, where she is applying and transferring her knowledge to others at the new enterprise.

Country Boys and City Girls

From the beginnings of the countryside's depopulation half a century ago, women have led Spain's rural exodus, and even in recent years have been more willing to move to cities than men. Men now outnumber women in Spain's rural areas, and the gap is growing,[30] a counterintuitive fact given that these regions are also aging quickly and that Spanish women, on average, live so much longer than Spanish men. The gender disparity in rural Spain matches or exceeds the disparities in countries such as China and India, where parents, who prefer boys, often select their children—through abortion or infanticide—on the basis of gender.* (Women migrate in higher numbers out of rural Asia, too.) The Spanish country girls may return one day, but when they are just old enough to leave, they do so much more readily than men, largely because men have better prospects for productive work in modern mechanized agriculture.

Where there is a shortage of women, one might expect that the women who stay back are especially attractive to men who want to get married, and that men will go to great lengths in preening themselves, getting an education, saving money, and doing whatever else it takes to make themselves more valuable in the marriage market. If that's the case, it is not working. The marriage rates in the countryside have dropped far lower than the out-migration of marriageable women explains. Bachelors, young and middle-aged, are in surplus.

In Spain and throughout Europe, far fewer men and women marry than a generation ago. In 2008, there were 30 percent fewer marriages among Europeans in EU countries than there were in those same countries in 1975. The men and women who do marry are about two and a half years older at the time of their unions than those who married in the 1970s. Later marriages, of course, mean smaller windows of time in which couples can have children, and the decisions of Spaniards to delay starting families has had the same effect it has had all over Europe. Although elsewhere in Europe a

* In Castilla y León the ratio of males to females is 106 to 100, the same as the national ratio in China and India. In Vietnam, the ratio is 98 males to 100 females; in Japan it is 95:100; in Indonesia it is 100.6:100. In the European Union as a whole the ratio is 92:100, but in Spain overall, the ratio of males to females is 96:100. Globally, gender ratios for different age groups break down as follows:

Sex ratio at birth: 1.07 male(s)/female
Under 15 years: 1.06 male(s)/female
15–64 years: 1.02 male(s)/female
65 years and over: 0.78 male(s)/female
Total population: 1.01 male(s)/female (2009 est.)
(Source: *CIA World Factbook*, September 2009)

higher proportion of children are born out of wedlock, later unions between intending parents are nonetheless still one of the chief reasons couples have fewer children. As Spanish women opt to reach for their potential as educated people and as workers, the balancing act to manage family, education, and work might be different without the presence of immigrants in Spain to work as maids and caretakers.[31] The low-wage, low-skilled newcomers have freed up Spanish women—and men—to seek skills and higher-value jobs.

In the case of rural women, whose traditional roles on the farm and in small towns offered neither pay nor social security, the chance to make a break has been all but irresistible. Even today, the participation rate of women in rural Spain's paid workforce is half the rate of workforce participation in the cities.

Again, put the factors together—women leaving small-town and rural Spain, delayed or demurred marriages, the surplus of bachelors, the aging of the population—and the result is what Spanish demographers warn is a "vicious circle of demographic decadence."[32] Some of these characteristic trends can be seen in aging places in the developed world and all over aging east Asia, too. The factors age the cities and countryside alike, though the process may run according to slightly different clocks, as cities initially enjoy a rush in of young people. Cities do not, however, escape the vicious circle forever; in fact they drive the forces that lead to demographic decadence. Still, there is an anomaly in rural communities that age because of out-migration: the aging countryside is going through a "masculinization," while the aging world overall is "feminizing."

One last melancholy fact for men in the era of global urbanization is that small-town and country women are desirable to urban men, but small-town and country men who move to the city struggle to succeed with city women.

Wanting More Children

"Spanish women are having fewer children than they say they want to have," observes one of Spain's leading demographers, Margarita

Delgado, of the Spanish Council for Scientific Research in Madrid. "We took a survey of ten thousand women and asked them a long series of questions about children, family, marriage, and related topics. What emerged was something like a mathematical formula that explains why it will be impossible for Spain to recover the higher level of fertility it had in past generations. Women have children too late. When asked, they say they want children, but not many. On average, they want two, but since they start having children at thirty, they do not have a big enough window of time to have two children. Our survey shows that it is economic factors that limit them. Their salaries are low, the family policies in Spain don't provide enough support for mothers, and there are too few public schools for small children."

Delgado complains that a lot of writers in Spain are convinced that the country needs large numbers of immigrants to overcome low fertility. The view is built on the fallacy that Spain could absorb as many immigrants as it would take to bring the fertility rate back to the 2.1 replacement level. "The numbers of people needed for that," she says, "would be so huge that there is no way the Spanish labor market could absorb everyone. And with the number of immigrants in Spain today, the immigrant women would have to have giant families to bring the national average up to replacement levels." Delgado and her colleagues calculate that each immigrant mother would have to have eleven children on average in order for Spain's population to stay even.

The answer for Spain, Delgado believes, is to make it easier for Spanish women to have the number of children they want. That means more provisions for day care, more work leave for mothers, and a bigger role for men at home. "Spanish employers think that women want to have children, and it is inevitable that they will leave the workplace. The reality in Spain is different. Woman actually have to work harder than men, and they do not miss a lot of work compared to men, either. What has been hard for employers to grasp," she says, "is that if we do not recover our fertility, it will affect employers, too, because of the shrinkage in the workforce. They also need to understand that in an aging population like ours, we will eventually get into a period where we are so old we lose our productivity. We are not there yet."

Delgado stresses, however, that there is no way to stop the aging of the population, only ways to cope with it. Even higher fertility rates, back to replacement rate or a little above, would only go so far to inject youth into the demographic profile of the aging society.

While economic pressures and ambitions keep women from having as many children as they say they want, it is almost impossible to imagine that Spain's women, or the immigrant women who come to the country (and soon find themselves at roughly the same fertility rate as Spain's natives), would turn back the clock on their independence. Women, especially women with fewer children, are a central part of the Spanish workforce today, and their presence will be needed in great numbers as the country ages. Seven out of ten working-age women with no children held jobs in Spain in 2008. About half of the mothers with one or two children worked. Delgado found, however, that there is an almost staggering difference between having two children and having three, the number of children that Spanish women find impossible to manage while holding on to a job. Among the country's mothers of three, a mere four out of every one thousand work.

No wonder Spain's families decide fewer children suit them best. Families may rue what they have lost as they make a transition to an aging society, but Spaniards, like those in nearly all the world's aging societies, would not surrender en masse the gains in education, economic power, and personal freedom that drive the change.

Not Getting Any Younger, by the Millions

In 2004, Spain's Ministry of Labor and Social Security published a census of how many people in the country needed care to get through the day.[33] It found that 1.125 million people, two-thirds of them elderly, lived with disabilities that prevented them from caring for themselves. They needed full-time help just to eat, take their medicines, bathe, shop, or to get in and out of their bed. Another 1.7 million people need more intermittent, but still reliable, care with their basic daily activities. In all, around 2.7 million people out of Spain's population of 43 million, or about one in every sixteen, needed help caring for themselves.

This is a dependency ratio of a different sort. Rather than comparing working-age people to those who are either too young or too old to be counted in the mainstream workforce, it counts those who need the hands-on help of other people. It counts the proportion of people who need a helper whose time spent offering care is time not spent doing something else, such as activities that are more educational, more fun (and less stressful), or productive. As the country's older population grows in relationship to the population overall, the ratio of people in need of such basic help will grow, too, and so will the ratio of people needed to provide the help the growing numbers of dependent people need.

The United Nations Population Division estimates that by 2050, Spain will have a higher proportion of people over sixty-five than any other country in the world, more than doubling from 17 percent in 2000 to 37 percent by midcentury. No country in Europe is getting proportionately younger. The proportion of Swiss people over sixty-five will grow 104 percent, Italians 94 percent, Germans 73 percent, and in the United Kingdom the proportion of people over sixty-five will grow by 56 percent.[34] Spain's population over sixty-five, immigration notwithstanding, is expanding fastest.

Translate the numbers into an estimate of how many people need help with their basic needs, and Spain begins to look like a country that is literally handicapped. Unless medical advances deliver millions of people from the infirmities they are now destined for, one out of every six to eight Spaniards will need another person to help with walking, going to the toilet, or doing some other essential activity that we all take for granted until it grows difficult. What then will be the ratio of helpers to the needy? Will it be one to one? Two or three to one? Ten to one? Because of sheer demographic pressures, the style of help will have to change.

Looking into the future from the 2004 count onward, Spain's Ministry of Labor and Social Security saw a nation of people overwhelmed by the demands of care. To many Spaniards, however, the weight of dependency on the nation's future had already arrived inside the family. The weight was borne largely by women who were still, by and large, young enough to work. In 2004, seventeen of every twenty care providers was a woman. On average, they were fifty-two years old, well below retirement age in Spain. The vast majority were family members: daughters, wives, and even mothers. The family members received neither salaries nor social benefits. Many were, in effect, reduced back to the labor status so many of Spain's women once had as unpaid, hardworking farm wives, except that they were now usually urban caregivers and did not contribute to families' incomes as rural Spain's women once did on the farm. To the contrary, they were hindered from earning money.

If the first decade of the twenty-first century portends the future, then by 2050 nearly every family in Spain may well require a caregiver. Families will either have to hire one or count on a family member to forgo time, and probably work, to provide the care for an older person.

"When We Get Old, We Are Going to Be a Bother"

Pilar and Daniel can barely sit still. They have been a little jumpy all day and anxious all week, ever since Pilar was asked to describe their experiences caring for her ninety-two-year-old mother. Boy, did she want to explain it. She needed to get it all out, and she pledged to tell truths that would be hard to hear but which everyone ought to know. When Daniel opens the door to their two-bedroom apartment, he offers a strong, two-palmed handshake. He's dressed in a well-worn sweater that covers a round, but not bulging stomach. His faded but ample hair is tied back in an unkempt ponytail that gives him an artist's air. When he releases his handshake he motions to the table where Pilar sits, barely, bouncing her hands on the table. She says hello and offers dinner, but her mind races ahead to what she is compelled to say. She will not return to the niceties of being a Spanish hostess unless she has aired her full complaint.

"I cannot stand it," she blurts out. "It is hell, I tell you, living hell. It is like being in jail. You have no choice but to adjust, but it is not easy and not satisfying. To start, when you reach ninety-two, like my mother—my father died at ninety-three, and my father-in-law also died at that age—everything depends on how you reach that age and whether you and your family can bear it. In my case, to be honest," she says, leaving no doubt that she is being very honest, "I would not choose to live the way my mother is living. I wouldn't choose it for myself or wish it on my family. I have to feed her and bathe her morning, afternoon, and evening. I feel kidnapped in my own house. That's the truth, and I am not going to go into the intimate details about when she soils herself."

Pilar and Daniel's apartment shows no signs of the infirmed mother's presence. It is comfortably cluttered with handmade blankets and souvenirs of their travels around the world with their adult sons. Pilar and Daniel have both been retired for several years. Neither has held a regular job since 2005. Pilar was an administrator at a magazine distributor. Daniel worked as a plumber, jumping from construction job to construction job. "I worked," he says, "I really worked. And now that I am retired, I am busier than ever. I get odd jobs from old clients. But really most of my work is here"—helping out with his mother-in-law and filling in on the household duties for Pilar.

The reason there is no evidence of Pilar's mother in her own apartment is because she needs space for herself. Mother is now tended to in an apartment down the hall.

"That's our apartment and I could get €1,200 a month in rent for it," says Pilar, "but when I see her so vulnerable I feel pity." And she feels stuck. "We have not thought about paying to bring in someone full-time. Frankly we don't have the money. And frankly, as much as I can't bear it, I also can't bear to leave her. Something always makes her unhappy and she's always saying, 'It's too hot, it's too cold, the TV is too loud.'" Pilar adds that her oldest son stays in the apartment with his grandmother at night while she sleeps, just so she does not feel she is ever left alone.

"I also believe," she says, "the relationships you had with your parents before are very important. Your memories and experiences of your parents affect what you can put up with later. My father was more understanding and full of life. Perhaps it was because he was an educated man." Pilar's eyes water and her face grows red. Daniel puts his arm around her. She breaks down into a full, choking cry. She wipes her face, but still cannot halt her story. "I discussed things with my father, but I never talked that way with my mom. What a difference between the two of them. My father was born without a hand. Maybe that gave them a different outlook, too. He struggled but was always positive and happy. My mother was jealous of my father and he paid the consequences. When your memories of a person are more positive, you can sacrifice yourself for that person. With him, when he needed help, I never felt burdened." Pilar says that despite her history with her mother, she takes good care of her. "We watch over her like a garden flower, because in spite of her character, she loves us in her way."

Pilar complains that the state provides few resources to families like hers. "Everything depends on who evaluates the older person." The government sent two different agencies to evaluate Pilar's mother and the observers saw her very differently. One said the mother was mildly senile, and the other rated her condition as far more severe. In the end, Pilar and Daniel were granted €200 a month. The money goes to pay someone to come in a few days now and then so that Pilar and Daniel can leave the house, have time with each other, and renew themselves. In addition, the state provides money for family caregivers to hire someone for a full month every year. That allows enough time for a vacation.

"I'm seventy-three years old," says Daniel, "but inside I feel thirty or forty. I have a lot of things I'd like to do. The fact is I would leave my mother-in-law in a residence and pay for her. I've done that every August, when I paid for her to stay at a clinic while we went traveling with our son. When we get old, we are going to be a bother, and I am very aware of this. I will make an effort then not to bother our kids. I'd check myself into a residence."

"If I have the money," says Pilar, "and I have my wits, I'd have someone come in and take care of me and have the children check up on me. If they didn't, I'd really be disillusioned. But I would not want them to do what we are doing for my mother. I would not want them providing the care day after day. We have adult children who live outside the city, and we can hardly get away to see them."

"I shouldn't mention this," adds Pilar, "but I have heard that the Socialist government mentioned something about euthanasia. The Popular Party [the Socialists' center-right opposition] does not even want to discuss this. We need to talk about it in Spain. If they implemented this, I'd be the first to sign up. There is no need to extend my life. I'd rather die than be a vegetable."

The Strains of Being No Burden

Spain, of course, has places where Daniel and Pilar can see just what it would mean for them to spare their children the trouble of tending to them.

Three years ago, when Josep Maria Mas's mother, Isabel Solà, turned ninety-eight, he had to put her in a nursing home in Barcelona. Josep Maria is sixty-six and went to call on his mother for her hundred and first birthday. He lives in a small, cramped apartment. He rents out one of the small bedrooms to a boarder to help make ends meet. For much of his working life, he lived outside of Spain. In his youth he worked in Switzerland and England, as a waiter. Then he ran a business making decorative custom metalwork. He lost his last job before he reached official retirement age. He worked for an Italian maker of pasta machines but the company went out of business. Other than his mother, Josep Maria has little contact with his family.

Walking into the room in the nursing unit of a city senior center, Josep Maria passes the various ages of aging man. On the ground floor is a boisterous room where some elders not much older than he are playing billiards and cards and laughing it up. Music from a dance class or exercise session down the hall fills the air. On the second and third floors, the rooms hold the somewhat able. They can walk and talk fine, but some are frail or demented. But the third floor is the place that announces the next-to-final destination. The hall is lined with wheelchairs with vacant occupants. A woman asks Josep Maria if he knows where her dinner is. He's blue even before he gets to his mother's room. Entering, he offers a loud, friendly hello. She is blind, and maybe deaf. He looks down at her blank, toothless face. She looks like a church icon of a skeletal soul crawling through purgatory.

"She doesn't know me," he says. On a previous visit he set up a series of family photographs for his mother to look at, or rather that he could describe to her. "She's gone. Happy birthday."

He leaves the room after a few minutes and searches out the nurse in charge of his mother to learn if there is any news, or a time when they expect her to die. He finds her. It is Nina from Peru. "I know your mother well," she says. "I even know her every bowel movement."

Asked whether anyone else in the room is over one hundred, Nina says there are always people over one hundred. She points out three women between 100 and 104, and then another who will turn 100 in three more weeks. "I haven't seen anyone reach 105 yet, though," she says within earshot of the 104-year-old. Nina relates that she has an autistic grandson who is cared for by her son at home in the city. She was able to get them here from Peru, where there are no services for boys like her grandson.

Another resident, sitting in a chair against the wall of the lounge, is a handsomely dressed woman with large glasses and a neat bun of white hair.

"Who are you here to visit?" she asks. She does not know Isabel Solà, because she has just come over from another home. "I was in a residence I really liked for three years. I had a lot of friends there," she says. "But it was private and expensive and I thought it was a burden to my nephews, who were helping to pay for it. I didn't want to be dependent on them, so I did the research and found this home run by the government and made the move." She removes some photos from her handbag. They show her now-deceased husband with her nephews when they were boys. "At the other place I was very popular. They even had a pet name for me: 'Little Sweetie.' Sometimes my nephews come and bring me back to visit my friends, and everyone greets me so fondly." She begins to cry. To cry her milky blue eyes out.

The nurse continues to feed the other centenarians. These are some of Spain's oldest living citizens, who lived through civil war, world war, authoritarian regimes, and national hardship. The Spain they knew and loved is gone, and soon they will be gone, too.

"I miss them," Little Sweetie says, recalling her loved ones and times past. Her head has nearly dropped onto her purse. "I miss everyone."

CHAPTER 4

HOW WE (REALLY) DO (CONTINUOUSLY) AGE

Some day, when you are old and wrinkled and ugly, when thought has seared your forehead with its lines, and passion branded your lips with its hideous fires . . . you will feel it terribly. Now, wherever you go, you charm the world. Will it always be so? . . . You have a wonderfully beautiful face, Mr. Gray. Don't frown. You have. And beauty is a form of genius—is higher, indeed, than genius, as it needs no explanation. It is one of the great facts of the world, like sunlight, or springtime. . . . You smile? Ah! When you have lost it you won't smile. . . . You have only a few years in which to live really, perfectly, and fully.

—Sir Henry Wotton, *The Picture of Dorian Gray*
by Oscar Wilde, 1890

OSCAR WILDE CERTAINLY UNDERSTOOD THE PSYCHOLOGY OF aging, but he couldn't have known the molecular science of it, which hadn't yet been discovered. Why do we age? It's not because time is jealous of youth. It's because our bodies destroy themselves at the molecular level.

Rusting Away, Cell by Cell

Everyone knows we age, but few of us really know how that happens. The topic is of immense interest to researchers, many of whom base their studies on what is known as the free radical hypothesis of aging. The theory identifies the cause of aging as the body's production of free oxygen radicals, also called oxidants. When an animal digests food, its body breaks the food down into molecules that can be delivered to the inside of cells. Eat a piece of whole-wheat bread and the body will break it down into glucose and then assemble the glucose into clustered chains of glucose molecules. Once inside a cell, the molecules are metabolized into usable energy by mitochondria, bacteria-like organelles that, through biochemical reactions, produce the molecules that are the body's chief source of energy. This conversion requires oxygen to unlock the energy from the glucose for cells to use. Out of the glucose and oxygen combination come energy, carbon dioxide, and water. The energy powers the body, the carbon dioxide is breathed out, and the water plays its various roles, supporting nearly every function in the body. While most of the oxygen ends up in the water, some oxygen molecules do not. They leak out of the process and become the often damaging free oxygen radicals. Caleb Finch, professor of gerontology and biological science at the University of Southern California at Davis, and coauthor (with Robert Ricklefs) of the influential book *Aging: A Natural History*, describes the free radicals as "chemical sparks," because they tear electrons and atoms away from other, whole molecules. That, in turn, creates still more free radicals and sets off a chain reaction that both produces more oxidants—as many as one trillion for every cell in the body—and weakens still more molecules. Steven Austad, Finch's sometime collaborator, likens the process to rusting. Just as an iron nail rusts and weakens when it is exposed to oxygen, a person ages and weakens as free oxygen radicals destroy animal DNA bit by bit and instigates the death of cells.[1]

Our cells make antioxidants that combat most of the damage that the ongoing barrage of free radicals might bring, but our cells cannot contain all of the damage. Even everyday activities can stoke the activity of free radicals and make the body's attempts to mop them up far harder and the destructive job of free radicals easier. Smoking, for example. A single cigarette sends a storm of free radicals into the bloodstream. A sweet tooth, a love of rich foods, medical treatment that relies on radiation, colds, influenza and other infectious diseases, many common forms of pollution, and some drugs all spur the creation of free radicals. So do physical and emotional stress.[2]

Yet the free radical hypothesis may not be the ultimate explanation of why we age. Free radicals play at least as important a role in preserving us as in wearing us down. They are one of the immune system's responses to infections, perpetually attacking and dismantling alien microbes that enter our systems. As the free radicals go on the attack, however, they cause collateral damage to healthy cells. In the end, then, this hypothesis may simply describe a function of the body that grows opportunistically more virulent as other causes trigger our cells to die off.

Elizabeth Blackburn and her collaborators at the University of California–San Francisco have discovered that high levels of stress damage the telomeres, the DNA-protein complexes that act as the protective ends of our chromosomes. Telomeres shrink every time a cell reproduces. Eventually telomeres are too short to contain enough DNA to allow cells to replicate. Different kinds of cells have different life spans and their telomeres shrink at different rates. An enzyme called telomerase, whose discovery led Blackburn (with Carol W. Greider and Jack W. Szostak) to win the 2009 Nobel Prize in Physiology or Medicine, sets the pace of the telomeres' decline and thus the pace of decay in the life of cells and the health of tissue.

Oxidative stress, when free radicals are in overdrive, shortens telomeres. Blackburn looked at patients under psychological stress and found their telomeres dangerously short. She also matched stress with the telomeres' length and with diseases such as heart disease. While, so far, only psychological stress, not physical stress, has been studied, Blackburn suspects that stress itself can take years off a life.

We are all subject to the cumulative changes in our cells that make us more frail as we grow older. Meanwhile we fight outside attacks on our bodies with mixed success. Violent assaults and accidents, physical wear and tear, emotional trauma, and our darker psychological inclinations can beat us down over time. Youthful exuberance, hormonally driven, urges teenagers and people in their twenties to take death-defying risks in their cars, in bars, in bed, and in sketchy neighborhoods. On the other end of life, gravity is a mortal enemy to older people. The hard floor is one of the world's most dangerous places. And everywhere, the environment intrudes. Being born in the era of modern public health and advanced medicine is enormously influential, but our cells are nonetheless dying every day, and despite our many individual differences, there is a general sequence to how we age, observable the world over.

One Decade After Another, Day by Day

Aware that we are aged from within and by external circumstance, let us take a clear-eyed look at how we really do continuously age. What follows is a rough ladder of the decades that traces what *tends* to happen to people over time, but not necessarily what happens to everyone or when. Most people are in quite good condition as they enter their sixth decade, but most is not all. Cognitive decline is a continuous fact throughout adulthood, but it unfolds slowly for some and jolts others. Many of the common conditions below are easily managed, yet many are hard to bounce back from. Some setbacks are discrete events after which we heal and move on, while others, such as immune disorders and the family of diseases called metabolic syndrome, including diabetes, usher in multiple maladies that compound one another.

Now then, we might as well understand that:

In our thirties, we:

- Begin to pull muscles and snap tendons more easily. Exercises and sports that require quick movement can end suddenly with a pop in the leg or, after a pivot, when the floor, not the basket, comes into view.

- See our metabolism slow. This makes it harder to stay trim. For men, big bellies come easily because the body begins to redistribute fat and lose muscle tone.
- Lose muscle mass and strength. The decline will not affect most people for some years, but those in highly physical jobs or with intensely physical hobbies will start losing out to younger people. Professional football players and other athletes in sports requiring strength and speed typically retire by thirty because their natural decline in strength already separates them from up-and-comers.
- Have another reason to avoid sugary diets and simple carbohydrates: an increasingly higher risk for diabetes, even for people who are not overweight.
- Have passed our peak brain power, which we achieved in our early twenties. Our mental decline, which begins around age twenty-seven, is gradual, however. The quickest, but still rather slow, decline affects our prefrontal and temporal cortices, which control our executive functions, including our judgment, planning, and strategic thinking. By our thirties, our episodic memory, which is our ability to remember episodes from our own lives, begins to slowly wane. Over the next three to five decades this loss changes how we handle information. On the plus side, we do continue to acquire information, and shifts in how our brain functions may actually enhance our ability to sift information and achieve a "mature" perspective on it.
- Cross into the period of life when cancer rates start to climb significantly from decade to decade until our midseventies, when the rate stabilizes. Getting older is a risk factor for getting cancer that increases every day. For the rest of our lives, daily conversation and news of friends make it seem as though we live amid a worsening cancer epidemic. Data from the U.S. National Institute on Aging help explain why. By age thirty-five, 90 of every 100,000 Americans have cancer; by age forty-five, 206 of every 100,000 have cancer. By age fifty-five, the number jumps to 574; by sixty-five, it climbs to 1,301; and by seventy-five, 2,234 people of every 100,000 will have some kind of cancer.

- Start looking around for men. The population of males begins to drop off around now. Males at all ages are more prone to disease and tend to suffer worse consequences from what hits them. They are more likely to suffer severe violence and die from it. By the time men enter their thirties, women their age outnumber them. The disparity will grow over time, affected by the severity with which men suffer nearly every physical, cognitive, and emotional insult. When they are young, they die in car crashes, and when they are old, broken hips kill them more surely than they kill women.

In our forties, we:

- Begin to become more susceptible to the three big eye diseases: cataracts, glaucoma, and age-related macular degeneration. (More on this below.)
- May feel beat-tired. It could be the result of physical inactivity (or the cause of it) or poor diet. It might stem from normal hormonal changes in the body—such as menopause or andropause—that wear us down. Fatigue might be the precursor to a more serious ailment. As a focus of research, fatigue has only recently come under intense study, and there is still no standard by which to measure it. Depending on the criteria, it afflicts between 5 and 20 percent of people over thirty-eight years old, but afflicts women two times as often as men.
- Start asking around for good physical therapists and orthopedic surgeons. By forty we are more prone to joint injuries, especially with our shoulders, wrists, knees, and ankles. Surgeries to fix them soar once we hit forty.
- Begin to re-hem our old pants. Time cuts down our stature by more than half an inch every decade. British researchers noticed that men who lost more than 1.4 inches in height in their forties and fifties had a 645 percent greater chance of dying in the next twenty years than men who lost less than half an inch.
- Feel our joints stiffen. Some of us start getting arthritis.
- Begin to see gray hair, or perhaps wish for it. Color begins to

go out of hair in some, and hair goes on permanent holiday for others. Going gray while balding? Enjoy it while it lasts.

- See bags under our eyes. The puffiness is the result of a more pervasive and accelerated decline in the elasticity and youthful color and texture of our skin. Part of the blame falls on our lymph glands. As we age past forty, our lymphatic systems progressively lose the ability to rid the body of toxins. When lymph glands go limp, we can "puff up."
- Get not-so-cute dimples. It's cellulite. Fat cells under the skin of men and women begin to leave skin with a dimpled orange-peel texture. For women the change is most visible in the hips and thighs; for men, the dimples are likely to spread around the neck and stomach.
- Are likely to see big changes in ourselves as sexual beings. In women, the progression through menopause begins, with actual menopause most often beginning near age fifty. There is such a wide range of experience with menopause that the end of fertility and monthly cycles are just about the only universals. Women in some ethnic groups tend to experience more severe physical and emotional effects than women in others. Surveys report that African-American women feel that menopause affects their health and psychological states especially strongly, while Chinese and Japanese women appear to feel the change far less. Researchers at UCLA found that memory and the ability to learn falters in about half of all women going through menopause, but that once they are postmenopausal, their cognitive functions bounce back.* While undergoing "The Change," hot flashes, night sweats, sleeplessness, and irritability are common but temporary complaints. More lasting problems are weight gain, loss of height, worse cholesterol levels, and a weakening of the bones. Many women will experience the gruesomely named "vaginal atrophy," in which declining levels of estrogen cause their vaginal walls to thin, lose moisture, and to grow inflamed. No wonder sex lives suffer. Pen-

---

* More soberingly, new research from Erasmus Medical Center in the Netherlands indicates that women who go through menopause early, in their early to midforties, are at higher risk for early onset dementia and death.

etration may become less pleasurable or even painful and lead to bleeding. Orgasms can be weak, elusive, and can be regarded indifferently. The need for passion and romance can become less urgent, too. In a 2009 industry-sponsored poll of twenty-five hundred American women* who were experiencing or had been through menopause, nearly seven in ten women reported that their symptoms negatively impacted their personal health and well-being; six in ten said menopause hurt their sex life, and around half said there were unwelcome consequences for their relationships with their significant others. The change in their sex lives, the women said, was what surprised them most. Some women, however, regard the change positively; many women find that the passage through menopause frees them sexually.

Men have their own problems caused by declining sex hormones. The effects of declining testosterone in men are often called "male menopause," which is nonsensical considering that "menopause" derives from the Greek terms referring to the cessation of a woman's monthly cycle. Lately, "andropause," a better deployment of Greek, and "man-o-pause," have been used to describe the male version of the change. Men produce testosterone all their lives. Levels ramp up in puberty and for most men peak in their late teens. Men plateau at the highest level for two or three decades and then, typically around age forty, their testosterone levels begin to drop about 1 percent a year. And even when the overall levels are high, the usable "free" testosterone may decline in older men, while unusable testosterone, bound to proteins, may stay high. This makes testing testosterone levels a knotty business, since levels alone do not reveal how the body uses the hormone. It also makes the prevalence of andropause a source of controversy. One confounding factor is that andropause is not caused by low testosterone alone, but by varying levels of a number of other hormones as well. Most men must live with the life-changing effects of falling testosterone, though not all. Some men feel

* The survey was sponsored by Teva Women's Health, Inc., a pharmaceutical company with products aimed at menopausal women.

only the slightest change related to sex hormone change, even into old age. Andropause also unfolds much more slowly than menopause. From age forty on, men begin to lose muscle, bone density (which usually makes them shorter), and their red blood cell counts drop over time. Dr. Jeremy P. W. Heaton, professor of urology at Ontario's Queen's University, cites six clinical changes that result from waning hormone levels in men: decreased sexual desire and erection quality, decreased intellectual capacity, decreased lean body mass, body hair and skin changes, and increased visceral fat around the organs in the abdomen, which ups the risk of diabetes, high blood pressure, heart disease, and stroke. Surveys of men from their twenties through their seventies show, generally, that by their fifties men grow dispirited by weak erections and low-volume ejaculation. Yet, while hormone levels may drop, men still produce enough testosterone to cause damage in an aging body, as the substance that once played a central role in building strength and reproductive capacity becomes a factor in the diseases of old age, including heart disease and cancer.

In our fifties, we:

- Are more threatened by the most potent risk factors: high blood pressure, high blood sugar, high cholesterol, excessive weight, excessive drinking, smoking (ever), heart abnormalities, and unmarried status (for men). In a recent study of more than five thousand men in Hawaii, those with none of the biggest risk factors had a six-time better chance (55 percent) of making it to age eighty-five as men who had six or more risk factors.
- Are more prone to break our bones. Contrary to popular belief, this is not just a threat to women's health.
- Think about new joints. By the fifties, rheumatoid arthritis and osteoarthritis begin to afflict great numbers of people. Up to one in five adults have rheumatic conditions, and in the decade after it appears, most start on some combination of steroids, painkillers, and joint replacements to help alleviate agonizing discomfort in the hands, arms, legs, neck, and back.

- Have more problems with receding gums, decaying teeth, more cavities, and periodontal disease. We are more likely to lose teeth.
- Retain less water, and start to dry up, sweating less and over-heating more.
- Have a harder time putting on weight, especially muscle mass and lean tissue.
- Do not taste or smell as keenly as before.
- Are at higher risk for heart disease. Postmenopausal women, formerly protected from heart disease by estrogen, are newly vulnerable.
- Get even bigger bellies (women), because our bodies are redistributing fat and losing muscle tone.
- If we smoke, we age prematurely, and the damage to our lungs begins to cut life short by an average of ten years. We lose our ability to withstand stress from recreational drugs and excessive use of alcohol. The American Heart Association reports that "middle-aged and elderly marijuana users increase their risk of a heart attack by more than four and a half times during the first hour after smoking the drug." Longtime abusers of alcohol will experience accelerated and premature aging, even if they now abstain. Nearly all the bodily setbacks that normally strike people much older will beset heavy drinkers in short order. Their motor functions will be particularly hard hit, their gaits and balance will suffer, and they will be racked by the mortal consequences of falls.
- Begin to see some effects of osteoporosis, especially in women, which will become more serious over the coming decades when bones become fragile and brittle. Women suffer more bone loss than men.
- Start forgetting things. Words we *know* become lost on the tips of our tongues. We forget tasks and lose track of what happened just a day before. One reason is that the hippocampus, one of the areas of the brain central to memory (and severely crippled by Alzheimer's), begins to shrink.[3]
- Start suffering eye problems in significantly greater numbers. Cataracts are the world's leading cause of blindness, but surgery is nearly always effective against it. Glaucoma is the

second leading cause of blindness in the world, following only age-related macular degeneration. After arthritis/rheumatism and heart disease, the loss of vision is the most likely hindrance to the everyday activities of people over seventy.

- Enter the high-risk group for osteoarthritis, the world's most common joint disease. It is most likely to be felt in the knees, hips, and small hand joints. Globally, it afflicts nearly one-quarter of adults over fifty. Overweight people are especially at high risk as they grow older. Osteoarthritis causes pain and often disability in about half of all Americans sixty-five and older but, for reasons not well understood, afflicts only one of three people over seventy in Hong Kong.

- Fear cancer whenever we sit down, if we are men. During our fifties our prostates will likely enlarge. Nine in ten men have benignly enlarged prostates sometime after age fifty. It may be hard to urinate at times, but the urge may come more often. It can be messy, too. And painful. Hopefully it is not cancer, though it is best to check. Prostate cancer is the most frequent form of cancer in men. Prognoses for men who are diagnosed early are good, but many men delay exams. Others have no early symptoms to send them to the doctor. The result: prostate cancer is also one of the biggest killers of men.

In our sixties, we:

- Worry about our hearts. Age is the number one risk factor for heart disease, one of the world's number one killers. In the developed world it is the leading cause of death, but 80 percent of deaths due to cardiovascular disease occur in low- and middle-income countries. In the United States, 83 percent of deaths from coronary heart disease occur in people over sixty-five. Worldwide, close to 30 percent of all deaths are from cardiovascular disease. Eighty million Americans also live with cardiovascular diseases, including strokes. The effects range from highly manageable to utterly debilitating.

- Are even more likely, if male, to have an enlarged prostate gland. The percentages of sufferers keep rising, year by year, affecting men's ability to sleep through the night and the number of times they urinate each day.

- Begin to feel changes in our skin. It becomes thinner and loses some of its ability to act as a barrier to keep our fluids in and foreign invaders out. The skin, like the rest of the body, heals ever more slowly and is more sensitive to chemicals, including medicines. Age spots appear, and the skin is less resistant to cancer.
- Look like we have bigger noses and ears, in part because of the loss of fat surrounding them.
- Lose some of our ability to regulate our body temperatures, and are prone more than before to both hypothermia and hyperthermia.
- Enter the high-risk group for cancer. If we are not afflicted by cancer ourselves, we almost certainly have friends and family who are. According to the U.S. National Cancer Institute, Americans sixty-five and older account for 60 percent of cancerous tumors and 70 percent of all cancer deaths. According to the NCI, "the age-adjusted incidence rate for persons aged sixty-five and older is ten times greater than the rate for persons aged under sixty-five. . . . Pancreas, stomach, rectum, lung, leukemia, non-Hodgkin's lymphoma, liver, kidney, and ovarian cancers account for two-thirds to three-quarters of cancer deaths in persons aged sixty-five and older. Over 75 percent of cancer deaths are due to urinary cancer, bladder cancer, colon cancer, and corpus uterine cancer. Half of the cases of breast cancer, often thought to be a disease more prominent in premenopausal women, occur in women aged sixty-five and older. Prostate cancer mortality is in a class by itself, with 92 percent of the deaths occurring in men aged sixty-five and older. Nearly 50 percent of brain cancer mortality and 60 percent of head and neck cancer deaths occur in persons aged sixty-five and older."[4] Particularly bad lifestyle choices, once enjoyable, now wreak damage. Lung cancer begins to take people in their sixties in large numbers, as damage done by the accumulated "pack-years" of smoking reaches the point of no return.
- Are likely to begin to lose hearing. Both the mechanisms of the ear and the ability of the brain to distinguish sounds usually

decline with age. One of the most common forms of hearing loss, presbycusis, affects both ears and reduces the ability to hear all kinds of sound. It strikes up to 40 percent of adults over sixty-five and 80 percent over eighty-five. Men's hearing diminishes twice as fast as women's.

- Begin to walk more slowly. The normal walking pace for healthy older adults is about one-fifth slower than younger adults. Older adults still walk nearly as much as they used to, but their steps are shorter. Arms swing less; hips, knees, and ankles do not stretch out as much; and the walk is more flat-footed. Walking around town, crossing the street before the traffic light changes, and dodging otherwise benign street life can grow challenging and limit people's ability to conduct their everyday affairs, especially for those whose hearing or vision has also worsened.

- As mentioned earlier, face the dangers of gravity. According to the Cleveland Clinic, falls are the leading cause of fatal and nonfatal injuries among older people. In the United States, one of three persons over sixty-five suffers a serious fall every year, usually at home. The BBC reports that in the United Kingdom, more people die from falls at home than in automobile accidents. Around two thousand elderly people die from falls every year in the United Kingdom, and three hundred thousand are injured. Older women have the highest risk. Falls are related to a wide variety of other health conditions. Injury from falls can lead to social isolation and rapid decline in health. Around one-third of the elderly who fall and break a hip are dead within a year. Fear of falling is also a serious problem that impedes people's ability to function independently.

In our seventies, we:

- Forget more, while the speed at which we process information slows down. Memory lapses are normal and there are good ways to cope and compensate. If you fear Alzheimer's disease, however, new tests can determine definitively both if you have it now, or will be stricken within the next ten years.
- Gain in the ability to put experience and learning into perspec-

tive, and to focus more on positive emotions. At the same time, several conditions associated with age, including hormonal changes and cognitive impairment, can lead to depression.

- Are less able to control how our bodies eliminate our waste. The walls of the bladder become less flexible, reducing the volume of urine we can hold. Our bladder muscles lose strength, which makes it harder to empty the bladder when urinating, which can lead to incontinence. One in ten people over sixty-five have trouble with bladder control. In women, the bladder can also prolapse, or drop out of place, which can block the urethra and make it harder to urinate. In men, an enlarged prostate gland may obstruct the urethra. The efficiency of the kidneys can wane, meaning blood gets filtered more slowly. That can make people more vulnerable to toxins and less tolerant of many medicines.
- Lose our senses. Literally. In our seventies, our eyesight and hearing are more likely to deteriorate in ways that affect our lifestyles. One of six people over seventy have significant problems with his or her vision, a rate that doubles for people in their eighties. One of four over seventy are hard of hearing. For about one-third of those with hearing loss, a hearing aid will offer relief.
- Lose our footing. More than seven in ten people over seventy have a hard time balancing, and around one in three has lost enough feeling in the feet to make walking difficult.

In our eighties, if we are still alive, we begin to succumb to the maladies that afflicted less robust people in their fifties, sixties, and seventies. In addition, we:

- Have increasingly high odds of suffering from dementia. The chance of getting Alzheimer's disease, the most common cause of dementia, doubles every year from age sixty-five on. People eighty-five and older have a one-in-two chance of having the disease.[5]
- Reach a point where the loss of fat under the skin makes our skin thin, saggy, and more easily bruised. Older people who shed large amounts of body fat may feel their skin is literally hanging off their bones.

In our nineties, we:

- Have outlived nearly all the people born the same year we were. Those of us who reach this age die in increasing proportions year by year, but in some ways may be heartier than many of our friends in their eighties. People among the oldest-old are often impressively resistant to disease.

If we reach age one hundred, we are probably genuinely surprised to still be alive, and even more surprised how many of our contemporaries have made it, too.

What the Doctor Sees

As the preceding sequence shows, we age relentlessly. Yet some of us seem to age more quickly or less quickly than others. Who is relatively young? Who is surprisingly old? We all have categories in our heads and use them for ready reference. First, we judge by looks, then we listen, and smell. Our senses are keen at picking up the signs of age, and among those things we measure the most quickly—hairlines, bent bodies, poor teeth, foul odors from the skin and mouth—none leaves a positive impression. Despite the well-meaning wisdom that warns against it, our quick and superficial judgment is nearly indispensable, not to mention hardwired into our brains. Just following the passage at the beginning of the chapter from *The Picture of Dorian Gray*, Oscar Wilde's hedonist Sir Henry also advises the title character that it is "only shallow people who do not judge by appearances."

He's right. Ask a doctor who works with the elderly. Doctors sum them up on sight, albeit with a well-informed eye. I ask a geriatrician friend to walk around a Chicago lakefront neighborhood that is popular with older retirees and to narrate his thoughts as we make our way down the sidewalk.

"I see lots of potential patients," he says with a smile, "and I can't help reading them as they pass."

A stylishly dressed older woman is walking purposefully toward a group of friends who appear excited to see her.

"There goes a thin, healthy septuagenarian female with twenty good years left," he says upon seeing her. "A woman like that who is active, moves quickly, and has high energy and friends, has already done most of what a person needs to do to live longer, and by the looks of it she has a lower risk for just about anything that might kill people her age."

Looking farther down the street, he sees a more troubling view. It is a man, and his gender alone is a warning sign in old age.

"There goes a guy in the early stages of dementia."

The telltale signs are the notepad held uneasily in his hand and the impotent smile on his face. "His family may well bring him in to see me soon. If they come soon, I can help slow his decline a little, but not as much as they hope or the drug companies say."

Then again, my doctor friend corrects himself, the problem could be that the man is on too many drugs for other problems and the pharmaceutical cocktail has disoriented him.

"There are drug complications with nearly every patient we see. Millions of older people have them, and sometimes they're deadly. Other times they create conditions that make people walk funny or act disoriented, and their doctors think they have dementia. That leads to more treatment and more drugs, and more problems. If I take a man like that off eight of the fifteen medicines he's on, he might not strike anyone as demented at all. His doctors are trying to ward off the so-called ravages of age, but are aging him prematurely instead."

Farther along on our walk we see a family together, the daughter in her sixties pushing the wheelchair of her father, who looks to be in his mideighties. Two adult grandchildren are also along for the stroll. The daughter talks expressively, and though her father is hunched over and breathing with an oxygen tank and air tube up his nose, he's engaged and nodding.

The daughter is giving him extra months or years of life, my doctor friend says. Sociable people, after all, tend to stay healthier and cognitively sound longer. He also offers some folk advice that he believes is clinically verifiable. "If you want to live a long life," he says, "marry someone who treats her parents well."

Just ahead is a similar scene with a tiny ninety-year-old woman in a wheelchair whose eyes are fixed in an intense but vacant stare. The chair is pushed by a neatly dressed woman in her midfifties. She is likely from Eastern Europe. The Chicago area is home to hundreds of thousands of immigrants from former Soviet bloc countries, and they often step into the U.S. economy behind a wheelchair. The younger woman has bleached hair and dark, high-arched brows drawn in eye pencil. Around her neck are two rows of pearls and on her fingers glimmer rings of another era. The caregiver talks to and pats the older woman.

"People make all kinds of bargains to get care and keep it," my friend says. "I wonder whose jewelry that is."

The Eyes Have It

One way to understand how we age is to consider in particular how our eyes change. Ophthalmologists say that nearly everyone needs help focusing on the printed page, and doing other close-up work, by age forty-three. Glasses help users overcome the weakening of muscles that come with age. "Your eye focuses on objects at different distances by contracting and relaxing the lens in your eye," says Dr. James Folk, professor of ophthalmology at the University of Iowa and one of the world's foremost experts on macular degeneration. "The reason we have to start wearing reading glasses is that we progressively lose the ability to 'accommodate.' You have a muscle in your eye called the ciliary muscle, that contracts to make the eye's lens fatter and able to zoom in to objects closer up. Gradually that muscle loses its ability to contract. You become presbyopic and need reading glasses."*

Folk believes the change is related to the overall decline in muscle strength. "It may be the same reason why a basketball player can't dunk when he's forty." Yet unlike the muscles or skills of athletes, Folk says, no amount of exercise or wisdom can make up for the loss of muscle power that hinders our ability to focus up close.

"There is no evidence that strength conditioning, or the ways you used your eyes when you were younger, have any effect on vision.

---

* When the ciliary muscles contract, they in turn relax the tiny zonular fibers that hold the eye's lens in place. It is the relaxation of the zonular fibers that causes the lens to thicken and enables it to zoom in.

Monkeys have the same kind of degeneration people do. People used to think that younger monkeys groomed older monkeys, but older monkeys never groomed younger monkeys because grooming was a showing of respect. But it appears now that the older monkeys just can't see the small things, like lice, to pick out. The older monkeys need reading glasses."

The eye, Folk says, is a good model for the aging body. "A person can have as healthy a lifestyle as possible, by not smoking, avoiding the accumulation of midbody fat, eat lots of fish oils and other antioxidants, exercise, floss their teeth, and still not control completely how the eye ages."

It is not a given that aging gets you a bad heart or bad eyes, Folk explains, but like cancer and heart disease, eye disease has a mix of genetic and environmental factors that are hard to figure out. "If you have good genes, a good environment, and you exercise, et cetera, you're likely to have good eyesight for a long time; but the opposite is also true: if you have bad genes, a bad environment, and you smoke and eat only bacon and eggs and lie on the couch, you can get heart disease, diabetes, and eye disease maybe by the time you're fifty or fifty-five. Most of us are in the middle. We have some good genes, some bad genes. And some people still get heart disease at fifty even though they are joggers and eat vegetables. They just have bad genes."

Folk also implicates inflammation, the same sort that contributes to other diseases of age, in poor eye health. "If you look under the microscope at macular degeneration," he says, "there is inflammation, and inflammation affects the life cycle of the cells in the eyes." He advises people to take the same preventative measures that doctors advise to lessen the severity of a potential stroke or heart attack: take an aspirin a day.

Bodily wear and tear, kicked off on the genetic level, also changes people's vision. The repair mechanisms are not perfect. Sometimes you build up abnormal proteins that you can't get rid of. People start to get cataracts—a clouding-up of the lens of the eye—beginning around the age of sixty. Cataracts are a natural part of aging, and most people who reach their late eighties will get them at some point. Cataracts are caused in part because the proteins in the eye are damaged by exposure to the sun. The underlying cause is not fully understood. One reason may be that when the sun damages the healthy protein, other proteins move in to repair the damage but over time leave small fragments of protein behind that eventually cloud up the lens.

Even as the body works to repair itself, it causes wear and tear. "The aging process is about how many times you replicate your DNA, and every time you replicate DNA and start a new molecule, there is some cross-linking of the DNA, and that may be the problem that is irreversible. If you remember Dolly the cloned sheep, she was cloned from older cells that had already been replicated. So Dolly only lived about a year, so she was more or less middle-aged when she was born because of her old DNA. I think in all these aging changes in the body and the eye, it is all wear and tear, inflammation, the repair's buildup of abnormal proteins, et cetera, so it makes perfect sense that you would get cataracts at sixty. If you have terrible genes, you might get them at forty; if you have terrific genes, you might not get them until ninety."

Folk adds that, "As people age they lose cells everywhere, in their lungs, in their brains. That includes the retina. In general, eyesight is not as good for people when they are old as when they were young because they lose cone cells and rod cells. But still most people can see 20–15 or 20–20, if they have no disease [and wear glasses], in their seventies."

In his own practice, Folk says he notices that most people do not "really begin to age" rapidly until they are seventy or seventy-five. "They are in good shape until then, doing pretty much what they want to do, but they seem to start falling apart around seventy-five."

One disease that can wreck vision, and which is emblematic of natural aging, is macular degeneration, the primary focus of Folk's research. Age-related macular degeneration commonly begins to afflict people in their sixties, though in rare cases it can strike people younger. About one in twenty adults between sixty and seventy get age-related macular degeneration. The odds climb from there. One in four people in their eighties suffer from it. Eventually it will strike anyone who lives long enough. Macular degeneration diminishes a person's ability to see straight ahead, though usually people with the condition have limited vision to the side. The disease takes two forms, wet and dry, though people can suffer from both types at the same time. The wet form, Folk explains, is caused when cells in the retina "just die off." People are born with enough surplus cells so the reduction does not affect the sight of most people with macular degeneration until they are beyond their midseventies. Folk's lab has been searching for the genes that trigger when macular degeneration presents itself. There are already some candidates, but, Folk says, there are lots of genes associated with macular degeneration, some of which make the condition appear faster, and some that keep it at bay. He suspects that the condition is actually a "bunch of different diseases," some of which begin to unfold when people are very young.

Loss of vision changes the experience of aging, but Folk notices that there is a wide spectrum of responses among his patients. "On one end of the spectrum are the people who really fight the effects of their vision loss. They remain active and have good support systems, have lots of friends, and get low-vision aids. They're doing pretty good in a year or two. They say to themselves, 'This stinks, but I am making do. I can read the newspaper with electronic magnification and so on.' And there is the other person who isolates himself, or herself, and doesn't do well at all. Such a person looks at the magnifiers and says, 'Nah, I don't like this and I can't use that,' and they tend to get depressed. A lot of it depends on social interactions with people. The difference in how they adapt is the difference in the kind of people they are, and you can almost tell when they walk in what will happen with them, whether they will make do with what they've got or whether they will isolate themselves and that will be it."

The eyes also act as the sentinel for other age-related problems. Folk sees patients who come to him believing their eyes are diseased, but who are in fact suffering from other age-related illnesses that affect their vision. "A daughter might come in with her father, who is complaining about his vision, when he really has early Alzheimer's disease." The patient may say he can no longer see the clock clearly. Folk offers a simple test, asking the man to draw a clock with the hands at half past four. If he struggles at it, you can tell right away that it is not a vision problem. Other neurological diseases impact vision, too. "The eye is connected to the brain, so you have to make sure that any vision loss is not central, and look, for example, at whether someone has had a stroke or a tumor."

Aside from diseases that affect vision, normal aging can have effects on eyesight that influence how people function as they go about their everyday activities at work, out in public, and at home. "Vision is the most important sense in that we use it the most and as it gets worse it becomes harder and harder for us to gather in information. Just reading papers, doing your checkbook [and other everyday tasks] keep you alert, and as people can't handle them, there is a tendency for people to do less and less.

"That's why it is important to have life habits that keep your vision as good as you possibly can," Folk advises. "It really is, as my mother used to say, 'use it or lose it.'" Poor vision also causes falls, trauma, and depression. "The biggest thing people complain about is that they can't recognize people who greet them and call them by name. They worry their friends will think they are snubbing them. They also can no longer talk to a person and look at their facial gestures, and that is hard for them because they lose their visual clues and isolate themselves from those situations."

The social glue that people need to cope with the limitation of age-related diseases is undone by the shame that afflicted older people feel. Loneliness and isolation in old age are sad in and of themselves.* They also hasten the diseases of old age. Tests on people in their fifties who describe themselves as lonely show that they are more likely than others to have constricted arteries, and eventually dangerously high blood pressure. It may come as no surprise, too, that loneliness is also suspect in contributing to the wear and tear on the body, because it raises the level of inflammation and stress.[5] Loneliness doubles the risk of Alzheimer's.[6] People who are lonely have higher mortality than those who are not. They are more likely to suffer setbacks, including cardiovascular disease, viral infections, hip fractures, and cancer.[7] Loneliness and isolation can also change our genetic makeup for the worse.

"[T]he biological impact of social isolation reaches down into some of our most basic internal processes: the activity of our genes," says Steve Cole, a researcher at the School of Medicine at UCLA,

---

* In 2007 the Association for Psychological Science noted that back in 1985 the typical American had three confidants, but by 2004 that number had dropped to zero. That's sobering arithmetic for our rapidly aging society.

whose team found "a distinct pattern of gene expression in immune cells" of people who were chronically lonely, finding that the genes that were over-expressed in lonely people included many involved in the activation of the immune system and inflammation.[8]

One Day at a Time

Some of what the time line reveals about aging must be read between the lines. Aging is a dynamic mix of cumulative effects that both diminish people's powers gradually and lead to seemingly rapid failures. The most widely used standard for well-being among the elderly, the Activities of Daily Living, or ADLs, covers peoples' ability to walk, go to the bathroom, and dress, bathe, groom, and feed themselves. There is, however, a difference between functioning well with ADLs and being fully engaged in a productive life. And there is an even larger difference between what it takes to be a valuable member of the workforce, volunteer corps, or a busy household and what it takes to have a functional, or even a richly fulfilling life. One may no longer be able to wield power tools carving wooden carousel horses with the other volunteer craftsmen at the Sarasota circus museum, but that doesn't mean you can't join the drum circle on the beach, advise on a board, or be engaged with your family and neighbors.

In an aging world that now expects older people to work and be economically independent longer, the differences matter. The levels at which older people can function matter for people past traditional retirement ages who need and hope to work more years. They also matter for shrinking families and overstretched governments that provide support for older people. They matter for pension plans and tax receipts. They matter for nations' economic competitiveness, particularly where—such as in Spain—businesses, governments, religious organizations, and civic organizations depend on older workers filling the creative and productive gaps left by shortages of young people.

"Aging is associated with chronic illness. As you get older, the number of chronic illnesses you have goes up," says Dr. Robert L. Kane, a world-renowned geriatrician and director of the University of Minnesota's Center on Aging. "It used to be if you got a heart attack you died. Now there's a 75 percent chance you'll survive, and the chance that you'll go on to get congestive heart failure. If you survive a stroke, you'll probably have some weakness and cognitive loss. If you get renal disease, you can be maintained on dialysis and then get a kidney transplant. Now we can replace joints, but the replacements never function as well, and in ten to fifteen years, the replacements need to be surgically swapped out again. And the big loss most people fear most is cognition. Essentially, bad things happen to you.

"The paradigm of aging is having multiple diseases interacting with one another," Kane adds. "Someone who is short of breath because of pulmonary failure and who has bad joints won't walk. One of the measures of aging is the response to stress and the ability to bounce back. In the elderly, one event leads to another. Being old is not an absolute sentence of frailty, but as you go down the list, people do get more frail, more dependent. They lose control of their car and their bowels."

On average, Kane says, the list of functional limitations goes up with age but does not go up to 100 percent. By the time people are eighty, 60 percent have some limitation on their ADLs. Long before people are limited in their activities of daily living, though, the rest of the world is already looking for signs of decline and dependency.

"There are all sorts of reasons there are more people in their sixties and seventies out of the workforce than in it," Kane observes. Older workers are perceived as expensive to keep on the rolls. There is a widespread concern they are unreliable and will need to take a lot of time off. Workplace data give a mixed picture. For one thing, it only covers people who are actually working, not those who have been cast out or who have removed themselves from the job.* Also, the statistics on older workers are mixed. According to the U.S. Bureau of Labor Statistics, the average annual number of missed workdays for all workers is around eight, but for those fifty-five to sixty-four it is twelve, and for those over sixty-five it is eighteen. But the percentage of older workers who miss days is lower than that of colleagues who are younger than forty-four. This information sug-

---

* Forty-one percent of people with two or more chronic conditions who are between the ages of forty-five and sixty-four do not work at all, according to the Center on Aging Society at Georgetown University.

gests that older workers are reluctant to take time away from the job, but that when they do, they face challenges—minding their own health, or tending to someone else—that make it harder to return to work quickly. Looming difficulties do not weigh heaviest on older workers, though. Younger workers with children at home have the highest stress levels.

It is nonetheless widely accepted that in just about every measure of cognition, people's abilities begin to decline ever more steeply beginning around age fifty. How functional people are in a challenging workplace as they age depends on how functional they were to begin with. In studies on cognitive memory, fifty-year-olds do better in general than eighty-year-olds, but the best prediction for the powers of any one person at eighty was that person's abilities at fifty, not some more general difference between fifty-year-olds and eighty-year-olds as a group. A person, in other words, is more likely to be like himself over time than like his age peers.

Kane notes the example of airline pilots. He worries whether seemingly healthy older pilots are at risk of having a heart attack. "You have to weigh that against their skills, which can be tested. If their skills are high, there is a benefit to keeping them in the air, but with a healthy copilot.

"It is very important," Kane says, "that we don't see age just as a number. Someone's chronological age is a pseudo-predictor that hides a lot about a person that makes him better or worse. Statistically someone may have a very high risk of dying, but in life they can still be very capable."

As we saw with the case of Spain, and as we are about to see even more dramatically in a very different place, when a society has millions upon millions of people aging along the sequence described above, and when that society is forced to compete with countries that have huge numbers of young people, change can arrive abruptly, sending shock waves across the land and affecting everyone, especially young people.

CHAPTER 5

JAPAN, LAND OF THE MISSING SON

Number of centenarians in Japan in 1963: 153

Number in 2007: 32,300

Expected number in 2050: 1 million

Percentage of Japanese population now over age 65: 21.5

Percentage projected to be older than 65 in the year 2050: 40

Expected decline of Japan's workforce between 2008 and 2050: 1/3 (from 66.5 million to 42 million)

Expected population decline in Japan by 2050: 41 million

Number of Japanese companies now operating in China: 20,000

TOKYO HAS MORE OLD PEOPLE THAN ANY OTHER CITY, A CLAIM that almost certainly could have been made any time over the last three hundred fifty years. Tokyo was already the world's most populous metropolis in the seventeenth century, two hundred years before Commodore Matthew Perry forced Japan to open to the outside world. Tokyo then had over a million inhabitants, roughly twice as many as London at the time. Today the number of people who live within the city's contiguous urban environs comes to 35.5 million people, and includes a bit more than one-quarter of the country's population. The population of metro Tokyo puts it at nearly twice the size of the world's other giant global urban centers: Mexico City, Shanghai, Mumbai, São Paulo, and New York, each with about 18 million people. That's a large number of people, but, amazingly enough, it's less than the number of people who are going to disappear in Japan.

In 2005, Japan became the first modern, industrial nation to shrink in population for reasons unrelated to war or disease.[1] Fujimasa Iwao at the National Graduate Institute for Policy Studies, a think tank that serves Japan's central government, predicts that by 2050 Japan will have 41 million fewer inhabitants, in effect dialing back the population to its level before 1950.

The aging of the country's population is as startling as its decrease. Japan, where 21.5 percent of the population is over sixty-five and 10 percent is over seventy, is, along with Italy, Spain, Korea, and Taiwan, one of a small group of countries that by some measure might claim the world's oldest populations. By 2050, 40 percent of Japan's 85 million people will be older than sixty-five.[2]

Imagine walking down the streets of Tokyo that year. School children and office and factory workers will be inside at their posts, but the shops, sidewalks, and cars will be filled with two generations of retirees, the younger group in their sixties, seventies, and early eighties; and, those one generation older, the faster-growing cohort of the oldest-old, reaching toward one hundred. Even on weekends they will dominate the streetscape, their numbers far outweighing those of the country's youth.

And the old will be ever more aged, chronologically, but at the same time probably healthier than their counterparts today. While the Japanese now live as long as any people in the world, epidemiologists have noted that many of the chronic diseases that afflicted Japanese elderly in large numbers in the past now strike down a smaller percentage of people, or kill them later in life. This healthier older population is coming to be a result of what demographers call a "fourth stage of epidemiological transition, the state in which the onset of degenerative disease is delayed,"[3] and even killers that we regard as inevitable consequences of aging are held at bay longer and longer.[4]*

* The concept of epidemiologic transition was pioneered by Abdel Omran, who in 1971, as a professor of epidemiology at the (continued on following page)

145

In the modern era, the country's people have not been as prone to heart disease as those in other developed nations. Diet is likely the chief reason for Japan's superior heart health. Cancer is a bigger killer, but the Japanese have smartly cut back on two bad habits that have been especially lethal to them: smoking, which leads to lung and other cancers, and eating large quantities of salt, which contributes to stomach cancer.[5]

Centenarians Everywhere

One is already more likely to meet centenarians in Japan than in any other country. Like Spain, the country is in the midst of a great-great-grandparent boom; the population of centenarians is growing at 11 percent a year.[6] In 1963, the first year records were kept, the country counted 153 people age 100 or over. In 2007, the count passed 32,300.[7] By 2050, Japan expects to be home to one million centenarians,[8] making them an ever larger group in a country that's contracting. While granted longer and longer lives, the Japanese who make it to such ripe old ages will find themselves in a country with fewer and fewer people to take care of them. Family members, especially, will be in short supply.

Demography is one social science that can offer a fairly reliable view of the future, and fifty-year projections, because they fall well within the range of the average human life span, are as foolproof as any prediction about human society. Of course, traumatic events—wars, disease, natural disasters, and other assorted mayhem—could

University of North Carolina, described how over time mortality patterns change with social and technological developments. Omran described three stages. In the first stage people tend to die from the basic scourges of pestilence (infectious diseases and parasites), famine, and war. Life in this stage is indeed nasty, brutish, and short. Lives improve and grow longer in Omran's second stage, when society masters nutrition, sanitation, and medical know-how. Death by infectious disease begins to recede and people are more prone to chronic degenerative ailments as they reach older ages. Omran stopped at a third stage in which chronic degenerative and socially induced diseases, such as some heart disease and some cancers and diabetes, become the dominant killers. Omran did not make it to a fourth stage in which even chronic and man-made diseases are overcome, though today the demographics in Japan and other countries argue strongly that such a stage is already upon us.

overwhelm all predictions. Japan's population projections don't take into account earthquakes and famines.[9] Nevertheless, the predictions still challenge every vision of the country's physical and social future. They are even starker compared to the trends in the rest of the world's population, which will grow at about the rate Japan is shrinking, reducing Japan ever more in relation to the whole of mankind. While Japan in 2050 will end up the size it was one hundred years prior, the rest of the world will have grown from 2.6 billion to 9.3 billion people over that same time. If the United States went through a Japanese-style reversal, its population would be 150 million in 2050, rather than the 420 million that the U.S. Census Bureau predicts.[10]

All of the industrial countries, and then most of the world will, eventually, follow Japan. The island nation matters because it is one of a handful of countries leading the way, and showing the world the consequences of contracting demographics, a shortage of young people, and a growing population of elderly.

Autumnal Youth

Tokyo, like the rest of the country, is suffering from attrition; more of its people are dying these days than are being born. The core of the city has also had its share of urban flight. And Tokyo, well ahead of the national trend, already had seen itself shrink nearly every year since 1967. In recent years, however, the population began ticking up. The national squeeze, it appears, is making Tokyo increasingly attractive to those outside the city living through the squeeze. In 2008, the city attracted at least eighty-three thousand more residents from elsewhere in Japan than it lost.[11] While the recent arrivals span all age groups, Tokyo's population—with a median age of around thirty-nine and a half—is a bit younger than the nation's, where the median age is four years older.[12]*

* Today, according to data from the IMF, Japan is one of eleven countries with a median age above forty; by 2050 there will be eighty-nine such countries, forty-four of them among today's developed countries. By 2024 the median age in Japan will be fifty.

Yet Tokyo's population is young only compared to present-day Japan. By global standards the population is quite mature, and measured against the city's own history, its people are antique. For much of the first half of the twentieth century, Tokyo was one of the world's youngest cities, as the median age there stayed about twenty-two, nearly half of what it is today. Tokyo nevertheless can feel quite young. Thirty-nine-year-olds today are likely to have fewer children than twenty-two-year-old Tokyoites in 1950; they also may well be single and frequent the city's unmatched assortment of bars and restaurants more willingly than they stay home for dinner. People in Japan postpone marriage the longest of any people in the world.[13]

Confirmed Bachelors and Bachelorettes

One often-talked about problem in Japan is the perceived crisis of the "parasite single," the young- to middle-aged single adults who will not move out of their parents' homes but who do not contribute to maintaining the households, either. The concern is mainly about women in their twenties or older who are among the 92 percent of single women who still live with a parent or two. Men, though, can be parasites, too. Viewed from the other direction, i.e., how many of Japan's elderly live with single adult children, the number is still an impressive 19 percent and climbing.[14]

The attractions for singles are easy to grasp. On the one hand, the Japanese government is among the most outwardly pro-family in the world. It has tried several measures aimed at encouraging multi-generational families to live together. On the other, as with many stridently pro-family policies, the result has been to accelerate the decline of traditional families. One typically well-meaning measure that has in fact encouraged people not to marry is Japan's promotion of multigenerational mortgages, which offer low interest rates but typically last up to fifty years, and sometimes longer. Tax breaks, too, encourage multigenerational living arrangements, which in theory were aimed at helping couples keep their parents with them at home, but in practice have provided great incentive for adult singles to stay in their parents' homes.[15]

Not every benefit is government induced. Singles get to keep or spend the money they earn. They can devote more time to either work or pleasure or both without the distractions of domestic duties, and they can, in most cases, bed down in surroundings far nicer than those they might afford if they rented or bought on their own. The press focuses on the negative sides of the single hangers-on, seeing them as emblems of decadence. That makes better copy than the bright side of the phenomenon, which is the fact that families are supporting the social and economic emancipation of their adult children. Workforce participation among women is three times what it was a generation ago, and workplace demands on women are on par with those made on men. The salary gap between the sexes has also narrowed considerably.

There is, however, a demographic price to pay, as nearly everywhere women have achieved some measure of equality. That price is, of course, the postponement of marriage and the delayed start of families. As researchers Naohiro Ogawa, Robert D. Retherford, and Rikiya Matsukura point out, marriage in Japan (as in Spain) is closely tied to couples' immediate plans to have children, and most do have their firstborn within a year and a half of marriage. Very few children are born to unmarried mothers—only 2 percent—and with marriage in Japan coming later than in other countries, family size is not just limited by the onerous economics of parenthood, but by the clock.

The fear that the parasite singles leave too many wombs in Japan empty reverberates in the halls of power where legislative attempts to coax the parasites out of their parents' homes are perennially debated. One proposal would tax adults who refuse to move into their own places, a measure that would have to be squared with the tax breaks that encourage parents and children to live together.

Where Youth Is Not Wasted on the Young

Tokyo has become the one city in the world where one's youth lasts longest, while at the same time it is a city where time passes so quickly that Tokyoites are near middle age before they know it.

Tokyoites, and those who long for the metropolis, hunger for the city's unceasing bustle, diversity of commerce, and convenience. Tokyo has become a kind of urban preserve in a state under demographic siege, the place that is still pulsing with youth, creativity, and the attention of the world as the country's other localities feel their vitality and critical masses wane.

Walking through the Red Gate that marks the entrance to the Hongo campus of the University of Tokyo brings familiar markers of campus life into view. Except for the rows of glistening unlocked bicycles, the shady campus could fit seamlessly into Boston, Frankfurt, or Canberra. Most of the buildings are forty years old or more, but new, architecturally daring laboratories signal to prospective students and young scholars that technological advances are under way. Starbucks has been given a beachhead on the main quad, too. Such small amenities are seen as necessary in the competition for students.

One of the evergreen verities of Japanese life is that admission to the University of Tokyo grants students an aura of brilliance that becomes a badge for life. Getting in still requires a dedication to academic toil. The process still begins when children are barely in school. Moms who may or may not want to dig back to juvenile academics still often spend years supplementing their children's lessons. Many Japanese grammar school and high school students still receive yet more instruction in the evenings and on weekends in the country's famous "cram schools" that can cost thousands of dollars a year. For the college-bound who are committed to the years-long grueling job of prepping for entrance exams, "crammers" are as unavoidable as ever. The demands of the extra cram schools entail commitment from families in terms of time, money, and emotional cost. The students crossing the quads of the University of Tokyo are likely to be beneficiaries of thousands of hours under their mothers' tutelage, of millions of yen in fees, and of the stress on parents and child of keeping students in their books.

Nearly all of the young people in view on the university grounds are single children or one of two. The costs of seeing three children through university in Japan, and the time sacrificed by mothers to get them there, is high. Most often, too high. In 2005, the Japanese

Ministry of Economy, Trade and Industry estimated that Japanese families spent between 13 million yen ($119,000) and 60 million yen ($540,000) to raise each child to age twenty-one. For a large number of Japanese families, the cost of raising and educating two or three children, not to mention the opportunity costs of keeping the children's mothers out of the workforce, is higher than their incomes.

As Japan has shifted from a country that is overwhelmingly young to one that grows inexorably older, children are not just more expensive than ever, they are more scarce, and thus highly valued for the places Japan needs them to fill. The number of children taking college entrance exams has dropped dramatically. From 2004 to 2005 test takers dropped by seventeen thousand. This sounds grim, but in a country that has half a million fewer eighteen-year-olds than it did in the mid-1990s, the decrease is impressively small. Today, three-quarters of Japanese high school graduates go on to higher education,[16] the highest proportion in history. Higher percentages of young men and women are entering colleges and universities, but the biggest change by far is among women. One in three female high school graduates continues her education today, about three times the rate of their mothers' generation.[17] When families are smaller, they tend to pour more money into higher education for their children, a practice that has helped women in Japan gain access to professions and other higher-paying careers that require university degrees. Nevertheless, the absolute number of students is shrinking and the percentage of high school graduates who are college-bound can only climb so high. Before long Japan will have as many open places in higher education as it has high school graduates.

To attract students, many of the country's six hundred universities and colleges are advertising aggressively and lowering barriers to admission. Some have moved to open admissions, scrapping entrance exams for essays and interviews. The strategies do not always work, because a higher degree is now so common that schools that do not help grads rise above the mass flounder. In 2006, Tohwa University, a private engineering college, announced it would close in 2009 because only 140 students applied for its 160 slots. The desperate chancellor said at the time, "There's no bright future [for Japanese universities]. It's time to quit before things get even worse." The Japanese education ministry reports that four in ten colleges failed to attract enough applicants. Some are bleeding money. A Standard & Poor's credit analyst called the financial straits of Japanese higher education a "life or death situation."* It is estimated that two hundred institutions will die over the next ten years. One university trying to rise above its struggling peers even instituted a "culture of golf" program and enlisted pro golfers as "professors." The school, Hagi International University, recently filed for bankruptcy. Part of its reorganization plan is to introduce programs that prepare students to care for the elderly.[18]

A Roundtable on Big Junk and Soggy Leaves

In this environment, schools that remain highly selective offer an ever more potent signal of their students' worth. Admission to the University of Tokyo and the handful of other top tier schools remains as prized and as hard won as ever. And their students often are indeed exceptional.

On a bright March afternoon, during the university's spring break, three students and a professor of sociology gather in a conference room in one of the campus's new showcase buildings, home of the Graduate School of Humanities and Sociology. Social science everywhere thrives on change and the clash of culture, class, and ethnic identification. Tokyo has undergone as much change as any city in the world over the past century. Its physical infrastructure was destroyed by violence twice, in 1923 by earthquake and fire, and again in 1945 bombing raids that wiped out three hundred thousand buildings and killed or wounded one in seven of the city's

---

* Businesses in Japan now also routinely worry about their future in a shrinking and aging country. Reuters reported in April 2008 that at Tokyo's version of Disneyland, officials are already fearful of how the park will fare in 2055, when 40 percent of the Japanese population will be over sixty-five. That does not bode well for a place where only 15 percent of the visitors are forty or older. "There is no way that the decrease in the population's parameter is going to be a positive factor [for Tokyo's Disneyland]," warned a grave analyst from Morgan Stanley. So, despite having two-hour lines filled with young people today, the Tokyo park has instituted annual passes for seniors, and begun to host flower shows and a circus in order to draw in older visitors.

inhabitants. Since the end of the war, it has been in a constant state of rebuilding and reconfiguring, even during its long economic downturn.

All the while, its population has remained, among cities in advanced industrial countries, uniquely homogeneous. Think of nearly any big city in Europe, and, especially, in North America, and change has come, and been caused by, new waves of residents of mixed backgrounds, languages, and cultures. In Tokyo, change comes amid a backdrop of cultural and ethnic continuity.[19] Of course, even in Japan there is more than enough diversity to keep social science humming. Japan also has more immigrants than it will publicly acknowledge. In the main, however, Japan has stalwartly protected its homogeneous ethnicity. So when students and a professor gather in a room to talk about the consequences of aging on life in Tokyo, their generalizations are sweeping, assured, unmuddied by ethnic politics, and apt to ring true.

Ikuko Sugawara is the young University of Tokyo professor gathering the students for the conversation. Her research explores how the Japanese make and maintain friendships as they grow older. Friendship, it turns out, has a strong relationship to how families care for one another. Japan's century of progress has fundamentally changed both. One of the sad findings is that as Japan ages, many Japanese past retirement are likely to find themselves friendless. Women fare better than men, especially women whose adult lives were spent minding the home, not work. Their world is likely to have been intensely social, and the friends and groups they chose while raising their children are likely to comprise their social circle when they are older. Older men, the ones who filled Japan's corporate ranks as factory workers or salary men, leave their social world behind when they retire. Japanese husbands spend an average of five minutes a day on housework and under half an hour on child care,[20] and they are virtually domestic aliens in retirement. Wives, Sugawara says, find older men's presence at home difficult to manage. Men don't fit into the social world of the women, and couples rarely have other couples as friends (the Japanese do not have a tradition of entertaining at home). Two nicknames capture the men's welcome home: "Big junk," because, like broken refrigerators and worn out chairs, they aren't cool or comforting, and are too big for the trash; and "soggy leaves on the ground," because they are drab, limp, and fallen.

Late life is a lonely period for men. In a survey conducted by Japan's Cabinet Office, two out of five men over sixty-five who live alone reported they had no close friends and one in four said they never saw their neighbors, far worse than women. Japanese newspapers report a rising suicide epidemic killing up to three hundred thousand people per year, of which the elderly account for one-third of the deaths. Of those who kill themselves, 73 percent are men. The suicide rate among men in Japan is far higher than in any other rich country.[21] So many hanged men have been suspended from trees in one wooded area near Mt. Fuji that the area has been dubbed "Suicide Forest." When Japan's suicide rate began an alarming climb in the 1990s,[22] a disproportionate number of victims were old, but in a country that historically regards elders as moral standard bearers, the trend seems to have unleashed devastating effects. Experts now say the suicide rate among the elderly has spurred a growing suicide cult among Japan's teens and young adults.[23]

Noe Morita, one of Sugawara's students, entered the University of Tokyo in engineering, which more than ever is a practical and almost inevitably lucrative choice, because Japanese industry is starved for young engineers. But students choose engineering less often, and millions of years of experience are walking off the nation's shop floor into retirement.

Had Morita stayed the course, she would have had her pick of employers. She changed direction while abroad as an exchange student in New York. There she met and befriended a gerontologist at Columbia University and the encounter woke her up to a reality facing her country that struck her as more pressing than the need to restock Japan's industrialists. Following the encouragement of her American mentor, Morita turned her studies to the aging population when she returned to Tokyo.

The choice was not wholly impractical. In Japan, where academics can be conservative and entrepreneurialism is stunted, fields that pertain to aging are wide open and waiting to be defined. Her research now compares aging in Japan to Denmark, which many in

Japan regard as the world's gold standard for quality of life among the elderly.

"There is a different assumption about who cares for you in Japan than in Northern Europe," she says. "Here we assume our families will be the ones around us, but in reality there is often no family to be there. In Europe, people expect to have a network of friends they can count on. In Japan, men are reluctant even to visit the sick."

One exception for men is their childhood friends with whom Japanese men say they remain soul mates. "These friends offer one of the few breaks men get from the social demands made by work and family," says Sugawara, drawing from the results of a survey of eight hundred people over fifty. "Men say that when they are with their soul mates, they can connect just as they had when they were young." But they rarely see them. Maybe only once or twice a year, if that. Yet they hold on to these friendships as their most important ones. Parks, shrines, banquet halls, and hotels all over Tokyo are crisscrossed with groups of excited, laughing senior citizens. They are the reunion groups, pulled together by self-appointed volunteers who organize get-togethers of their school and university chums.

Attitudes toward aging are rife with contradiction. When the troubles of old age set in, Sugawara says, people don't stop visiting friends because they are heartless, but because they know that illness is a sensitive issue. They feel that their friends may not want to be seen in their reduced condition. This vicious circle leads progressively to more isolation. Those who are ill but have family members willing to care for them retreat into their homes, or into the homes of their children.

"I lost my grandfather this year," volunteers Kazunori Inamasu, another graduate student at the roundtable. "He didn't want to be seen by others, and insisted only the family take care of him." Inamasu, like his peers, says that he expects, and is expected, to play a central role in the care of his parents. It is a conservative point of view that students say their generation still shares. When these students talk about their futures as caregivers, they do so with resignation and some melancholy, knowing full well the weight of the duties. On family matters, it is common for people to project conservative expectations, but then forge ahead in new directions when they get to the mileposts of adult life.

Japanese parents may have a more realistic view of how their children will treat them when they are old and dependent. The Mainichi Newspapers have been asking Japanese families a series of questions to determine how the nation's values are changing over time. The survey has revealed there has been a staggering drop in the percentage of adults who say they expect to be cared for. In 1950, two-thirds of Japanese women said they thought their children would care for them; today the numbers are closer to 10 percent.

Yet traditional attitudes persist because the nation gives up family traditions more slowly than have other advanced industrial countries. The traditional Japanese home houses several generations, and nine in twenty Japanese over sixty years old live with their adult children. That is a high proportion for the developed world, where the norm is around one in five seniors living with their children. Judging by the trend line, Japan will get there, too. In 1970, only two in ten older Japanese lived without their children. Rising divorce rates, small families, shame, and the long lives of those who have outlived their spouses have created an epidemic of solitude. Four million Japanese elders live alone, often in a deadly detachment from their families and society outside. In the nondescript apartments that filled in the flattened city after World War II live some Tokyoites who have grown old in the complexes. They mix with other, financially depleted elderly who have moved there for the low rents. Among these elderly, residents have formed ad hoc task forces to discover the bodies of dead neighbors, to stem the bane of corpses of loners left for months to rot.[24]

Japanese also combat the dangers of loneliness among elders in particularly Japanese ways. Little robot dogs equipped with sophisticated animatronics provide their keepers with companionship and can monitor their vital signs, beaming signals out to family or health-care workers when the sensors flash danger. There are also teakettles that send reassuring signals when they are heated up and area rugs that ping over the Internet when they are stepped on so that distant loved ones have evidence that everyday activities are proceeding as expected.

Tokyo Teens

The Japanese capital's size accounts for some of its peculiarity. There are enough people with nearly any given interest to support commerce aimed—often on a surprisingly large scale, and with great sophistication—at their group, no matter how mainstream or weird. There are huge shopping and entertainment districts for the young. Shibuya, the busy neighborhood for teens and young adults, is often given star treatment in films set in Tokyo. Japan's youth culture is not a violent response to an aging society, but is nevertheless a powerful one. Youth hit the streets with fashions that offer an overt assertion of babylike and childlike cuteness. In other countries, fashion-forward young teens and young adults assert their place in an adult world by eroticizing violence with daring clothes, and street fashion takes on dark tones that intimate control by force or sexual assertion. In Japan, fashion is more likely to turn as radically away from adult norms, even gangster norms, as possible. From radically prim to over-the-top cartoonish, from toylike to hermitic, fashion in Shibuya and Japan's other centers for young people separates younger Japan from the country's drift to gray. It also insults and exploits the Zeitgeist of the maturing mass, but it does nothing to change the demographic future of the nation. If anything, the assertions of Japan's youngest generation will compound the aging of their country.

It's in the youth districts that Japanese young people search for their own stories. Some come in the latest fashions. Shibuya's denizens pioneered the massively baggy kneesocks that pushed the Prussian military style of school uniforms to extremes. The neighborhood also gave birth to dueling teen cults. One is that of the *ganguro* (which connotes "black face" in Japanese, but also sounds close to the English "gang girl"). These are Japanese girls and young women who dye their hair blond and darken their skin by spending long hours in tanning beds. Bleached teeth, stark black clothes, bleached blond hair, and improbably tall platform shoes were the initial building blocks for the look. Back in 2000 it was all the rage. The *ganguro* girls caught pop cultural fire then and spawned pop stars, magazines, and manga that picked up on their look and lifestyles. *Ganguros* are less present in Shibuya now, but the current crop has pushed the fashion past all limits, and the girls involved traverse the neighborhood's pedestrian streets and bright cafés like performance artists defying everything the aging culture values. In their looks, they utterly reject the aesthetic of fine jet-black hair and pearl white skin. They are grungy, gamey, and unwashed (but perhaps not by American or European standards) in a scrupulously clean society that demands bathers scrub every fleck of dirt and dead skin from their bodies before they enter a bath. They hang together in groups of like-minded girls but cultivate an image of rootless sexual promiscuity, desiring men neither as friends nor as fathers of a coming generation.

Eroticized Day-Glo Shirley Temple Psychopaths

Getting dirty and raunchy, and even emulating American gangsta culture are predictable rebellions for youth, but just how aggressively do attacks by rebels with frills, ribbons, and giant silk Hawaiian flowers in their hair push Japan's generation gap? One riff on *ganguro* fashion is the more darkly tanned *Yamanba* or "Mountain Hag." The latter dress for battle in taffeta layers of baby-doll pink and Dreamsicle orange, and their war paint is panda makeup, bright white lipstick and eye shadow. Cute, charm-bracelet bobbles hang from their hair and clothes. And they are coifed, with hairdos either wildly frizzy or aggressively limp, like plastic baby dolls that have weathered a typhoon. Some still choose blond hair, but others are topped with mops of hair in kiddy colors popular in crib toys and Flintstone Vitamins. The ensembles of the *ganguro* clans and their successors flaunt the mien of eroticized Day-Glo Shirley Temple psychopaths. The extremes of cult fashion don't come cheap, and having bewildered parents who are nevertheless willing to underwrite the creative passions of a single child helps a younger generation maintain its sartorial extravaganza.

Fashion in Japan is as fleeting as it is anywhere, maybe more so, and the rebel look of tomorrow may adopt Elizabethan gowns, kimonos, Chanel, sci-fi, or the animal kingdom. What's astonishing is that in the land of the single-child family, where one of the culture's most repeated clichés says the nail that stands up is the nail that gets pounded down, such rebellions capture so much popular attention and even drive cultural change. In the moment that this page is being written, the more flashy *ganguro* styles are yielding to ultrafeminine takes that stress extravagantly expensive clothes and accessories, where the party dress is a symbol against the powers-that-be.

The girly styles now have crossed into men's fashion, too, and the symbol of male youth in Japan is the slender male gamine with a large leather purse. In a country where the work ethic once routinely drove students to the brink and where intense academic and economic competition demanded extreme diligence from young people, the youth of Tokyo now have the time and money to hone their elaborate rebellions. Even as rebels branded—self-branded, too—as profligate, dirty, and slutty, kids are still valued highly enough to demand and get their way. The maverick girls in Shibuya seem to be screaming out that adulthood can't have them for a while yet. Even the radically juvenile, however, see the day coming, and if it comes late enough, they will welcome it.

If one makes a practice of asking Japanese youth how they see their futures, particularly within their families, they consistently answer in similar ways. In a fast-food shop in Shibuya, for instance, two *ganguro* women offer a picture of their middle age.

"We'll still need steady jobs then," says one, struggling in English but then switching to Japanese to ask her friend the right words. She works, she says, in a nearby fashion accessories shop. "I hope to find a boyfriend who can love me and marry me. I really do. I feel this very strongly. But I probably won't marry until I'm thirty at least."

Her friend elbows her, makes an exaggerated frown with her white-panda eyes, as if to say, "Don't change, don't sound so stodgy."

The girl goes on, though. "I'd like children, a boy and a girl. But I may still be living in my parents' house, or them with me. This is Japan."

Her timing will be important. East Asian women have a very short few years to engineer relationships that will allow their expectations to match the reality of their future families. Like the girl in the café, most see themselves ready for marriage beginning in their late twenties, only a couple of years before men start seeing them as too old, at around thirty, to be marriageable.[25]

Café Society

Tokyo's young and older denizens mix in unexpected ways. One place they are meeting, and not quite meeting, is the twenty-four-hour manga café. Tokyo has hundreds of them. Open around the clock, manga cafés give refuge to people who want quiet time among Japan's comic books and animated films. Most are part of franchise chains and have a preassembled look about them. They are rarely greeted with unalloyed enthusiasm. The reasons are evident to the eyes and nose when one enters one of the many cafés around Ikebukuro station. Around two and a half million passengers make their way in and out of the station every day, and, it seems, many have little inclination to head to work, and many more don't want to head home. They become denizens of the manga cafés instead. The cafés, which often occupy ground floors and basements, open narrowly and then snake into warrens of private cells. (Some new ones have more open, modern designs.) Upon walking in, one is likely to be greeted by a sleepy teenager who sells a ticket that entitles the bearer to snacks, soft drinks, and unchecked use of the café's library of comics, videos, and computer games. Down a narrow hall is a library section. Stacks on the right have the comics for Japan's males—shelves and shelves of them, including some series that have hundreds of issues stretching back decades. Start at one end of the male section to find the books for young boys, fantasy stories, and joke books. Work down the shelves and the appropriate ages climb. There are slightly racy titles and more violent ones for teens; lurid tales for men; and then, at the end, perhaps in their own rack, the over-the-top x-rated volumes filled with cartoon fetishes for tied-up schoolgirls, zeppelin-breasted nurses, and dripping flesh.

Across the narrow hall is the collection for female customers. The magazines are noticeably neater and less used, but no less plentiful. Here are found love stories and tomes of girls leaving home and finding themselves toyed with and toying with men. There are also the powerful princesses and sorceresses and the animal tales. And the manga that feature Japan's fashion-forward rebel power girls, sometimes as heroes, but interestingly, often as villains. Readers cheer for them both ways.

Walk farther to come to the warrens—cubicles of various sizes equipped with one chair or two, computers, and DVD players. These are the escape hutches for the lonely boys and young who want to retreat away from the world of work and school. They don't date; they lose themselves in Japan's fabulous fantasy universe. If need be, they make love alone, on the page or over the Internet.

The world of fantasy has led to a spasm of public concern in Japan that decries the dissatisfaction of women in the real world, who must vie for attention with the sexual escape of virtual and comic book Japan. In the manga cafés resides a population of single-ton children—boys and young men—forging solitary lives, frustrating the singleton children—girls and young women—on the outside. Where young people have little need, or little desire to work, they buy time, and the boys and men in Japan's forty-five hundred manga cafés buy lots of time alone. One disturbing, recent study showed that 80 percent of the country's manga cafés are homes to some of their customers, who rarely leave for a night elsewhere, and in some cases, rarely leaving to see the light of day. And for many, the cafés are a cheap hotel, if for instance, one has missed the last train home. Or the last train home over the last few days. Walk down a level or two, and there is the floor that has showers, or maybe cots and showers. Don't ask too insistently on what goes on down there, but it is where the older men tend to spend their time.

Train Man

Are the loners the norm? Hardly. Manga cafés are just one group on a constellation of marginalized youth in Japan. Another group, the Geeks, or Otaku, are techno-crazed manga and anime superfans who inhabit Tokyo's shopping district for electronics, the neon wonderland of Akihabara Electronics Town. Akihabara has long been the place where shoppers flock to buy electric and electronic products of all sorts.

Want a robot to feed Granny? On the sidewalk outside of Akihabara's dozens of electronics department stores, there's likely to be a robot dishing space food out to another cyborg. Around the neighborhood, the Geeks can be seen dressed in meticulous costumes that re-create their favorite comic characters. What the fashion plates around Harajuku Station and in the streets of Shibuya spend on their getups, the Otaku spend on "cosplay" (costume play) outfits and to stock up on electronics and their favorite entertainment. In one sense they exist at the center of Japan's most powerful and popular pop culture machine, but they are so deep in the center that they are also distantly removed from the mainstream.

So profuse are the Geeks in Akihabara that sociologists liken the neighborhood to ethnic enclaves in foreign cities. A few years ago, a Geek famously, and perhaps apocryphally, intervened to stop an abusive man from accosting a pretty young woman on the train. The story of Train Man became a multimedia sensation, the basis for comics, a movie, and a TV series.

Perhaps one reason the Train Man, a Cinderfella geek steered to the mainstream by a traditionally pretty girl, hit it big in all media was that his story is reassuring in a country which feels, justifiably or not, deeply threatened by all the nails sticking up among the nation's youth. Japan has had radical moments in its history before, where young people violently muscled their way into the headlines with group action. The 1930s and the 1960s each saw periods of that. The current revolution is a quieter one that insinuates itself into the fabric of the family, where young people act unchecked by brothers and sisters, or disappoint, embarrass, or turn against parents who have no other children to turn to.

It seems that the Geeks, perhaps even more than the girls in Shibuya, have not removed themselves from more traditional Japanese dreams and expectations for their later adulthood and family life. The rap on them is not that they don't want to meet women, but that they can't. At least in Akihabara, girls who love electronics and manga are also among the in-migrants, and can be seen in their cosplay garb. Ask the males the same questions about their futures, and their answers are as conservative as the women's. They want children and expect that there is a good chance they will have to take care of their parents. One fellow browsing on the DIY computer floor of the gargantuan Yodobashi Camera store—walking around it is akin to being inside a computer—reluctantly offered his view: "I'm spending my parents' money in here. I think they expect me to be a good son."

Remember, a larger percentage of young men are going on to higher education than ever before in Japan, too. Most of the Geeks are college educated or college-bound. That doesn't mean they will be socialized. But in a one-child culture, loners, like rebels, have a disproportionate role in shaping the future. They are partners with the more conventional university men and women in shaping Japan's demographic drift, since they, too, will delay marriage and have small families or none.

Shopping for Lucky Red Underwear

Elsewhere in Tokyo another group gathers in another neighborhood. They are mostly women, but not because the neighborhood is geared toward fashion or wayward girls. This is Sugamo, home of the Togenuki Jizo Temple. Like Lourdes, Sugamo attracts the old and sick, who come to make an offering in hopes they will get cured. The restorative power of the temple's Buddhist figure is thought to be more potent on some days than others, and on the few especially propitious dates, the area around the temple throngs with many elderly.

The street, officially called Sugamo Jizo Shopping Street, is just short of a mile long and is home to a pedestrian mall with around two hundred shops that cater almost entirely to older customers. Curbs have been lowered to minimize the chance pedestrians might trip. The streetscape becomes a sea of bobbing gray hair. Like the fashion outcasts, the Geeks, and of course, for the mainstream shoppers and luxury buyers, the elderly migrate to their own, impressively large city within the metropolis. The scale of Tokyo makes it possible.

Shops on either side cater especially to the older set with canes that are painted or delicately carved, hats, traditional cakes, bedding, and sleepwear. Small stands sell a nostalgic mixture of traditional snacks, many cooked on the spot. There are sweets such as cakes in the shape of the temple's *bodhisattva* and savory pies molded to resemble good luck coins. But there are French-style cafés and bakeries and Japanese restaurants, too. This is not a street Tokyo's seniors visit to comparison shop for toileting aids, incontinence pads, or other concessions to decline. The district is full of life, and by design it reminds shoppers of their past joys and current capabilities. The street is full of vendors selling the tools of arts and crafts, T-shirts and jackets that blend the traditional with contemporary fashion. There are also stores that sell baby clothes and finely sewn stuffed animals, perhaps the finest baby clothes and stuffed animals in the world. They look to fit the cribs of wee Victorian aristocrats, and the prices for the miniature goods are also fittingly luxurious.

Doting on grandchildren is more affordable in places where family size is a fraction of what it once was. Several stores specialize in frumpy fire engine red underwear and long johns meant to bring good luck. The underthings are reserved for days when children or grandchildren are taking exams or otherwise need good fortune.

When asked, the local McDonald's agreed to allow customers to bring in outside food so that they could sit and have coffee with friends without feeling the pressure to spend more than they are comfortable spending. Or to spend less on themselves and more on their grandchildren. It is the only McDonald's in Japan that bends the rules on food. The neighborhood's shop clerks, mostly women in their teens or early twenties, must be patient.

"You have to learn to be calm," says one eighteen-year-old shopgirl in a pink smock who shares a temperament with the cashiers in Florida. "Older people go over things a few extra times, and they ask a lot of questions. Some of them are nice and some quite mean. You can't take it personally. I like old people."

Sugamo's place as a hub for shoppers, nearly all seventy or older, is relatively recent. It grew organically as the visitors to the temple grew more numerous over time, the result of Japan's expanding elderly population.

Today, the transformation of Sugamo continues. Residences and assisted-living facilities are springing up around the temple. Senior housing has chic locales in Tokyo, and Sugamo is one. One nearby assisted-living facility requires between $1 million and $2 million to buy into, and is home to retired executives and other well-heeled clientele.

The people who come to Sugamo offer insight into Japan's longevity and Tokyo's attractions for its older citizens. Most of the shoppers have arrived on their own, navigating the city's complex network of trains and streets that wind in all directions past often nameless buildings in apparently random order. If cognitive fitness depends on daily challenges to the mind, living in Tokyo handily beats nightly sudoku puzzles. The city is stressful in that it is a constant puzzle, but it is safe, so older people can get lost without fear that they will get threatened.

"The city helps keep us in good shape," says a woman on Sugamo Jizo Shopping Street with her husband. Call them Fumiko and Hideki. She's sixty-eight and he's seventy. "We climb stairs down to the trains; we climb them up. The city is hilly so we get some exercise. And there are always new things." The couple has come by commuter train and city subway to Sugamo from forty minutes away. They say they are going to visit a friend in a nearby home for old people and offer a visitor an invitation to join them.

A few blocks away, they come to the home, a new building with an inconspicuous front. They say that it is assisted living. Inside, the front lounge is filled with women, most of them thin and as old looking as human beings get. They are greeted by the home's director, a quiet man in his early thirties. He confirms that the ladies on view are nearly all over ninety and that one, walking along the wall holding a rail and being held up by a nurse, is 102.

Immediately, something strikes a foreign visitor as strange, and it is hard to put a finger on it. Then it hits. All of the caretakers are Japanese. It is Japanese people taking care of Japanese people. They share a language, a cultural history, and nonverbal communication is accurately summed up and acted on. When the nurses and aides call the residents by honorifics, it sounds right. That homogeneity is rare in places where care jobs are relegated to immigrants.

Fumiko and Hideki's friend is Hideki's former boss, once the editor of one of Tokyo's big papers. He paid $1.2 million to enter the home and loves it. When asked how he spends his time, he says he is studying classic Buddhist texts. In archaic Chinese. Why? Because each year he takes a trip to China with his grandson and they visit historical and sacred sites. This year, he and his grandson, who's thirty-five years old, climbed the Great Wall together. Asked why he needs assisted living if he walks the Great Wall of China, the old editor says he needs someone to cook and make his bed. He's widowed. Would he consider living with his son or daughter? No, he says, they should lead their own lives. But what about tradition in Japan that dictates children care for parents? He says tradition is not always reality. "It is good to be old in Japan," says the editor, clearly speaking as someone who can afford what's good about it. "Old people have the best health in the world; we have money, we have peace and security. We've won at life."

A Family History

Wake Lankard is an American man who works for a Japanese company; he is also an accidental industrialist, for his life in metal-forming began as an English teacher in Tokyo. He started his journey into the future teaching children at a day school. A year later he was teaching adults. At six feet tall with a bright, ready Matt Damon smile, Wake has a willingness to be a bit silly and can laugh at himself enough, and with enough dignity, to endear himself to the often reserved Japanese. One person particularly drawn to him was Naoko Shibayama, a recent college graduate not too old for a schoolgirl crush on an English teacher. After several unsuccessful attempts to arrange an accidental meeting with Wake, Naoko finally ran into him outside a coffee shop she knew he frequented. Now they are married.

Wake's mother-in-law, Setsuko Takahashi, began her adult life in a bad marriage. Though the couple had a son, the marriage ended. Destitute, with a baby to support, she took a job as a bar girl. On the job, she met Naoko's father, Masanao Takahashi. He was a young, independently minded engineer who worked in his family's small metal-forming shop. His parents objected to their son dating a bar girl. She was, they thought, beneath them. Out of pride, perhaps, she had not let on that she hailed from a once honored, aristocratic family.

Mr. Takahashi married her anyway. With him at the lead, the family business, Taisei Industries, thrived over time as the Japanese auto industry grew. It is one of the Japanese auto industry's suppliers of steel parts. The relationship has allowed the Takahashis the comforts and status of Japan's modern upper class. Today, Taisei sells millions of dollars' worth of steel parts a year and employs 220 people.[26]

That Wake ended up with a family in Kamakura was a great stroke of luck.

"My family," says Wake, "is the story of aging Japan. In October 2008, my wife and I took in her ninety-two-year-old great-aunt, Mina-san, who had a stroke six months before and lost all use of her left side. She stays in an extra room in our house, which has been rigged up with closed-circuit night-vision video cameras so my mother-in-law can keep a watch on her from the other rooms in the house." Mina-san is the sister of an uncle who died at 104.

Wake's Japanese house is the size of a three- or four-bedroom house found in an American suburb, spacious by Japanese standards. The extra room the great-aunt occupies has come to be the care station for an unbroken chain of needy elderly relatives. Japanese tradition demands that daughters and daughters-in-law take care of their in-laws and, when necessary, their own parents, aunts, and uncles. For the willing, there is almost always an elderly relative around to care for. Wake's mother-in-law has been taking care of older relatives nearly without interruption since she was a teenager. Mrs. Takahashi began by taking charge of her grandmother's care, then her parents' and her husband's parents'. After that, the uncle.

Nowadays Mrs. Takahashi keeps going, with lots of help from her daughter Naoko. The weight of Japanese tradition bears heavily on her. Often in the Japanese multigenerational home each generation gives and receives care in varying degrees over time. The old often care for the very young, and older children care for the very old. This may sound like the natural order of a family, but in practice it is rare in the developed world.

The shrinking of family size in Japan has had a strong influence on the intergenerational quality of Japanese families, too. Women who marry are more likely than ever to marry a man who has no brothers. Since it is customary for aging parents to live with their eldest sons, and because any son in Japan is now likely to be an eldest son, young and middle-aged married women in Japan are highly likely to live in a house with their husbands' parents. And if the woman is an only child, she may well live under a roof with her parents.

The mixture of tradition with Japan's new demographics means that one in three married women, at the ages when they can have children, live in three-generation households, sandwiched between their own children and parents or parents-in-law. No doubt the number would be higher still, except that Japanese women, for obvious reasons, don't all accept the prospect of living in a three-generation household enthusiastically. There is a vicious circle forcing ever smaller families, precisely because women—who generally don't relish spending the prime of their lives caring for young and old together—postpone or refuse marriage and motherhood.

As Mrs. Takahashi's experience seems to show, once one surrenders to an obligation, its duties can go on without end. In Mrs. Takahashi's case, each time she fulfilled one obligation to care for an aged relative, another obligation sprang up. There is still the expectation in her family that she will also take care of the next needy old person in line.

And judging from the care given the aunt, love is certainly at work, too. At dinner, Mrs. Takahashi leans in close to hear her aunt speak, nodding attentively and kindly, though the old woman's patter is mostly the same all day, every day. Mrs. Takahashi often takes the aunt around town. She probes her network of friends for places her aunt might go where the older woman can visit with people she might enjoy. After calling on a string of sterile, institutional adult day-care centers, Mrs. Takahashi dug deeper into her social resources, looking for a place that felt more homelike. When she heard of a traditional-style Japanese home in Kamakura run by a fiftysomething divorcée, she planned an outing for the whole family to take Mina-san there and check it out. There, a ninety-one-year-old woman played piano, another nonagenarian lady practiced her French with guests, and a dapper octogenarian man who identified himself as a "volunteer" popped around to play the board game "Go" with men even older. Mina-san loved the place, and sweetly sat, slightly engaged, at whatever table she was shown to.

"I'm on My Eighth!"

Now in her early sixties, Mrs. Takahashi is more familiar with her routine than she'd care to be. "I have always cared for an older person," she says with exasperation. "I'm on my eighth!" The experience has given her a system designed both to keep watch on her aunt and to give her some freedom. It was her idea to put in the cameras to monitor the old aunt. That way she can go about her business in the house. With a kind but forceful efficiency she hoists and prods Mina-san to the table, to the toilet, and to an occasional meal out. Mrs. Takahashi's keen-eyed force of will is persuasive, too. As if by instinct, Mina-san responds obligingly to Mrs. Takahashi's signals, heeding the daily rhythm of the family.

Miraculously, six months after Mina-san's stroke, and with no medication, she had regained all her motor control and again eats well, using her chopsticks. Moreover, despite her advanced dementia, she can still recall and perform all the steps in a full tea ceremony. The carefully choreographed meditative ritual is one of the centerpieces of Japanese cultural life, and Mina-san in her prime was a tea ceremony instructor of the highest rank.

The old woman loved the Kamakura home. At the other day-care centers, inevitably decorated like preschools, Mina-san sat passively at the long tables, watching other people performing tasks they had first learned when they were small children, folding origami cranes or cutting out paper dolls. At the home-style center, Mrs. Takahashi told the director that Mina-san was a master of the tea ceremony, and straightaway an assistant produced the ritual equipment: elegant earthenware tea bowls, a bamboo whisk, a wooden scoop, and the green tea powder that is foamed up in hot water. Mina-san took charge and expertly whisked up the tea, as the staff and other clients circled around, referring to Mina-san as *sensei*, the respectful word for "teacher." Mrs. Takahashi felt that the center was a great find. It did not infantilize her aunt, but created an atmosphere where she felt not just tended to, but honored.

Mina-san is afflicted with the paradox of memory loss in old age: able to invoke memories of events and practices acquired years ago, she is nonetheless unable to hold on to new information even for a few moments. Ask Mina-san to recount when she served tea at a tense 1941 meeting, and most days she can tell the tale. It occurred before the bombing of Pearl Harbor, and brought together her brother, an ardent opponent of Japan's militarism, and General Hideki Tojo, Japan's bellicose wartime prime minister. She relays keys details: who was in the room, where they sat, the tenor of the harsh words traded. Then remind her, when she stands from the lunch table for the fourth time looking urgently toward the toilet, that she paid a visit there moments ago, and she knows nothing of it.

Luckily, her disposition during the busy days is sweet. She even plays well with Wake and Naoko's two-and-a-half-year-old daughter, Aika. Both play with stuffed animals and both keep their beds piled high with plush bears and bunnies. Neither can focus on anything for long, and the aimless flitting around the house of the youngest family member amuses the oldest, and vice versa. Mrs. Takahashi is both bound to the house and needy for time outside it. Minding the moving bodies often falls to Naoko, but the daughter, like her mom, craves time away. She can go for days without a break.

As if four generations traversing the house weren't enough, Mina-san also has a rotating crew of caregivers, subsidized by government assistance, who add to the mix.* There is an overnight helper, a

---

* In Japan, the cost of home care is divided among the central government, the prefectures, and local cities and towns, with some contribution from recipients or their families. The program is, in part, an insurance scheme, but premiums do not come close to paying for it. The program was created in response to a public outcry for a system to help Japan's women, who are burdened with providing care, but are often themselves in their later years. The level of care is based on an evaluation that places recipients in one of six categories of severity. Mina-san, because she recovered from the physical effects of her stroke, does not qualify for full-time care. When the program was enacted, in 1997, the Japanese government vastly

divorced woman, who comes to relieve the family a couple of nights a week. The government subsidies discourage families from relying on a single, full-time caregiver. Policy makers know how domestic duties can get heaped on Japanese women, and dividing a family's care among several workers safeguards workers, who cannot easily say no to families, from exploitation.

The Professional Bather

Then there is Mr. Shimono, who is very important to the household. Once a law student whose prospects soured, Mr. Shimono worked as a manager at a fast-food chain. "I didn't like it, and another worker in the restaurant had a book with advertisements for jobs. There was one that described Japan's aging population and said they were recruiting caregivers. I thought that if Japan was aging, this would be a good career. But I expected the job would require a license. It didn't. Just four days of training. Nothing medical, just the system for bathing people and how to work with people who cannot walk," he says.

His educational background and gender make him an anomaly in the caregiver universe. He says that his wife never really supported his decision, but the job is working out. The peculiarities of Japan's home-care system have, in short order, created some giant companies that send out legions of workers to people's houses. Shimono's first two patients were a married couple, both over ninety-five years old and immobile. The husband had diabetes and his wife a broken hip.

"When I began with them, the job was very hard. And in addition to me, there was a helper who took care of the food—in the Japanese system, caregivers are not allowed to cook. There was also a housekeeper and the couple's two adult children, who lived nearby."

Both clients died soon after he began with them. Shimono can

underestimated how many people would need it. Twice as many people as expected obtained help, but because the aged population is the fastest-growing segment of the population, the gap between the original estimates and reality is expected to widen ever more, creating a fiscal emergency for Japan.

handle around ten families at a time. The relationships are usually short.

Shimono says that his goal is to have his own agency. The Japanese government structured care so that instead of families having one caregiver in charge of all of a recipient's needs, there would be a rotating crew of people, each with their own functions. That way, the logic went, the work could be professionalized and the workers would not suffer from the emotional attachment that comes with tending to one patient over long periods. Nor would the job subject the workers to abuses from families who demanded more than the caregivers were charged with doing. "Before the current rules, families were asking the caregivers to do everything, including walking the dogs," Shimono says, reflecting on one of the complaints that led to stricter rules.

The business of bathing alone might be enough to support one. It is quite a business even for one man. In the last eight years Shimono has served as bather to over eight thousand old, gravely sick, and nearly dead people, and to five thousand different families. For most of that time, his role, he says, has felt like that in other jobs. He has tried to do a good job, but has felt little bond with those he has bathed, or with their families. But over time it has come to mean far more to him.

Bathing in Japan has a spiritual dimension that at the start he was personally familiar with, but had not put into the context of those he was washing. Beginning with one older woman, he grew sensitized to the special place baths had as people were dying. In this case, the family impressed on him that the old woman was asking when Shimono would come to bathe her. He bathed her, Japanese style, managing to submerge her fully in a warm tub, on her last day. Later he received a heart-felt letter from the family thanking him for his efforts and expressing how much the bath meant to the woman, who was fearful of meeting her end without it. As people near death, many elderly request, as their last wish, a Japanese-style bath. When they feel that they may not get one, they despair.

With his changed perspective, he changed his practices, too. Now he often gets letters from families thanking him for the service and describing how very important the baths were to the dying relatives.

"The letters," he says, "make me realize how important the seemingly small things in life can become to the people I serve, and that nothing is to be taken for granted." Certainly not water, nor the human touch.

The Business of Family

Wake's father-in-law, Masanao Takahashi, began work at Taisei Industries when he was twenty-three in 1963. "When I started working for the company every worker in the factory was younger than I was," he recalls. "There were only five managers older than me, and they were between thirty-five and forty years old. We didn't hire anyone over forty. We thought we couldn't use them. Every year we'd hire about ten new people, between fifteen and eighteen years old. They were farm boys from the countryside, like the new factory workers in China today. They finished middle school, but had no skills. Typically they'd stay for ten years, rethink their goals, and move to a bigger company or off to Tokyo."

In 1973, Japan was hit by the Oil Shock, when the Arab member states of OPEC halted oil shipments to countries, including Japan, that had supported Israel in the Yom Kippur War. Subsequently OPEC raised the price of oil fourfold, a disaster for Japan.

The Shock helped push Japan's rapid conversion from a low-cost economy to a "high-value" economy. As the cost of goods and labor spiked higher, Japanese industries turned more intently to automation. Robots, not farm boys, were the fresh additions to the assembly lines.

By many measures, the Shock proved a blessing in disguise, propelling Japan to focus on cultivating a highly skilled workforce and using the technological tools that boosted productivity and were energy efficient.

There was another factor at work in the transformation, however. In the 1970s, Japan's working-age population, people fifteen to sixty-five years old, stopped growing. Compared to other industrialized countries after World War II, Japan's postwar baby boom was exceptionally brief, lasting only four years in the late 1940s. In 1948 and 1949 the country enacted and reworked the ominously named Eugenic Protection Act to give Japanese women unlimited access to legal abortions[27] and both women and men access to sterilization. The law was inspired in part by American-born theories on eugenics and Nazi German laws aimed at promoting a genetically strong race. One of its goals was to allow Japanese women to abort pregnancies that resulted from unions with foreign soldiers during the postwar occupation.*

Today the law remains controversial on account of its origins, but there is no doubt that it has changed Japan. Once given a choice, the Japanese took it, and the country's birthrate dropped 40 percent. By the mid-1970s, young workers in Japan would never again be as abundant as they were before, and the average age of workers never as low, as the society was set on course to "gray" over time.

Mr. Takahashi says Taisei had to learn how to balance the usefulness of younger and older workers. When computer-aided design was incorporated into the business, beginning in the 1970s, growing in sophistication ever since, many of the older Taisei workers—still not all that old—were reluctant, or unable, to learn the skills necessary to use it. The company needed workers who were both highly skilled and young enough to feel comfortable with the changing technology. As with all marketable goods and skills, when supplies are low, prices are high, and the young workers brought on for the new tasks were as valuable as any at the company. Now at Taisei, there is a large contingent of older workers, because they still have valuable skills that are hard to replace. But Takahashi is cautious with them. "My philosophy is that if a worker is over sixty, I don't give him a job of magnitude. He may decide to leave at any time. Nevertheless, we still rely on many of them."

Capable older workers are a bargain for Japanese companies. Taisei's employees receive a large, onetime retirement payment at age sixty, when they are officially expected to hang up their work clothes, or at least give up their regular full-time status. Small

---

* As a bulwark against the creolization of the Japanese race, the government facilitated the segregation of prostitutes so that some would work only among foreigners. The law was also invoked to justify forced sterilization and abortion in the government's efforts to contain leprosy and genetic disorders.

manufacturers offer about half the sums offered by Japan's giant manufacturers, such as the automakers or large electronics firms. Longtime shop floor workers at Taisei receive $80,000 to $100,000, but at Toyota they might get $160,000 to $200,000. These sums, combined with savings over their careers, are often annuitized by the workers, a conservative financial strategy designed to give them income from their investments, but also to shield them from the cruel forces of the Japanese financial markets.[28] And from the machinations of a financial services industry marred by a history of scandals victimizing overly trusting retirees. Retirees also receive pension payments from Japan's social security system.

After its older workers officially retire, Taisei offers them a chance to work at the company at a reduced wage. The practice is common in Japan. Two-thirds of the country's firms offer similar arrangements. Smaller firms that offer lower retirement packages have a lot of success rehiring retirees who need the income more than those from bigger firms. It's a good deal. Workers' wages, together with their retirement income, approximates the full income workers made before their official retirement. The arrangement apparently suits Taisei's older workers particularly well. Most of them do stay on at the company.

The Japanese know that they live long lives and feel compelled to continue to sock money away even in their sixties and beyond. That's hard to do without work.[29]

Japanese employers and employees are more willing to stick to one another after retirement age than in other countries. Better than six in ten men in Japan are still at work if they are between the ages of fifty-five to sixty-five, the decade-long window that includes most countries' official retirement ages. In the European Union's fifteen original states, only about four in ten men ages fifty-five to sixty-five work.[30] A breakdown of the age group into more limited ranges shows how the Japanese are outlasting their counterparts elsewhere at every stage during that ten-year span. Nineteen of twenty men aged fifty-five to fifty-nine have jobs—four times the chances that a man the same age in France will work.[31] Forty percent of men sixty to sixty-five still work. The Japanese government has been successfully experimenting with ways to enlist older workers as a front line against the effects of a shrinking workforce.

At Taisei a glimpse of the group of older workers yields a mix of men and women, few of whom would be the first choice of an employer with lots of options. Of course the older workers talk up their skills and willingness to stay as long as they are wanted. Nevertheless, meeting them feels a bit like meeting the ranks of aging citizens thrown into soldiers' uniforms in a last-ditch attempt to defend the homeland. Some appear strong, capable, and ready, while others are hardly front-line material. Older workers have many strengths, but whether they can be relied upon to keep a country's cutting edge as its workforce declines by one-third and its population of young people withers, remains to be seen. The battle plan so far is to raise the mandatory retirement age from sixty to sixty-five, a transition already in the works—and to offer a vast assortment of training programs for workers at or near retirement. There are also a growing number of public and private employment offices that focus on placing older workers.

The early efforts have not been as promising for seniors looking for new positions as it has been for those who are hired back by their old firms. One of the new employment agencies for seniors has fifty-seven hundred seniors in its system, but finds it can place only about one-fifth of them. More will need jobs over time. Economist Marcus Rebick, the director of the Asian Studies Centre at St. Antony's College, Oxford, studies poverty among the elderly in Japan. He notes that Japan's poverty rate among the old is among the highest in the group of OECD countries, and that the story of the poor in Japan is overwhelmingly a story of the elderly.

"The proportion of poor elderly in Japan has been going down slightly," he says, "but their numbers are climbing as Japan ages."

The most vulnerable groups, Rebick says, are those who were self-employed, worked for companies with poor pension plans, and above all, are widowed women whose husbands' pensions couldn't support them over a long life.

At the employment agency for older workers, applicants desperately want work, and the agency's manager says a surprising number have even expressed a willingness to work abroad in developing countries,[32] where their cost of living would be lower, household help would be available, and where, some say, they could pass on their skills.

In many cases, continued employment also gives them the income to help support their extended families. Sometimes that means helping pay for programs for their grandchildren, but often it goes to help fund the care of parents in their late eighties or nineties. "Retirement income," says one sixty-nine-year-old worker who says he hopes to work for years to come, "is too little for me to get by, so I have to keep working." For his mother, he chose a nearby nursing home so he could visit her after work. He knows, he says, he may be visiting her for years.

The Rock-Hard Biceps of Another Mr. Takahashi

Some of the older workers at Taisei remain remarkably fit, even into their sixth decade of work. One seventy-year-old factory worker, also named Takahashi, began at Taisei twenty years ago after he retired from a job as a door-to-door deliveryman for a rice company. In that job he carried six tons' worth of sixty-kilogram rice bags from a truck to people's doorways every workday. Takahashi is a short, compact, wiry man with a full head of unkempt white hair. When asked to make a muscle, his eyes twinkle and he nods assuredly and smiles, showing a broad set of original teeth. Rolling up his sleeve, he flexes, and a rock-hard ball of a biceps muscle pops out of his thin arm.

"My father is ninety-three, and my mother is eighty-six," Takahashi says, "and I have the bloodline for a long life. Many of my friends aren't working, but I am glad I am. When I come here, nothing makes me tired."

This Mr. Takahashi now works as a welder on prototypes, a less stressful version of the job he did a decade before. He also conducts training for younger workers, a job that offers unexpected challenges for him, because Taisei, strained to find young Japanese workers, has been taking on more foreigners.

Each year, Taisei brings five or six foreign workers into its Fujisawa plant. Officially, Japan puts its count of immigrant workers at around 1 percent. This appeases the popular desire of the Japanese to preserve their nation's ethnic, racial, and cultural cohesion. Regulations governing whom Japan allows to become permanent residents—citizenship is nearly always out of the question—are highly restrictive by world standards. That such policies have survived as the Japanese economy and culture have globalized is a testament to how deeply Japan's wish for national purity runs. In an aging country with a workforce that stagnated and now shrinks, those demands conflict with the practical requirements of families and businesses that need bodies to fill caretaking jobs and workbenches. Outside the bounds of the immigration policy, however, is a labor policy that allows businesses to bring in foreign workers from a select group of countries whose citizens Japan feels are both primed to work for reduced wages (often for long hours and little time off) and hail from Asian cultures, or places that Asians, including Japanese, emigrated to in years past and are therefore ostensibly simpatico with, regarding Japanese ways.

Outsiders Needed But Not Wanted

It is hard for anyone to take root in a new culture, and especially hard for foreigners to do so in Japan because the country is so profoundly suspicious of outsiders. Immigrant workers often sign on for three-year tours as "trainees," though they are frequently placed in unskilled work that requires and gets no training. Others enter as "returnees" of Japanese ancestry, who are eligible to stay indefinitely, or else stay illegally. No matter how they arrive individually, as a group they provide the indispensable glue that keeps the Japanese economy together.

One scholar with personal and professional insights into Japan's push-and-pull policies toward foreign workers is Dave Aldwinkle, an American-born professor in Hokkaidō, Japan's big northern island.[33] Aldwinkle, who also goes by a Japanese version of his name, Arudou Debito, is that rarity in his adopted home, a naturalized citizen. Writing in the *Japan Times*, Debito noted that whole industrial sectors in Japan now depend on foreign labor. Some major voices of business, such as the chairman of Toyota, Hiroshi Okuda, and the Japan Business Federation, have declared that

Japan must formalize a policy that attracts foreign workers on better terms.[34]

To Masanao Takahashi, Japan's reputation for exploitative ethnocentrism is a stain on the country, partially justified but not universally deserved. His family, and his wife's family, have long been internationalists. On a trip to Bali in the early 1990s, Mr. and Mrs. Takahashi met a hotel waiter who announced that he very much wanted to come and work in Japan but needed money to do so. Rather than dismiss the request as one more ruse by a conniving local, the Takahashis thought it over.

"There had been so much ill will for Japan around Asia that I felt an impulse to provide another view of our country. That we can be generous and open and that Japan is not home to all evil people, but a nice place," he says. "I had a home he could live in, and I was in a position to give him the job he wanted."

The next day, the Takahashis presented the Indonesian five hundred dollars in cash, telling him that it would take care of about half the airfare to Tokyo, and saying that if he raised the rest, he could live with the family and work for the company.

About a year later, the family heard from the man. He had scrounged up the money needed and was heading to Tokyo. He stayed in Japan for eight years, living for some of the time with the Takahashis. He learned Japanese and returned to Indonesia to become a tour guide in Bali serving Japanese tourists. "He has a terrific reputation," Mr. Takahashi says with pride. "People really love him. One of the big tourist magazines picked him as the best Japanese-language guide in Indonesia."

Walking the Factory Floor

The Taisei factory itself is hardly a design gem. It looks like other factories that share the nearby industrial landscape. The front building is a bare-bones office where the white-collar jobs get done, often by managers dressed in the same jumpsuits the factory workers wear. Behind the office stand the factory buildings, where the company turns out whatever its chief customer, a supplier to Nissan, demands.

American visitors to the shop floor might not sense the company's need for foreign labor and might even overlook the presence of immigrants entirely. The first group they would pass would be hard to pick out. They are Nikkeijin, ethnic Japanese, or fractionally ethnic Japanese, who are descendants of emigrants from Japan who went to South America in search of agricultural work. Most of the early émigrés ended up as plantation workers. A quarter of a million found their way to Brazil but they settled all over Latin America.*

Their presence in the New World was a response to the demographic crises of the time. In the early twentieth century, common wisdom in Japan held that the country could not support its 50 million people. There were too many idle young men in the countryside, most of whom were not firstborn sons and would not inherit family land to work on. The "surplus" males were a burden to their families and an impediment to Japan's modernization. With government support, a wave of Japanese found new lives in South America. As farm workers, they were welcome. Large plantations were short of workers at a time when world demand for South American crops, such as coffee and cotton, boomed. Today, there are six generations of Japanese descendants in South America.

The ethnic Japanese in South America today have, by and large, risen well above the status of plantation workers and tenant farmers. Some of Brazil's largest agricultural growers' groups are dominated, for instance, by ethnic Japanese. Descendants of Japanese migrants make up a disproportional number of their countries' professionals. It is a far better legacy than the one Japan established in the early twentieth century in neighboring Asia. The country's need to alleviate its perceived overcrowding crisis was one of its primary justifications for colonialism in East and Southeast Asia.

Today Japan still struggles to make peace, politically, with the countries that bore the brunt of the military and colonial policies Japan employed to manage its demographic destiny.

Over the last century the demographics of Japan and South America have flipped. Now in the same way that Ecuador sends workers to Spain, South America sends workers to Japan, and the country that was once so desperate to jettison its own people in the face

* Brazil is also home to 1.3 million citizens of Japanese descent.

of "overpopulation," prefers them above all others as it grows its pool of immigrant labor at home. Beginning in the late 1980s, when Japan's economy was at its strongest and Brazil's was weak, Japan eased residency requirements for Brazilian-Japanese, and the small number of immigrants that had been "returning" to Japan rose. The automotive and electronics sectors have been willing to employ them in impressively large numbers; today there are about 275,000 Brazilian-Japanese in the country.[35]

Dangerous, Dirty, and Difficult

The Nikkeijin on the Taisei shop floor hail from Brazil and Peru. On closer look they do not appear the same as their Japanese coworkers. Far from it. Some have red hair; their posture doesn't yield when superiors walk near; and they look like imports from the *mestizo* mix of urban South America.

One station down from the Nikkeijin are three Chinese workers in goggles and work clothes. It is impossible to see their faces in detail, but when they speak they reveal their nationality. Their tones, gestures, and carriage signal they are not local. The Chinese workers come to Taisei on the three-year trainee program. It won't be three years for long, though. The need for workers is too great and no company wants to spend the effort to acculturate and train workers and then lose them just as they are getting up to speed. In 2008, in response to what manufacturers described as an urgent need, the government began to debate extending the trainee program to five years. As soon as discussion began, passage was nearly inevitable. Little by little the barriers to immigrant labor, and eventually to more foreign settlers in Japan, are falling, a trend that is growing fast. Even more than Spain, Japan works to attract foreigners with cultural connections to its people, but as in Spain, Japanese employers can grow wary when the connections take such firm hold that immigrants venture beyond their workplace.

One of the top managers at Taisei, Mr. Tada, sees the extended stays as a mixed blessing. "If they stay longer, the workers tend to get into trouble. They get houses, start families, and their lives get complicated."

But the wary Tada, who is sixty-eight, nevertheless sees the need to allow for some such trouble. "Thirty years ago I would not have been allowed to work at the company at my advanced age. But the government now subsidizes us to keep workers on into their sixties. That's good for us, because we can't hire young Japanese people."

The increasingly well-educated young Japanese tend to refuse jobs with one of the so-called "Three Ks." The term describes the conditions that Japan's younger generation avoids, at least for the money employers offer; in English the "Ks" are translated as the Three Ds: Dangerous, Dirty, and Difficult.

"For the migrant laborers, the work here is something they want." Tada says that in the trainee program, the foreigners earn about half of what a Japanese counterpart would take home. The company also offers small bonuses if the foreigners pass a series of Japanese language tests.

With the Chinese, Taisei's success has been mixed. Of the first group of six Chinese trainees, three did not complete their tenure. One ran away and was never heard from again. His escape cast him into Japan's immigrant underground. Press accounts of illegal immigrants in Japan estimate their number at between 220,000 and 250,000, with 10,000 new arrivals a year. That is under one-quarter of a percent of Japan's population, and would hardly rate a blip on the radar in countries that are Japan's economic peers. The United States, where 4 percent of the population is comprised of illegal immigrants, has nearly fifty times as many undocumented workers as Japan. Great Britain and France, each with less than half Japan's population, have more than twice as many undocumented immigrants as Japan. Those that do remain in Japan have had to rely on stealth—their own, their friends', and their employers'. Everyday Japanese law enforcement depends on the omnipresence of an inquisitive police force aided by a populace willing to report the smallest anomalies on their streets. And no matter how restrictive life seemed to be as a Taisei trainee, the Chinese runaway almost certainly passed into a world of work where abuse and hardship are rampant and unchecked.

From 2004 to 2005, Sharon Noguchi, a staff writer for the *San Jose Mercury News*, researched immigrant communities in Japan on a Fulbright fellowship. She followed illegal workers in Japan who lurch from job to job, tracing leads to small factories, food processing plants, and services that employ them. One worker she followed held thirteen jobs in eleven years. This is the well-worn path of such workers everywhere, but in Japan, where they are considered criminals and feared by the public, employers know there is virtually no protection for their charges whatsoever.

Even workers who arrive legally can slip into the realm of the easily exploited. Upon their arrival, foreigners typically have to surrender their passports to their new employers, a practice that keeps the new boss in nearly complete control, unless the workers skip out without their papers, which makes them even more easily abused by whatever employers pick them up. Once in the illegal realm, their wages are a small fraction of those of legal workers. If they are women, they are at risk of being coerced into becoming sex workers. Social security and health-care benefits, of course, are out of the question.

Another one of Taisei's Chinese trainees who didn't work out was apprehended by police in Tokyo for wandering around without his Alien Registration Card, and was deported. A recent spike in Japan's still-low crime rate is often blamed on foreigners. The rhetoric can take on hysterical tones. Japan's former conservative justice minister, prominent politician Kunio Hatoyama, caters to fears by promising to drive down crime rates by tightening up "immigration management."[36] One member of Japan's Parliament speaks of the one million foreigners in Japan forming murderous, thieving gangs. A mayor of Tokyo talks about the foreigners who are "all sneaky thieves,"[37] and the whole nation has been enlisted as watchdogs to make sure foreigners in the country have the proper papers.

Even people who do possess papers but forget to carry them are subject to severe sanction, including deportation. In such an environment, it was inevitable that the second Chinese trainee would be arrested after a dunderheaded attempt to save himself a little money. He climbed an electric pole in an effort to siphon power from a neighbor to run the household appliances in his room. In China, law enforcement could barely be expected to weigh in on such a small matter, encouraging, at best, that the two parties work it out themselves. In Japan, the act, committed by a foreigner, was regarded more gravely. Tada says the behavior, being so far from the Japanese norm, mystified him. The promise that Chinese culture is close enough to Japanese culture to facilitate an easy blending of the foreign workers seems to have left both parties scratching their heads.

One other thing a visitor needs to have pointed out while traveling the roads in Taisei's industrial district are the small worker dormitories where the foreign trainees are put up three to a room. That is far better than many accommodations in China, but for the Chinese in Japan, the dorms, and the reduced wages, can be a reminder that the Japanese have not brought them in to give them a middle-class life in Japan, but to compete with China.

Taisei already has one operation set up in China. For now it is mostly a design center, and does not do any manufacturing. That may change soon. Mr. Takahashi believes Taisei will hold on to its domestic market of supplying parts for Nissan cars built for Japanese consumers—the plant so far does not build for cars sold abroad. But he adds that a shrinking Japan forces companies like his to have global strategies for both markets and workers. Yasumasa Ishizaka, managing director at Lotus Capital, a Japanese private equity fund that serves some of the country's largest institutional investors, says that aging demographics are forcing Japan to invest aggressively in younger countries. Capturing some of the economic growth in those places, he says, is essential for the support of an older Japan. The automakers Taisei supplies have been devoting billions to plants in emerging markets to combat their swooning businesses at home. Latin America and the Near East received giant commitments even during the global downturn in 2009 and 2010. Industrial, financial, and consumer products companies have, overall, picked up the pace of their emerging-market investments in order to replace once robust (and captive) markets at home. "Japanese companies are seeing markets in ever more exotic lands," wrote the *Financial Times* in July 2010, "as an aging population and changing consumer behavior continues to cloud prospects at home." No wonder Mr. Takahashi also does not have much faith that midsized manufacturers like Taisei will command the important place in the Japanese economy that they have today.

"Of the many friends I had in manufacturing," he says, "most are gone. They've sold out their plants to make money on the real estate which was, they believed, more valuable than the business. Few people want to bother themselves with the day-to-day trouble of having employees, dealing with the government, staying competitive globally, while making things in Japan." The drift saddens him. "Manufacturing produces goods of real value and gives people good jobs. It doesn't sink in. The model for Japan in the future is to make money from Japanese factories in foreign places where other people will do the work."

Japan Goes to China, Again

As the supply of workers shrinks, the economic power of skilled young Japanese workers grows. Employers cope. One way or another they will find solutions to the demographic crunch. Increasingly they cope by arbitraging youth, choosing less expensive younger workers abroad. Today, there are approximately twenty thousand Japanese companies with operations in China. Together they directly employ about a million Chinese workers.

But the number only hints at the willingness of Japanese industry to shift the "dangerous, dirty, and difficult" work to China and to its abundant youth, whose labor can still be purchased at low cost and whose enthusiasm can be stoked by the promise of a growing economy. Behind the Japanese factories are thousands more Chinese firms that act as suppliers to the Japanese firms. The suppliers, very often companies created by Chinese entrepreneurs, serve up parts and services that go into the end products that pour out of Japanese-run factories in China. These new businesses are re-creating clusters of companies that are the new versions of the prized networks of suppliers that made up the heart and soul of Japan's industrial rise in the last century. The countries, like China, that have large numbers of energetic young people to employ are where such new industrial clusters are built today, and where aging Japan turns to hold on to what it still has.

Mr. Takahashi is sometimes invited to lecture young Japanese on the importance of manufacturing to Japan's national strength. Yet underlying his plea is a dark realization: even the young people who brave the Three Ks risk having everything pulled out from under them as Japan's companies seek aggressive solutions to the nation's receding demographic wave. The percentage of Japanese college students enrolling in engineering and other technology-related fields is declining about 10 percent a year, a rational response in an economy where the premier employers seek foreign engineers abroad to replace their own high-wage workforce at home. Even parents hesitate to push children into engineering fields that they know Chinese, Indian, and Brazilian engineers can fill for one-tenth to one-third the Japanese starting wage. The country's Ministry of Internal Affairs estimates that Japan is short half a million engineers in digital fields alone.[38] Japanese industrial associations make a valiant attempt to lure people into the empty jobs. They produce glossy ads aimed at glamorizing engineering. Individual firms offer signing bonuses to talented workers who agree to abandon their companies and move, a practice that not long ago would have been impossible in a country where it was once shameful to jump corporate ship.

Yet the companies and the country cannot escape the forces they also feed. As the population shrinks and students become more valuable, they drift to fields such as law and medicine that are less dirty, and, perhaps more important, less likely to be undercut by industries aggressively seeking ways abroad to avoid the shortages and costs at home.

Those who see a world in which jobs move because costs are lower abroad or because workers in rising economies are especially diligent will find a more complete picture of the dynamic of globalization in Japan. The shifting demographics change the value of work and the workers. Premium workers in advanced countries are not losing their value but gaining it, yet their premium place in the market forces global solutions that devalue them.

The theme is frequently echoed in the corporate marketing of large Japanese companies, which have made sounding the demographic warning bell part of their mission. The 2007 Corporate Responsibility Report of Konica Minolta, the big imaging company, stressed both that Konica Minolta was working hard to bring Chinese employees in China up to the standards of the company's best and that it had instituted strategies to manage Japan's population slide.[39] Japan, which was once steadfastly committed to managing and manning its own economy, now seeks to lash its fortunes to countries that can fill the gaps caused by its demographic shift. This strategy carries the risk that factories—and eventually Japan's service and creative industries, too—will be cut even further. Honda Motor Co. was the first Japanese car company to build an entire factory in China devoted to making cars for export back to Japan. In August 2009, the Asian *Wall Street Journal* reported that Indian technology and outsourcing firms, which had long been refused business by Japan's homegrown firms, were suddenly adding thousands of employees to serve some of Japan's marquee "national champion" companies, such as Hitachi, Fujitsu, and Nissan (which might affect the Takahashis' fortunes). "And with Japan's aging populace . . . ," said the paper, "Indian companies expect much more business in the future." Japanese companies have geared up quickly in China, too. In Dalian, a former Japanese colonial outpost on China's east coast, Chinese news sources report there are fourteen thousand Japanese-speaking software engineers creating code for everything from heavy machinery to Japanese computer and console games, some for Japan, but more for foreign markets destined to grow.

A New Family Business?

Back in Kamakura the Takahashis are now considering what to do with a rambling house they took over when the old uncle died. Mrs. Takahashi's latest plan is to turn it into a day-care center for seniors. It would give the people who use it dignified care surrounded by a traditional home in a natural setting. And considering how many old people Japan will soon have, it would be a good business, she thinks. Then again the big house might be a nice house to retire to, not to mention big enough for three generations.

CHAPTER 6

CHEATING DEATH,
ONE MOLECULE AT A TIME

WE BEGIN TO DIE WHILE STILL IN THE WOMB. THE NOTION IS paradoxical. How is that possible?

The answer, in part, is that even at birth we gain the health benefits of the modern world. And, just as important, we still live in a world that dispenses good health and longer life spans in unequal doses, depending on where, when, and how a person enters it or grows up. The effects of circumstance are not always obvious or easy to predict. How well our minds and bodies hold up as we age, compared to those of our contemporaries, calls on the complex mediation between the genes our forbears endowed us ("If you want to live a long life, choose the right parents"), the stress of our surroundings as we come into the world and grow up, and the lifestyle choices we make.

How mothers treat babies in the womb makes a difference in how well people survive to adulthood. Cancer that strikes at eighty may have had its genetic triggers timed by the environment that one's mother lived in while she was pregnant. Alan Jones of the University College London's Institute for Child Health calls the period before birth and during infancy a "window of opportunity" when genes can be "programmed" for good (or ill) health through epigenetics, which he describes as the delicate interplay of genes and the environment. Epigenetics, Jones stresses, has a bearing on the whole of a person's life.[1]

188

When there is an epigenetic change, DNA reacts with chemical groups that have the power to activate or deactivate genes. What epigenetic change does not affect is a person's genetic makeup; rather it affects how the genes we have activate, stay dormant, or change function.

The environment is often what stirs epigenetic change. If, for example, a mother places her unborn child in contact with synthetic hormones (perhaps they were prescribed to her or introduced through everyday foods), the baby may react abnormally to natural hormones later. The unborn pay lifelong consequences, too, for a mother's stress (it can forge extra-reactive nervous systems) or hunger (it can cause the body to hoard calories, stored as fat instead of muscle). A child of an emotionally abused mother may suffer consequences of the abuse, too (by being prone to depression, which is a killer in old age).

The Good News

But if we begin to die in the womb, we also can begin to live longer than we might otherwise have, if we are lucky to have good prenatal care. Thus does the quest to extend the human life span begin early. Fates that were once immutable are now often transformed by medical intervention.

The moments just before and at birth, so vital to a person's long-term health, have been recast from being one of the most dangerous periods of life for mother and child into a moment of opportunity when medicine can intervene and make a dramatic difference in how long and how well a child lives.

Mothers who are given a simple test for Group B Strep—a condition that can afflict adults without their feeling any symptoms, but which can lead to meningitis, and then to cerebral palsy in newborns—can be given antibiotics to ward off all the complications for their newborn. A simple blood test can identify up to fifty disorders in a newborn. It happens shortly after birth when a doctor or nurse pricks the bottom of a baby's foot and transfers a drop of blood to a small piece of filter paper. A laboratory analyzes the sample for mostly rare conditions, but conditions that, untreated, can handicap a child mentally or physically for life, or cut the baby's life short, or both.

"I'd say this [has been] the biggest change in the way I practice medicine over the last twenty years," says Dr. Rebecca Unger, a pediatrician affiliated with Chicago's Children's Memorial Hospital. "When I started, we tested for five things. Now it's ten times as many and we can do things about the conditions we discover." If a blood test finds a baby is one of [every] forty thousand newborns who suffers from a condition known as SCAD, a simple change of diet can help the child thrive when it otherwise would have faced life-threatening seizures and severe problems in breathing. The foot prick can also reveal which of every twenty-two hundred newborns is at risk for hypothyroidism, a condition that leads to cretinism, a stunting of physical and mental growth.

"If the lab test is positive for any of them, it is treated as an urgent matter," says Unger. "The lab tracks us down wherever we are, tells us the problem, and that way we can adjust to the baby's needs right away. This has made a huge difference in the health of otherwise very troubled children and their families."

Until recently there was a widespread and justified fear that the technology to save premature babies, those born before the thirty-seventh week of a pregnancy, had moved so fast that babies being saved too often were afflicted with severe health problems and went on to need lifelong care. Babies born prematurely face higher risks for a number of conditions, including cerebral palsy and mental retardation. The costs to support the children could be high and ongoing. Preemies often have a difficult time breathing. Worldwide, between 5 percent and 10 percent of all newborns need to be resuscitated. In the past that usually required oxygen therapies to make up for what the babies' small, weak, and frequently collapsed lungs could not provide. Oxygen can be highly toxic and too much of it makes babies prone to a battery of serious complications, too, including cancer.

Today, preemies have a far better chance. They can, for instance, often breathe on their own, provided that they are given a pulmonary surfactant, a substance that does for a baby's lungs what bubble-strengthening chemicals do for detergents, keeping them nicely round and inflated. "I used to think the hardest part of my job was seeing the preemies squirm for breath in the neonatal unit," says Unger. "I hated it. Now most of those babies breathe fine on their own."*

When medicine helps babies come into the world robustly, they ease those babies on the long road to healthy later years. In the developed countries, where the average life span continues to lengthen, early intervention today may offer longevity gains for some years to come, provided modern lifestyles do not negate all the gains.

My Very Own Epigenetic Identity

Much as we are intellectually aware that we are being affected by our environments, it's impossible to compare our real-world epigenetic selves with some theoretical version of our epigenetic selves. But a few people have a special opportunity to note and consider their epigenetic reality.

As it turns out, epigenetic change is nearly always readily observable in identical twins. It can occur before, at, or long after birth. I happen to be an identical twin. My brother and I share exactly the same basic genetic architecture. We are, in essence, clones of each other. Even today, years past age fifty, our faces, voices, postures, are all spookily alike. Yet some factors in our environments, or perhaps in the womb as well, have made us different in some subtle and not so subtle ways. I was bigger and healthier at birth. I came home with my mother; my brother stayed behind for a month in an incubator. I am taller than my brother by two inches, but my brother has always been able to beat me in a foot race. I have a heart arrhythmia that is the result of an extra bundle of nerves around my heart. Before I had surgery to fix it, my heart sometimes beat as fast as a hummingbird's

---

* The ability of doctors to save premature infants can, ironically, lead to more aggressive triage that needlessly ends a baby's life. In China, where the One-Child policy usually limits families to just one or two children, premature babies are often denied care and all but abandoned in hope that they will die. Families prefer that mothers try again in the belief that a child who lasts to term will be a healthier one throughout life. Families take the chance so that the one child they are allowed is, in their view, the best child possible. The triage against children also strikes healthy infant girls but does not come without anguish. The sadness Chinese women feel for the abandoned, and killed children, is a frequent subject in Chinese memoirs, talk shows, and letters to the press.

heart. My brother never had the problem. I lived in the tropics for many years after I finished college, so I am prone to skin cancers in a way he is not. The sun blasted me with more photons and at fuller strength than he was ever subject to. That energy insinuated itself into my genes and changed their structure. Though I have no serious complaints yet, doctors scare me with the statistics of the likelihood that my genes will be triggered later on as a result, and cancer will, if I live long enough, likely follow. Like anyone, I try not to dwell upon this glum information.

In the standard teaching on genes, my children and my brother's children are, genetically speaking, half siblings. But if my prolonged and intense exposure to the sun has changed the epigenetic facts of my body, my children and grandchildren may be more prone to skin cancer than are my putative "half children" conceived by my brother. It is not because my genome has changed. That is not possible. It is because the software that turns the genes on and off in my body has been reprogrammed in a way that my brother's has not. In other words, the software that works on my genes has changed.

Considered on a larger scale, the growing study of epigenetics may help show how the choices of one generation have profound effects on the health and longevity of the generations that follow. Put differently, if we can understand what we are doing to ourselves today, we may be able to help future generations live longer.

I'm a Taurus, What Are You?

Once overlooked differences early in life can have big consequences. It turns out, for example, that when flirters at the local bar ask "What's your sign?" they are inadvertently conducting a little bit of research of their flirtee's potential for epigenetic misfortune. Since the 1930s, demographers have been intrigued by the possibility that the month, season, or year during which a person is born is somehow linked to the chances of dying young, having health problems later in life, and surviving into old age.

The modern inkling that birth dates matter was launched in the 1930s by Yale University geographer Ellsworth Huntington, a real-life Indiana Jones-style globe-trotting scholar who was a giant in his field and in the popular imagination in his day but is now largely forgotten or dismissed. Late in his career, with a series of grand Near East adventures behind him, Huntington hung up his boots to plumb new mysteries in Yale's library and the file rooms of town halls. His first stop was the massive reference set, the *Dictionary of American Biography*. Huntington combed through each of the 10,890 entries and collated the ages of death of all the luminaries profiled and then matched their ages to the months of their births. Huntington discovered an unexpectedly large cluster of famous people born in June who died a couple of months shy of their sixty-ninth birthdays, and another implausibly large group born in February who died a month shy of their seventieth birthdays.

When Huntington pored over public records all over the United States, he found similar patterns. What distinguishes the strain of thought Huntington launched from the divination of ancient stargazers is that Huntington was looking for environmental influences here on earth, while the astrologers link fate to the movements of stars. The sun, naturally, is a star, and it turns out that the sun and its seasons have much to do with genetic triggers that influence how we fare as we grow older.

Today there's no controversy over the fact that environments affect our health or how long we live. But some recent discoveries, this time not from anthropologists but from medical clinicians and epidemiologists, seem to show that the environment works on our molecular/genetic destinies more than previously imagined.

In the 1970s when Anders Forsdahl, a doctor in Norway, noticed that lung cancer and heart disease among his patients could not be as firmly linked to the lifestyle choices science usually counted as being the most potent factors in leading to the two diseases. Their levels of wealth (Norway was a fairly egalitarian place in the 1970s) mattered little. Even smoking seemed a relatively insignificant factor.[2]

Forsdahl, also the son of a physician, had replaced his father as the district doctor and public health official in a remote northern part of the country. He knew the living conditions of the region's different ethnic groups well. The strongest link he could find to the diseases was to the places the patients were born and whether or not those places had comparatively higher infant mortality rates. Heart disease and lung cancer sufferers tended to come from parts of Norway where higher percentages of young children died, and the Norwegians who were free of the diseases more often came from parts of the country where children had a better chance of surviving their first years. Scandinavian records of people's birth, health, and the circumstances of death are detailed, descriptive, and span back into the nineteenth century, sometimes longer.

Looking at data on health and death rates, while matching the records to the months of birth (albeit in ways more sophisticated than Huntington's simple correlations), reveals whether conditions in the earliest days of life in Norway have serious long-term consequences. Measured against the rest of the world (and especially measured against their Russian neighbors), Scandinavians are generally long-lived; the research was aimed at teasing out the differences in health and life spans in an otherwise fairly homogeneous group.

Gabriele Doblhammer of the Max Planck Institute for Demographic Research has surveyed hundreds of studies on the environment and lifelong health.[3] She concluded that there are widespread differences in people's life spans that line up with their months of birth. The differences in the Norwegian countryside are linked to seasons, so that people in the Northern Hemisphere do better, by and large, in the months during which people in the Southern Hemisphere fare less well. A big reason for the differences is that early in the twentieth century, when today's older people were born, mothers were sicker in some months, or seasons, than in others. Because the health of the mother is essential to the lifelong health of her child, the general healthiness of the time of year back when the older Norwegians surveyed were in utero makes a difference to their health in their later years today.

It is a general finding, and more meaningful across big groups than for any one individual, but it points to the role environments play in how well we live. It is easy to understand how living in a city with killer smog or toxic water could lead to masses of early cancers and deaths. The Norwegian examples, and research in Sweden, too, were drawn from mostly pristine places where there were no modern environmental toxins but plenty of environmental stress.

Swedish studies have also focused on people whose life span and general health may have been influenced by the timing of famines in the last two centuries. Famines do not just deprive those who live through them, but inform the lives of their offspring, too. Studies of periods of feast and famine in Sweden have shown that children of famine victims, even children born after famine ended, and grandchildren, lived less long when compared to children and grandchildren of mothers who did not endure a famine and were not descended from a mother who did. (Famines, on balance, tend to shorten the lives of people who live through them, but famines also seem to lengthen the lives of a smaller number of people whose bodies are made more resilient by the genetic change wrought by environmental stress.) Pollution, dietary changes, the stress of war or persecution are among the widespread environmental triggers that affect how genes turn on and off, and which, in turn, affect our physical and mental well-being and how long we live.

Considered on a larger scale, the growing study of epigenetics may help show how the choices of one generation have profound effects on the health and longevity of the generations that follow. Studies do not show merely that mothers or children died earlier when the mothers have undergone stressful times. Stress on mothers, and in some cases, fathers, too, seems to affect not just their children, but also their grandchildren and great-grandchildren. That seems to be true even if the younger generations never experienced in their own lives anything like their progenitors' stress. Research is now honing in on whether there are inheritable triggers that work on genes that pass down from parent to child over two to four or more generations, but are over and above the human genome, which does not undergo the same change over time. Inheritance of an "epigenome" may turn out to be one of the major influences that separates people by health, length of life span, and even partly differentiates their personalities and cognitive functioning.

Old and Creepy

An understanding of the environmental effects on the life span leads, of course, to the human desire to find what changes in environment might lengthen it. This is where one of the superstars of aging research comes in, a small worm that researchers call C. elegans, short for *Caenorhabditis elegans*. The worm is just about as long as a sesame seed, and, left to itself, C. elegans basically does three things with its life: squirms, eats bacteria, and poops. C. elegans is transparent, a fact researchers like when they play around with genes and cells. It is also a tough little worm. Some of its kind survived the concussion of the in-air explosion of the space shuttle *Challenger*. It can also survive a deep freeze in a sort of hibernation, then thaw and come out squirming. What the worms do not survive well is time; their natural life span is just two weeks. Nevertheless, they make great collaborators; three Nobel prizes have been awarded to researchers who work with the worms.

For those researchers who regard aging as a disease, the C. elegans makes a good case. If they are made to live in a petri dish and are given enough food to live on, and subjected to no outside stress in the form of disease or trauma, C. elegans still die. That means that something internal to their makeup is killing them. Yet because the organism is pretty easy to work with, and because its genome has been as thoroughly sequenced as possible, researchers have used C. elegans to see how to play around with genes in ways that extend its life.

What's more, the tiny worm's genetic makeup is close enough to that of more complex organisms, such as the human one, to shed light on aging in general. In the lab, mutations of the worm can be created by engineering bacteria to carry genetic materials that, once the bacteria are eaten, start changing the behavior of select genes in the worm. As with humans, C. elegans have genes that control growth and aging by regulating hormones that influence growth and aging. When those genes are altered, the way organisms grow and age also changes. In a series of experiments led by Cynthia Kenyon at the University of California–San Francisco, the teams turned off the expression of a gene in C. elegans known as daf-2. The gene encodes a hormone receptor that rests on the membrane of the worm's cells. Normally the gene enables a hormone that speeds aging in older worms. Humans have the hormones insulin and insulin growth factor (IGF 2) to perform a similar job. When the gene was turned off in the worms, they lived twice as long.

If that seems miraculous, the state of the longer-living worms in their new old age was just as impressive. When normal C. elegans worms reach the last day of their two weeks on earth, they still poop and eat, but they can no longer crawl. The changed worms were squirming all over the place in their third week and also seemed able to resist diseases, toxins, and stress (such as cold and heat) far better than normal worms. They are super-worms. Similar gene mutations in yeast, fruit flies, and mice that attempt to regulate the hormones that influence growth and aging have also extended the life and vigor of those creatures.

Would it work in humans? Kenyon says there is some intriguing, still unpublished work that the world will be very interested to discover. In the meantime, she offers a prelude in the studies of human centenarians, who she notes also often have modified genetic pathways that distinguish how they regulate hormones, and who tend to be particularly good at warding off disease and dealing with environmental stress. In the meantime, until experiments reveal whether we can reengineer the life span, the worms remain a particularly good way to shed light on the fundamentals of how we age. It is all about how well we deal with the insults that environments throw at us and how our bodies turn on themselves as we grow older. Our genes turn on and off the mechanisms that age us, and between us there are enormous variations in how our genes are expressed.

Is Regeneration Degenerate?

There are other ways that life might be extended in the future, and they derive from the basic fact, as anyone who has received a transplanted heart, liver, eye, or kidney knows, that one human can possess certain physical elements useful to another.

Researcher Tom Rando does not believe that science is likely to make any breakthroughs that will keep people alive and healthy into extreme old age. One problem, he says, is that some of the very same processes that keep you healthy when you are young turn against your body as you age. Nevertheless, he has found a way to make damaged older bodies, the kind that usually heal very slowly if at all, mend quickly. Rando himself is slight, trim, bald, and disarmingly cheerful in the way a scientist having fun in a cutting-edge laboratory ought to be. Rando is also exceptionally curious, one of those people you suspect knows more about everything than you know about anything. Coincidentally, he is also a bit ageless. At fifty years old he looks closer to thirty.

Rando, the possessor of three Harvard degrees, including a Ph.D. and an M.D., owns a résumé with enough positions on it to fill a research institute, but his main job is as director of a lab at the Stanford University School of Medicine. There he and his work group investigate the biology of muscle cells and their interplay with muscle stem cells. Their findings help explain why muscles regenerate, and how they weaken as people grow older. Given his youthful mien, it is reasonable to wonder whether, in a locked cabinet, Rando has stashed a secret serum he is not yet sharing. This is the heart of Silicon Valley after all, and money is already pouring into research that tries in all sorts of ways—mechanical, electronic, and biological—to extend life. Time on earth is the ultimate scarce resource and one prize that, so far, money cannot buy enough of. In the Valley there certainly lives a titan or two willing to make any effort to obtain a vial promising another hundred years or so of life. The old morality tale does feel as though it may play out here, where many of the world's greatest fortunes, ingenious minds, and prodigious egos combine.

Dr. Rando has no youth potion, but the success of his work on healing has also versed him in the social dimensions of aging, from inspiring to ghastly.

Over time, mammals lose their natural ability to regenerate their muscles. Despite Rando's skepticism about radical life extension, he does believe medicine may be able to help people maintain their regenerative powers longer. Rando's lab is located behind locked doors on the fourth floor of the Palo Alto VA Hospital, which also supports his research. Reaching it requires walking through the hospital past veterans, many crippled by war injuries that speed the physical decline that would normally come later in life. People left disfigured, hobbled, or immobile struggle against the accelerated decline that comes with atrophy and despair. Head injuries lead victims down a steep slope to the confusion and memory loss that usually strike at later ages. The wars in Iraq and Afghanistan have had a particularly punishing effect on the heads of American soldiers. Veterans' hospitals expect they will be caring for such injured soldiers in large numbers as the wounded experience premature declines. There is no mystery why an agency charged with mending hurt soldiers would support Rando's investigations on healing. Or why Rando brings such passion to his work.

The Trap of Building a Better Mouse

One finding from Rando's lab is that muscles often have a dormant ability to regenerate themselves. Muscle stem cells, called satellite cells, reside in muscle tissue and switch on to heal damage in the muscles of the young. Satellite cells, however, do not turn on as regularly in the old. The stem cells are there; they could wake up to trigger healing, but they do nothing. The cells are "deaf to the muscle's cry for help."

"The older a body gets, the more likely it is to scar when it's injured," says Rando, "and scarred muscle, and scarred skin are less functional. Scarring is one of the things that goes wrong with age." To get to the root of the problem, Rando and his team took older mice, whose muscles regenerated poorly, and young mice whose muscles healed at a good rate, and, through some very delicate surgery, joined their circulatory systems together for six weeks. In effect, Rondo created May-to-December rodent Siamese twins.[4]

Rando's team then injured the skeletal muscles of the older mice, the kind of muscles that help them move. Lo and behold, Rando says, "the older mice healed at a remarkably faster rate," similar to the young mice. To double-check that the age difference counted, older mice were connected to each other. They did not heal faster. Livers also regenerate slower in older mice, but when they are conjoined with younger mice, their livers heal faster. Rando speculates that it isn't the stem cells of the younger mice that are making the difference, but the "chemical soup surrounding the cells." Old soup doesn't promote healing.

Finding what in the soup of the younger mice makes the difference, Rando cautions, will be a long and complex task, requiring the testing of thousands of proteins, lipids, and sugars in the bloodstream. Rando also cautions that the experiments studied acute injuries, not gradual loss of muscle function over time.

"The wear and tear of aging is still enigmatic," he says. Ultimately, however, the results may help combat degenerative diseases, including Alzheimer's, as science learns how to coax dormant cells back into their roles in regeneration. That's the good scenario.*

The Rectangularized Life

In the mouse experiments, the benefits to the older mice ceased as soon as their connection to the younger animals ended. Rando cautions against assuming his experiments could be applied to reverse the effects of normal aging or to extend the natural life span far beyond its natural limits. Our bodies have mysterious traps against such enterprises. The body's suppression of the healing role of stem cells might be an evolutionary response to suppress unhealthy growth in bodies that are no longer growing. In younger animals, rapid growth is a good thing. In older animals it is an illness.

"The stem cells wait for a signal, and if they are 'artificially' signaled, that could trigger cancer," says Rando. A therapeutic approach that looks to sustain healing of chronic decline flirts with unleashing a more destructive response in the body. "There will be trade-offs," he says. "Medical science is better at fixing what's broken than at preventing what goes on naturally."

This is not a magical world, he continues, where everyone will be allowed to play tennis like a teenager, "but most people have a view that diseases will be fixed and their lives maintained and that science can rectangularize life so that people will be healthy until the time they drop dead." By "rectangularize," he means maintain ample function as long as possible. For most people, the picture of health

---

* People have contemplated the blood of the healthy as a cure before. In a telling of the tale of Exodus in the Midrash, a Jewish collection of commentary on the Hebrew Bible, Pharaoh is advised to seek a cure for leprosy by bathing in babies' blood and then he slaughtered Hebrew infants to get it.

will remain an imperfect triangle, with a fat base that represents robustness in youth, and a taper toward the top representing the decline with age. So for now, Rando limits his therapeutic advice on warding off the ravages of age to "eat well and exercise."

What then are the ethical challenges of Rando's finding? "Well, I think what really scared people about the mouse experiments," Rando says, "is the prospect that our research would encourage older people to find ways to surgically connect themselves to children in order to cure themselves."

What's surprising is not that people would imagine such a scenario, but how easy it is, with the prospects of longer lives for those who can "arrange" for such a connection, to see how such a market might spring up.* In a world that is getting increasingly older, and ceaselessly in search of prolonging the vigor of youth, it would seem all but inevitable. Prospective mothers who fear they are too old, or too busy, or too beautiful to carry their own child already have the option of employing younger, reproductively fit women to carry a child to term. One can even buy the healthy eggs of younger women that he can then have implanted in the bodies of still other women. The market for both is robust and commands high prices.

In the case of human eggs, demand among women in wealthy countries has encouraged a shady world market in which women from poorer countries sign up with clinics that dose them with potentially deadly hormone treatments to spur their bodies into making sellable eggs.[5]

---

* University of Chicago law professor Richard Epstein made a stir in 1998 with an op-ed in the *Wall Street Journal* that proposed a market in which people could sell off human organs, from the dead and the living (in the case of kidneys and other organs that people might reasonably expect to live without). His argument: better to have two hundred people alive with one kidney each than one hundred people alive with two kidneys. Critics complained such a system would encourage exploitation of the poor and otherwise vulnerable. Epstein, a formidable libertarian intellectual, entreated critics to put aside their ethical squeamishness.

In 2007, the *Chicago Tribune* reported on a Pakistani village where residents engaged in the global gray market for organs and walked around with large purple scars over where their kidneys used to be. Human rights groups have long charged China with harvesting the organs of political prisoners, whose executions are arranged on demand so as to secure the most valuable hearts, lungs, livers, corneas, and kidneys. The Chinese government rejects these accounts.

In cosmetic dermatology, one of the prime sources of collagen used in injections that bring youthful fullness to women's lips and mask wrinkles is derived from the cells of an infant boy's penis. Baby foreskin is also used as fibroblast, which can serve as a base for growing great lengths of skin unattached to a human body and useful in the treatment of burn victims or people who have somehow lost their eyelids. Fibroblasts are also used, dubiously, in beauty creams said to promote skin rejuvenating collagen when applied. Measures of the ointments that can treat a skin patch the size of a square of chocolate are wholesaled to physicians for around a thousand dollars. Evaluating the efficacy of foreskin-based remedies in February 2009, *Scientific American* said that the treatments for scars appeared effective. The journal doubted the fibroblast creams brought any help for wrinkles.[6]

If there ever did arise a market for human-conjoined blood sharers, in which young healthy healers agreed for a fee to attach themselves to the sick and wounded, demand would likely far outstrip supply.

Even if old and young are not tethered together literally, the demands of a society where the older population grows more rapidly than any other group will give rise to a society that mines and extracts the powers of youth in challenging new ways. The health and welfare of the young and old will be bound together in ways that push far beyond our current fiscal, social, and ethical boundaries.

In a variation on the mice experiments in Rando's lab, researchers led by Noriko Kagawa at the Kato Ladies' Clinic in Tokyo announced in June 2010 that they had transplanted the ovaries of fertile mice that were about three and half months old into the bodies of no longer fertile female mice who were seventeen and a half months old and just three weeks shy of beginning to die naturally. Kagawa reported that every one of the rodents with a transplanted ovary began to behave like young fertile mice (mating with young males) and also lived up to 40 percent longer than expected. Kagawa speculated that humans might gain some of the benefits the mice with transplanted organs did if women had their own ovarian tissue removed and frozen at younger ages and implanted back in when they grow older.[7]

This brings up another possibility in an aging world. If people who had children early in their lives fear that their first generation of children will themselves be too old to care for them when they are in their late eighties or beyond, older adults may begin to have children later in life, long after the time that menopause normally puts a stop to such hopes. Ninety-year-olds could then have their own children, in their twenties or thirties, tend to them instead of counting on their more elderly children or strangers. There are already strong hints of this strange world to come.

The tools fertility doctors have today are already helping to push the boundaries of childbearing years and can even allow older grandmothers to carry babies. If advances in reproductive science eventually allow generation gaps between parents and their children to stretch to six or seven decades, we may create a future where childbearing and parenting are what people look forward to in retirement. All those singleton grandchildren? Grandma can give birth to someone for them to play with. Does that sound absurd? In 2006, in Redding, California, sixty-two-year-old Janise Wulf, a blind, diabetic grandmother to twenty and great-grandmother to three, gave birth to a healthy boy. The redheaded child was the second for Wulf and her third husband; his older brother was born three and half years earlier. Both were the result of in vitro fertilization.

Wulf told the Associated Press that her late-in-life pregnancies were groundbreaking for older women. "Age is a number. You're as old as you feel," she said. In 2008, a seventy-year-old grandmother of five from the northern Indian state of Uttar Pradesh gave birth to twins, also after in vitro fertilization. She underwent the treatment so that she and her husband could have a male heir. One might imagine that the adult daughters of the new mom/grandma grew upset upon learning that the family farm would now go to a new infant brother, except for the fact that their seventy-seven-year-old father had hocked the family land, sold the water buffaloes, drained his bank account, and borrowed eight thousand dollars on a credit card to pay the in vitro fertilization fee. The twins were born small and whisked away into incubators too quickly for the mother to hold them. "I just want to see my new babies and care for them while I am still able," she said.

Can We Keep Getting Older?

How long will the trend toward longer lives actually continue? Opinions are all over the map, themselves a reflection on the pitfalls in prediction. Is age, like height, a characteristic that can change enormously with the right diet and environment, but has a genetic limit above which people are unlikely to grow? For years, anatomists wondered how tall Dutch people could grow. The storybook picture of the Dutch—think of the boy who stuck his finger in the dike—is of a squat, sturdy people. Today, young, tall, blond tourists often approaching seven feet have become walking advertisements for Holland on city streets around the world. After a rapid growth spurt following World War II, the Dutch have become the world's tallest people. Dutch men, on average, grow to five feet eleven inches (180 cm), and women average five feet six inches (168 cm). Nutrition, including lots of calcium-rich dairy products; health care, which in Holland is universal; and high-quality public health systems get the credit for elevating the Dutch.

Nutrition and access to health care are also factors in elongating life. From 1981 to 2007, the life expectancy of the Dutch has gone up nearly seven years. The number of years the Dutch live in good health has also climbed. Elevated height and estimable health often go together. A study of fifteen thousand men and women, between forty-five and sixty-four years old, not in Holland, but in Scotland, found that "height is inversely associated with . . . coronary heart disease, stroke and respiratory disease mortality among men and women."* Being tall distances one so well from disease that the scholars found that even when they matched the effects of height on longevity against the effects of social class, height was a more powerful predictor of how well individuals warded off heart disease and stroke. For years scholars wondered when the Dutch would stop growing, since their added height pushed them higher and higher, above even other Europeans. Well, since 2001, the Dutch seem to have leveled off in height, perhaps because they

* The Dutch joke that their added height is an evolutionary adaptation to growing up below sea level. Water flooding through breached dikes overwhelmed their shorter countrymen and only the taller ones reproduced.

have reached the ideal balance of diet and genes that puts them at their limit.

There are alternate scenarios on aging that veer far from the mainstream predictions of government head-counters and UN number crunchers. Even without considering such cataclysms as war, pandemic disease, or environmental meltdown, some reputable seers at world-class universities, think that life expectancy may go *down*, not up.

S. Jay Olshansky, public health scholar at the University of Illinois at Chicago, is one. He is one of a growing number of epidemiologists who see the rapid rise of obesity, and the concomitant diabetes and vulnerability to strokes, as great and fast-developing threats to life span. Today's teenagers, Olshansky says, will likely end up the first generation in the modern era to live shorter life spans than their parents. That will not alter the coming graying of the world's population. Older people will still become a larger and larger proportion of the global community (because family size is shrinking so dramatically), but the older population of the future may not be as old, on average, as today's.

The disputants debating the long-term future of aging do agree on some incontrovertible facts: the number of old and very old is climbing, and we all have a lot of work to do to figure out how this change will affect us personally and communally in the next few decades.

The Bionic Man, at Last?

Science will get better at forestalling the diseases and conditions that weaken and kill people. It may even devise human immortality. Some solutions will be biomechanical, outfitting people with machines that replace body parts. Operations to implant manufactured joints, engineered bits of bone, and lenses on the eye are practically rites of passage for older people who can afford them. My eighty-nine-year-old aunt has had two hip replacements, two knee replacements, and lives with silicone lenses that replace her formerly cloudy cataracts, and until very recently attended lectures, took part in a book group, played bridge and golf every week, walked through the woods daily, and, in her own halting, deliberate way, contra danced.

As miraculous as these advances are, they will someday soon seem simplistic exercises in carpentering human flesh. The next wave of advances will involve computerized bionics with microelectronics. Already these tools—implanted into the brain—connect to the nervous system and help some people with paralysis or lost limbs walk and move their arms. Researchers at Rutgers University in New Jersey have created a bionic hand with computer controls for each finger; the hand is so well attuned to the nerve impulses of the wearer that it can be used to play simple piano pieces. Perhaps better known are cochlear implants, with which deaf people receive a form of hearing that connects them electronically to the world of sound.

The list of new developments keeps growing. For around fourteen thousand dollars, Japan's Cyberdyne Inc. offers a semirobotic exoskeleton that can help older people walk longer distances and lift household loads. Want to haul around five hundred pounds of gear in a backpack on an all-day hike? The U.S. military and engineers at the University of California–Berkeley have a suit that lets wearers carry that weight as though it were just ten pounds, and still lets the hiker jog up hills almost normally. One day, a version of these suits may help grandma get grandpa from the chair to the bed, then on the way back to grab a broom and lift up the piano.

Rob Spence, a Canadian documentary filmmaker, lost an eye as a result of a gun accident that happened when he was out shooting cow pies in a field as a child. In his late thirties, he began working with a team of engineers and vision specialists to develop a cyborg eye, or "eyeborg," to replace his damaged one. While Spence will not be able to see with his new eye, which is still in the works, it will be implanted with an eye-shaped wireless camera that can broadcast and record video of all that he turns the eye toward. Spence has posted a video on the Web that shows the removal of his blind eye in preparation for the insertion of the eyeborg.[8] It all points to a multimachine future where prosthetics do not just replace body parts but redefine experience. Spence's eye, like others in the works at labs elsewhere, can theoretically record every moment of his life following the implant. Together with a device that serves as a recording ear, and a computerized database technology that can tag and index the recording, this set of technologies can make up an electronic memory that can be played back whenever the owner's natural memory needs jogging.

Remembrances of Memories Past

Computer pioneer Gordon Bell, now in his seventies, works on a lower-tech version of such a project at Microsoft. Called "lifelogging," Bell's goal has been to record nearly everything about his everyday comings and goings and to store it electronically forever. He has been at the project, a kind of virtual hoarding, in one way or another, for nearly a decade. On a lanyard around Bell's neck hangs a digital camera programmed to take a picture of whatever lies ahead every thirty seconds. Another lanyard holds a digital voice recorder, about the size of a pack of gum, that records every sound Bell encounters. Material piles up. Among his hundreds of thousands of digital pictures are fifty thousand of his family. Bell never deletes an e-mail and has more than one hundred thousand messages stored on his computer. His philosophy is that electronic memory is so cheap—thousands of books worth of information can be stored on memory cards that cost less than one hardcover book—that it costs nearly nothing to have a complete play-by-play of all of one's days on earth. Better to clutter up a memory card, than to clutter one's mind, which can be freed for more creative thinking. Also, when one's memory begins to fade, there's a reminder from every thirty seconds of one's life that is there, on a screen for reference. Prosthetic memory. And a hint of immortality: a whole life on a wafer.

Meanwhile, in the last few years a number of companies have sprung up with computer programs designed to stem memory loss and other cognitive challenges faced by older consumers. Often the companies have psychologists and doctors on their boards or in the executive suites, and their programs are carefully designed to drill older people with tests of their ability to recall data and recognize patterns such as audio signals. The companies support and produce research papers meant to bolster their claims that their drills do, for a time, stave off and even reverse cognitive decline.

The products are sold to senior centers, communities of older residents, nursing homes, and individuals. What is little mentioned are the effects the drills have on their subjects' self-image. When they are first tested, it may be in an environment in which the subjects are led to believe they must be drilled because they are in decline. But over time, the programs may lead them to believe the subjects can overcome their stereotype and gain confidence, a turn of affairs that on its own improves performance. It is infant science, but it garners tremendous publicity for results that are usually underwhelming.

The Hard Questions We Don't Have to Answer Yet

Any contemplation of further extension of the human life span, whether that lengthening comes from better prenatal care, genetic tinkering after birth, dependence on other humans' bodies, or implanted computer interfaces, to say nothing of ongoing improvement in more standard therapies and medicines, quickly arrives at a host of deeply unanswerable questions: We may well be able to live longer, but why do we want to do so? Who will benefit from these new technologies of life and who will not? Who will pay for them, one way or another? What might it mean that humans might someday meet their great-great-great-grandchildren? Will relentless extensions of the life span, widely used, make some populations even older than they would be, thereby further burdening their societies with even more ancient humans? Could small, rich nations enjoy collective fates quantitatively different from those of other countries? And perhaps most unanswerable of all, how old is old enough?

CHAPTER 7

THE TWISTING FATES OF THE
SCREW CAPITAL: ROCKFORD, ILLINOIS

ONE MIGHT SAY ROCKFORD IS NEAR CHICAGO. THE CITY IS ABOUT ninety minutes northwest on the Jane Addams Memorial Tollway. Most Rockfordians, however, have spent much of their lives emphatically refuting the idea that their city is anything like Chicago. A Rockfordian might more naturally mention the cluster of world-class, but unheralded, aerospace companies in the city. Or the airport that covers more ground than O'Hare, but receives few passenger planes. Or a handful of cafés and a couple of chic restaurants offering promise to a downtown otherwise marred by empty storefronts.

Rockford is a hybrid of urban and suburban, where few buildings climb above ten stories. Single-family homes line neatly divided lots in neighborhoods that encircle active and dormant industrial buildings. The city has more than its share of baronial mansions to brag about, but then one might mention how much less than baronial their market value is today. There is the recently renovated Burpee Museum of Natural History that boasts a real T-Rex skeleton, which will be the centerpiece in the city's new scenic riverwalk. The Rockford MetroCentre, an arena where the Rolling Stones played in 1981, now attracts some metal and country acts and monster truck shows. There are minor-league hockey and baseball teams, an art museum, a fine professional symphony, and repertory theater, the kinds of institutions that industrial midsized midwestern cities could have easily supported when they were richer. Up until now, Rockford has held on to the kinds of once-stalwart arts organizations that are struggling, or folding, all across America. There is still some old money in town, and an ever older audience to match.

When Rockford Hummed

For much of the twentieth century, Rockford was one of the richest twenty towns in America. Per capita, it may have had more millionaires than any other sizable metropolitan area. The city has ample charms and deep strengths, but they are the charms and strengths that the midsized powerhouse cities of industrial America achieved in good times gone by. Though incomes now fall below the national average, Rockford still attracts shoppers. The city is rimmed with every major big box retailer and restaurant chain in America, though it now has some big empty boxes and abandoned car lots. Much of the city still feels normal, eminently suitable for bringing up children—especially for parents with jobs good enough to underwrite private or parochial school tuition.

It is also a good place to grow old. It costs less in Rockford to buy a house, fix a car, hire a good lawyer, or get an immigrant to provide twenty-four-hour care at home than it does in more thriving cities. The community networks are strong. Church attendance is high and the city has an ethnic club, with clubhouse, for every group. There are separate clubs for the Poles, Italians, Germans, Mexicans, and the city's Swedes and Norwegians, who still strongly invoke their separate ethnic identities. The clubs survive because the old-timers still fill them, but most feel the clubs' days are numbered. Some would be gone already if they didn't give their halls over to slot machines and other games of chance. Among Rockford's retired set, the clubs are a constant topic of conversation, and among Rockford's workers, the bartending jobs (complete with tips) within them, are jealously sought and guarded.

Rockford spreads its industrial footprint across the midpoint of the northern extreme of Illinois, near the border of Wisconsin. With 157,000 people, it's the 146th largest city in America. Some cities grow steadily over time. Others, like the industrial orphan towns in the Midwest's automotive belt, shrink steadily. Rockford did not sink into recession with the rest of the nation when the economy plummeted in 2008. The city was already deflated, so it moved from recession to depression, posting jobless rates that were among the highest in urban America.

Nostalgia recalls Rockford's prosperous stretches as stable, but in truth prosperity grew from churn and tumult. At the time of the American Civil War, the city barely existed; the Industrial Revolution called Rockford into being. In every decade from 1880 to 1930 the city's population grew at a double-digit pace. Immigrants poured in from rural America and from central and northern Europe. The early rush of Swedes, and to a lesser extent other Scandinavians, is still evident in Rockford today. Nordic surnames fill the cityscape on signs for stores, services, hotels, factories, museums, and political campaigns. The immigrants brought industrial skills that helped make Rockford a powerhouse in America's industrial heartland.

Dozens of furniture factories made the city the number two center of furniture-making in the country, behind Grand Rapids, Michigan. Many of the small houses on the city's oldest blocks, in a now crime-blighted neighborhood, show off remnants of the exquisite wood moldings, staircases, and fireplace mantels that immigrants carved for their families. The city continually reinvented itself as the demands and sophistication of the American economy changed. Rockford became an industrial town that other industrial towns depended on, making the machines that make other machines, and pouring out an endless stream of parts from which industrial America was fashioned.

As the 519 square miles of cityscape changed with the rise and fall of local businesses, and with the trappings of its civic wealth, Rockford manufactured nicknames, too. It was called the "Forest City" and the "City of Gardens" because European immigrants and their progeny encouraged parks, and set aside a generous seven thousand acres of public green. The name that stuck, however, followed the industrial expansion of World War II, when Rockford was home to a group of companies that made industrial fasteners: the joints, clips, rivets, nuts, bolts, and other tools that help the world fit together. Rockford is still the center of one of the largest concentrations of fastener makers anywhere, thus its preeminent nickname, "The Screw Capital of the World."

Now, however, Rockford is known for being home to one of the most troubled public school districts in America. Low graduation rates, violence, and entrenched gangs plague the city's classrooms. Rockford may be even better known for its unemployment. The city is a de rigueur stop for politicians who promise to put people back to work. Rockford is regarded as middling as Middle America gets. Where better to pronounce that China, the banks, bloodless multinationals, and the government have hurt the heart of the nation? Politicians, however, do not mention that for the world's most competitive enterprises, middle-American places such as Rockford are too middle-aged, too middlebrow, or too fat in the middle. Or that it makes enormous economic sense for money and jobs to move where workers are both young and eager, where college grads work for less than Rockford's high school dropouts, and to where the Middle Kingdom can be served.

To hear its citizens tell it, especially the white and black families that have long called the city home—not the Hispanic families or the blacks that have recently moved from Chicago and Milwaukee—the city simply cannot hold on to its young people. Although the out-migrants are by no means all white, the effect of the youth exodus shows up most strikingly in the changing age profile of the city's white population. Over the last two decades, Rockford's nonwhite population more than doubled, which allows Rockford's boosters to claim the city is growing, and, despite its economic woes, to suggest Rockford is on an upswing of sorts. Joel Cowen, a demographer at the University of Illinois College of Medicine at Rockford, attributes some of the influx of new residents to the outflow of the older ones. As former residents left their homes, and the value of their houses dropped, low-income minority families moved in. Most are Hispanic and most of the Hispanics are Mexicans who tried to settle in higher-cost U.S. metro areas but were priced out. Cowen says the housing in Rockford is cheap enough to allow them to stay in the United States provided their breadwinners are willing to make the longer drive into metro-Chicago from Rockford.

Rockford has other newcomers, too. The city has nearly one thousand Burmese refugees. The vast majority of Americans have never set eyes on anyone from Burma, but among Rockford's 157,000 residents, they are a visible group. Sizable Central European communities made up of relatively recent arrivals from the former Communist bloc have also taken root. What looks today like a clear picture of a largely white midwestern American city on the wane, may instead be the beginnings of new retooling at the hands of the city's new Americans, for whom the city offers both a way to escape population stress at home and a chance to find opportunities in the stresses affecting Rockford.

A Franchise Operation

The new Asians and Europeans often interact with the older whites as caregivers, which is one of the few business sectors really growing in Rockford. Kathy Wetters, a former industrial engineer who now runs a franchise of a national home-care agency in Rockford, made the switch because she saw elder care as one of the city's most promising economic niches.

Wetters was trained at Georgia Institute of Technology, one of the world's premier engineering schools. Her speech still has a Southern lilt and charm, but she relates the details of her life with matter-of-fact precision. As an engineer, she worked in a series of large plants that employed five hundred to twelve hundred workers. In the early 1990s, Wetters, who was stationed in northwest Illinois, grew restless in the work, and began to wonder, as future entrepreneurs are wont to do, whether she could apply her skills to a small business of her own.

As Wetters cast around for a business idea, she got a firsthand lesson in caregiving. Her mother was diagnosed with cancer, and her husband's mother entered a long-term care residence. "I learned how we worked together as a family, how great hospice care was, and what it was like to provide long-distance care to a parent that was in another part of the country." Where the aging population is growing, family members often get thorough, if informal, training while caring for a loved one. Sometimes care is technically straightforward and other times it demands the precise application of technical skills. Caregiving demands emotional intelligence and strategies, too. The professional ranks of caregivers are filled with people such as Wetters, who find the work sufficiently challenging and engaging to embrace it as a career.

Wetters thought she could wed her experiences and expertise as a trainer to a home-care business. Like Mr. Shimono in Kamakura, Japan, she saw promise in a graying population. "First we thought about what we would enjoy. We have two sons who were already educated [and we were done with that], so we wanted a business that would give something back. We researched the demographics. Nonmedical care is private pay [so people spend their own money on it], and we saw an aging population with a sufficient number of people to sustain a private pay care service."

Wetters had noticed that in Rockford, blue-collar families get together to pay the bill for their parents' care. "There could be six kids who pay, and they do pay. The more families struggle, the more they are careful to pay their bills. It's their work ethic. They also know that the people they're paying are working hard for their money. It's the more affluent families you have to worry about. They let things slip."

Wetters says that lately she has been placing caregivers in more homes where adult children of needy parents are trying to restart a career or are struggling to establish themselves in a new job late in life. In Rockford, that often means they are trying careers that take them out of town. In general, her business thrives on the needs of far-flung families.

Often the children want to find ways to keep their parents from doing otherwise simple duties that are dangerous in old age. "One son in Texas came home to visit his frail mother and when he saw her cleaning house, he realized he needed to step in. But the mother is so cussedly independent, he really had to insist she take our services. Other people hire us just to keep a parent company."

The starting hourly wage of her workers, $8.50, Wetters says, is generally lower than Rockford's blue-collar wage, and pay tops out at $11.50. Many of the people she hires were aides in nursing homes; they have burned out on that kind of institutional work. In the United States, low-level nursing-home workers do not last long on the job. Turnover rates nationally hover around 80 percent, and in many homes they exceed 100 percent, which means a home loses more workers a year than it has on staff at any given time.

One way to enter the home-care business in the United States is to purchase a franchise from a company that supports franchisees with marketing, training, and management guidance. For Wetters, one of the largest franchisors, Home Instead Senior Care, had grown so successful that franchises in her region were all spoken for. Of the eight hundred Home Instead franchises worldwide in 2009, about half of them had been added since 2005.

Wetters turned to another, smaller but fast-growing franchisor, Right at Home, Inc., which had 185 U.S. outlets in 2010. In 2003, Wetters became franchisee number twenty-eight, and now she has three branches.

The Rockford operation is run out of a bare-bones office on the second floor of a cluttered strip mall. She vouches for the workers she places. Because Rockford employers have cast off white-collar workers along with the rest, she, like those hiring in Sarasota, has lately moved educated, native English-speaking workers into jobs she once filled with either less-educated locals stuck in the near-minimum wage economy or with foreigners looking for a foothold in the American workplace.

On principle, and because the law demands it, Wetters does not discriminate according to race, but does not find the same is true among the white families who use the service.

"The ethnic mix is an issue for the people we work for," she says, "I grew up in the South and saw racism up close. It nonetheless shocked me up here to have families call me and tell me what races they didn't want in their houses. In some families, skin color is more important than any superior reference.

"It puts us in a dilemma with their care. They would often rather have a white person who came from Poland three weeks ago and speaks no English care for them than someone with dark skin who grew up around the corner and has virtually everything in common with them. It boggles my mind."*

Ships, Trains, and Trucks

Rockford's economy is part of an industrial complex that is compelled to shed American workers, in good times and bad. Over the first seven years beginning in 2000, U.S. industrial output climbed steadily higher, while at the same time, industrial employment shrank by about 3 million workers. That is to say that U.S. industry made far more stuff, with far fewer workers. Josh Bivens of the Economic Policy Institute in Washington, a think tank that is generally pro-labor, notes that the withering of jobs in manufacturing marked a turning point in the American economy. "From 1964 until 2000, U.S. employment in manufacturing was between 17.5 million and 19 million people." But following 2000, he says, there was an "unnatural" drop in the manufacturing workforce. According to EPI survey data, Illinois, Rockford's home state, lost around 80,000 jobs between 2000 and 2005. Only the much more populous states of California, which lost 269,000 jobs, Texas, down 136,000 jobs, and New York, which lost 105,000 jobs, fared worse. When manufacturing jobs disappear in developed countries, steam goes out of one of the great engines for propelling people into the middle class. In the United States, as manufacturing jobs fell away, the wealth gap widened, concentrating more wealth among America's rich and relegating once socially mobile families to the lower reaches of the middle class, or worse. Manufacturing jobs fell again in the post-2007 recession, during which the Midwest's auto sector also collapsed. As this book goes to press, there is no firm count on the automo-

---

* Sometimes the mind-boggling goes in the other direction, however. In October 2009, Charles Wesley Mumbere, a Ugandan native who had lived in Maryland and Pennsylvania for twenty-five years, returned to his native country. In the United States Mumbere worked multiple jobs as an aide in nursing homes. The Associated Press reported that Mumbere, age fifty-six, surprised his friends and colleagues with the news that he was leaving the country to become a king of the Bakonzo people of the Rwenzururu Kingdom, also known in Uganda as the Mountains of the Moon. Mumbere said he had trained to be a nurse's aide because of the job security.

tive manufacturing jobs lost, but the U.S. Federal Deposit Insurance Corporation estimates the losses between 2005 and 2008 at a minimum of 140,000 and adds that the final calculations will likely be hundreds of thousands higher. Those job losses, in part, contributed to a historic shift in the U.S. economy, when for the first time ever wages and income supports paid by the government exceeded those paid by the private sector. Globalization and automation, the FDIC worries, mean millions of manufacturing jobs across the economy are unlikely to return. The long-term trend, in good times and bad, bodes against it. The pressures on older workers will increase, the risk to the nation's financial system will intensify, and a road to the American middle class and a traditional retirement will shut down.

Tellingly, one of the most impressive job creators in the U.S. economy became the logistics industry that coordinates the movement of goods across the country and around the world. The old manufacturing centers of the United States that grew up because of their proximity to roads, rails, rivers, and canals have been reshaped by a building boom of gargantuan warehouses, many put into place to hold the growing volume of foreign goods coming into the country. The shift is part of the dynamic that is aging Rockford, and lowering its expectations for what it can attract. One of Rockford's economic development dreams is to sell the city to the world's movers of goods now that so many of its makers of goods have moved on.

Hard times accelerate corporate cost-cutting, which often means finding ways to cut jobs at home and move production to low-cost climes. In boom times to come, companies will again ramp up production, but more of it will be abroad where young workers are cheap to hire, and not in the United States where incumbent older workers are expensive to keep around. Every port and land-shipping hub in America expects trade volume to grow significantly and localities are investing heavily to make sure they can meet the future traffic. When the new, wider Panama Canal opens to speed the transit of cargo ships to America's southern and eastern ports, more warehouses will spring up to house more foreign-made goods, and the demand for older industrial workers will continue to fade. The trade literature of the logistics industry now routinely offers advice on how to accommodate older workers with devices that help them lift and move goods. Receiving, storing, and shipping the goods made abroad does not pay the rank and file what they earned when they made goods. Blue-collar warehouse workers[1] typically earn less than $10.50 an hour, and the work is often seasonal or part-time.

Who You Gonna Call?

From 2001 to 2009, 5.3 million American workers were cut from manufacturing. In the third quarter of 2009, the U.S. Bureau of Labor Statistics reported there were roughly 6,000 "mass layoff events" that together idled about 620,000 workers, a historic high. One in five of those out of work were over fifty-five. The proportion tracks closely with the overall place of people fifty-five and over in the national workforce, but it does not include the large numbers of older workers who were not laid off, but rather given incentives, or forceful suggestions, to retire early or take disability. In 2009, the number of applications to the U.S. government for social security and disability benefits more than doubled, to 465,000, over the previous year, as employers made it clear that older workers were not wanted. The Social Security Administration expected its numbers to climb by only 315,000 as the first wave of baby boomers reached retirement age that year, and the number that actually moved to retirement proved an expensive surprise.

As manufacturing lost jobs, women, for the first time in U.S. history, came to outnumber men in the workforce. The inversion follows two trends: a higher percentage of women are in the workforce and a declining percentage of men. One reason women's jobs are more plentiful is that they fill more of the service economy, including health care, which grows ever larger as the older population grows. For new jobs created in Rockford, women seem to be the preferred hires, not just in home care and health care, but also elsewhere on the low rungs of the service economy. Call centers have converged on Rockford to capitalize on the city's low wages and desperation for work. Call centers offer employees day and night shifts, which suit adults who want part-time work, have multiple jobs, or are also caregivers. Businesses employing older women are the heroes of

Rockford's troubled job market. Financial Management Systems, a national collection company, has been ramping up in Rockford. If there is any place the company can find empathetic representatives to fill the open slots for "Entry Level Student Loan Collector" and "Wage Garnishment Specialist," Rockford is a good place to look. FMS's director of branch operations told the *Rockford Register Star* that company officials were excited about hiring more people in town. "The priority is to see how many people we can put to work in Rockford," he said. Rockford's woes will help in two ways. The labor pool for FMS will grow as more people in Rockford need new jobs, and so will the collections business.

Older workers may be losing their chances to rebound, too. Most remain out of work six months after they lose their jobs. Only one-third find work within a half year of losing a full-time job, and when jobs come they are very likely to pay less than the job lost. The Urban Institute reports that 43 percent of older workers who lost one job and moved to another earned one-quarter less than their previous salary, and more than a fifth of reemployed older workers took to jobs that paid half their former pay, or less.[2]

No wonder older workers often choose to retire early. If U.S. Social Security pays, on average, a little less than half (45 percent) of what older workers make on the job,* and older job seekers are either stymied in the job market or relegated to jobs in which they may earn, after taxes, barely more, or often, less, than what they would receive from Social Security alone, it is hardly crazy to stop work and collect Social Security. And no wonder government sources of income now outweigh private salaries. Those who are out of work, but have some pension income, can easily match what they would make were they to work.** The literature of empowerment and the rhetoric of legislators trumpet an age when older Americans will

---

* The Congressional Research Service reports that for Americans over sixty-five, the average annual Social Security benefit in 2008 came to $12,437. The median income from all sources for the same age group was $18,208, but one-quarter of Americans sixty-five and older received less than $11,140.

** How one fares in or out of work at later ages in America depends much on the kind of pension one was left with when the job vanished, and one's age and Social Security eligibility (or one's ingenuity in getting on to the Social Security disability rolls).

be able to work as long as they are able. But in the job market as it is, the message to millions of older workers is that they are barely worth more than if they did not work at all.

Of course, people compete for jobs more fiercely if they really need the work. People who are forced to retire early have often just finished the most expensive times of their lives, and are just beginning to rebuild their savings. Children are out of the house; expenses for their education may be through or winding down; the end of the mortgage may be approaching. The last ten or fifteen years on the job are a prime time for catching up on savings before retirement. Losing a job means losing the chance to save. Instead, what savings exist get drawn down as debt piles up. Even people who do not lose their jobs are often strapped in retirement. More than half of the country's retirees call it quits with less than fifty thousand dollars in savings, which in practice means they are destined to live on Social Security or some form of public income assistance for the poor. Or, if they can, to go back to work.

Despite the hardship older workers face finding jobs, even low-paid ones, as a group they are highly willing—or, perhaps, resigned—to work past traditional retirement age. Though seven in ten American workers say they plan to work "in retirement," that does not mean they are destined for jobs. Of the 6.6 million Americans over sixty-five years old who either worked or wanted to in 2009, only half were employed.[3] Only one in three retirees today (most retirees, of course, are no longer considered to be in the workforce) have had any work at all in retirement.[4]

Overall, the official unemployment rates for workers over fifty-four years old register below those of the general population, but the statistics are misleading. Because older workers have less luck in finding jobs once they have been released from a past employer—it takes them an average of thirty-four weeks to find new positions—they tend to drop out of the official count of job seekers. That count includes people who find part-time work but does not include those who have given up looking because they could not find any job after searching for months. Moreover, the most commonly used surveys of older workers include only those who have managed to survive the workplace and stay in it.

The velocity at which older workers have lost their jobs during the recession points to how vulnerable and disposable the class can be. In December 2009, the U.S. government reported that more workers over fifty-five were counted as unemployed than at any other time on record and that their numbers represented a 50 percent jump over the year before. In the two years leading up to 2009, the unemployment rate among workers aged fifty-five to sixty-four tripled, while for the population overall it merely doubled.[5]

An Unemployed City

In challenged industrial cities such as Rockford, finding new work is particularly difficult. Where people do work, it is often part-time, and often lower-wage. Wetters, at her care agency, not only hires better qualified people than ever—because better qualified people are among the jobless—but hires many who need flexible hours. Often they piece together a new livelihood by holding several lower-paid jobs, and often they need to keep time free so they can tend to family members who need them. People who work as caregivers are often among the 30 percent of Americans—65.7 million people—who are also unpaid caregivers of family members, and who, on average, put in nineteen hours a week of work for elderly parents and other loved ones.[6] Wetters employs workers who are between twenty-five and seventy-five years old, but most are fifty and older, in the age groups when people are most likely to be caring for a family member themselves.

Older and better qualified workers might not appear as plentifully on Wetters's work rosters if the international trade picture were different for the United States, or if global firms and the world's consumers did not also regard Rockford as over-the-hill. Rockford's slide in some ways repeats the busts of the city's boom-and-bust past. Places that are overreliant on manufacturing get whipsawed by economic currents more than do highly diverse local economies. But other long-term trends have made Rockford's recent slide more definitive, and ominous. The city's marquee companies, most of which were once family-owned, formerly employed tens of thousands of workers. One by one, the firms have been absorbed into larger global conglomerates or into the stables of private equity firms. Rockford once headquartered nearly all of its large employers; today only one big firm still calls the city home. New, outside employers have extracted value in the usual ways: cutting workers, outsourcing abroad and automating, and consolidating plants and pruning the wages and benefits of workers they kept and hired. The multiple wage structures now common in U.S. factories have taken hold in Rockford, too, so that workers with seniority get paid according to schedules that give them more per hour than newer hires, who are kept to lower wages and benefit plans for their whole careers. This, of course, stokes intergenerational resentment on the shop floor, too. The younger workers may never achieve the lifestyles or retirements of their predecessors, though they are expected to perform as well or better—more reasons for management to lay off or buy out the older workers.

Airplane Auguries

As companies moved production abroad, they retained employees who had the deep expertise needed to gear up foreign operations before they retired for good. For several years preceding the Beijing Olympics in 2008, the nonstop United and American Airlines flights from O'Hare International in Chicago to Shanghai or Beijing were solidly booked weeks in advance. The sight on these flights was always the same—extra-large business class seats filled with row after row of portly men carrying the jewels of American industry to the newly growing industrial clusters in China.

There could be no happier sight for the advocates of late-career workers. These planes were filled not just with the well-tailored executives and moneymen who usually take up the premium sections on international flights, but with a whole new class of knowledge worker, too—engineers and blue-collar workers who knew the ins and outs of their companies' production lines back home. Balancing drinks in one hand and flipping through thick, black notebooks with schematics for plants and logistics with the other, these travelers personified every virtue that champions of older workers promise. They knew all the twists and turns in the production processes. They were exceedingly loyal to their companies; through years of experience they had come to see their colleagues and bosses as family. Unlike younger workers, who might also get sent to China for the home team, they did not wonder how they would parlay their experiences into jobs for other companies. They did not want to uproot themselves completely from their home communities. Gen Xers and millennials may regard themselves as God's gifts to their employers; they may demand responsibilities that leapfrog them ahead of older workers. But the seasoned company soldiers with their undaring haircuts, wedding rings, and paperback thrillers carried their companies' fortunes as dearly as their own.

Often the men who made the trip were retired, but lured back as consultants by their companies to work out production in a new China factory. One fifty-eight-year-old man from a town not too far from Rockford, who traveled to Shanghai in 2007, told a fellow traveler that he had retired two years earlier but that his old manager had recently called to ask if he had ever been overseas, or would ever want to go. The man said he rarely left the state, let alone the country, but he took the job. Now, he said, he was spending months at a time in an industrial city between Shanghai and Nanjing, at his old Illinois company's new operations headquarters, building farm and construction equipment for the Chinese market and for export.

"I love it," he said. "The food is sometimes a problem, and I don't like to drink as much as my Chinese hosts want me to. I can't go to church and worship with Chinese people. I can't even bring in Bibles for them. But the workers are great—hardworking and so young. They look up to me. I'm older and they want to know what I know."

He talked freely. He needed to talk. He said he could never do the work had he not retired. Union rules would not allow it. He knew he played a role in making the jobs held by his former union friends at home vulnerable, but said the change would happen no matter what, and he might as well earn the money and get the experience. Profits were high at his company that year, he said, and China was cited as a highlight by management when the yearly results were announced. The stock price was high, too, and the traveler had company shares in his retirement plan.

But months after the plane ride, at lunch near one of his company's Rockford suppliers, the man felt less sure of his footing at work. Tensions were higher now that his company and its partners were laying off thousands more workers in the United States. Their China operation, he said, was not contracting, so he was as busy as ever. Many of his friends at home, though, had been eliminated from the company. "It was just recently when they were offering everyone all sorts of incentives to put retirement on hold. Now the same workers are standing in line for jobs at Home Depot and Wal-Mart for one-fifth the wage."

Once jealously courted, mature workers have found, unfortunately, that even their plans to find lower-wage jobs are mirages. The need of older people to work longer to make up for the failure of their pension plans has not been matched by the need of American businesses to employ them. A study by two economists at Wellesley College, Courtney Coile and Phillip B. Levine, predicts that about twice as many workers over fifty-five will be forced to retire compared to the number of older workers who will find a way to hang on to their jobs past the time when they intended to retire.[7]

Even jobs in niches that seem relatively secure can make older workers suddenly vulnerable to redundancy. Defense and aerospace companies, recently accustomed to a flush pipeline of U.S. security and wartime spending, now widely expect dramatic reductions in orders in the near future. (Industry consultants and defense department insiders do not how America's outsized defense budgets could be practically or politically sustainable.) At the same time, these industries are home to one of the country's oldest skilled workforces and they expect, as the spending cuts come, to lose a whopping 40 percent of their workers to both early and standard retirements. The losses will leave a giant "knowledge gap" at the companies, which raises urgent concerns for the companies' long-term health and the technological leadership of the U.S. defense sector. For Rockford, as an aerospace center, the change could offer one more blow.

Especially since there are too few skilled younger people to fill the knowledge gap left by the retirees and there may be, in a contracting environment, too few prospects for secure aerospace jobs that would lure in large numbers of outsiders to town, or would justify expensive programs to train large numbers of natives.

When jobs are in short supply, the ability of older workers to compete successfully against younger job applicants can be a mixed blessing. When older workers do succeed, it can have lifelong consequences for those they have displaced. In Rockford, for instance, where the overall unemployment rate was historically high in 2010, older workers were so plentiful in the job market that they competed fiercely with workers in their late teens and early twenties. If the trends in Rockford that divide the low-end workforce by age fall in line with national trends—anecdotally they seem even more acute—the job experience of the older workers may put them ahead of inexperienced younger ones.

Older workers in search of any paying job at all now snatch up entry-level jobs in Rockford that in the recent past were reliable first steps into work for teens and twentysomethings. "You have the ability [as an employer] to choose from higher-educated, more experienced, and higher-quality workers," says Kristen Lopez Eastlick, of the Employment Policies Institute in Washington, which keeps an eye on the Rockford jobs picture. "Those youth don't have a chance."[8]

In weak job markets, it's tough to split up jobs between the young trying to break into the market and the old trying to keep a place, even a reduced one, in it.* Western European countries have experimented with various strategies to ease late-career workers out of the job market to make room for younger ones, but youth unemployment, as high as 40 percent in much of Europe, has just grown more entrenched. And now, of course, most developed countries

---

* An analysis by Bloomberg News (relying on data from the U.S. Department of Labor) shows how prominently older workers now fill jobs traditionally available to U.S. teens over the years 2008–9 in food preparation and service. For example, teens aged sixteen to nineteen held 240,000 fewer jobs, but adults over fifty-five held 128,000 more jobs. In sales, teens were down 532,000 jobs and the fifty-five-plus set up 822,000. In office and administrative work, 553,000 fewer teens were employed, but 1,091,000 more of the older adults held jobs.

are raising the retirement age. Most puzzling perhaps, is the failure of the mass educational initiatives in Europe to make young people more employable. One stream of criticism argues that much of the young population in Europe is now overeducated, which makes many workers too expensive to hire for the jobs European firms might otherwise create and fill. In this line of reasoning, Europe pours too many resources into advanced schooling for its young people, and into paying for university and other postsecondary education with precious public funds. At the same time, the argument runs, the policies delay the entry of a big part of the population into the job market, and thus shortens their working lives even as their natural lives grow ever longer. If people start on the job in their late twenties, wind up out of work in their mid- to late fifties, and then typically live into their eighties and beyond, the burden on their earning power can be overwhelming.

Not Learning the Invisible Curriculum

In Rockford, as everywhere, the longer that young people are made to look for work, the worse their long-term economic prospects get. They lose income and the raises that grow over time. Lisa B. Kahn, a Yale economist, found that workers who began their work lives in the recession of the 1980s started at such low wages that even with annual raises, it took ten years to get to the wage level they would have achieved had they been hired in better times.[9] They lose early years of savings when money put aside compounds the longest and most potently. Worst of all, perhaps, unemployed younger workers miss out on the "invisible curriculum" gained on the job, the stuff beyond textbooks that grooms one for the working world. This includes the social skills and political savvy one acquires in the workplace. Young workers, for example, typically have more room to stumble and make their way through the pecking order on the job. Bosses know new hires have things to learn and, should a younger worker lose a job, the experience of the failure can help in the next round.

That's not to mention the specific skills that workers learn early on the job. "The interpersonal interactions and relationships [young workers] develop during those early years stay with them forever," says the director of a Rockford program designed to groom basic workplace skills for job seekers. "[The jobs young workers do get] is a valuable experience for them to have."[10] If youth unemployment proves more durable than unemployment among other age groups, the building blocks that help societies pay for themselves can weaken over the long haul. When employment is on a more even keel, younger workers build up their financial resources—earning power and savings—so that they can support dependents who do not work, such as children and retired parents. If not directly, then at least through their taxes. And, importantly, work helps them pay for "visible education," including vocational training and degree programs. If successful aging is more likely to result from cumulative advantages over the course of life, the fate of Rockford's unemployed young people bodes trouble for their future and their city.

Worker Against Worker

Countries build their futures on comparative advantages, too. And the competition that pits older workers against the young in lean job markets grows out of the past and plays out for years to come. The more young workers that a country can employ, the more likely it is to accumulate savings and investment capital. The Asian miracle economies all boomed when their young workforces were most engaged. China is in such a stage now. Its workers are producing and its savings rate as a nation is very high, as are its surpluses in trade and currency. Japan went through a similar stage, and in the 1970s people thought Japan would not slow down until it took its place as the world's largest economy. The United States was in surplus when the postwar boom and the baby boom generations were younger, working, and providing the country with investable capital out of America's cumulative savings. Demographically, the United States is not as challenged as the more rapidly aging countries of Europe and east Asia, but if youth unemployment stays high, it will negate and even reverse the demographic strengths the United States ought to gain from its young workforce.* In Rockford, for one, there is justifiable fear that a whole generation of young workers, if they stay in town, will languish there. Or worse. "What research shows is individuals who are unemployed as teens are often not keeping up with their peers many years later," says Lopez Eastlick.[11]

And then there is the flip side. The invisible curriculum young job seekers learn in a weak market contains lessons in dependency and discouragement—two trends that stand out in the era of high youth unemployment. In a recent survey of American adults eighteen to thirty-four, the Pew Research Center found that 10 percent had moved back to their parents' homes as a result of failed job searches or fears that their current jobs were not secure.

The weak job market may also be causing Americans to delay or give up on starting families. The national birthrate in 2008 was one and a half percent lower than the year before, but down twice as much in Illinois. Rockford hospitals reported a 4 percent drop in births over the same period. Marriages are also down.[12]

Driven Out

In the United States, as in much of Europe, the social security system is contributing to a vicious cycle that encourages the unemployment of older workers. Unemployment itself has become one of the criteria by which former workers are deemed eligible for disability insurance. Looser standards for disability often encourage unemployment among older, less-educated workers. What's more, Western governments have often allowed companies to extend disability benefits to workers facing mass layoffs. The benefits use government money, but are offered in exchange for company commitments not to relocate altogether and not to fire even more workers. The incentives keep older people off the job while at the very same time the system in the United States, as in most of Europe, now requires that active

---

* In mid-2010, the youth unemployment rate in the United States was 29 percent, its highest level since statistics were first gathered in 1947. In Illinois, the rate was 40 percent.

workers wait one, two, or three years longer than they once did in order to collect their standard retirement benefits.

In the United States the conflict has created a peculiar pattern for older workers. "We've seen the numbers of very old workers, those over sixty-five, go up, mostly because they are going back to work part-time," says Susan Houseman, senior economist at the W.E. Upjohn Institute for Employment Research at Kalamazoo, a Michigan research center that focuses on employment issues. "But higher participation is not there among those aged fifty-five to sixty-five, particularly if you look at less-educated workers, and mainly the men being driven out of factories."

Houseman's research also ties the unemployment of older workers to globalization. In 2009, she published a widely reported critique attacking the way the United States calculates both its trade statistics and its GDP. Houseman suggested that worker productivity in the United States was overestimated because government numbers mistakenly counted low-cost imported goods as higher-cost final products in cases where the goods ultimately were sold out of a U.S. factory. In a city like Rockford, where manufacturers create finished goods out of vast volumes of imported parts, the standard accounting makes the companies' production lines seem far more potent at creating wealth than they really are. The errors in reporting also help explain why manufacturing wages have headed down even as worker productivity has seemed to head up. In years past, productivity gains had always been accompanied by wage increases. That is what once made Rockford a golden town for blue-collar workers. Their wages went up as their employers grew into more sophisticated domestic producers. Globalization reversed that equation, and the recent increases in productivity are largely a mirage created by cheap imports that go into American goods. In Houseman's reckoning, the arrival of imports is a chief cause of the rapid destruction of manufacturing in the United States. The United States may brag that output from manufacturing peaked even after millions of manufacturing jobs were destroyed, but an important part of that U.S. output is an illusion. So much so that Houseman suggests the United States revise down its tally of the gross domestic product by as much as 8 to 10 percent a year.

In Rockford today, retooling for a new job often means acquiring skills in health care, an industry that has rapidly become one of the region's biggest employers. Three of the four largest employers in the region are hospitals (the Rockford School District is the largest single employer) and the tenth largest employer is a network of clinics.[13]

On paper, the age demographics of Rockford make it seem younger than Sarasota, Florida, but that masks some important statistical similarities that would not surprise Rockfordians, who all seem to know someone who has moved to the Florida city. One real way the two places are demographically similar is that both have a high proportion of non-Hispanic whites and their white populations are markedly older than their smaller nonwhite populations. Yet, atmospherically, the cities feel very different. While Rockford disperses people all over the globe, people from all over the globe come to Sarasota.* The economy of Sarasota stands or falls on the ability of the resort town to rejuvenate successive waves of older newcomers. The economy of Rockford, however, offers constant reminders

* Oddly, if Rockford's citizens are leaving, they are once again lagging behind a national trend. Joel Kotkin, author of a number of influential studies on urban and suburban life around the world, notes that in the 1970s, each year about one in five Americans moved to a new home, but now the number is closer to one in eight, the lowest number since the U.S. government began to track mobility in 1940. "In 2008," he writes, "the total number of people changing residences was less than those who did so in 1962, when the country had 120 million fewer people." Kotkin's observation may or may not apply to younger people in Rockford, but it is dead on in describing older age groups in Rockford. Midcareer Rockford natives with families and older citizens stay put. And, in fact, they are planted whether they like it or not. Home values in Rockford are far from high enough to help a family swap into a new home either in more prosperous places or the posher retirement communities like Sarasota. College-educated children just entering the workforce can leave because they don't need mom and dad to sell the house in order to resettle somewhere else. The biggest draw out of Rockford is Chicago. Yet in America, when young adults move, they tend to move farther away than in the past, with a higher percentage moving out of state. But perhaps the most entrenched bunch are the people with young families, two incomes, and a nice house and yard that they would have a hard time equaling in more vigorously percolating parts of the country. And in an era where aging parents are as likely to help middle-aged children with money, child care, social connections, and other services, nearby family offers a compelling slew of reasons to stay. The reasons why most of the country is not as mobile as it once was intersect with the economic and social changes making Americans older. As Kotkin says, "After decades of frantic mobility and homogenization, we are seeing a return to placeness . . ."

that its natives are redundant to local enterprise once they reach their midfifties. The white populations in both places are old, but only the Illinois city's economy reinforces what is "aged" about its own, while the Florida city's economy accentuates what is vital. In Sarasota, the sixty-year-olds are the "kids," while in Rockford, the fifty-year-olds face a social and economic milieu that signals they are getting on.

While Rockford's median age of 34.4 is about a year and a half younger than the national median, the median age for its blacks and Hispanics is about twenty-six. The median age of the non-Hispanic whites in town—still about 70 percent of the city's population—is 41.8 years old, nearly five years older than the national figure.

The huge gap between the white and nonwhite population shows how disproportionately young the minority population is and how old the majority population is. It's a huge difference. "Is the majority white population in Rockford going to get older and older?" asks Joel Cowen, the demographer at the medical school, rhetorically. "When you see that 70 to 80 percent of the people moving to Rockford are minority, and middle-class educated people are moving out, it is hard to see it any other way." Cowen says that there are no hard numbers on who leaves, but rather that it is nearly the universal observation, and obsession of the city.

Please Stay Here

Rockford's current mayor, Larry Morrissey, was elected on a platform that promised revitalization strategies to bring the departed natives back to town. Morrissey, a political novice and independent, won the office at age thirty-six and challenged an entrenched, partisan political culture. He knew why people leave Rockford. He himself had moved to Chicago to practice law and escape a town he once believed was in inexorable decline. It is not unusual that Morrissey's law degree led him out of town. "One of my first meetings when I returned home was with the Rockford Area Economic Development Council to talk about attracting and retaining young people," Morrissey recalls. "I thought the conversation felt like some kind of science experiment and I felt I was the subject of the experiment. The older members were talking about their kids leaving the city and never coming back, and I was seen as the guy who did come back. I was twenty-eight and came back to be part of my father's law firm and for the opportunity to get young, talented people, to make Rockford cool. I also had two goals for myself, to live in a cool loft. They were nonexistent so I had to create them. I bought a thirty-thousand-square-foot building for fifty thousand dollars and did that. And my second goal was to get to and from Chicago, so I started working on getting passenger train service back between the cities. We're still working on that one."

Morrissey hired a consultant to study what Rockford needed. "She concluded we needed a cool city, one that was clean and green and that had bike trails along our riverfront." Morrissey tested the thesis by taking an apartment over a downtown bar. Others followed. "I asked myself if this is what younger people want, and the answer was yes it is. My generation is interested in shared community assets, not just two-acre homes on the edge of suburbia. We have urban areas we can 're-pioneer.'"

Education is one of the best predictors of who leaves Rockford. Sadly for Rockford, the college-educated natives that are so hard to keep are also the sort of residents Rockford most craves. They are wanted because they are the class of Americans that starts businesses, and gives stability to schools and local institutions.

"In the past, Rockford had a chance to have the kinds of institutions that would help us have the kind of workers we need today," says a staff member of the Rockford Area Economic Development Council. "We could have had a university here. The powers-that-be back then thought that having a big university here would discourage people from heading into the factories after high school."

If the local myth of Rockford's refusal of a comprehensive university is true, the fears of the industrial big shots have proved prescient. Rockford's best-educated young people often do leave and become resources in other communities they move to. But the big shots did not have it all right. Midwestern universities are also the magnets for industries that need bright, highly skilled workers. Michigan's Detroit and midsized factory cities may be atrophying, but Ann Arbor, home of the superb University of Michigan, is a hub for many of the world's most technologically advanced companies, such as Google, and myriad start-ups. The multinationals that gobbled up Rockford's premier manufacturing firms crave and need top talent. If they cannot sell the talent they need on Rockford, they set up shop where they can attract people, in the United States or anywhere else that works.

The Fate of Cities

In city halls and economic development offices across the country, and around the world, officials obsess about how to attract and retain young, well-educated professionals. The desire is articulated most famously by Richard Florida, a geographer now at the University of Toronto. In series of energetically written books and articles, Florida has brilliantly, but controversially, argued that the fate of American cities in the Information Age depends in large part on their ability to serve what he famously labeled "the creative class." The class is made up of the obviously artsy—musicians, painters, and writers, some of whom work away in garrets and lofts, and some of whom attach themselves to the mainstream corporate, government, and institutional economies. Creative directors at ad agencies and jingle writers are probably more vital to a place's verve than its Van Goghs and Emily Dickinsons. Importantly, however, many in the creative class are not so artsy. They are engineers, scientists, philanthropists, educators, and many other kinds of knowledge workers who stir a region's cultural and intellectual stew. They can be young, midcareer and older, but if they are creators and innovators, the young will attract the old and the old will attract the young. The creative classes also crave a dense concentration of cultural assets. They want café society, a music scene, arts that speak to the present. Opera companies, symphony orchestras, and museums that ape royalist European warehouses of culture are fine, Florida says, in effect, but they are not enough to lure and hold on to the creative class. Young creators and innovators do not move to Austin, Texas; Boulder, Colorado; or San Francisco just for the work. And they do not move to Brooklyn, Shanghai, Barcelona, and Tokyo because those are the very best places to see Impressionist painting, Picassos, or porcelains. That may be part of it, but mainly they come for the culture they contribute to as a class. The culture that keeps them both caters to their sense of the new, and is created by them.

What the creative class yearns for is also precious for people who want to re-create themselves and who relish ever-changing environments. That includes middle-aged and older people in search of new friends, positive challenges, and an atmosphere that can shake them up intellectually and aesthetically.

"College towns are an increasingly popular choice to empty nesters because they offer access to great health care, substantial amenities, and diverse, intellectually stimulating communities," writes Richard Florida in his 2008 book, *Who's Your City*.[14] According to Florida's taxonomy, empty nesters are people aged forty-five to sixty-four who are old enough to have seen their adult children move out, though, importantly, he also includes people who may be childless, including gay and lesbian adults without children. Madison, Wisconsin; Boulder, Colorado; Minneapolis, Minnesota; and Columbus, Ohio, among other big university towns, have seen a large influx of empty nesters.

The trend, though, does not have an upper age limit. College towns in the United States and Canada have become popular places for retirees to move to. More than five hundred American universities now have programs designed specifically for older adults. The enrollees stay engaged and the schools earn tuition at a time when many colleges and universities need to find ways to fill their desks and bursaries. For developers building sites for the oldest Americans, college towns are seen as strong attractions for the seventy-and-older set. The firm behind the Glenridge in Sarasota, for example, now focuses entirely on projects in college towns. People usually move into a continuing care community when they can still go to theater and sports events. The college town developments appeal especially to committed alumni who still feel a strong attachment to their old schools. In practice, however, residents do not have an easy time taking advantage of all the amenities in cities that cater to students. But the atmosphere of the cities and the camaraderie with fellow alumni has strong appeal nonetheless.

Take a Second Look

Economic development offices cannot provide everything Richard Florida says cities need to thrive. Rockford's does not have the power to move a big university to town. They can, however, promote the amenities that make members of the creative class take a second look. Rockford's young mayor, for one, ran on a platform that links the city's future to the improvement of its green space, a livable downtown with stylish cafés, restaurants, and a lively nightlife. He's spurred projects on every front he promised. Rockford's own Rick Nielsen of Cheap Trick ("I Want You to Want Me" and other megahits) has embraced the vision of a resurgent city and is behind a project to build an eight-acre entertainment district that would include music venues, a convention center, and a museum for his vast collection of guitars. And hidden in plain sight beyond all the smokestacks, assembly lines, empty stores, and burgeoning health clinics is a creative city bursting to get out. Rockford may be America's 146th largest town, but it is replete with some of the world's best makers of things. There are thousands of engineers, one of Richard Florida's favorite group of creators. They have, according to the economic development council, made Rockford the nation's tenth most prolific producer of patentable products and processes.

It is possible, however, that the city sees itself as too burdened by its age to move into a more creative gear. "We have an aging population and it's getting poorer," reflects City Administrator James Ryan, who works under Morrissey. Ryan sees the standard of living declining with few ways to pull it up. He blames the shift in spending that has redirected public money to security and to the care and maintenance of an aging population. For example, in Rockford, the city struggles, he says, to pay the rising costs of increasingly frequent ambulance runs to fetch older people from their home. "Our challenge in this city is that so much money goes to maintenance and not to investments in the future."

As for Morrissey, he takes a more positive view. "I tell people that the Renaissance did not begin in Rome; it began in Florence. Families there were patrons of the city and allowed creativity to flourish. We are on our own and we can't expect Washington or the State of

Illinois to bail us out. If cities are going to recruit people back, they will have to fight their own fights."

Part of the civic discussion centers on the cities Rockford might emulate.

The Promise

Another once-hammered midwestern city that nonetheless elicits envy in Rockford is Kalamazoo, Michigan. At its height, Kalamazoo was also the picture of an industrious and prosperous city, where large family-owned companies delivered decades of economic growth and a measure of social stability. It, too, is home to a symphony, theaters, and arts centers, all worthy of much larger cities. The stage was set for a crippling economic upset in 1995 when one of the city's major employers, the 110-year-old Upjohn Company, was merged with Pharmacia, a Swedish drug company. Upjohn employed twelve hundred workers in town, a large percentage of them well-paid Ph.D.s. Once it was no longer locally owned, Upjohn abandoned Kalamazoo, and after two subsequent purchases and mergers, every Upjohn job was gone, as were many of the knowledge workers who manned them. The poverty rate in the city climbed, and middle-class families abandoned the public school system. Population growth turned negative. The city's population demographics were not old by national standards—a large college and university help keep the age stats for young adults high—but there was a paucity of families with young children, and the local birthrate barely approached the magic 2.1 level of replacement.

Happily, not every engine of wealth deserted the city. In a surprise announcement in November 2005, the superintendent of the city's public schools announced the Kalamazoo Promise, one of the most generous pledges in American history. A group of anonymous donors had pooled their resources and pledged to provide every schoolchild in the city with tuition money to attend any public college or university in Michigan. Those children who started in the Kalamazoo school system in kindergarten and graduated from high school would have all their tuition paid. The program's finances are a guarded secret, but when rumors surfaced that the stock market drop of 2008 threatened its viability, the administrators issued strong reassurances that the fund was in no danger. The magnitude of the commitment, and its durability, leave other communities dumbfounded and jealous.*

In 2010, the program was seeing its first college grads complete their studies, and altogether was providing school money to more than 860 students.

"The idea was that the Promise could be a tool that could accomplish many things," says Michelle Miller-Adams, a political scientist who wrote the first comprehensive study of the Kalamazoo Promise. "It is about place-based economic development. The Promise doesn't require students to do much more than live here, go to school here, and graduate. The whole idea, though, is to build local assets, and eventually to draw many new families into the school system and the community."[15]

Place-based economic development seeks to set up a bulwark against "the world is flat" creed propounded most famously by Thomas Friedman, whose bestselling book features the phrase for its title. The idea is that virtually any job in manufacturing or the information economy can be snatched from one part of the world and moved to any other. Friedman's description of the world holds the multinational corporate imagination captive in the same way that Richard Florida's strong opposing view on the value of local strengths appeals to local boosters. In locales adjusting to the dynamics of aging populations, the seemingly contradictory points of view describe complementary phenomena. The world may indeed be flat for many nimble enterprises, investors, and workers. They propel the dislocation of industries from places such as the industrial Midwest and the manufacturing centers of high-cost

---

* It may be ironic that a family widely suspected of funding the Promise is the Strykers, whose $36 billion namesake company is one of the world's largest suppliers of hospital beds. Market research by BizAcumen reports a growing worldwide shortage of hospital beds that is directly the result of the growing aging population. Stryker has been a stock picker's favorite in a turbulent market and has done well. Thus, it seems, the most ambitious plan to retain young people and families in an American city may be underwritten by a firm whose impressive fortunes are directly tied to an aging society.

European countries. But if place really did not matter, the world would have far less motion of capital, goods, and people, which move to capitalize on the advantages of place. China may be propelling the dislocation of older workers in the United States, and it may play a role in the tragically high rates of youth unemployment in Europe, Japan, and parts of the United States; but every vibrant jurisdiction in China also knows what local steps it must take to attract young people to its realm. It must do what the Kalamazoo Promise aims to do—build a critical mass of people who can pour their lives, skills, and treasure into that place. Localities offer tax incentives to businesses; they promise local investment from government-connected sources; they say they will train workers on the public dime.

Often these incentives work. Often, too, they lead to boondoggles. It turns out that companies that chase incentives once will do it again when better deals from other places come along. The Kalamazoo Promise is an attempt to draw in families first, not companies; firms, proponents hope, will follow later. Education is a good that people will relocate for, and when it is offered, young families can fill in the demographic gaps.*

In the first years of the Kalamazoo Promise, public school attendance spiked up. Kindergarten enrollments nearly tripled. Hundreds of families moved to town once word of the Promise reached a national audience. Real estate agents in town were besieged with calls about the local housing market. New homes sprang up. In a school district where six in ten of the students were low-income minority children (Kalamazoo had recently been embroiled in a painful battle to desegregate the schools), middle-class white children showed up in numbers not seen for years.

"The donors in the town," speculates Miller-Adams, "were probably reading Thomas Friedman and Richard Florida, and they saw the devastation and poverty that overcame Flint, Michigan, when

---

* Recently, IBM chose to locate a facility in Dubuque, Iowa. Rockford tried to make the list of candidate cities but failed. Dubuque was chosen not because IBM could lure workers and their families to Dubuque, but because the city is full of highly educated workers and families who are committed to stay following the city's investment of hundreds of millions of dollars in civic revitalization.

the auto industry moved out." And they saw the Kalamazoo Promise as the way to save the town from the worst side of globalization, and to capitalize on its promise, by stocking the city with educated young people and fighting off the aging and denaturing of their place.

Where the Elite Live, and Don't

There seem to be some cities and towns in America that liberally plant their natives in all the country's major metropolises. Often they are the prosperous suburbs of formerly prosperous industrial areas. Their emigrants are the educated class that fills the professional and executive ranks of more animated places in the United States and abroad. Call on a big law firm in New York City and there are likely a few lawyers there who went to high school in Shaker Heights outside Cleveland. Northern California venture capital firms may feel like they are homegrown in California, but ask if anyone is from Bloomfield Hills near Detroit and it's likely there are a few. Tour a temple in Toyko, and the American tourist with her head in a Lonely Planet guidebook is very possibly from Chesterfield or Town and Country, Missouri, outside St. Louis, but living in Tokyo selling insurance.

Rockford differs from America's suburban pockets of prosperity that mint a national class of well-educated elites. Rockford is not a suburb; it does not produce a huge population of knowledge workers. Not only do fewer than half of the city's public school children graduate from high school, but a very low proportion complete a college degree. Among medium and large metro areas in the United States, Rockford ranks among the lowest in terms of the percentage of college graduates in town. Janyce Fadden, the impassioned president of Rockford's economic development council, has made raising the number of college grads in Rockford one of the business community's top priorities. Fadden notes that every percentage point gained in grads would yield about $240 million extra income to the community, and if Rockford could reach the national average, it could be over $1.5 billion richer. The gap creates demand for educated outsiders, and despite the city's paucity of college grads, it has an above-average percentage of engineers in town. But the pull is not strong enough to keep the kind of critical mass of younger educated workers in town that would be big enough to lure others seeking a larger coterie of younger, like-minded transplants.

"We try to network newcomers in the community," says the economic development executive. "We have parties where they can meet others in their stage of life and who share the same concerns. We hook them up with local organizations to get them to volunteer and plant a stake in the community. We get them to sign their kids up for youth sports leagues and help them find a church. They say they try to make the city home, but they don't feel at home enough to stay. I talk to them after a couple of years, and often they say they've given up on Rockford. The city is too cliquish, they say. They go to parties and have a hard time finding people with their interests; everyone just talks about high school. They tell me they are leaving."

Caring for Nurses

Health care is another niche in which Rockford must compete aggressively for skilled workers. The stakes are economic, but they are also social, and, for its aging citizens, mortal. "What does our workforce look like? It's aging," says Dan Parod, who runs human resources at Rockford Health System, the largest hospital group in the region. "Eighty-five percent of our workers are female, and their average age is between forty and forty-five," he says, adding that a large number of them are due to retire out of the system over the next decade. One of three employees in Parod's system is a nurse. "We need a lot of nurses, because the boomers and their parents are aging, and that population needs nurses. As go nurses, there goes health care. The demand is going way up. And there is a huge nationwide shortage that we fall into."

By 2025 the United States is expected to be short 260,000 nurses.*

---

* Nurses are in short supply all over the world. In June 2009 the *New York Times* reported that Czech health-care providers faced such a severe dearth of nurses that they had to offer extreme incentives to attract help. A thirty-one-year-

That may sound grim, but it is far less frightening than the standard estimates of a few years ago that warned of a shortfall of one million nurses by 2018. The difference is that the recession, combined with the prospects of high pay and job security in nursing, has caused a surge in nursing schools and students. In 2010, there were more new nurses in their early twenties than there had been since the 1980s. The demand for nurses has pushed up incomes so that a nurse can earn as much as a well-paid physician. It is the impulse of the Japanese bath attendant Shimono to secure a livelihood among an aging cohort writ large. Globally large.

The growing population of older Americans is bound to tip the health-care industry. Parod sees that future more clearly than most. Among his barometers in Rockford are the help-wanted ads in the local papers and online in which entreaties for health-care workers take up more space than *all the other ads put together*. Another is the course of the local economy where, as in Sarasota, the big hospitals are now among the most important economic drivers in terms of revenue and employment. Only the school system—not any of Rockford's factories—employs more people.

Another telling detail for Parod is how much effort and discussion on issues relating to older patients consume his hospital's staff and executives. "The medical costs of the end of life are some of the biggest costs people will ever have to pay [or have paid for them]," Parod says. "What's happening [as a result of the aging population] is that patients in the hospital are much sicker than they were ten years ago. As a result, the intensity of health care is much higher. We have four hundred beds. The overwhelming majority of them used to be for general health and a smaller number for critical care. Now it is the reverse." From Parod's watch as employer, the new

old nurse in Prague was enticed to renew her contract at a private health clinic with an offer for free German lessons, extended vacation time, liposuction, and silicone breast implants. All of that came on top of a $1,400 a month salary, which is not high by Czech standards. "We were always taught that if a nurse is nice, intelligent, loves her work, and looks attractive, then patients will recover faster," she told the paper. The offers of free or discounted plastic surgery have become a force in the Czech marketplace. Czech nurses, on account of their low pay relative to other countries, have been leaving the country in large numbers. Twelve hundred went to Germany and the United Kingdom in 2008.

intensity of care for an older population causes his staff of nurses to age faster on the job because of the relentless physical and psychological demands. In talks with nurses who retire early from the job, Parod learns nurses who once offered lots of care and attention to their patients, who gave them back rubs and baby-powder massages, feel overly pressured in the new environment that demands quick-moving medical care.

The physical demands of working in a hospital often become too much by the time nurses hit their midforties. "They leave direct care [in the hospital] in search of other less strenuous and stressful options, such as working for an insurance company or something besides hospital or home care, something where they don't need to put in twelve-hour shifts and can semiretire or at least not work beyond their full capacity."

One reason they semiretire is that they are also family caregivers for spouses or aging parents. "When nurses enter the system at age twenty-five and five years later want to have children, we can offer them day care at work. But now with so many nurses in their forties and fifties, we have many who are wondering about elder care. Boomer nurses want to care for their parents within the family, but we need them to take care of patients. They don't want to do both, so if they are taking care of their parents, they may quit."

Importing Nurses from the Philippines

As a result, nurses are now recruited from outside the United States. One in three of the nearly half-million nurses added to the workforce between 2001 and 2008 were foreign born. "Nurses are now the biggest export from the Philippines," Parod notes with some dismay, though his facts are dead-on. In Rockford, Filipinos have come in impressive numbers to fill the gaps in the health-care workforce. A large Filipino ethnic society has been added to Rockford's mix of ethnic clubs. One of the city's largest Catholic churches now fills up with Filipino families and the new pastor is a Philippines native, too.

Ten percent of the population of the Philippines, or around 8.5 million people, works abroad. They leave in the prime of life and in effect take 23 percent of the working-age population, the cream of the country's workforce, with them. Remittances home from workers abroad is the single largest contributor to the country's GDP. Millions go to work in aging Asia as nurses and aides, factory and field-workers, and, among women, as hired caregivers for young children and aged adults. Filipino men get dispatched in large numbers to work construction crews and pipelines in the Middle East, according to the booms and busts of the markets there. One million Filipinos live and work in Saudi Arabia. When Dubai was in its frenzied building mode, a quarter of a million Filipinos worked there, building up the city and supporting the service economy. But their wages in the desert cannot compare to what their professional countrymen earn in the high-income countries of the aging West.

For historical and economic reasons, though, the United States remains the golden destination for Filipino men and women, and health-care jobs offer the best road into the country. The disparity between professional incomes in the Philippines and the United States is so great that eight thousand doctors in the Philippines have enrolled in nurses' training so that they can make the trip to the United States, where immigration rules favor foreign nurses over foreign doctors. One of Rockford Health's competitors, Parod notes, a regional network of Catholic hospitals, OSF Healthcare, sent a team of nurses and executives to Baguio City on the east coast of Luzon, to recruit one hundred nurses. They found thirty-five they would hire. The OSF team also went to London, not to hire British nurses, but to lure foreign nurses working there to come to the American Midwest. Recruiters found that London attracted such a wide variety of expatriate nurses that they could find a diverse group that could match the ethnic diversity of the U.S. patient population with a one-stop shop.

Why Jocelyn Came to Rockford

"I didn't really want to go abroad," says Jocelyn, a nurse from Manila who moved to Rockford to take a job at OSF in 2006 when she was twenty-six years old. A fair, slight woman, Jocelyn wears designer jeans and jeweled eyeglasses. She shares her story over dinner with a small gathering of her countrymen in a ranch house in Rockford. As the guests enter the house, they complain good-naturedly about the icy walkway hardened by one of the coldest Januarys in recent memory. Inside, the house is full of light and the table full of fried noodles, adobo pork, boxes of Kentucky Fried Chicken, and soda pop. To the suggestion that the meal might not be what one would expect in a gathering of health-care professionals, one of the men replies, "Yes, but it is so good! And besides, this is more or less what we would have in the Philippines."*

Though Jocelyn is a newcomer to America, her husband first arrived in the United States when he was in grade school and he speaks like a Rockford native. She had wanted to be an interior designer, but chose nursing at the insistence of her mother, who Jocelyn says once wanted to be a nurse herself but was forbidden to go to college. "I'm an obedient daughter, so I listened to my mother. You could say I relived my mother's fate because she had to obey my grandmother. In the U.S., kids follow their passion, but in the Philippines kids follow their parents. I'm afraid of hospitals, I hate the smell and the stress. No one in my family had ever been in the hospital. I didn't know anything about nursing except that it was something you did if you wanted to marry a doctor. The only thing I really knew was that you get a hat and a uniform. I only knew that because I used to watch the American TV show *Doogie Howser, M.D.*" Jocelyn scored high on the nursing students' entrance exam and was admitted to a top school. That was it. She would be a nurse. "It was good to be in one of the top schools."

Jocelyn and her classmates were recruited for jobs all over Europe and the Middle East, but had very little contact with the hiring institutions. Every interaction goes through an agency hired by the foreigners. OSF used a Florida agency that specializes in Filipina nurses, and it did all the prospecting and prescreening in-country to get OSF good candidates. Jocelyn did not want to go abroad, so she made half-hearted commitments to several agencies. Ultimately, though, she felt she could help her family if she left the country.

* Diabetes is on the rise in the Philippines, growing 2.5 percent a year. If the trend continues, one in twelve Filipinos will suffer from the disease in 2025.

"The quality of life for my family is just average at home and my parents have no savings. My mom didn't force me to leave the country, but I saw the need. If I went to America I could make a big difference. My sister graduated from university with a degree in clinical psychology and she was recruited to be a psychologist for autistic kids in Saudi Arabia, but she ended up as a domestic helper there." After OSF offered Jocelyn the job, it took her five years to complete the professional exams and immigration paperwork required to get on the plane for the United States. "I had no idea what they might pay me and I would have taken anything just to get to the U.S. But OSF had people greet me when I arrived and help me get settled. I was put up for three months in the Marriott Hotel. Wow! And then they gave me three thousand dollars tax-free to help me get settled in town. I didn't know the difference between Rockford and Southern California. They said it was snowy, and I thought that sounded fun, that I would go skiing and build snowmen—in reality it is really cold. But with three thousand dollars, I could have put a down payment on a nice house in the Philippines. My first day's salary was more than I would have earned in a week at home, and my first month's was more than I would have earned in a year. I was already earning more money than my father, who had spent twenty years in the Philippines military and was a captain in the navy. I saw that if I could earn this money, I could help a lot, especially with my young brothers and sister. I could bring my family a higher standard of living."

While many of the factories in Rockford have gone to the two-tier wage structure, the hospitals that recruit foreign nurses to Rockford start the Filipinas at the same salary and benefits they offer American hires. As employers, they scrupulously monitor the workplace to ensure as best they can that there is no favoritism along ethnic or national lines.

Why would immigrant workers who often come willing to work for less than they are offered be put on equal terms with the local workforce? In the local factories, young Rockford natives often cannot extract the same terms for their employment as those enjoyed by their seniors. Both arrangements are the function of the global market for young people in an aging world. In the first instance, the young workers are groomed for jobs that must be imported, but in the latter the Rockford natives possess skills that can easily be outsourced to where young people are more plentifully cheap and easily mobilized.

Living in a NORC

On Rockford's northeast side, if you travel up Pleasant Valley Boulevard, past Carefree Drive, then turn left, you come to Sunnyside Drive. It's a subdivision of well-kept, but generic, recent-vintage family homes. At two in the afternoon the neighborhood looks nearly deserted, but at the end of Sunnyside, beyond the houses, cars and people move in and out of the Cloisters of Forest Hills, a three-story condominium complex that is all but hidden from the main road. The building has dozens of apartments that circle around a glass-covered atrium. The trellised roof is big enough to cover a bar, patios connected by paths, and a free-form swimming pool that emanates a tropical blue glow after the underwater lights switch on at dusk.

Most people in Rockford have never heard of the Cloisters, and the fact that a residence like it exists in town comes as a surprise. There is another surprise inside. The majority of the residents are retired Rockforders, most of them women older than seventy, many widowed. The tables around the pool are often filled with older residents talking in small groups, playing cards, or working on sizable jigsaw puzzles.

The complex was not built for older people; the older residents found it and, through strength in numbers, more or less took it over. The conquest began slowly. Its origins are rooted in the fears inspired by homes such as the picture-perfect two-story houses nearby on Sunnyside Drive, where stairs, paved walkways, and driveways (which get slippery in the winter) play into the menacing hands of gravity. Nationwide, single-story homes are gaining in popularity. (When baby boomers bought houses for their growing families they preferred two-story houses like those on Sunnyside, but as they have moved into new homes once their children left and their knees started creaking, single-level homes have taken on new appeal.) The elevator at the Cloisters, therefore, was the chief treasure worth having.[16]*

The canes, walkers, wheelchairs, and bent backs of the groups gathered midafternoon on the atrium's patio make it plain why stairs make a former home worth leaving. "Before my husband died," says one woman, "I remember thinking that every step he took was like climbing a big dangerous ledge, and lots of times I would have to hold him up, even though I am not that strong and my bones aren't what they used to be. If he fell, we'd both be in danger." She said that today, if she stayed home, no one would help her on the stairs, so she came to a building with an elevator.

The Cloisters also feels safer than these women's old homes in other ways. It is well lit and, unlike the quiet neighborhoods up the street, there are usually other people around willing to lend a hand or to consider that something such as a neighbor's absence from a favorite dominos game looks suspicious.

Once a few older people found that the place suited them, they encouraged their friends to move there, too. "What we like about it is that we own our own places and can stay independent," says a slight ninety-two-year-old man whom the ladies describe as "the fella we all spoil and want to marry, if he didn't have a wife." The man looks around for nods of agreement and continues. "We own our own places; that's very important. No one can move us out unless we say so."

Recent prices for one and two-bedroom units in the complex ran less than eighty thousand dollars, making life far less expensive than just about any similar option in one of the nation's continuing care communities. The residents of the Cloisters are far more typical of the elderly in America, who overwhelmingly prefer not to go to the more structured arrangements of senior living communities. Only about 11 percent of older Americans ever live in any of the places designed especially for older people. That includes local hometown

* Boomers would probably do better if they used stairs more, not less, and planning too far ahead for old age by buying a flat house in one's fifties may mean the day when the house is really needed due to one's immobility may come sooner than it would have in a house that demanded daily workouts on the stairs.

versions of everything Sarasota and other retirement destinations have in abundance, from posh adults-only golf communities for the very active to assisted living for people who need help with the activities of daily living. (About 45 percent of Americans use nursing homes at one time or another, though these are often for rehab and not long-term stays.)

The Cloisters in Rockford, however, has by happenstance turned into a de facto community for the aged. Though the residents take rightful umbrage at any suggestion they have created a senior residence ("This is not an old people's home!"), the halls and lounge areas sport many of the touches of an organized senior community. Nearly every door is decorated. Dolls, wreaths, and pictures perk up halls. They also give older residents with dimmed vision and occasional moments of confusion extra visual and tactile cues to find their way after dinner at a neighbor's. Vans from Meals on Wheels park outside to deliver several residents their supper. Groups get together and travel en masse to cultural and social events elsewhere in Rockford. Neighbors idle on their interior balconies looking down on the pool, sometimes waiting until a neighbor or the super can let them into the apartment they've locked themselves out of. No one formally organized a system for lockouts, but the self-organized one works very well.

Still, when one asks the ninety-two-year-old gentleman whether there has ever been any discussion about setting up a battery of services that could help with some of the frustrations in an aging population, he again surveys the women at the table and offers an opinion. "I think we would regard any services like that as a serious negative. You wouldn't want nurses coming in and out, or people being wheeled in on their hospital beds. As far as I know, no one wants an organized meal service where someone carts in food on trays. That's not what we want here. We own our homes and this is just a condominium, not an institution."

Without meaning to do so, the Cloisters has taken its place among a growing number of highly localized communities of older people who work together but do not give themselves over to the more formal structures of communities planned for people their ages. Called NORCs, short for Naturally Occurring Retirement Communities, these discrete areas where a large percentage—usually 40 percent or more—of the residents are elderly, have become a feature of an aging world, especially in cities home to large populations of elderly who prefer their own homes and hometowns. Some NORCs take shape on city blocks where people have lived side by side for decades and have aged together.

The idea of the well-organized NORC originally took shape in New York City, where over the last few decades residents in many large cooperative buildings and rental apartment complexes were not moving out as they aged. In the mid-1980s Jewish philanthropies in the city began to consider how to bring a basket of services to the elderly in their own homes. There would be case managers for people who needed help coordinating their care. The UJA-Federation, New York's premier Jewish philanthropy, set up a program that today serves tens of thousands of older New Yorkers, bringing to them social workers, educational programs, and planned activities for days and nights out among the city's theaters, parks, and museums. Perhaps most important, it created structures where older people could come together.

Though the arrangements at the Cloisters are still far less inclusive than in other self-organized communities, state social service agencies in Rockford, for example, do provide a selection of services to residents that can grow over time. Will the Cloisters go more in the direction of NORC programs in New York, Boston, and elsewhere? As the residents age there, it very well may. It is also likely that informal self-organized communities of the elderly such as the Cloisters will become more common. Common even in communities once firmly identified with a young America.

"The majority of adults in the United States live in suburban environments that are great to raise kids in but lousy to age in," observes sociologist Andrew E. Scharlach, professor of aging at the University of California–Berkeley. "In suburban environments the distances from one person to another can be great and the places depend too much on the automobile, which make them difficult for older people who often have to limit their driving, or stop it altogether." A 2007 analysis of U.S. census data by the Brookings Institution[17] found that American suburbs are the fastest-aging places in the country. People who chose suburban living for their young families decades ago still like their houses, yards, and friends. The patterns hold in old-line metro areas such as New York and Chicago, but is also strong in the Sunbelt, where vast, once very young suburban landscapes of places, such as Metro Phoenix and Atlanta, will see a "senior tsunami" as their residents age in their longtime homes and communities.

Scharlach says that older people often mischaracterize their long-term needs when choosing where to live. Retirees have become part of the general demographic shift in America, which is now away from core urban areas into suburban settings that isolate them. "We don't realize the value we place on social connections and on social capital, and too often we take for granted the social connections we have made over time." This, Scharlach says, is part of the story of the invisibility of older adults in society. Late in life people often inadvertently sever their social connections. "Kids expect their moms and dads to move in with them when they grow dependent, but that ignores how over the past fifty years or more, mom and dad have developed relationships in their churches and synagogues, in the local markets, among their neighbors."

All of these are important but subtle connections and often people do not realize their importance until they need them. "We have the idea that when mom moves in, we will replace all of that for her. But we can't." Emotional well-being is at stake, but so is health. It is natural to think that moving an older parent into one's home, even if it puts distance between old friends, is a life-saving strategy. Scharlach points out, however, that there is "plenty of evidence that people who have social networks respond better to health insults, and there is some evidence that they live longer, too."

Scharlach believes retirement communities are great for the people who like them, and he praises the sense of community that they create. Nevertheless, he says, "there is a question of access and a disparity of opportunities" in a system that makes retirement communities accessible to only the fraction of the population that can afford to live in them. "More than half of Americans above retirement age live almost exclusively on Social Security. That's not a whole lot of money. We have to structure the communities people are already in so people can stay in them."

What Scharlach prescribes, the residents of the Cloisters have already created for themselves. When they sit around their pool with the old friends they have coaxed to join them as residents and the people they have come to know since they moved in, talk rambles far and wide across politics, family, and condo business, but it returns often to the streets, stores, theaters, ethnic clubs, and workplaces of the Rockford where they spent seven, eight, nine decades building a life. About half of the residents report that their children and grand-children live elsewhere in America. "I could never tell my kids to stay here," says one of the women, "but I would never live anywhere else."

A Company Is Forced to Change

For thousands of people in Rockford, one manufacturer, the Wood-ward Governor Company, was the center of their working life for decades. Woodward, which makes energy control products, has been an important presence in the Rockford area since the 1870s. It was one of the groups of companies that high school graduates once depended on to all-but-automatically offer them a job. Woodward employees were intensely loyal to their employer, and with good reason. One might not relish every post the family-owned company assigned over a long career, but Woodward's workers long felt the force of the company's family-like values that made the workplace pull together.

"A big part of my life was taken up by the company and the people I knew there. Outside of work, my friends were Woodward friends," says John Elliott, a worker who began at Woodward in his teens and stayed until the company began to send strong signals that employees of his generation ought to leave, and offered incentives to get him out the door when he was in his early fifties. When Elliott played baseball, or took a weekend trip, his work pals were his companions. The clubs he belonged to were dominated by members from Woodward. For many families, Woodward was the company that hired their parents, their brothers and sisters, their aunts and uncles and cousins. In-house doctors, dentists, and nurses treated sick employees and their families. Long before family leaves were regarded as enlightened policies, and before they were mandated by law, Woodward actively encouraged them. "A big part of the Woodward culture used to be you were hired for life if you did what you were told," says a current executive. "That's not so anymore."

Older Workers, Teenage Wages

In recent years Woodward has more reliably instilled job insecurity, even in obedient workers. For older workers, the company has become something of a revolving door. It lets them go, brings them back for brief periods, or hires older workers who have never set foot in the company before, but come in at a low starting salary. It is still regarded as a great place to work, and the company gets high marks when compared to some of Rockford's other large employers, but it is more a nimble global conglomerate than a family these days—because it must be.

Woodward moved its headquarters out of Rockford to Colorado, and now has other important manufacturing centers in other U.S. cities, in Japan, China, and elsewhere. Woodward's China business made the company a favorite of investment portfolio strategists, who have repeatedly sung Woodward's praises on the strength that the development of China's urban infrastructure creates vast demand for Woodward products. The company sees it that way, too, and in 2009 announced a large expansion of its China business and plans to export more products out of China to other Asian countries. Its Rockford workforce is a fraction of what it once was.

Change in the company did not sit easily with management or employees. Woodward was, however, buffeted by global market forces that forced its hand. In the 1990s, when the aerospace industry was roiled by cuts in U.S. defense spending, Woodward suffered its first loss in its history, a shock that spurred drastic cost-cutting. Carol Smith, a human resources manager, describes those first waves of cuts, when many Woodward employees were enticed to retire early. "We offered an extremely generous package to early retirees. Workers who were age fifty-five or older and had ten years of service received a sum for every year at Woodward, a ten-thousand-dollar bonus, and a defined benefits plan [which gave them a traditional pension]."

Following the September 11, 2001, terrorist attacks in New York and Washington, the company cut back again. Among the company's products are governors that regulate the flow of fuel, water, and air in a wide variety of settings. Woodward products are used in conjunction with a huge variety of industrial applications essential to everyday life. Most of what it makes is deployed where energy is used, where it is converted from one form to another, where it flows through, and where its flow must be controlled. Woodward products are found everywhere in America's, and the world's power infrastructure. Because the aircraft industry is one of Woodward's main niches, when the 9/11 attacks hit, and the future of aviation was in doubt, Woodward cut from every limb of the company, and also from its core.

"It was a mistake," Smith says in retrospect. "A lot of people walked out the door who had skills and knowledge we still could have used access to. We lost experienced workers and important mentors." The company, which is now prosperous, finds that it often hires back the workers it lost, but they return as temps and part-timers. Smith also describes a revised attitude for older workers at Woodward. "The bad economy," she says, "actually stabilized our workforce." Which is to say that workers are nervous about leaving.

"From our standpoint we look for those workers fifty-five and older. They are more stable, their loyalty is better, they're more reliable." Smith says that it is harder to teach the attitudes needed to succeed at Woodward to younger people. "I just met with a young man who at nineteen is quitting to sell cell phones," she says, bewildered. "He said he wants more flexibility. Maybe he lives at home and has too much stability outside of work." Workers in the past, particularly the postwar generation that were John Elliott's peers, always thought they would do better than their parents. Smith thinks younger workers today do not see how they will even equal their parents. Rather than work hard and obey, younger workers choose lifestyles over money. If cell phone sales allows for more pleasures outside work, cell phone sales it is. Smith shakes her head. "Young workers, though, have their advantages. They catch on to computing immediately, and can do everything with it. Older workers are scared by the computers on the job. Some just can't make it."

Of the 206 workers Woodward took on in 2008, it let go twenty for poor performance. "Eighteen of the twenty were older workers who thought the work, the machines, and the computer screens were too complicated." Smith says many of the older workers could have stayed with the company. Woodward tries to move its hires to areas they can perform well in and tasks that do not require facing a computer. But, she says, the very pride and work ethic that makes older workers desirable can also get in their way. "When we look at the older generation here, older workers don't seem to have the same math skills as some of the younger ones; they can't think as quickly. We try to place the older ones in spots that are not too uncomfortable for them. We ask them a lot of questions before we hire them and we show them the machines. . . . But their pride won't allow them to say they're not up to the job." They'd rather struggle at tasks they do poorly at, Smith suggests, than admit they are not up to them.

Woodward would seem to have good reasons for steering its older hires first to jobs that require more brain than brawn. Some of the older workers dropped out, but others did fine. The physical work capacity of older workers falls far short of their younger peers. "The average physical work capacity of a sixty-five-year-old is about half that of a twenty-five-year-old worker," concluded a team of Canadian researchers in a review of dozens of recent studies on workers' physical abilities over time. "In general, functional capacities appear to decrease after the age of thirty with the declines in physical work abilities occurring at a younger age and exceeding those of either mental or social abilities. . . . These declines are associated with reductions in cardiovascular, respiratory, metabolic, and muscular functions, which are small to begin with, but culminate in an appreciable decrease in functional capacity between the ages of forty and fifty." Between ages forty and sixty, workers' capacity for sustained physical work drops by about 20 percent, and the decline accelerates thereafter.[18]

How Postponing Retirement Prolongs Learning

While older workers remain closer to their mental peak than their physical peak, how well one takes on new complex tasks depends very much on the kinds of work and intellectual challenges one is accustomed to. Older workers who have been lifelong learners on the job tend to continue to learn on the job as long as they stay with it and are in good mental health.

Woodward, which has no mandatory retirement age, can count on long, productive years from its engineers, lawyers, accountants, marketers, and managers who choose to stay on the job past their fifties and sixties. Some evidence suggests that one reason many older workers may not be up to date on computers is that they have expected to retire before new computer skills would have been demanded of them. If economic circumstance has now forced them back to work where computer skills are needed, they are out of luck. Recall that Robert Kane, the eminent geriatrician at the University of Minnesota, noted research that older workers tend to be most muddled in workplaces where technology changes often.

Yet, *adapting* to technology is also a skill, and with the right economic motivation (or fear) it may be better mastered. Older workers with more current computer skills, contrarily, tend not to be those who expect to exit the workforce in the near future. And relatedly, workers who expect to work past traditional retirement, and have incentives to learn new computer skills, learn better than those who plan to leave. Another noteworthy discovery is that workers who have learned new computer skills tend to be more enthusiastic about working more years than they were before they were tech-savvy.[19]

But there may be other factors at work, including the sober intuition of early retirees. Workers who hide their shortcomings may not be simply unable to take on unfamiliar tasks, they may be in declining health. There is some suspicion, for example, that the reason many early retirees (perhaps not those who were pushed off the job, but who elected to leave) suffer cognitive decline and health reversals after they leave the job is because they were in decline while they were on the job, but they didn't acknowledge it to others, or perhaps to themselves. Once they are no longer at work, they may look for medical attention they had put off.[20]

Early retirement, of course, can also improve people's general health and spark people to take on, and succeed at, new challenges, provided they do not suffer from a rapidly debilitating condition like Alzheimer's, wrecking memory, mood, or reason.*

A Life of Hard Work

At age eighteen, John Elliott began at Woodward at the bottom. He delivered parts to production lines within the factory. Over the years, he worked various machines, and then moved to service the company's customers in the field. He was a salesman and quality control manager. "I was in hydraulic controls for half my career," he says, "and then I transferred to the aircraft division." After thirty-five years of making, selling, and patrolling machines, he can take them apart and put them back together again, and knows every shortcut to get them humming again. He has the kind of deep knowledge that human resources manager Smith said left the building when the payroll reductions grew too indiscriminate. Elliott's last job at Woodward was serving as the assistant to the vice president in charge of public affairs.

"Woodward was one of the great Rockford companies and I was proud to be part of it. When I worked there, I was always very conscious that if I was out and about, even on my off-hours, I didn't want to embarrass the company."

Elliott, who says he loves to work, did not take a vacation day or sick day in his last ten years at Woodward. His first day off the job was the day he began his early retirement, at age fifty-three in the year 2000. "I don't have any regrets about leaving the company. But I thought the end came up awfully fast. I only had thirty days to make a decision." Elliott counts himself among the more fortunate of those Woodward encouraged to leave. His offer came with a good package, but, he says, the signs that the company expected him to go were delivered according to the science of modern workforce reduction, which demands that workers guess as to the potential cruelty of

---

* A 1999 Finnish study by J. Ilmarinen and J. Rantanen that tracked older municipal workers over more than a decade showed that one in three of the workers over fifty-one who were deemed poor at fulfilling work duties became disabled within four years of their evaluations. One in ten were dead by age sixty-two and only one in forty remained on the job at age sixty-two.

their employers, and be made to think the worst. Such tactics usually dodge the charge of age discrimination, in part because they offer a bittersweet measure of mutual benefit, and in part because those who take the packages are usually made to sign agreements that they will not sue. Vetted by lawyers, these tactics are a legal mix of cajoling and coercion, but to those who live through them, they feel like age discrimination with a velvet glove.

Elliott saw this firsthand, as he was subject to intimations of stronger downsizing tactics and less generous packages to come, and saw colleagues after him who were steered out on much harsher terms. After thirty-five years on the job Elliott felt too shocked to feel betrayed. The feeling hit him later on. Today, he has a mix of emotions, proud of the company and the years he worked there, but dismayed that the company that was his life could cast him out so forcefully. The most bitter part of the separation for Elliott, and his wife, Diane, was the loss of company-subsidized health insurance. "We were misled into thinking we'd have the same insurance as before." In practice, the Elliotts were saddled with a yearly insurance bill for a whopping $22,000. For the average earner in Rockford, that bill would consume nearly all his after-tax income. That, too, feels like age discrimination. For the Elliotts, it is an enormous burden, but they can cover it.

It helps that both John and Diane work. "People don't realize that when they retire it will cost more than when they worked," says John. "The reason is that you have more time. One of my friends who was let go—he didn't get the early retirement package—had to dig into his 401(k) retirement funds early. Now a lot of people are saying they have to work until they die."

Elliott, who has a hard time being idle for any reason, finds that even he is working more than he would otherwise choose to. One reason is that after years of relying on the Woodward pension plan, he was given a lump sum at retirement and forced to decide what to do with it all at once. "Our investment advisor put it all in the market in 2000 just before the Tech Bubble collapsed. We're a conservative family, and that was a big unknown. Nearly all our money was gone." Even a lifetime of private savings can offer little if the timing of one's retirement coincides with the all-too-frequent market meltdowns. Retirees are no longer long-term investors, and do not always have the luxury of waiting the years or decades necessary for their accounts to drift back to whole.

Going with the Flow

After suffering the loss of their retirement funds, John received a lifesaving call from a former colleague. "He was looking for someone with experience with Woodward controls." In 2002, Elliott started a consultancy expressly to work on projects for three other industry executives who themselves had started a business to service old Woodward equipment. "I started working with hydroelectric controller-governors that regulate the water flow through turbines used for power generation."

Many of the projects he was called on required him to repair Woodward equipment that the company could no longer service. Traveling to hydroelectric sites all over the world, Elliott routinely encountered dams that still had Woodward machines that were fifty years old, and sometimes older. He knows how to fix them, and it has made a good business. "I am earning more now than when I was with the company," he says. Elliott, who rarely left Illinois during his career at Woodward, now travels throughout North and South America to some of the most beautiful wilds in the hemisphere, to places where turbines in dams are powered by rushing rivers. Lands he knew little about before his new job, leave him breathless. Coming from the flat plains of the Midwest, he finds that the mountains of Oregon and Washington have given him a new sense of wonder. He marvels, too, at the equipment he helps keep running, some of these machines icehouse-sized and built in the Great Depression but still able to provide power and water to millions of people. Perhaps most surprising to him is his new view of how water flows, and how, over short slices of time, a rushing river is worth hundreds of thousands of dollars as it passes through dams. And he sees how without him there to untangle crises, without his experience at hand, the conversion of big flow into big dough might not happen. He compares himself to the younger engineers working for power utilities at the job sites. He says they are smart and capable and ready to learn, but lack the cumulative experience often needed to execute a sure fix. "I have the experience at troubleshooting the equipment, analyzing the structure, and know-how to use the resources at hand," he says. "I can eliminate a lot of root causes while younger people may not be able to break down the problem to work through it. They tend to reach for a quick fix that often means I will have to step in later. Someone could work at a power company for ten years and never see a problem. I've seen a lot of problems. I still see something new on every job, but I have the tools to make the fix."

Over the same time Elliott's work life has been transformed, the three-person start-up of Rockford industrial refugees is now a firm of seventy-five people, not counting the ten or twelve who work on contract like John. To some, this collection of castoffs might now appear to be part of a core creative class, though in America today they are part of a mass movement among one of the most creative classes of all, older entrepreneurs.

John's consultancy is not the only evidence of the creative business-stirring of older workers. Following John's retirement from Woodward, he and his wife, Diane, took on another business, too. "We bought a half acre, and ice cream came with it," John says about land they bought that was home to a seasonal soft-serve stand called The Dairy Depot. It needed sprucing up when the Elliotts took it over, and they did all the carpentry, painting, and mechanical work themselves. John's years at Woodward served him well. "I can fix anything," he says, "and a soft-serve ice cream machine is like a mini version of a power dam. If I couldn't service the machines, I know we couldn't make the business work." During the three-month summer season, the Elliotts serve eighteen thousand cones and sundaes in eight different flavors.

Entrepreneurs with Old Networks

While Rockford's college-educated young adults head for the exits, there are good reasons why an older entrepreneur might stay. Rockford has a pool of connections that can be networked. Elliott's consultancy could be run out of a mountain aerie with a phone and

Internet connection, but it would never have started, or flourished, without the people in Rockford who knew his skills and his manner and who trusted him. And what he learned in thirty-five years at Woodward made his consultancy possible.

"It is interesting to think about entrepreneurship and the advantages older people have when starting a businesses," says Dane Stangler, an analyst at the Ewing Marion Kauffman Foundation in Kansas City, an institution devoted to researching and promoting entrepreneurship. Stangler's research focuses on the connections between business start-ups, economic growth, and the fate of cities. "When you consider that people's life spans are growing longer by more than a year every decade, and when you think about what it will mean for people who retire at age sixty-five to still have twenty-five or more years to go, one starts to imagine how powerful their huge, deep well of networks can be in getting their own business off the ground and running."

Experience and networks count far more than money for entrepreneurs, Stangler says. That is where the older entrants, such as John Elliott, have colossal advantages. "There is also a viral element to entrepreneurship. The more people you know who are entrepreneurs, the higher the chances you will be one, too. You begin to see it as a conceivable option. A lot of entrepreneurship depends on exposure."

Entrepreneurship is often less the pursuit of the American dream than a reaction to the realities of the workplace. The average time men stay on the job as employees has dropped by six years since 1980 (women stay on the job slightly longer than men). "This is undoubtedly a phenomenon related to there being no lifetime employment anymore. A lot of people are pushed into entrepreneurship," says Stangler.

Many start-ups take on tasks that were once done in-house at bigger companies. "When Boeing builds a plane," Stangler notes, "it needs hundreds of companies to support it. A lot of new small companies do research and development for big ones." Then there are those companies that are designed mainly to be low-cost home businesses, but which nevertheless have potential to grow. Amazon.com and eBay allow others to set up shop and sell through their online portals, and together they have facilitated the creation of half a million businesses that sell out of virtual concession stands on the bigger sites. Stangler says that no one has a handle on the incredible diversity of new businesses being started.*

Old Innovators

Better understood, however, is who is starting all the new enterprises. Think beyond the idea, fed by the mythology of Silicon Valley, that most entrepreneurs in the United States are male tech hipsters with whiz-bang ideas, a little angel money, and a garage lit by midnight oil. The conventional wisdom is not altogether wrong. Maverick young techies are out there and they are one of the prime sources of the innovation that feeds growth and change in the economy of the United States, and other countries where business start-ups are valued and promoted. Stanford economist Paul Romer has long argued that economic growth depends to a great degree on the schemes of young creators, who in general tend to be—if not more skillful—more radical innovators than their older peers. Economic growth occurs, in his view, when resources are recombined in innovative ways that increase their value, and requires young thinkers, including entrepreneurs. Silicon Valley venture capitalists are famous for their dismissal of entrepreneurs over forty, and thirty already looks a tad long in the tooth for them, too. Chris O'Brien, a columnist for the *San Jose Mercury News*, one of the daily papers that cover Silicon Valley, caused a stir in late 2009 when he relayed remarks by Douglas Leone, a partner at VC giant Sequoia Capital, before an audience of students from MIT's Sloan School of Business. Sequoia, Leone said, focuses on entrepreneurs under thirty because those who are older aren't innovative. Leone also said he thought that in online fields, such as social media, younger entrepreneurs are a better bet because they are the users.

In fact, younger entrepreneurs are, proportionally, a shrinking

* While job instability spurs some people to start businesses, it dissuades others. Labor economists note that when unemployment is high, people in more stable jobs stay at them longer than they might have in a better economy. This is called "job lock."

group when compared to their elders. Entrepreneurial activity among Americans eighteen to forty-four years old has dropped significantly in the past decade. Among those under twenty-five, the rate is down the most, about 30 percent. At the same time the place of entrepreneurs over forty-five is growing, and among a newly studied group, entrepreneurs over sixty-five, the rate of entrepreneurship is impressively high: nearly one in every twenty adults in that age group starts, or tries to start, some sort of business.[21] In the United States, one in ten workers is self-employed, but among workers over fifty, one in six is self-employed. The more representative vision of the contemporary American entrepreneur might be a man or woman, fifty or older, who is capable of innovation but somewhat less likely to rewire the world. The great strengths of the older entrepreneur, after all, are his or her connections to businesses and processes in place.

Stealing the Promethean Fire?

There is some concern that the aging of America's entrepreneurial class could, over time, cost the nation some of its potential to innovate and grow. Countries such as China and Brazil have large groups of potential young entrepreneurs standing in the wings who could steal the Promethean fire that has led young American entrepreneurs to shake up everything from the information economy to the uses of our DNA. Countering that worry perhaps are some better promises. One is that older entrepreneurs will create jobs. Small business is America's greatest jobs engine. Stangler points out that of the millions of jobs added to the U.S. economy since the mid-1990s, nearly all of them came from start-ups that grew large and from small business. Payrolls at the old Fortune 500 industrial companies, on the other hand, are dramatically down. Another promise is that older entrepreneurs will be an increasingly central group within the creative class, revitalizing where they live. One reason people start new businesses is because they believe they can do a job or create a product that is better than what is already on the market. That's a pretty good description of the process of innovation. In addition to creating jobs and pumping up productivity, entrepreneurs are customers for the services and equipment other companies sell, and part of the creative mix in creative destruction. In Rockford, they may be the best chance to bring back the very industries that cast them out.

A Grandmother's Labors of Love

The generations in Rockford, and in America more generally, divide time and money in another realm outside the workforce: the economy of "grandfamilies." In it, grandparents, many of whom no longer work, are pressed to support and care for their grandchildren.

In a modest two-bedroom apartment in a housing development built to be affordable to families on government assistance, lives a sixty-three-year-old grandmother—call her Yvonne Flowers—who tends to her "grandfamily." At present, this includes two of her thirteen grandchildren. The apartment overflows with life. A forest of plants fills the living room. Kids' drawings fill the walls.

Yvonne is a nurturer. God, she believes wholeheartedly, sends her signs and counts on her to tend the living. Once, Yvonne recalls, her heart stopped for twenty-five minutes. A nurse at the hospital later told her she flatlined, but God intervened to save her. In prayer, Yvonne asked to live so that she could see her granddaughters, call them Tina and Val, grow up, go to college, and get married.

So far, the deal is holding. Yvonne survived near-death, and today lives with kidney disease by walking around with the portable apparatus for dialysis. She also suffers from diabetes, which requires daily insulin injections, usually administered by a granddaughter. Yvonne, though, still shops, cooks, cleans, and takes Tina and Val to church.

Yvonne has beat her odds. The medical literature on aging suggests that older people who worship in congregations or engage in regular, private religious observances tend to fend off death more successfully than those who do not devote themselves to religious practice.[22] The earthly reason for the benefit seems to stem from how religious practice offers fellowship, and thus wards off the symptoms of loneliness and isolation. Prayer and meditation can also influence how the body handles hormones that influence mental health.

Just how deeply Yvonne feels connected to her family and social network comes through in nearly everything she says. Her father and mother, though deceased, remain a strong presence in her life. To Yvonne, they still mediate her spiritual life and inform her commitment to her grandchildren. When she communicates family values down to the younger generation, it is with the voices of her parents in her head. The story of how her family moved from Alabama to the Northern states and how her father went from being a coal truck driver to a respected minister is often told; and the family photo album is well thumbed. When Yvonne recounts her story, her sixteen-year-old granddaughter is sent to fetch all the photos and mementos that go with it, and she knows precisely where everything is. The granddaughter also fills in when Yvonne struggles for a detail. These are tales ofttold, a hero's quest that took a black family out of the American South in the era of segregation and was aided by providence to gain respectability in a new home. Her family is not the traditional nuclear family she grew up in. It is extended and, in the past, would have come apart if Yvonne had not worked mightily to pull it together.

Yvonne was formerly a hairdresser and a cook. She worked in schools, in the homes of wealthy, white families, and in Rockford's social clubs. "In 1989, I left work in Rockford and went to Ohio to take care of my mother, who could no longer get around. My father was too old to help her, so I moved in and took care of her for two years." Yvonne says that her mother had run into trouble at a local nursing home that refused her good care. She suspects there were racist reasons for the poor treatment. "It was a town where they had the KKK, and I heard a lot of horror stories there."

Obama's Doctor on Institutional Racism

In general, African Americans use nursing homes far less than white Americans. Dr. David Scheiner is a white physician in Chicago who, prior to the 2009 presidential inauguration, was Barack Obama's longtime doctor and discussion partner on health-care policy. Scheiner, a thin, bald, bookish rapid talker known for spending far more time with his patients than the conventions of modern

American medicine encourage, listens for health clues in conversation and often hears the points of pressure, and of pride, within the families of those he treats.

He says that over the years, he has become a de facto geriatrician. He has a touch of Borscht Belt in him, too, and trades jokes with his patients so regularly that some come prepared with new jokes to tell him. Scheiner says that his patients have grown old with him, and for the most part, he adds, "they are in surprisingly good shape. I actually wonder how long they can go on in such good health."

Today about 70 percent of his practice is made up of African Americans in their sixties and older, including many in their nineties. Scheiner observes that among these patients there is a very strong distrust of institutional care. "The black families I see will avail themselves of all the social services and public supports they are entitled to," Scheiner says, "but they will make whatever arrangement within their families or extended families to keep elders out of nursing homes. People have this notion of the black family in America being this irreparably broken entity, but when I compare how my black patients care for members of their extended family— with grandparents caring for grandchildren, and nieces caring for their elderly aunts, and so on—I often think it is the families of my patients who are white that are more likely to be broken. The kids are separated from the parents, who are often left to fend for themselves. The families arrange for institutional care or for someone to come in—an immigrant caregiver, maybe—to pick up the roles the family members should be filling."

Yvonne, in Rockford, was a young grandmother at forty-six when she took in her then baby granddaughter, Tina, in 1993. A second grandchild, Val, who turned six in 2010, will likely still be part of the household when Yvonne reaches her midseventies.

Busy, Overworked Grandparents:
Granny Is the New Mommy

Yvonne's commitment to her grandchildren mirrors a resurgent role for grandparents in the United States. Drawing in part from

U.S. Census data from 2000, Amy Goyer, of the AARP Foundation Grandparent Information Center, reports that "30 percent of American children under age five are cared for by grandparents on a regular basis; 6 percent of all children live in grandparent-headed households in the U.S.; and 2.4 million grandparents in the U.S. are responsible for basic needs of grandchildren living with them." Goyer also notes that today, the grandparents who take on parental duties are rather young as a group. Seventy-one percent are younger than sixty. The expense of taking on grandchildren can have grave financial consequences in the long run. "Grandparent caregivers often spend down their retirement savings and are forced to give up their jobs to raise grandchildren. About 20 percent of the children being cared for by grandparents are living in poverty, with a higher incidence of physical, mental, and learning disabilities, and a third have no health insurance."[23]*

In the United States there is an even chance that a child in the primary care of a grandparent is cared for by a single grandmother. Only a very small percentage are cared for by single grandfathers. In many cases, too, the income offered to grandparents with dependent grandchildren by government assistance programs is an essential support, without which many grandparents simply could not, or would not, take on their grandchildren.

For Yvonne, who has the energy, spirit, and love to care for her two grandchildren, money is short. She has few work options, and probably could not return to work if a job opened up. She has two serious chronic conditions and a six-year-old at home, and grandparenting is her "job." Many grandparents with grandchildren to support find that the needs of the children force them back into the workplace when they thought they had retired. Many others find that having grandchildren at home keeps them from working. The local job market, child-care options, and the availability of income assistance influence the choice.

Yvonne's sons help out, but money that the threesome at home counts on often does not come through. "Santa promised my granddaughter a computer this year," Yvonne says pointedly, "but that didn't work out." Social workers in Rockford say it is unrealistic for

---

* The numbers for impoverished children in the U.S. are about the same.

grandparents to expect money from their children to help; they are rarely willing, and usually unable to contribute.

Grandparents of every racial and ethnic group are taking on more duties with grandchildren, though among African-American families the role of grandparent as guardian is pronounced. About one-quarter of guardian grandparents in the United States are African American, which is a little less than twice the proportion of African Americans' place in the U.S. population as a whole.* In Rockford, and throughout America, there is now the growing phenomenon of the dependent great-grandchild, a child born to an unwed teenage mother who is herself still the legal ward of a grandparent.

The Gigantic Economic Value of Grandparents

"Nearly all of my caseload, 93 percent, involves encouraging grandparents to take on their grandchildren and to keep the kids out of foster care," says Cheryl Davis, a social worker at Lifescape Community Services, a Rockford social service agency deputized by the State of Illinois to work with families and assign funds in cases where biological parents have for one reason or another been deemed unsuitable to care for their children. There are social and psychological reasons to place children in need with family members rather than foster care. Children seem, in general, to fare better with family members rather than in foster homes. And for the state, placing a child with family is far less expensive than foster care, too. Nationally, the average public cost of placing a child in foster care is about twenty-two thousand dollars a year, but placing one with a grandparent is just one-fifth as much.

Sometimes the parents themselves make the choice and abandon

* Non-Hispanic black Americans under the age of eighteen make up about 14 percent of the national population of children. Seventy-two percent of African-American children born in the United States are born to unwed mothers, compared to 40 percent of children born to unwed mothers overall. In 2007, there were 1.7 million American children born out of wedlock, a 25 percent jump since 2002. Of course, not all children born to unwed parents are born to teens. Nevertheless, after a fifteen-year decline in the rate of teen pregnancies, the numbers began to climb again in 2007.

their children. Sometimes the parents are jailed, or dead, or too abusive, or too much under the influence of drugs to be allowed a choice. Davis says that her requests usually meet strong resistance. "The grandparents often are not prepared or they are too stressed out to take on the responsibility. They may be at a point in their lives where they feel they can't handle it. A couple in their fifties may be looking forward to retirement and a big vacation they've planned for a long time, and then here come three little ones and they get very upset. I'd say in 50 percent of my cases, grandparents have a hard time with the idea, but end up doing what they can to make sure their grandchildren do not end up in foster care."

About one in twenty children in the United States are cared for by one or both grandparents, but Davis says the ratio for her jurisdiction is high and going higher. In 2009, her agency, which is not the only one serving Rockford, successfully convinced more than one hundred grandparents to take in grandchildren. But, she says, the numbers have been climbing with the bad economy, and her office was on track to handle two and a half times the number of cases of 2010. Despite the rise, she says, the public service agencies don't reach the large numbers of families that are off their radar.

Grandparents provide broad and underappreciated safety nets for families all over the world. Often they do so because they have the means and the time, but often their help demands heroic sacrifices. Usually when the issue of dependency arises in relation to aging populations, it is the worries about dependent elderly that come up. Yet older people often provide services at little or no cost, and most often actually pay out of their own pockets to provide services that keep the rest of productive society humming in the workplace and consuming outside it.

Recently Davis has helped organize community meetings she calls Grandparent Summits in Rockford to provide services and a sounding board. The most common regret grandparents express is that they are robbed of the experience of being a *grandparent,* and instead are put in the role of being a parent, with lots of extra baggage. "They have to start with the grandchildren's necessities, instead of spoiling them. They have to provide discipline, food, and set boundaries, rather than be the grandparents who indulge their grandchildren." Grandparents also ask for ways to alleviate the isolation their guardianship causes. Time the grandparents might otherwise spend with friends their own age, or in activities outside the house, gets spent instead on providing what the grandchildren need.

Moreover, the grandparents' efforts may be out of step with how people think children ought to be raised today. And they have ideas about spanking and other discipline that may not work, especially for older people whose grandchildren can threaten them. Not every "grandparented" family is as effusively loving as Yvonne's. Failed parenting has consequences across generations. Children who, for example, were abused are more prone later to be abusive parents and abusive caregivers. And their children can be abusive wards in their grandparents' homes, too. "We're seeing a rise in elder abuse right now," says Davis. "It is coming from cases where the child was in an abusive home." Davis sees a good number of the most troublesome cases work their way through the public agencies.

Overall, however, the grandparents provide family services—emotional values aside—on a massive scale. Using a conservative calculus, the Urban Institute estimates that in 2002, in the United States, grandparents—acting either as full-time or part-time caregivers—provided $39.2 billion worth of unpaid services to their grandchildren. When the care for older parents, spouses, and their own children is added in, Americans over fifty-five provided $100 billion in family care. Davis notes that among the clients in her caseload in Rockford, the grandparents who care for grandchildren are also caring for even more elderly parents or adult children who need support, too. In many cases, of course, these loving and self-sacrificing women will work until they literally drop—felled either by accident, or disease, or the accumulations of old age—at which time someone will have to care for them, too.

VULNERABLE, CHERISHED, FRAIL, KIND, BOTHERSOME, SWEET, EXPENSIVE, WISE, LONELY, AND IRRELEVANT: HOW DO WE SEE THE ELDERLY?

HENRY OLSEN LIVES ON THE NORTHWEST SIDE OF CHICAGO. AT ninety-one, he's wiry and ruddy-cheeked, and beneath his red watchman's cap, his thin, gray hair mats to his head. Henry's large glasses, circa God-knows-when, overwhelm his face and bounce on his boney nose when he talks. He nudges them constantly to align with his pale blue eyes, always blinking. Henry's nylon Windbreaker is also too big for him. Old pictures show him as a slight man, which makes the big jacket a mystery, as if it were something that he picked up for nothing. His frugality is extreme, and the striking, cumulative results of it recently put Henry in grave danger. In what would have been a tragic irony, Henry's life savings nearly ruined him. Without an extraordinary intervention, he may well have ended up penniless in a state nursing home, where he would have died alone.

Henry's caretaker today is Jenny, a fiery, middle-aged Puerto Rican grandmother who doesn't mind teasing him or bossing him around. She has also taken charge of the house. She says hers is a hard job, but Henry is basically healthy and friendly, an improvement for her. In one recent case, her elderly charge coughed rivers of blood. In another, a woman in her late eighties called her "momma" and acted like an infant. Then there was the lady who sat stonily in a recliner for weeks without saying a word, then one day just stood up.

Henry, however, talks a lot. He can be rude. "When I started, he told me to go to hell if I fought with him," says Jenny. "But I had to. He didn't hire me, and he didn't want me, but I still had my job to do. He was eating out of the same pot for weeks, scraping the mold away and cooking the rest. He ate off the floor. I had to tell him I was there to cook for him."

Henry is also sexist in his commentary, which is no surprise to his caregivers, but it is probably unwise, since in the last two years he has had eight women caregivers in the house and the women have all but taken complete charge of his life. His caregivers see him as an old-school racist, too, with an attitude likely learned in Chicago's older days of tribal neighborhoods.

But Jenny, who is dark-complexioned, does not hold Henry's prejudices against him. Old-school racism is one of the conditions of the job, like cleaning up blood and sputum or making small talk with a catatonic. On Jenny's days off, two black women, one Jamaican, replace her and there is no stereotype Henry leaves out when describing them. That's who he is, and the time he came from, Jenny says. No matter what, he still needs care and she's obliged to give it. And besides, over time, she says, he's learning to respect others more.

Henry has nice things to say about some of the women who have helped care for him, though the compliments, too, can be intemperate. "Every girl," he says, "has a different story to tell. A girl from Africa told me how to use a drum. I had a quiet Chinese girl from Taiwan who was like Suzy Wong [the Hong Kong "hooker with a heart of gold" from the 1957 novel and hit movie and play]. She really touched my heart. She had a couple of daughters and owned a building and said I could paint her in the nude. I would have done it, too, but she went to work in a chop suey joint before I got around to it."

Henry speaks plainly about what he hopes his "girls" will get around to. He asks Jenny for blow jobs. She sternly deflects the requests. Enduring them is also part of the job, but Henry's sexual badgering upsets her.

Jenny warns that Henry is in a foul mood because he has been forbidden to speak to his neighbor, who nevertheless has been poking around the back porch trying to get Henry's attention. Henry, Jenny says, believes his neighbor is his only true friend and he does not trust all the other people coming in and out of his house. He's afraid they are going to take everything from him.

A Chicago Boyhood

But after ten minutes of careful listening, Henry wades into conversation. A question about his childhood in Chicago of the 1920s cheers him up. Full of nervous pep, his talk is fast and unmediated as he recalls his life in exquisite detail. Born in Chicago to Norwegian parents, he attended the city's giant Lane Technical High School, where he emerged with high marks. Following graduation he earned a job at AT&T's Western Electric division and proved himself a gifted technician. Shortly after he began working, Henry's parents bought the house Henry still lives in, which he shared with his brother Arne for more than sixty years until Arne died in 2006. Meanwhile Henry was assigned to small district workshops and big factories that turned out telephones and nearly all the kinds of equipment needed to keep the phone system up and going. Western Electric's factory complex outside the city employed forty-five thousand people back then and over time the company provided a road to the middle class for hundreds of thousands of people, including large numbers of white immigrants from central and northern Europe who congregated in neighborhoods around the plants.

But Western Electric started to slide toward oblivion in 1984. It stopped making telephones in the United States in 1986 and came to a final end in 1995 when its assets were split up among a number of other American telecommunications companies.

By the fall of 2008, a few weeks after Jenny began work in the house, the place was still a maze of stacked papers piled high with every scrap that ever entered the house. Arne and Henry had hoarded everything.

"There were boxes and boxes," Jenny recounts, "filled with

T-shirts, women's underwear and negligees. There were big stacks of letters, in English, all about sex, from a woman in Mexico." There were untouched groceries from 1989. The stench of mildew and rodent pervaded the house. The mold and animal dung were a life-threatening hazard to Henry, who relies on a cardiac pacemaker. The stench, now confined to the still untidy basement, wafts up from the cellar door, but the house gets a daily wash of fresh air and it's the aroma of a hot lunch that dominates the dining room.

Recently, with help, Henry found some sixty-five-year-old pictures of his family, brown and spotted but still in frames, and, in an attempt to resurrect his more normal past, Jenny tacked the photos up on the walls. One shows Henry with friends and family in Norwegian skating gear as if they are out of a Sonje Henie film.

"Yeah, uh-huh, that's us. We're in Norway," he says. Asked if he skated in Chicago, Henry says yes, and points to a picture of himself on the ice with friends in a local park. "I had a girl and we went skating. She was real nice to me, and I liked her. We'd twirl around the pond and I saw her a lot." Tears come to his eyes, and he's soon overcome. "She liked me, and I liked her, too. I don't know why nothing came of it."

He talks on and on, nearly uninterruptedly, describing classrooms, teachers, parties, workmates, family members, and the recent injustices perpetrated by government officials who have stepped in and taken charge of his life.

The Frugal Millionaire

In the 1920s, AT&T began one of the world's first employee stock ownership plans. Henry acquired a small number of shares, adding more year after year. For decades AT&T stock was the most widely held stock in the world, and a reliable performer. Hundreds of thousands of employees took advantage of the company's share-purchase program, though few had Henry's discipline or longtime horizon. Later in life he changed jobs and became a technician at Zenith back when Zenith, a company that pioneered the remote control and "pay television," was one of the leading makers of TVs and radios in the world. (Zenith lives now in name only, its remnants long since transferred to a Korean conglomerate.) He received Zenith stock, too. Meanwhile his AT&T stock grew in value.

"Little by little, my shares piled up. They split and split again, and what do you know?" Henry asks rhetorically. His investment history flies in the face of the accepted wisdom that argues against betting too much of one's nest egg on just a few stocks. He rode AT&T and Zenith all the way up and had the luck or smarts to get out at the right time, before the forces of global competition wrecked both companies. With poor timing he would have been wiped out, too.

Henry has lived long past the companies he worked for, an increasingly common experience. Former icons of economic permanence, such as Western Electric, are now proof of impermanence in an age where, on average, large public companies last for no more than fifty years. For those lucky few, such as Henry, who play their financial cards right, the compounding that comes with reaching age ninety can be spectacular. So much so that the world's newspapers in recent years have carried recurring stories of frugal blue-collar workers and teachers who were stealthy long-term investors and left large sums to unsuspecting charities or schools.*

Henry is frugal, but if he was once stealthy, he can no longer keep his own counsel. "Today I am worth four million dollars," he

---

* A few of the recent bumper crop of unlikely millionaire benefactors: Michigan teacher Edna Diehl, who died at eighty-eight in 2006, willed $1.3 million to the district she worked in for twenty-nine years. • Sheila Mair, eighty-eight, a "modest," retired teacher in Scotland, who passed away in 2007, left £4 million to charities in Scotland. • Friends of Toronto elementary school teacher Roberta Lantry, who worked for fifty-five years and died at eighty-nine, "didn't know she had two nickels to rub together" and were surprised by her C$4.3 million bequest to the Nature Conservancy of Canada. • A ninety-one-year-old tool-and-die worker who retired in his early fifties left $600,000 to a Michigan hospital after freezing to death in January 2009 in his home after his electricity was shut off due to an unpaid bill. • Walter Schmitt of Gresham, Nebraska, a ninety-four-year-old retired blacksmith who never went to college and never married, lived in "Spartan quarters," and dressed in bib overalls, left $3.5 million to the University of Nebraska in 2009. • Joe Temeczko was a solitary handyman in Minnesota, a Polish immigrant who once worked on the Statue of Liberty, and someone people mistook for a homeless "bagman." He died at age eighty-one, one month after the September 11, 2001, attacks on the United States. Just before he died he altered his will, leaving $1.4 million to renovate a park in New York City to commemorate the 9/11 victims.

announces. Like other myriad facts of his life, the stunning admission just tumbles out. He smiles, then sits up straight. "That's right, I have four million dollars. How about that?"

This isn't the claim of a mad old man. His appointed attorneys confirm his accounting is up to date. But it's an astonishing admission for a man who minutes earlier seemed to border on paranoia. Because Henry's memory remains sharp, his hearing good, and his conversation highly articulate, people easily overlook his dementia. It results from damage to the frontal lobes of his brain, the centers of logical thinking, self-awareness, and social moderation. The condition robs Henry of much of his judgment.

The open, unfiltered quality of his conversation may also be a symptom. Hyperorality, a symptom of dementia that causes sufferers to put inappropriate objects in their mouths, may cause Henry's lewd advances toward Jenny. Henry's condition may have gone undiagnosed for years, maybe decades.* Frontotemporal dementia accounts for less than one in twenty cases of the 4.6 million new cases of dementia worldwide. The population that shares Henry's condition in the United States is between 140,000 and 350,000, which is still large. Barring a radical breakthrough, that number will climb as the population of elderly grows disproportionately to the whole population. By 2040, when all living baby boomers will have passed into the group at highest risk, the world's population of demented will climb to 81 million people, more than three times today's afflicted.

By Henry's own account, his younger brother minded much of their business, and while Arne lived, he held things together for both of them. But eighty-seven-year-olds cannot take care of their ninety-year-old brothers forever.

---

* In a 2003 study in the *Annals of Internal Medicine,* a team of American researchers concluded around one-half of dementia sufferers are never diagnosed. Olsen's dementia, so far, has spared him the impulse to wander far beyond his own yard and neighborhood. Among the demented elderly the tendency to wander can be so strong it has become a focus of public health and safety officials. In May 2010 the *New York Times* noted that for the first time—and for the foreseeable future—the most common cases of missing persons now handled by some large police departments involve elderly victims of dementia.

The Sharks Move In

After Arne's death, Henry grew depressed and lost control of his daily affairs. A faraway cousin appeared at Henry's house and went through the brothers' records. She then hurriedly found a lawyer and soon pressured Henry into signing a power of attorney that granted her control of all of Henry's assets and created a draft of a new will that granted her all of Henry's estate. Before the papers were finalized, money began to move out of his accounts. Henry wandered among the small neat yards of his neighborhood talking openly to anyone who would stop.

A middle-aged neighbor, an unemployed man with time to spare, took an interest in the ramblings of the old man. The two talked daily. Henry laid out his current situation, his loneliness, his frustrations, and his finances. Again, in short order, the neighbor presented Henry with a new set of papers assigning the power of attorney to him, which would have transferred to the neighbor control of everything Henry had. The neighbor removed items from the house and began selling them online.

The cousin, sensing her plan unraveling, alerted lawyers in the office of the Cook County Public Guardian, a government agency charged with taking care of citizens—children, disabled adults, and frail elderly—who cannot run their own affairs and are easily, and too often, abused or exploited. A social worker from the Guardian's office visited Henry. He resisted, but the social worker persisted with the investigation. Recognizing a pattern of financial abuse, which Guardian staffers see hundreds of times a year, the office moved in and put a legal wall between Henry, his cousin, and the solicitous neighbor.

"Our experience shows that if we didn't act, Henry would have soon lost everything," says Wendy Cappelletto, an attorney for the Cook County Public Guardian who is in charge of getting elderly victims into the Guardian's protection. "I am convinced that Henry's money would have drained away, his house [would have been] remortgaged, and the money spent and he would have been placed in a nursing home to wither away alone. I suspect the neighbor also has a version of Henry's will lying around, too, with the neighbor as beneficiary."

"Someone Is Going to Have to Care for These People"

Following the social worker's report and a medical exam that diagnosed Henry's dementia, Henry found himself a ward of the county. The Guardian's office lined up caregivers to help him at home and hired lawyers to interview him and help redraft his will so that it was in line with lifelong goals of his that are surprisingly philanthropic. Among the papers that emerged out of the vast piles in the house were hundreds of small canceled checks, most for twenty-five dollars, sent to a wide assortment of charities over the years. Meanwhile, Henry's house is getting a hundred-thousand-dollar makeover that clears away the hoarded mess, replaces mold-infested walls, and rebuilds them, shores up the structure, replaces tumble-down steps, and installs a new roof.

"We use his money on him," Cappelletto says, "and it is making a big difference. He likes us now, and trusts us. It's good he has the funds."

Henry's story might seem extreme, but the most extreme facts of his life are the ones that are now, or soon will be, universal. That he had no children or reliable relatives to care for him in old age makes Henry more of a trendsetter than an outlier. In the coming half century, much of the world will be childless or so separated from their one or two children that hundreds of millions of people will have no more familial resources than Henry has had.

"We see it already in Chicago," says Cappelletto. "Our job is to serve people who have no one else to turn to, whether because they have no family or friends to help; their families are dead or far away, abusive or uninterested; [and] sometimes because [these family members] were abused as children by our wards. Our rolls are going way up and they are nowhere nearly as large as we expect them to be as the population of people in the older age brackets goes up and up. It's going to be someone's job to care for all these people, and I have a hard time seeing how society will manage. It's a big, big problem."

Henry will likely live three or four more years. If he makes it to one hundred, he'll probably make it another two years after that.[1]

One hopes he'll enjoy the rest of his life in his own, tidy home, free from abusers and fear, telling the tales of his life that bring a distant time vividly into the present for those lucky enough to hear them.

Legally Scamming the Elderly

Henry's case is not unusual. Older people often have significant sums of money that younger people want so badly they will counterfeit friendship in order to quietly steal the desired assets. But what happens when money is lost but no law is broken? What is the definition of mental incompetence and what is the difference between that and plain old bad judgment?

In the United States, the sales practices that the financial services industry used with the elderly have come under extra scrutiny since 2007. That was when the credit crisis caused all sorts of shaky retirement schemes to collapse; the courts were then besieged with suits brought on behalf of elderly investors claiming their financial advisors should have taken their elderly clients' expressed wishes *less* seriously and their age-related needs and addled brains *more* seriously. In other words, the suits on behalf of older people are demanding that older people should have been discriminated against by younger people.

This is a strange and slippery slope. Age discrimination, as it is described in the literature on aging, occurs in everyday social settings, in commerce, and in the workplace, and is a practice that both mocks the intelligence and wisdom of the elderly and fails to take full account of the epidemic in dementia. Discrimination happens when people deny or defer the reality of aging, but also when they exaggerate it, or sometimes, take a person's aging for what it is, then exploit it.

The case of Robert J. Pyle, a California widower in his eighties, became a cause célèbre epitomizing the seeming contradiction between the elderly's demands for independence and society's insistence that the elderly receive more attention and care. Charles Duhigg of the *New York Times* wrote about Pyle's plight in a long story on Christmas Eve 2007, and the story, a real-life holiday weeper, pitted one man's pride and frailty against greedy friends and the cold, impersonal whims of the marketplace.[2] The story also spawned a flood of comment by senior-law lawyers, watchdogs' newsletters, and outraged citizens, all of which was matched by a public campaign by the insurance industry to discredit Pyle.

In 1999, Pyle, a retired aerospace engineer, was a man of some financial means who once had coordinated teams of engineers on highly complex technical projects at defense contractor Lockheed Martin. Pyle owned a house worth $650,000 and had half a million dollars stowed in the bank. But Pyle's emotional resources had been low after his wife died, following a lengthy illness. After many months of solitude, Pyle warmed to a neighbor, a single mother in her forties who stopped by to chat and made him smile.

With Pyle's encouragement, and his services as a driver, the woman found work as a cleaner. Pyle, who controlled his own finances, began to lend the neighbor money for her rent. Later he lent her money for a bail bond to spring her from jail after she was caught shoplifting, and still later he paid bail for her boyfriend. He lent them $40,000. Pyle told the newspaper none of it was repaid, but he also said that didn't deter him from cosigning for two cars for the woman and her family. In all, he lent the woman about $209,000, either directly or in deals with her creditors, and gave her at least twice that much in cash.

Mr. Pyle's stepchildren made halting efforts to inquire and intervene, but shied away from fully interrogating him out of respect for his privacy and dignity. Pyle apparently offered no information to them because he was ashamed. Short of money, he obtained a large loan against his house, but not enough to dig himself out of debt. He refinanced his home again, through a broker who extracted $33,000 in fees on a $352,000 loan, and soon found he could not make the monthly payments. A spokesperson for the loan company told the *Times* that they did not "have a responsibility to tell him this probably isn't going to work out . . . [or] to tell [customers] how to live their lives."

The lender moved to foreclose and seize Pyle's house. He refinanced again, on worse terms. Pyle tried to refinance his house once more, but was rebuffed by a nineteen-year-old mortgage broker who said Pyle was too great a risk. Instead, the young broker offered to buy the house himself and negotiated a price 20 percent below the house's $539,000 appraised market value. Ruined and broken, Pyle moved into a small room in his stepdaughter's house from where he pondered how he had engineered his Job-like fall.

Unlike Job, Pyle will not have God to restore him, but since he's a Californian there is the hope of a remedy from the state's courts, which tend to side with underdogs. At age eighty-one, Pyle filed suit to recapture some of the million dollars-plus he had lost over the previous eight years. The companies and salespeople he dealt with are the defendants.

The case would be merely a curiosity except for the fact that, in the United States, lawsuits by people who are competent to deal with most daily activities are claiming that their age alone makes them plainly incompetent to handle their financial affairs. So much so that the bankers, brokers, and other people who have financial dealings with the elderly ought to have taken extra careful measures to protect their clients from their decisions, no matter how forcefully or freely expressed.

In California, the state's law against elder abuse makes the suits promising because it sets the standard of financial abuse as anything "obvious to a real person." Pyle was not acting strangely, or suffering from obvious (to a physician) brain damage. Pyle was just old. A bit forgetful, very lonely, and, according to some of his older California friends, part of a generation that is too trusting.

Pyle was plainly abused by a succession of low-life characters and predatory financial institutions. But was it bad behavior plain and simple, or was it a special form of bad behavior that preyed on the age-related limitations of an old man?

Despite claiming in his suit that he was incompetent, Pyle told the *Times* that he still meant to hold on to his independence, or what was left of it. To give Pyle's paradoxical argument for autonomy the benefit of the doubt, it sure seems as though he had some method to his madness when he refinanced his home three times at absurd prices, hoping perhaps that he could stay in the house on the banks' dimes while the clock ticked down on his last remaining years. One facet of the U.S. mortgage market laid bare by the financial collapse is that older borrowers were sometimes party to the schemes of shady brokers that gave the older residents homes they could live in for a while, even if they could not otherwise afford them. Pyle, after all, found three institutions and completed three rounds of complex paperwork to get each of his deals done. He managed to get all the legal work arranged for the sale of his house. These aren't trivial tasks.

So, which is it? Should Pyle be accorded his independence and respected as an autonomous person? Or, should he be protected? If it is some measure of both, that may not be so easy to arrange unless we are willing to aggressively evaluate the cognitive state of older people before they are in crisis. Or, alternatively, specify an age, say seventy-three, when Pyle says his troubles began, at which the elderly are officially dubbed vulnerable and their independence is challenged. The lawsuits aim in that direction, but people who are still capably in charge of their affairs will push back, and will be quick to hire lawyers of their own should others threaten their autonomy.

Checking Out the Big Ears and Saggy Cheeks

The cases of Henry Olsen and Robert Pyle are disturbing, in part because it is so easy to see how they happened. Old people get lonely and vulnerable. And their frailties are easy to identify. Almost everyone can do it—and does.

Even by age two, children can already estimate the ages of adults around them. We get better at estimating ages as we mature, and by adulthood get very good at sorting people by age and at estimating, within four years, how old they are. Mostly we look at others' faces to judge.

We rely on several clues based on what we all know about the way people change over time. Matthew G. Rhodes at Colorado State University has cataloged the changes to faces.[3] In childhood, as the face grows, it gets remodeled. Brains are large in young children because their brains are more developed than their physical features, such as their jaws and noses, which take awhile to fill out. Eyes look big, because the other parts of the face are still relatively small. (It is a little harder to judge the age of older people with eyes that are big relative to the rest of their faces.) Foreheads grow and slope more, noses and nasal bridges fill and create a more angular impression. Overall, features appear to move up the face as the jaw grows in.

At age twenty, when most people have stopped getting taller, the face is still a work in progress. Noses and ear cartilage get bigger and the skin of the face changes, growing less smooth. As people get into their thirties and beyond, the tissue that connects the skin of the face to the bones underneath stretches out, and the fat under the skin begins to disappear, making the whole face sag. Smile lines, wrinkles, and ripples appear. Skin gets thinner, more translucent (Photoshop-in smoother skin on an older person's picture, and age estimates for that person will get wildly inaccurate). Hair grays and thins. We lose some teeth and the others change. Eyebrows grow thicker. There are also cranial changes that alter the geometry of the face. Changes in the eyes are one of the biggest clues (masking the eyes thwarts good guesses, which is why older people often look better in sunglasses). When people size up others, they look at multiple clues, and the aging face offers such a profusion of clues that they can be checked and cross-checked against one another. If the skin looks great after dermabrasion or plastic surgery but the whites and pupils of the eye look more timeworn, that may make age seem more indefinite, but not unambiguously younger.

Clues in the face are so plentiful and powerful that even machines can read them. Automated facial recognition is already in place at public places and businesses throughout the world. Facial recognition systems capture images of people who pass within a radius of forty yards or more of a video camera; and, with an algorithm that accounts for the subtle changes in the way a person looks over time, the system matches a person's face as it appears in the present to a database of faces kept in a computer server. If the face on camera is also in the system, the system will most likely make the match.

Some systems claim to get accurate matches more than 90 percent of the time. (In 2009, I attended a demonstration by a Southern California company that sells facial recognition systems to the U.S. military, and went with my identical twin brother. The system could tell even us apart.) Computer scientists in China and Australia[4] have been developing algorithms for "automatic age estimation," which identify the age, not the identity, of persons from their faces. The system analyzes facial features against a massive database of faces pictured at different ages. The experimental version has been surprisingly accurate and hard to fool.

It is not hard to imagine the Big Brother-uses of facial recognition software, whether it searches for people's identities or their ages, or both. But should there be alerts when older people are amassing in larger than usual numbers in the malls, trains, bus stations, and public squares? In Tucson, Arizona, software tells local officials there is a traffic snarl about to unfold. In China, where the over-fifty population is the group most likely to gather, protest, and make a ruckus, officials may have strong reasons for knowing how old people are when they enter a public place.*

Look Your Age

I am three years older than Susan Boyle, the frumpy midlife sensation whom audiences laughed at when she galumphed on stage for the first time on *Britain's Got Talent*. The legend that grew out of Boyle's smashing success on the British talent show was that she had tried to screw up her courage for TV talent contests in the past, but had buckled out of fear that youth and beauty were valued above vocal talent. Even when her former vocal coach encouraged her on to *Britain's Got Talent*, he reportedly warned Boyle " . . . she was too old and that it was a young person's game." If, like Susan Boyle, the person is doughier than the television norm, that adds extra years to audiences' best guess on age because people on TV

---

* A Chinese friend of mine, a computer scientist I met in Silicon Valley, was one of the Tiananmen Square protesters during the violent crackdown in Beijing in 1989. He did a postdoctoral fellowship at a West Coast university, where he specialized in optical identification systems. Today he runs a company in China that provides the Chinese government with intelligence surveillance systems, the kind meant to quash events like Tiananmen before they happen. Two groups that often try hard to command attention of the regime with demonstrations in China's public places are older farmers who have been pushed aside (and often have been forced off their land) by development, and the religious group Falun Gong, a spiritual movement made up mostly of middle-aged and older people.

are expected to do everything possible to make themselves look as young as possible.

So if Susan Boyle looked like a real forty-seven-year-old, her apparent age in Television Land was nearer to sixty. The audience for the show, perhaps prompted by the hosts, screwed up their faces and shook their heads as Boyle took the stage. The talent judges asked what she had, and Boyle wiggled her hip suggestively like a cartoon streetwalker, accentuating the first impression that she was a dotty old hag with a foolish dream to be a sexy pop star.

Of course, the whole Susan Boyle episode may have been a clever ruse. Television producers have in the past habitually craved shows that serve the eighteen-to-thirty-five-year-old demographic. But in aging societies where money, and the power to decide how it is spent, still often resides with baby boomers and their parents, reality shows such as *Britain's Got Talent, American Idol,* and *Dancing with the Stars* have shown the power of programs that attract older viewers, even if they attract them unintentionally. In the United States, baby boomers watch some thirty-nine hours of television a week, twelve hours more than the generation recently out of college, who are glued to the Internet and their cell phones. *Variety,* the entertainment trade magazine, reports that the median age of the audience of the major U.S. television networks is now north of fifty, older than the eighteen-to-forty-nine-year-old demographic big media long coveted most.

Appealing to older audiences makes economic sense. *Dancing with the Stars* and its equivalent shows in other countries aim squarely at the idea that vigor, risk-taking, and sexual display are appropriate at any age. It sets us up for a world in which people add years to their lives but don't add restrictions. A world where one can act young, provided one consents to a few constrictions: if you sing past forty-five, and are not already a pop star, sing stirring ballads from musicals; if you dance and aren't already a rapper and a grinder, stick to ballroom. Unless you want to be a novelty act, the public expects you to act your age.

Will that change? Biology and society will have a say, and they may not agree.

Seeing the Old People

As the world around us ages, we will be summing up older people in our view more often, not less. Want to make a quick trip to the grocer? Avoid the line with the octogenarians, or speed up the line by helping the older people empty their carts. Want to get across town by car? Watch out. The driving population is aging. By 2030 in the United States, one in four drivers will be over sixty-five years old, up 10 percent from today. At the office, in the mall, or in the park we will be watching people's gaits, listening for quick clues to whether they are coherent, unduly grouchy, or too trusting. We will be navigating a world that is home to ever more people in the stage of life when people with age-related setbacks are omnipresent.

The complaint that society ignores older people will soon be an absurdity. Too much of society will *be* older people. Daily life will mold to the contours of an older world, and our instincts and generalizations about older people will often guide us whether or not we have a firm idea of how to define who's older, who's old, and who's extremely old. Stereotypes about older people will have more influence on our daily interactions, not less.

Our heads are filled with stereotypes, and when we journey through an ever-older world we will reference them. A body of scholarship is taking shape in academic psychology that describes the complex factors that produce stereotypes, and it is overthrowing the conventional view that stereotyping is always bad, that it is a "pathology of social cognition, neither based on experience, nor changeable based on experience."[5]

David J. Schneider is a professor at Rice University in Houston and author of the 2004 *The Psychology of Stereotyping*, an exhaustive exploration that has become a central text on the topic. Schneider notes that since the 1930s, there have been more than five thousand empirical studies looking at the psychology of stereotyping. Unsurprisingly, the inquiries picked up steam as academic interest in ethnic, racial, and gender divides exploded, in parallel with civil rights movements across the globe. As attention turns to the politics of an aging world, academia has begun to shine a brighter light on the attitudes underlying age discrimination.

Schneider's own conclusions draw from contemporary cognitive psychology. Cognitive theories probe the fundamental processes that make intelligence happen. A core belief in the field holds that intelligence is a collection of sets of information and a mix of processes that combine and configure information in them. One of cognitive psychology's powerful early insights is that it is in people's "cognitive nature" to categorize other people as "buckets" for traits, physical features, expectations, and values.[6] We fill people with collections of features that become their stereotype, because our cognitive processes are constructed to do just that. In this view, stereotyping is a "central, primitive, hardwired cognitive activity." To give it up, Schneider says, we would have to abandon our ability to generalize, a bargain no one would make.[7]

Beginning in the 1970s, psychologists started to look beyond how we tended to place other people in certain categories and began exploring the underlying cognitive processes that lead people to stereotype others, tying stereotyping to the fundamental ways people process information. Rather than always being the product of corrupt minds or diseased culture, stereotyping is something people just do.

Why People Don't Like Old People

Many of us know healthy, active, vital older people who defy the usual negative views of the elderly. But they don't just fight for dignity with younger people, but also with peers. A number of studies show that older adults who perform under the shadow of stereotypes acquire the traits of that stereotype. Make them believe their class has poor memories or cannot do math as they used to, and they will wilt on memory and math tests.

Thomas Hess at North Carolina State University tested the memories of two groups of people between the ages of sixty and seventy. The first group was issued the test after being told that those in their age group, because they were older, could be expected to perform poorly. His experiment was designed to create the impression that the test givers had already stereotyped these older test takers and looked down on them. "Such situations," Hess reflected, "may be a part of older adults' everyday experience, such as being concerned about what others think of them at work having a negative effect on their performance—and thus potentially reinforcing the negative stereotypes."

The experimenter took pains not to stigmatize a second group in any way. Not only did the first group underperform the second group, but the differences were greatest among the subjects who had the highest levels of education. "The positive flip side of [the experiment]," Hess said, "is that those who do not feel stigmatized, or those in situations where more positive views of aging are activated, exhibit significantly higher levels of memory performance. . . . The take-home message is that negative social factors may have a negative effect on older adults' memory performance."[8]

In a three-year study of Americans between the ages of seventy and ninety-six, psychologist Becca Levy and her colleagues at Yale University yielded the startling finding that elder individuals' own stereotypes about aging influence how well their senses work.[9] The elderly legitimately complain about hearing loss; it is one of the most common hardships of aging. Yet the Yale researchers found that subjects who had the most negative view of aging suffered the greatest hearing loss over the thirty-six months. Looking at other cultures, Levy discovered that elderly who live in lands where the stereotypes are less stigmatizing and more reverential suffer less hearing loss.[10]

Stereotypes of the elderly, it turns out, are a complex mix of positive, indifferent, and negative, and views of the elderly as warm and caring, or ineffectual and incompetent can be just as commanding in our calculations as the most boorish insults.[11] And while some cultures may hold the stereotypes in slightly different measure, the mix of views appears to be fairly universal. Studies conducted by Harvard's Amy Cuddy and others looked at attitudes held by about twenty-four different American social groups: Asian Americans, disabled people, homeless people, and so on. Over and over again, "elderly people" were described as highly warm but incompetent. The only other two groups that were described similarly were disabled and "retarded" people. Other studies show that the stereotypes attached to age override the powerful gender stereotypes that people hold about men and women. Both old men and old women are typed as being less ambitious, less responsible, and "more feminine and less masculine" than young people of either sex. Ouch!

Pan-Cultural Ageism

In an international study that looked at the attitudes of college students in Belgium, Costa Rica, Israel (Arabs and Jews), Japan, Hong Kong, and South Korea, students everywhere saw elderly people as warm, lacking ambition, and incompetent. Everywhere, too, the young people viewed older people as low-status. In a study that focused on Hong Kong, attitudes toward the elderly were particularly demeaning. "Ageism," says Cuddy, "is pan-cultural."

Modernity may be to blame, Cuddy and her colleagues say. When societies move from farm to city, industrialization lowers the status of older people in several ways. It increases their numbers by giving them longer lives, institutionalizes retirement, and denies older people their status as productive participants. Modernization has tended to make people's skills obsolete as they age and leaves them inept in new fields, and therefore troublesome to employ. Modernization has also set young people in motion, creating a transient class less tethered to older relatives for practical and emotional support. And tied up in all of the change is the devaluation of the older person's role as wise one. Books, newspapers, electronic media, and peers all inform younger people about what's current, while older people's memories, and the oral traditions they carry, no longer hold much stock.

Cuddy's analysis most likely describes the attitudinal backdrop to the aging of the world's population that will be in effect for some time to come.

"We know that stereotypes are pretty sticky and that they are maintained over time in the face of lots of counterevidence. . . . Even as we all age, we tend to think of old age as a point off in our futures," says Jim Sherman, a veteran professor and Indiana University psychologist with a full, white beard and white hair, who graduated from college in the early 1960s and has been teaching for more than forty years. "My friends all talk about the elderly as people in their eighties, but, hey, we're elderly."

Sherman was one of a group of academics who advised Barack Obama's first presidential campaign on strategies to unseat commonly held stereotypes that conservative Americans often hold about Democrats, urbanites, and minorities. If ethnic or gender typing is an analog to stereotyping of the elderly, society is in for a long run of negative attitudes and everyday practices, by young and old alike.

Similarly, a look at ageism in Tucson, Arizona, one of America's top destinations for retirees, found that the concentration of older people magnified negative stereotypes of the elderly. Locals held particularly strong and harsh opinions about how the elderly supposedly snarled up traffic, and how they were "despised" for dominating local political debates with calls for lower taxes and cuts in education spending for the young.[12]

Why We Fear the Old

Robert Butler, the pioneering gerontologist who died in 2010 at the age of eighty-three, popularized the term "ageism" in a large body of work on the subject that he began in the late 1960s. He was also the founder, president, and CEO of the International Longevity Center, one of the world's leading institutions for research and advocacy on issues related to aging. Writing in 2006, Butler argued that ill-treatment of the elderly stems "from deeply human concerns and fears about the vulnerability inherent in later years of life" and that these feelings "translate into contempt and neglect."[13] There is, in this view, something primal and "innate to the human condition" in the way we categorize and then demean older people. If Butler, who was a psychiatrist by training, was right, the mistreatment of older people is like the revulsion toward lepers. We fear that if we get close or extend a kindly hand we'll end up as they are. Except, in the case of lepers it is untrue—leprosy victims do not spread the disease to people who pass by them. In the case of the elderly it is inevitably true. Thus ageism's omnipresence.

Butler's view draws on the tenets of "terror management theory," a strain in psychology that grows out of the work of anthropologist Ernest Becker in the 1960s and 1970s. Very simply put, the theory holds that people spend their lives engaged in the work of survival, managing the terror of death and avoiding thoughts of their demise. To the theory's adherents, our need to avoid the terror of death gives rise to religion (people often grow more religious as they age), the formation of groups, and the willingness to see older people as beings very different from ourselves.

According to Butler, ageism is expressed in the everyday language used to describe old people, terms such as "dirty old man" and "greedy geezer," which he says would never be acceptable if applied to any other group. As derision goes, "dirty old man" and "greedy geezer" (which was new to me) do not seem to approach the iniquity of racial epithets, but Butler may simply be too polite to record in print nastier names. Then again, in polite circles, milder terms hurt more.*

In sum, it is absolutely true that social and personal mistreatment of older people is rife. One of the chief arguments of this book is that vast, unremitting forms of discrimination against older people are key forces in the workings of the world today. Yet the literature and public advocacy that describe age discrimination are packed with so many charges that they often seem to compete with one another or to cancel one another out. The voices for the elderly are so steeped in complaint that they often seem to be striving to reinforce a stereotype they deplore, that of the elderly as incoherent, ornery, and demanding.

One hears, for example, the passionate complaint that the elderly are singled out by society at large, that they are marginalized, and not treated equally or valued for the contributions they can make. The elderly should, for example, be afforded their independence as long as possible, and be full participants in matters regarding their

---

* In Great Britain, road signs that portray the silhouette of a bent over man and woman with walking sticks warn drivers to slow down in areas where older residents congregate. Formerly the signs were joined by the words "Elderly People," in bold letters. Officials removed the text after it was deemed "ageist" and now face a campaign to remove the graphic portion on the grounds that even elderly people these days are not as bent as they used to be and that the picture stigmatizes them. That leaves the problem of what to show or say on the signs, to persuade people to slow down when speed limits alone won't do. One suggestion is to treat the areas as school zones, where drivers do slow down, but that might raise the question of treating the elderly as children.

housing, their financial estates, and their medical care in deciding their fate as they near death. All are complex issues.

But there are equally passionate counterclaims that older people, out of pride or fear of others, hold on to their independence too long and end up isolated and at risk of neglecting their own needs, and of getting hurt with no one around to help. There is also the concern that older people have exceptional needs arising from the loss of their mental and physical powers and from the diminution of their social status and financial wherewithal.

Such complaints have their quotidian side, manifested, the anti-ageism literature points out, in implacable insults buried in everyday conversation. Ageism shows in the way people speak too loudly and too simply to older people on the blanket assumption that they can't hear well or digest information quickly. "Ageism is also perpetuated by the ways in which our society talks about older adults," notes materials from the Canadian Network for the Prevention of Elder Abuse. "It is common to see ageist language in medicine, law, and social sciences, when terms like 'the elderly' and 'the aged' are used to refer to older adults. Both of these terms give the impression that most older adults are mentally and physically frail. Health journals sometimes include people in their fifties as 'elderly.'"[14] Then again, complaint, just as vocal, comes from the other direction: people too seldom adjust their message to accommodate for elders' loss of hearing or diminished ability to grasp new, complex information or tasks.

In a similar way, voices have risen against employers and pension policies that urge, or force, people to retire in their fifties, sixties, or seventies. At the same time they denounce arrangements that push older people to work because government and private pensions do not dole out enough money to allow older workers to retire. Advocates for the elderly protest that older people—because of the expense of providing them with income support, health care, and other services—are made scapegoats for the government deficits that exist today and loom even larger in the future. That, in fact, there is a *plot* against the elderly by the economic elite.[15] But the advocates also worry that governments have vastly underfunded the costs of the coming boom in the aging population.

What are we to make of the seeming contradictions in the way all of us, young and old alike, perceive the elderly?

They are all true. The elderly are as diverse a group as humankind.

My Fiftysomething-Year-Old Wife, the Teenager

As brilliant as humans are at discerning true ages, we also have a generosity in our perception that allows us to see our friends, ourselves, and others we cheer for in a youthful light. On the stage, my wife, Sara, looks eighteen. She tells me so and from the distance of my seat in the theater, and from our closeness of heart, it does not seem far-fetched. "You know, everyone's telling me that they thought I was a teenager up there," she said after a recent performance as one of the schoolgirls in *The Mikado*. "They say I'm so energetic and coquettish. It's a good thing I dye my hair." Sara is a marketing executive by day, but at night she is a singer, a mezzo-soprano with a warm but big voice. She appears in operas, light operas, and musicals in houses big and small, often in the role of a tittering maid or young mother. She recently had a part written for her in the annual revue put on at a local university's faculty club, where the old professors have adopted her as the house starlet and like to dress her up. In the last show she played a sexy French philosophy student. Costumed in a beret, tight red dress, and fishnet stockings, she raised an eyebrow, and when she rhymed "Sartre" and "Descartes" in a French accent her audience hooted and *ooh la la*'ed.

To many of the people in the audience, I am certain Sara does look eighteen. The audiences for opera, operetta, and faculty clubhouse reviews are filled with people for whom a midlife ingénue is young enough. Their hearing and eyesight are forgiving, their imaginations flexible. But even for the musicals that bring in younger audiences, age brackets are stretched freely. In a recent revival of *The Music Man*, the mayor's wife, the mother of an Iowa teen girl, was played by a woman in her eighties. The director of the production was a super-fit dancer in his late fifties, and may have lost track of how old the character of the mayor's wife should have been. She was the dotty, fussy old lady in the script, so naturally she ought to be eighty, right? Perhaps when we cast our contemporaries and older friends in younger roles, on the stage and in life, we cast ourselves as younger, too. That can confuse beholders, but, then again, age and social roles now seem meant to confuse, often in wonderful ways.

We may have lost track of what ages once went with what social roles, and we might be clueless about what a typical mother looked like half a century ago. A cougar? A fifty-five-year-old man in the audience who sits with a ten-year-old girl could be her father, her grandfather, or a first cousin. Directors, who may not have children of their own, lose track of what traditional families look like, so that craggy women old enough to be great-grannies are cast as mothers of young children. Think how grandmothers now confuse everyone. In the real world, grannies can be far less wrinkled than the women who play mothers on stage. They are nearly as likely to have iPods as their grandkids, to go to the gym, and to be distance runners.

Viewed from the distance of the stage, some of the grannies and grandpas in the audience look, if not eighteen, maybe somewhere near forty-five. They ought to. They use all the same tricks that the actors use to reengineer their appearance: pricy, sophisticated cosmetics, dyed hair, false hair, false eyelashes, fake tans, pinked cheeks, polished teeth, nips, tucks, and injectables. Performers, meanwhile, often have the physical fitness and grace that help them simulate younger age. For them, succumbing to the obesity epidemic is professional suicide. Even eighty-year-olds had better be lithe, and ought to dance.[16]*

Despite all her paint, prosthetic aids, and good habits, my wife still may not look eighteen up close. We're both past midcentury. We've lived more than half of our lives together, and I think, on close inspection, we look the same age. Thirty-five.

---

* Then there's song, too. Researchers at Britain's Canterbury Christ Church University followed twelve thousand singers in choirs around the world, and found that singing gives the muscles of the upper body a meaningful workout. It delivers the benefits of aerobic exercise, reduces stress, increases alertness, and cuts recovery time from bacterial infections. The experience of some of the subjects suggested, but didn't definitely prove, that regular singing cuts the recovery time for heart attacks and stroke. So strong are the benefits that the researchers are now pushing the British National Health Service to prescribe singing to prolong general health.

CHAPTER 9

CHINA: WILL IT GROW OLD
BEFORE IT GROWS RICH?

Number of people in China over age sixty in 2009:
167,000,000

Estimated number in 2050: 438,000,000

AT THE CENTER OF OUR GRAY NEW WORLD STANDS THE MIDDLE Kingdom. China. Why? The people of Japan and the countries of southern Europe may be older, the aging industrial workforce of the American heartland may encourage businesses to move jobs abroad, and the burdens of Western welfare states, including the United States, may weigh heavily on the world's economic health, but no country feels the benefits and challenges of an aging world more than China. The country supplies an aging world with the young workers and consumers that global businesses crave and, at the same time, it is one of the most rapidly aging places on earth.

China's supercharged cities, which have driven the country's economic miracle thus far, have done so in large part by unleashing the energy and brilliance of the country's young workforce, and by systematically pushing aside whole generations—up to 70 million people—of workers, most in midlife, who have been marginalized in China's new market-driven universe.

How Rich Will China Become?

Economist Robert Fogel looked into China's future in a startling essay in the journal *Foreign Policy* in January 2010.[1] "In 2040," Fogel predicted, "the Chinese economy will reach $123 trillion, or nearly three times the economic output of the entire globe in 2000. China's per capita income will hit $85,000, more than double the forecast for the European Union, and also much higher than that of India and Japan. . . . [T]he average Chinese megacity dweller will be living twice as well as the average Frenchman . . . [and] China's share of global GDP—40 percent—will dwarf that of the United States."*

That's an aggressive estimation. The Chinese economy would have to compound annual growth of about 18 percent a year to reach Fogel's estimates. That is a much higher growth rate than the country's already historically high rates. The mainstream predictions about China are more in line with that of the Carnegie Endowment for International Peace, which pulled together data from global investment banks, financial services firms, the International Monetary Fund, and the World Bank to paint its picture of China's future. It sees China's economy first matching the United States' sometime in the early 2030s, and then pushing about 20 percent higher than the United States by 2050.[2] Fogel's predictions for China exceed even the rosiest estimates on growth offered by the Chinese government or the banks and investment funds that exalt the country's prospects in order to lure money there. And his views will come as outright relief to a growing number of economists and others inside Chinese and Western think tanks who look at the future shape of

---

* Although Fogel predicts the U.S. economy will fall to a mere 14 percent of the global whole, he does not see per capita GDP of Americans falling behind China's. His picture is gloomier for large European and the Japanese economies, which he sees going through a status shift that on a much bigger scale is akin to the shifts transpiring in the beat-up industrial corners of the world, like Rockford; these places, once near the top of the world's wealth pyramid, become relatively less affluent and less consequential in the world economy and increasingly subject to the whims of outside competition.

China's aging population and see the country's prospects stalling or even reversing.

But Fogel has compelling reasons that other prognosticators overlook. He has seen how China pours educational resources into its young people so that they become highly skilled workers in an increasingly technologically driven world economy, and he's seen how the country has marshaled resources to create dozens of mega-cities meshed with massive new industrial infrastructures.*

Gigantic Numbers

Tally up any fact about the Chinese population and the big numbers offer surprises. It is no surprise that China, with 1.3 to 1.6 billion people—there is no sure count—has a gigantic population of older people. In 2009, China was home to 167 million people over sixty years old.[3] By the benchmark year of 2050, one in three Chinese citizens, at least 438 million people, will be over sixty.[4] If they were their own country, China's senior citizens would be then the third largest country in the world, behind only India and China itself. Every older age group will see dramatic shifts. Those sixty-five years

---

* China's growth, and the aging of other economies, may show, above all, that countries and families respond to change in unexpected ways, and engage in massive innovation that can have counterintuitive results. Who would have imagined that pro-family initiatives, particularly in east Asia and southern Europe, would reduce populations so dramatically? Fogel is almost certainly right to see education as a propellant of economic growth. Yet in the early twenty-first century there are strong signs that the economic promise of education is wilting in some places. The youth of western Europe and Japan have never been better educated, yet they languish in the job market after they receive their impressive degrees. Might not China's educated young people do the same? Maybe not in great numbers now, since those entering the workforce today expect to care for parents, but in the next generation, when parents have better means to support their singleton children. Extrapolating from the trends in China in the 1980s would have given a very poor picture of China in the second decade of the twenty-first century. Economies and social milieus are complicated systems with billions of variables, the most transformative of which are people in search of well-being, however they define it. If anything, the past century of tumult and reinvention in China shows how dramatically a large swath of the world can change its rules and global status and how creatively its families adapt as their lives are repeatedly turned upside down.

or older, who as recently as 2008 accounted for less than 7 percent of the population, will make up 20 percent of the country.

As with many other aging nations, the number of older people will be going up at the same time China's overall population is in decline. Barring a radical unraveling of China's "One Child Policy" that limits families to one or two children, China's population will begin to decline in 2035, after having added 200 million to 300 million more people since the year 2000. The portion of the Chinese population that is working age will nose-dive by midcentury, too. In 2008, about 75 percent of the Chinese were between the ages of fifteen and sixty-four, but by 2050 that group's proportion will shrink to 66 percent.

People are expected to live longer, too. In a country where the current life expectancy is about seventy-three overall, residents in China's better-off eastern cities are already living, on average, into their eighties, right up there with the world's longevity champs in Japan and southern Europe. By midcentury, the national average should approach eighty, too. That means far more elderly for the country to care for, and a shrinking group of workers to support them. The shift is already apace. By age sixty, nearly all Chinese workers have retired from their long-held company or state jobs, which means that given China's age structure today, it is in the midst of a retirement avalanche. Over the ten-year period that ends in 2015, the number of Chinese over sixty years old will double from 100 million to 200 million.[5] Today, for every ten working Chinese there are two elderly dependents, but by 2050, there will be six elderly dependents for every worker.*

The Washington-based Center for Strategic and International Studies frames the shift another way: "In 1975, there were six Chinese children for every one elder. By 2035, there will be two Chinese elders for every one child. During the single decade between 1995 and

* In 2010, the U.S.-based National Bureau of Economic Research tallied, for Asia, the change from 2008 to 2050 in "population ratio of the old," which counts those under sixty-five against those older. In Japan the proportion climbs from 17 percent to 38 percent, Hong Kong from 11 percent to 33 percent, Korea from 7 percent to 35 percent, Singapore from 7 percent to 33 percent, Thailand from 7 percent to 23 percent, and Taiwan from 8 percent to 26 percent. (http://www.nber.org/chapters/c8144.pdf)

2005, China added 107 million working-age adults to its population. During the single decade between 2025 and 2035, it will subtract 79 million."[6] And here's one more way to look at the aging of China's population: by 2025, China will be home to one-fifth of the world's population, but home to one-fourth of all people over sixty-five.

Seeing Isn't Believing

The aging of China is hard to see on the typical tourist jaunt or business trip. Its renovated big cities are bustling with young people out on the streets and in the hotels and tourist attractions. Factories and offices seem as though they are versions of Western and Japanese workplaces, just bigger and filled in with young actors playing the roles of the people who have, or once had, those jobs oversees. Well, the young certainly are not playacting, but they do create a kind of discrete tableau for the world looking in. A land that appears infinitely stocked with youth is aging so fast that soon China will have more people retiring every year than entering its workforce.

While places like Shanghai and Beijing are aging rapidly, they are not growing old nearly as fast as the poorer parts of China, which send their most able earners out to Beijing, Shanghai, and other more bountiful markets. By 2025, many of China's poorer provinces and metropolitan districts will be considerably older than the rest of their richer cousins. The province of Heilongjiang, in the extreme northeast of China, is home to 36 million people (10 million in the city of Harbin). Part of China's rust belt of giant, obsolete, heavy industrial regions, Heilongjiang has been shrinking due to out-migration since market reform began to gain its footing in the 1980s.

The aging of Asia may have started in Japan, but other Asian places have caught up quickly, and may one day see aging Japan as a relatively young place. By 2025 the median age in Heilongjiang will be over fifty-one years old.[7] The median age in Japan in 2025 will be fifty. Heilongjiang will have traveled the age curve at twice the rate of Japan.

China's government-run dailies follow demographic issues closely. Even amid the mind-numbing listings of government initiatives, the news on the population front jumps out. There are routine, but always growing tallies of the country's elderly, statistics that track the effectiveness and lapses of the country's population-control programs, and news about the Party's latest paternalistic take on how to manage the size of the world's biggest "family."

Yet another stream of demographic news grips the government-approved headlines: the fate of China's highly mobile migrant population. Though China is Communist in name, in the era of market reform it has reverted to relying on families to provide support for one another, pooling their savings and earnings to provide for multiple generations, from infants to great-grandparents. Yet market reforms have also put the country literally in motion and spawned a vast culture of migrant workers and transplants. In 2010 at least 200 million earners were separated from hometowns and families. That puts China's traditional family structure under enormous strain. It is hard to imagine that China's urbanization is still in its infant stage when one beholds how the influx of young migrants has already doubled and tripled the size of the country's biggest metro centers and filled new ones built from scratch. Yet predictions out of the Chinese State Council's Development Research Center show that the government expects urbanization to drain the countryside and rural regions of another half-billion people.

The Party's Power over Families

China, under Mao Zedong, vacillated on whether the Chinese people were duty bound to limit their families or to grow them. Over the first three decades of Communist rule the government would go through periods when it ineffectually encouraged couples to limit family size by spacing out the births of the children. But at other times, at the overt urging of Mao, it went through periods where it encouraged them to have many children; when, as in the former Soviet Union, mothers with ten children were celebrated as heroes of the nation. Campaigns in the 1950s and 1960s created a highly fertile baby boom that added more than half a billion people to the country's population.

Mao's desire to multiply the Party's minions did not mean that he, or the leadership around him, had any extra love for the traditional Chinese family. To the contrary. Under Mao, the government developed elaborate campaigns and systems that undermined the family, and were designed to put a wedge between parents and their children. The template of the traditional, cohesive Confucian family, which venerated elders and ancestors, was viewed as a competitor to the new Socialist order and its egalitarian aims. What's more, the production of people in China was regarded, in accordance with Party ideology, as a complement to the production of goods, and the state's role as central planner in family matters was often as resolute as its role as steward of China's steel factories and collective farms. Families were to be big, but not strong.

Yet the days when the Chinese Communist Party pinned its authority to its ideological devotion to a classless society are dead and gone. The calamitous effects of the Cultural Revolution killed it. Mao officially began the Great Proletarian Cultural Revolution in 1966 and it ended between 1976, when Mao Zedong died, and 1978, when Deng Xiaoping consolidated his power. The Cultural Revolution embroiled the country in a political civil war that pitted the young generation of Chinese—including preteens, high school kids, and university students—against what Mao labeled "The Four Olds": customs, traditions, habits, and ideas. Parents, teachers, and leaders were all suspect in a new order that was to turn the time-worn veneration of elders upside down.

The violence and poverty wrought by the Cultural Revolution left the Communist Party nearly bankrupt until Deng Xiaoping ushered in another about-face. Under his rule, every tradition and institution in China was again reevaluated, and those that the Party deemed useful to righting the country were rehabilitated. Deng forced the Party to embrace global capital and Western capitalist ideas, and to bet that it could manage a turn away from redistributed Communist ideals and still stay in power. Skillful leadership, enterprising people, cooperative foreigners, and a measure of luck have helped the Party ride the development wave. Deng once observed, "There are those who say we should not open our windows, because open windows let in flies and other insects. They want the windows to stay closed, so we all expire from lack of air. But we say, 'Open the windows, breathe the fresh air and at the same time fight the flies and insects.'"

And when market reform began, the traditional family—once again exulted by China's leadership—reasserted itself as the central support in people's lives. China still lacks a comprehensive, national social security system robust enough to support both its rural and urban elderly, and families now must provide the time and money to raise children and to send them to school (though migrant families often have no good schooling options and have to depend on more informal, ad hoc schooling they arrange themselves). The country relies on far-flung workers to send money home to support their families, and, indirectly, their old hometowns. Official reminders—and edicts—that children and parents be true to their traditional familial duties are necessary because in China's supercharged era of change, family ties often fray. In an aging society, where hundreds of millions of elderly will depend on an increasingly burdened younger population, abandonment of traditional family support would imperil the mass of older family members left behind. China now must decide how much it will push development at the cost of the security of its aging population.

Beat the Clock

A smiling ninety-year-old woman sits in a cheap lawn chair planted next to her half-demolished house in one of the oldest neighborhoods of Nanjing, China. She reaches out her hands for passersby to say hello. One of eastern China's oldest wells for drinking water exists around the corner from her place, and lately, now that the city's piped water has been shut off to local houses, it is again indispensable. Most of the neighborhood has been torn down, and old movie posters flap on the walls of some of the nearby ruined homes. The neighborhood is slated for redevelopment; soon high-rise offices, apartments, and shopping centers will stand where some families have lived for centuries. Photocopied signs printed on alarming Day-Glo yellow, green, and orange paper have been glued to cover nearly every blank surface of interior and exterior walls, and even every window.

They advertise services that will move residents out on a moment's notice. The old woman lived with her middle-aged son, his wife, and a granddaughter in their one-room house, which has been defiled with thousands of the move-out signs. They are a form of terror that local developers connected to the government use to bully people from their homes. Some families are gone; they either could not take the pressure or negotiated a settlement and moved elsewhere with the money.

Others wait in hope of better settlements, or because they cannot imagine leaving their ancestral homes. Most of those who are left are older and, surprisingly, it is often the older residents who are most willing to take a stand. When most of the homes have been razed, the ones left are called "nail houses" because their residents, like the woman in the lawn chair, are too stubborn to extract. Or, their removal is, for a while, too shameful to enforce. There is even a nursing home that is refusing to move. The residents know that once their neighborhood is gone, they will be relocated to cheap government housing where they have no family, no friends, and no historical connection.

"If I die here," says the old woman in the chair, "I die happy. If I die there, I will be alone."

The Chinese cityscape has been transformed by cozy relationships between local officials and real estate developers (which themselves can be government-owned firms). The vast usurpation of property from China's older citizens is often driven by officials who can enrich themselves when old homes are cleared and new ones built and sold. These schemes, which are everywhere in China, have become the most corrosive, and intractable, issue in Chinese politics, as Party elite and their confederates, in effect, reassert the worst of the landlord system, which the Revolution was to have overthrown. China has found it hard to square the demands for growth with clean government, since officials are the ones who are expected to drive growth and are thus in the center of the activity.

The Party's stake in China's development is now so thorough that it has bet its political legitimacy on its ability to deliver ever-improving economic fortunes for its people in a mostly market-driven economy. The full weight of the state is devoted to creating prosperity before the aging population threatens to close the window on wealth. The country finds itself under such enormous pressure because its transition from a country with high birthrates and high death rates to one of low birthrates and death rates happened faster than with any other large country in the world.

And for distinctly different reasons. In other, wealthier Asian and western European countries—as we have seen in the cases of Japan and Spain—where low birthrates are near the level of China's, declines in family size came not by design, but as a result of other factors. Prosperity, advances in public health, urbanization, and the education and employment of women were key to these transformations. Once masses of people moved to cities, birthrates dropped, the proportion of dependent young children declined, worker productivity went up, and a higher percentage of working-age people held paying jobs. The result was that even as the pipeline of young people into the workforce stabilized or shrank, the number of people willing to work went up.[8] Since more productive workers tend to earn more money, the change also helped build richer societies. Eventually, the economic rewards that come from high numbers of workers and few dependents butt up against a rising group of older dependents.

Other higher-income Asian countries are trying to manage that change to stave off the threat to their standards of living. Massive infrastructure investments in countries such as Japan and Korea have focused on the productivity of the shrinking workforce by raising education levels, designing ever more automation into the workplace, expanding work options for women and older people, and developing trade strategies that complement their highly paid domestic workforce with the outsourcing of low-value work to low-wage countries, such as China and Vietnam.

The Chinese state, in contrast, used a wide array of coercive tactics to force the transition on its people. China's evolution works in reverse order, creating for itself the kind of prosperity that would have otherwise stirred the shift in population that its government legislated. When China builds cities, lays roads, unlocks new land for development, funnels money into promising industries—when it moves officials around from city to city, legislates for or against foreign competition, stokes nationalism (usually on trade issues), or promotes international harmony, and when the state weighs in on family matters—all is aimed at the country's economic development. If China often seems like a super-aggressor in matters economic, it is because that is how it must act for the sake of its people and for the political health of the Chinese Communist Party. Over the past thirty years, the intensity of the country's development effort has lifted more than 400 million people from the deepest depths of poverty and created a middle class that rivals in size those of the United States or western Europe.

But the development program still has a long way to go. Over the last three decades, between 20 and 30 million people entered China's workforce for the first time. Over the next two decades, about 2.5 million people a year, mostly young, will begin looking for jobs. The country must get them to work for the sake of present stability as well as to support its future. If the country gets rich fast enough, its challenges will be better met, but if it stumbles, the family may have to account for even more. So far, the picture is mixed, but considering the strain, Chinese families, driven by emotion and necessity, have proven remarkably resilient and adaptable.

The Party and government objectives announced after nearly every big political conclave identify China's rush to gray as a major challenge to the nation. And always, the discussions are underlined by what is perhaps the most pressing question about the country's future: Will China grow old before it grows rich? The question is a twist on the preoccupation of previous generations, when China's population growth raised the specter of a Malthusian collapse. Planners feared that China's natural growth could lead to an ecological collapse and forever prevent the country from modernizing, let alone growing prosperous.

Family Planning

"DO A GOOD JOB IN FAMILY PLANNING TO PROMOTE ECONOMIC DEVELOPMENT" exclaims a propaganda poster from 1986, seven years after the inauguration of the One Child Policy, in the province of Liaoning, in China's northeast. The painted poster features the profile of a fair, dark-haired, not-overtly Chinese-looking beauty whose image would fit just as well in an ad for beauty face cream in Rome, Mexico City, or Tel Aviv. She sports a stylish short haircut, arched eyebrows, mascara, and ruby red lips. She is a new image of a modern woman in China. In the Communist era before 1980, the image of the Chinese woman had been largely desexualized. The military-style suit that was the staple of the Chinese wardrobe was formless. Beauty salons were nearly unheard of, and women were as likely as men to have simple bowl haircuts. The family planning poster shows a new feminine ideal: the modern, glamorous woman with a stake in China's development. In her delicate hand rests a transistor radio, antenna extended. Doves, flowers, and the Chinese flag flutter in the foreground, but behind her head and in the distance is the high-rise skyline of the kind of modern city China could not claim in 1986, but had its sights on nevertheless. The woman's adoring eyes focus above the radio on a naked baby floating, doves all around, in a bubble of light. The poster unequivocally links modernization with the control of fertility, selling the good life to those who comply and promote the government's One Child Policy. The poster is a benign face of the most intense efforts to control human reproduction in the history of the world.

"When China adopted a one-child-per-couple birth limitation policy in 1979, the state claimed dominion over the most intimate personal behavior of its people, sovereignty over the production of life itself," writes Tyrene White, a political scientist at Swarthmore College, in her book *China's Longest Campaign*. The volume caps an extraordinary twenty-year-long study of China's "birth planning" programs, during which White delved into Chinese archives and conducted extensive interviews with officials engaged in the effort as well as Chinese citizens who did and did not comply. (White does not call China's policy "family planning," since it was up to the state, not families, to plan how big they ought to be.) Although China had encouraged limited families throughout the 1970s, it did not previously coerce women to limit how many children they had, or punish them if they had too many.[9]

Support for the One Child Policy among the country's top leadership was unified and, until recently, staunch. The support for the policy stayed strong even as China, overall, grew less ideological and put more faith in Chinese families to run their own affairs. The state then granted vast new freedoms that let people lead lives in styles of their own choosing. Yet when it came to decisions about childbirth, the state remained deep inside the family, and over the years implementation of the One Child Policy was unremitting.

In cities, where people could be more closely watched, and where officials were most supportive of the policy, the policy worked. In the countryside, where farmers had strong practical needs for boys to do field work and support them in old age, as well as strong desires to have boys carry on their family names, families devised myriad strategies to circumvent the one-child rule. Officials in the countryside, who themselves were often inclined to larger families, often helped families skirt the law and avoid its harshest penalties. (One reason the Chinese census figures are so unreliable is that children born outside the limits of the One Child Policy are hidden from the census head counters.)

On the whole the policy succeeded in drastically reducing the number of dependent children that Chinese families and the nation would have had to support without it. In 1963, China added forty-three new mouths to feed for every thousand of its people; in 1982 it added twenty-two; in 2003 it added only twelve. Over that same forty-year period, on average, the number of children born to a woman in China dropped from about six to between 1.4 and 1.9. The Chinese government estimates that the first thirty years of the One Child Policy prevented the addition to its population of 400 million people—a number comparable to the current combined populations of the United States and Mexico.

Although the logic is not spelled out in the economic platforms of the Party, the link between the One Child Policy and economic development was explicit in the years following its beginnings. At the very least, limiting the reproductive choices of China's huge baby boomer population, which in 1979 was already having families, would save the bankrupt China treasury the cost of educating and employing a new cohort of children. Unchecked, that cohort would have been twice as large as China's boomer generation. Tyrene White traces the government calculus back to a study conducted for Deng that summed up how much money the government had spent on services for the 600 million Chinese newly brought into the world since 1949, when the Communist era began. The total came to 4 trillion yuan, which at the time of the study translated into $1 trillion ($2.8 trillion at the end of 2009). Faced with the cost of feeding, clothing, housing, educating, and employing a newly larger population, and, perhaps more important, the political cost of failing to provide for the people, Deng moved quickly to limit China's population growth nearly as soon as he took power.

Once the One Child Policy was in place, the Party and state also set about reversing decades of revolutionary doctrine in order to bolster Confucianism and its emphasis on filial duty. In other words, the pragmatic, scientifically driven Party, which on one hand used all the power of the state to destroy the large traditional family, turned, on the other, to the old-time metaphysics in which Chinese families paid obeisance to elders, and, importantly, to ancestors in heaven in order to gain their earthly and celestial reward. If Chinese people again put stock in the importance of their roles in the order of the universe, the system of familial supports could regulate itself. The approach harkened back to a much different time and economy. In an agricultural society, adult children were more likely to rely on their parents for their livelihoods, since their fathers owned the family farms and passed them on only at death. When children provided support, they did so as dependents and earned their keep in exchange.

Xiaomei Pei, a U.S.-trained sociologist who heads the Gerontology Center at Beijing's Tsinghua University, points out that while Chinese people are quick to say that caring for elders is part of their cultural and religious tradition reaching back centuries, they conveniently forget that over most of their history, the traditions were practiced when the average life expectancy in China was no more than thirty-five. The demands on pious children were much lighter then. When parents got sick, their illnesses tended not to linger. They, like everyone on the globe before the advent of modern medicine and public health, tended to be able one day, sick the next, and dead shortly thereafter.

Six Elders Per Child

By 2010, thirty-one years of the One Child Policy made it the most durable mass campaign of all, and, in terms of its goals, the most successful. It ran longer than all of Mao's reign. Several well-connected policy institutes in China, including the prestigious Shanghai Academy of Social Sciences and the Chinese Academy of Social Sciences, have recently advocated revisions to restrictions on births, and the policy has been relaxed somewhat in areas—such as Shanghai—where birthrates are regarded as too far below even the one-child allowance. (When China's well-connected intellectuals take such unequivocal positions contrary to the prevailing rules, it is often a sign that the government is lining up support to back an imminent change in policy.) The fear is that China's workforce will shrink too rapidly and that the aging of the country's population will reach a stage where the older population swells at an ever-faster rate, so fast and so disproportionately to the rest of the population that the lopsided demographics of the country would be very hard to stabilize or reverse.

The One Child Policy could just as accurately be called the Six Elders Per Child Family. When the policy is strictly followed, singleton children have two parents and four grandparents to look after them when they are young. Common wisdom about the current generation of Chinese children is that they are spoiled by their doting relatives. Older observers complain about the overfed "little emperors" who always get their way. And there is some empirical evidence that children *are* overindulged. In 2004, a group of epidemiologists from Sweden and China surveyed body mass indexes of more than fifty-six hundred children under age six in Beijing, where nine of ten children in that age group were singletons and where children are highly likely to be cared for by grandparents. They also conducted interviews with a sampling of them.[10] They found that when grandparents were in charge of cooking and feeding their grandchildren, the youngsters were far more likely to be unhealthily fat. One reason was that the grandparents, who were often denied foods they liked when they were young, prepared dishes, such as large plates of dumplings, noodles, and steamed buns, that were high in sugar and fat. Grandparents told the team that they had little to do all day while their grandchildren were in school, so they spent a lot of time shopping in the market and cooking, and food piled up as a result. Meals were designed around the preferences of the little ones, not the adults.

The researchers also found that grandparents in Beijing regarded heavy children as healthy children and that the fatter their children grew, the more successful they regarded their care. They believed fat little children would grow up to be taller, thin young adults. Thin grandchildren, on the other hand, were pitied as sickly. One grandmother told the researchers, "[The parents] cannot say that I haven't done my best in looking after the child if the baby is big."*

Later, when a singleton child works, he or she may well have four grandparents and two parents to support. The 1-2-4 family pyramid is what the state has created, and what the state now leans on to provide family support. The burden is light when there are six adults looking after one child, but overwhelming when there's one adult child helping to support six adults. And in China, the law demands that children support their parents.

Dishonorable Children

China's laws also allow parents with grievances against dishonorable children to sue their offspring for alimony.** In Changyuan County

---

* Chinese grandparents are not the only grandparents whose grandchildren grow fat on their watch. A team at the University of London looked at records of twelve thousand British three-year-olds and discovered that the risk for obesity was 34 percent higher for children cared for by their grandparents than those raised primarily by their parents. Diet was part of the problem, but so was lack of physical activity.

** Singapore, the southeast Asian city-state where three out of four citizens are ethnic Chinese, has allowed parents to sue their children for support since 1999. Singapore has one of the world's lowest fertility rates (1.28); population aging and shrinking dependency ratios have led the government to compel adult children to shoulder the burden for their parents' care. According to *Today in Singapore*, the city-state's court heard 127 cases in 2008. Since the law's inception, judges have in central Henan Province, the local government grew so alarmed at the declining willingness of children to care for their parents that it adopted work rules for government employees that link their professional advancement to how well they perform their filial duties. The county sends out officials to interrogate family members to see if their relatives on the government payroll perform their family responsibilities. "Officials should possess traditional values of filial piety and family responsibility, which are the foundations of a successful career," the county's Party head told a local newspaper.[11]

Nanjing, one of the few cities in China with a civil court devoted entirely to family matters, has seen cases of negligent adult children spike in recent years. According to one judge in the court, a Party member with little legal training and a talent for browbeating adults into behaving according to traditional values, the most frequent excuses that adult children give for withholding or pilfering money from their parents is that the cost of apartments—either their own or that of their parents'—is too high. Cases almost always avoid trial because shaming family members works often enough, the judge says. His court is the last resort for desperate family members in the city. Before matters reach him, local governing committees in the families' neighborhoods are charged with working through solutions, something that works only if both parents and adult children live in the same neighborhoods.

"One of the measures that neighborhood committees have been trying lately," the judge says, "is to try to publicly shame the family into working things out." It's being tried in other Chinese cities, too. The *Shanghai Daily* reports that one neighborhood committee in the city inflicts public shame on errant family members first by issuing warnings to the offender. Money isn't the only issue. If, for instance, a child does not visit a parent at least once every two weeks, he or she gets warnings. If the child still stays away, there is a seven-dollar fine.

tended to side with elderly parents, ruling in their behalf 80 percent of the time. Caseloads jumped following the global financial crisis in 2007 when large numbers of families could no longer afford nursing home charges for elderly relatives. Faced with a crisis that could drain state funds, some legislators in Singapore called for stricter laws, but some of the city-state's most visible activists for the elderly charged that stiffer laws would drive adult children further into desperation and leave elderly that had a modicum of familial support with none at all.

"Although paying respect to parents is essential in the Chinese culture," the *Daily* declared, "the tradition is fading as more people who live apart from their parents are too busy to visit regularly." Following the warnings, the committee posts the names of the offenders for the whole neighborhood to see.[12]

An older couple in booming Dalian took a novel approach to the problem. A story in the local paper there reported that a well-off man in his sixties named Lin and his wife enjoyed a pension of RMB 4,000 a month (about $600 in 2010), but missed their children when they failed to visit. They offered their two sons and one daughter contracts that paid RMB 1,000 to those who visited at least twice a month, and threw in bonuses for when they brought the grandchildren.[13]

Of course, it is this same pyramid that has been the foundation of China's economic miracle. Because parents had fewer children to support, they could participate more fully in China's workforce. When there are only one or two children in the dreams of young adults, they need not rush to have children. They can enter the adult workforce young and stay in it. They can migrate to other parts of the country. They can marry late. They can entrust the care of their one or two children to their parents, who usually are still young enough and able enough to take on child-care duties. Grandma can chase junior around and wait at the school-yard gate to take junior home, while Grandpa does the shopping and prep for the day's meals. As a result, China counts the highest rate of employment among working-age teens and adults of any country in Asia.[14] In boom times, China's working-age women, with one of the world's highest workforce participation rates, are as likely as men to hold a job. Allowing for the vagaries of Chinese job statistics, that would seem to put Chinese women close to full employment.[15]

Daughters Are Better

Meanwhile, in China's cities, the old rules on filial piety are being rewritten. In the year 2000, about 40 percent of urban Chinese over age sixty had their own places, but by 2010 more than half lived without their children. The percentage is expected to keep rising. In the cities, older residents may live on their own either because they want their own places, or because their children have moved away.

In the countryside, the incidence of "empty nesters" whose children no longer live with them has also soared, largely because their children have moved. The rise of households where parents lack the familial support they want has contributed to an epidemic of loneliness in China. In late 2009, the head of the China Aging Development Foundation made national news when, at a high profile conference sponsored by the Chinese Academy of Social Sciences, he revealed that suicide rates among the elderly in rural China were nearly five times the world average. The *People's Daily* carried the remarks in a story headlined, "Filial Duty Not a Fig Leaf for Blemishes of Old-Age Social Security."

The old rules are getting a rewrite as daughters, for the first time, are emerging as parents' favorite children, particularly if they are city girls. The new view of girls is that they are more willing than sons to provide their parents with money and emotional support. It has become an article of faith among east Asia's urban families that daughters will serve elders better in old age than sons. In the cities, offering support means working visits into a busy schedule, now that China's older urbanites are more likely than ever to live in their own homes and not with their children. Daughters, the new view goes, are more willing to make the time.

"Urban couples all think girls are much better than boys. Girls are more thoughtful, especially toward their parents," Feng Xiaotian, a Nanjing University sociologist, told Melinda Liu at *Newsweek*. In a recent poll by a national newspaper, 29 percent of those surveyed preferred daughters, edging out the 28.4 percent who preferred sons.[16] Farmers may still favor boy children, but in urbanized Asia, the experience of relying on sons has brought enough anecdotal evidence of heartbreak to make new mothers talk about preferring girls. In Korea, where Confucian family values have long held sway, parents now often sex-select for baby girls.*

* In rural fruit-growing areas of China where girls are preferred for the small-motor skills that make them more adept than boys at picking berries, families select for girl babies.

No matter how individual families worked out who supports whom, one aim of the government of the One Child Policy and the reassertion of traditional values was always plain; to hold down the government's spending on social welfare programs for as long as possible.

The Dangers of a Youth Population

There might be another, more personal reason Deng moved so quickly on the One Child Policy. Deng once confided to the legendary Motorola CEO Robert Galvin that the reason he authorized the use of deadly force to put down the young protestors during the Tiananmen Square Uprising was that he linked it to the worst days of the Cultural Revolution. Back then, Deng's own son was heaved out of a window and paralyzed for life. Deng told Galvin that Mao had turned the country over to teenagers, who terrorized and vandalized the nation; and he, Deng, knew he could never turn over the country to a youthful mob again.

The "youth bulge" in China's population in the 1960s was seen as one of the causes of the country's extreme radicalism—just as the street protests and violent political action in the United States, Europe, and Japan have often been attributed to youth bulges there, as well. With a One Child Policy, Deng could engineer a Chinese future free from another, possibly radical and calamitous youth bulge. Rather than compete with a younger generation the size of China's baby boom generation or bigger, Deng, on behalf of older generations, could direct the state to limit births and blunt the rise of a rival horde.

As China changed its family structure, it remade its education system, too. Ideological education was suppressed, while China's schoolchildren were molded into the kinds of students and future workers that global businesses needed if they were to use China as the place to reproduce their enterprises outside their high-cost home bases. As time went on, the skills of young family members were honed to meet the demands of these foreign enterprises coming in as well as those of the Chinese companies taking their place.

Now China produces more university graduates than India and the United States combined, the large majority of them trained in highly pragmatic disciplines—sciences, engineering, and business—with no ideological training at all. China is today a place where an entire workforce in a high-priced country could get replicated with far younger workers, with up-to-date skills and a willingness to work for wages that are a small fraction of their counterparts' abroad that they have displaced.

The One Child Policy was at the core of the social restructuring and what has followed has driven China to the top rank of world economies.

A Candid Conversation with Mr. Gao

In a textile factory about an hour and a half outside of the center of Nanjing, an unmarked textile factory sits on an otherwise bare piece of land in a newly carved-out industrial park that runs for several kilometers along a wide stretch of the Yangtze River. No decoration or even a corporate logo clutters the inside of the factory, either. The large mantel in the lobby once intended for display shows only a large brownish water stain on top of gray cement.

The production-line manager, Mr. Gao, extends a beefy hand, though he is otherwise slight, bald, bespectacled, and, in his white short-sleeve shirt and ill-fitting black pants, a little generic-looking, the Chinese incarnation of Dilbert's boss. He leads the way to his office where seats are offered at a folding table and where tea leaves, added by Mr. Gao from his personal stash, are dropped into paper cups.

Mr. Gao has worked for the company for thirty years, beginning when it was a large state-owned firm with several thousand employees producing heavy cotton cloth, such as that used in blue jeans and tarps. Back then, the factory was in the city of Nanjing. After the mill went private in the 1990s, the company rented out its old factory and moved to its current location.

Today Mr. Gao has two hundred employees, less than one-twentieth of his former workforce; but he says the factory's annual output of six hundred thousand meters of cloth is about the same as it was before.

"But the workers are much younger," he reports, "and we don't keep them as long. It used to be they worked for us until they retired and we were responsible for everything, including their care when they got older. Now we just pay salaries and make a contribution to their social security."

The textile company's roster is much reduced, but the company is still on the line to pay some pension money to the older workers it let go. Mr. Gao says that the pension costs don't hit the company's operating revenue, but come out of rental income on the old factory building in Nanjing. He says that the land is also due to be redeveloped, which will bring even more money.

"When we had the mill in the city, our workers were city workers, but now that we are out here, we use rural workers, but they don't like to work here unless they can live somewhere near Nanjing, so we have a dormitory on the edge of the city and we bus them here every day."

To keep his workforce flexible, Gao says the company will only hire workers for one year at a time, and makes them sign a new contract every year. His method is common, but it is also the subject of a lot of official hand-wringing. Publicly, the central government is pushing for longer-term employment commitments from bosses, which would require them to build some job security and benefits into workers' contracts. But locally, companies try to stay as flexible as they can, because they, too, exist at the whim of global competition in the textile market. Locally, provincial governments have not insisted on more regular employed workers or benefits and pensions, because they collect taxes from the businesses and like to stay on their good side so that they can keep their localities' marks high when it comes to development.

To remain competitive, factories have to keep labor costs as low as possible. "I hear a lot of talk about wage inflation, but I have not raised wages here in about six years," Mr. Gao says. "And there's no shortage of recruits. Young people want to live in Nanjing." He says he would not take on older workers even if they worked on the same terms as his rural migrants.

"Younger workers are more efficient, and the group we have now is far better than the older group we let go. Young people have more incentive to fight for their own lives. If you're older, you might have savings and then not work as hard."

He also describes how competition from India, Vietnam, and Cambodia was beginning to take some business. "I've had to move to a more skilled workforce to compete, and the young people we hire—we look for people with leadership skills—are easier to train." The salary for most of them is RMB 1,000 a month, or less than $150.

The Unpaid Multitudes

Yet despite the exceedingly low wages paid to China's new class of young factory workers, their wages were not the only bargain the world gained from them. Their employers, and the global customers who bought from them, also realized, then and still today, the benefit of the labor of hundreds of millions of unpaid grandparents in China who provided and still provide most of the family services for the mass of the nation's newly employed and its more rootless underemployed, the 150 million to 200 million people the country labels "surplus labor."*

For economic development to work, the families have had to be pushed to organize themselves so that the young adults can work, often very far from home, and the older adults can provide family services at home.

The forced demographic shifts that made the Chinese economy such a success are now shaping up as the country's biggest challenge. The 150 million Chinese—equal in number to the entire U.S. labor force—who make up the first generation of workers that migrated following Deng's reforms will begin to retire in 2015. That is the year a woman who was twenty in 1980 will reach the retirement age

---

* Businesses and government think tanks have been worried about labor shortages since 2008. But as every economist knows, another name for a worker shortage is "salary shortage," and China still has a huge reserve of potential workers who can be coaxed into workplaces with higher pay.

of fifty-five. Pension reform is coming to China that will eventually cover far more workers, but neither the current generation nor the earlier generation of workers will get much, if anything, out of the revamped national system, which will aim instead to provide for the newest entrants to the workforce and those who come after. China's high savings rate and some of the pressure young workers face to leave home—and send money back—are responses to how impoverished and selective the country's pension provisions have been.

The achievement of the economic goals in the era of freer markets required a social structure that made older Chinese unemployable in the new economy. Market reforms and the closing of state-run factories put between 40 million and 70 million mature workers out of their jobs. What is more, older workers were commonly regarded as damaged goods, as paranoid or crazy, too marred by the mass political campaigns of the older Communist regime to be of much use in a fast-moving, market-driven China.

But "damaged" older people could be trusted with the nation's children.

There is a troubling contradiction in how China regards its late-middle-age and older citizens. The country puts great stock in their contributions within the close quarters of the family, where they can do unpaid service and offer a stabilizing role to the society, but from on high, in business and government circles where important decisions are made, the status of China's older citizens often leaves them expendable. Their marginalization is all the more puzzling since the state and Party leadership is filled with older people in powerful positions, so much so that China often seems like a gerontocracy.

Park Yourself Right Here

A party erupts early every morning in Ritan Park, one of Beijing's most verdant public spaces and one of a few large recreational parks in a city woefully short of green space. The celebrants are thousands of high-spirited retirees who, between 7 and 9:30 a.m., may make Ritan Park, de facto, one of the largest senior centers on the planet.

The park is surrounded by Chaoyang, the eastern district of Beijing that is the most rapidly developing and most densely populated part of town. The site is central enough that it draws older people every day, the way fireworks or a rock concert would draw in a younger crowd on a summer night. Before seven in the morning, the boulevard that separates the park from the surrounding neighborhoods is largely free of Beijing's notorious traffic. Even the city's usually ubiquitous taxis are scarce. Yet this is the hour the sidewalks swarm with fit, elderly pedestrians aiming toward the park.

In a small, red gazebo, a well-pitched pick-up choir delivers pop oldies, which for this group includes revolutionary tunes from the 1950s and 1960s, accompanied by a bookish keyboard player and leather-jacketed accordionist in huge aviator sunglasses. "Sailing the Seas Depends on the Helmsman," a rousing anthem to Mao Zedong, collides with the strains of Ricky Martin's "Livin' la Vida Loca" blaring out from a boom box. Martin's number serenades four long lines of boogeying women, some of them who have clouds of permed white hair that bounce to his beat, and others who move haltingly to their own rhythm while they slap their legs and torsos to stir their inner energy. Move them near a drum circle in Sarasota and they would fit right in.

Amid the dueling sounds is the park's largest group, a few hundred practitioners of tai chi, split according to their abilities, into groups of fifty or so, all moving in graceful slow motion, creating their silence amid the walls of sound. Martial artists with swords and poles fill other groves in the park, as do groups of men and women playing a variety of paddle games and badminton. There is a popular section for singers of Beijing-style opera, where a few sing and many listen, and another where a man with a case full of harmonicas of all sizes invites older women to come sing as he plays.

There's even a clearing for kite flyers. Lone walkers can be seen circling the park. Most walk facing front, but a couple make their way walking backward. From out of sight comes an occasional bloodcurdling scream. Someone somewhere in the park is finding another way to release bad qi. And one man, who looks near eighty and wears a gray shirt with a black suit jacket and brown pants, waltzes under the trees with a piece of clothesline loosely draped between his outstretched hands. Asked why, he says he lost his wife some years ago.

The park is full of dancers. Yan Ping, a barrel-chested, eighty-three-year-old, commands the center of the park's roller rink, where Chinese disco music blares from a tinny PA system. He blithely dances solo in a sea of nimble, older couples. He's taller than most, perhaps because every bone and ligament in his body pull straight up like a ballet dancer about to pirouette. Rosy-cheeked Yan sports a thick, white Elvis-style coif and has a bright smile only slightly marred by one brown front tooth.

"When I was young I was in the army," he says in a booming voice. "After that, I was an urban planner in Beijing. I smoked and was so overweight at 103 kilograms [227 pounds] that I had to wear a special girdle and suspenders to keep my stomach in the right place." Yan Ping then picks up his now-imaginary belly from around his waist and hoists it toward his chest. Then he hunches over.

"I was badly out of shape, I never exercised, and my back was bent over my desk all day. I retired at age sixty-six. Around then, in 1992, I met some professors from the Beijing Dance Institute and they gave me some video of the world dance championships. It had tangos, waltzes, and a lot of other things on it."

He demonstrates a bit of every dance he mentions, and then asks whether the dance he was doing was recognizable. "You probably don't know it because it's out of fashion now," he says, "an Italian dance from the eighteenth century." He reports that he dances for two hours in the park every day and has lost fifty kilos (110 pounds) since he began. Now he is a teacher, he says. "I have a fourteen-year-old girl in my neighborhood who I teach. She's better than the dancers on TV, and on Friday and Saturday night we go dancing in another park."

The party atmosphere in the park in the morning makes it a good place to visit with older Beijingers, and to piece together bits from the lives of a group that has seen nearly unfathomable tumult, but is nevertheless still vital, social, and for the most part, to hear the Ritan Park revelers tell it, happy and prosperous. Ritan Park sits on the edge of the capital city's embassy district, and many of its regulars are current and former members of Chinese officialdom. Others are former workers in state-owned industries, whose transformation left them without their old jobs, but by good fortune gave them a stake in Beijing's booming real estate market. Others have missed out on the riches the boom delivered but have pensions, work, or family that help them get by.

The Good Life, for Official Residents

The morning crowd includes older Beijingers lucky enough to have official residency status in the city. The demographics of the capital city run along two tracks, notes Yehua Dennis Wei, a geographer at the University of Utah who specializes in the globalization of Chinese cities. There are the long-term, officially recognized residents, the people whose families are rooted in the capital and who preceded the great influx of money, and the people who flowed in over the past three decades.

They, along with their counterparts who have official residency in Shanghai and Nanjing, are among the oldest groups in China.* The families of the native Beijingers have one of the lowest birthrates in the world. Outside China's most prosperous cities, people cook up all sorts of schemes to circumvent the one-child rule and have more children; but in Shanghai, Nanjing, and Beijing, the birthrate among the core population is barely one child for every two families.** Without migrants to Beijing, the city would be shrinking in population. Yet a second group, comprised of young migrants

* Life expectancy in the large, prosperous cities in China is among the highest in the world, exceeding the national averages for Japan and Spain (Hong Kongers live the longest, on average, of any big-city dwellers anywhere).

** Hong Kong, where there is no One Child Policy, has seen a dramatic rise in the number of women, and couples, who have no children. The territory's total fertility rate, according to Francis T. Lui at Hong Kong University of Science and Technology, is below one, and 30 percent of the city's women who are in their midforties have never borne children, a percentage that is climbing fast. Hong Kong's experience may be an unwelcome sign for those in China who believe the One Child Policy ought to be reversed in order to prevent population aging. If China continues to urbanize, it will likely see low fertility rates whether there is a One Child Policy or not. South Korea and Taiwan also have lower fertility rates than mainland China.

from all over China and the world, Wei notes, more than makes up for native Beijingers' unwillingness to have more children. Because young migrants choose Beijing, the city is one of the fastest-growing metropolises in the world.

Ritan Park's morning crowd comes rain or shine to celebrate its blessings as well as to extend them. They come, in part, because it costs nothing for them to get in. Their residency IDs let them pass through the gates. Roughly half of Beijing's population would not have that privilege. A ticket costs one yuan, about fifteen U.S. cents. That's around the price of two steamed buns stuffed with eggs and leafy vegetables that are sold outside the park.

Creating a Younger Beijing to Serve the World

Near Ritan Park, in Beijing's Chaoyang District, is the city's new, gleaming Central Business District, a planned downtown that now boasts more high-rises than the major European capitals, with most built since 2005. The status of the city's older residents is closely tied to Beijing's development boom, and the CBD itself has changed the fates of thousands of older people, some for better, some for worse. It also explains why thousands of older people flock to Ritan Park each morning.

Before market reform, Beijing had no need to develop the kind of business district that one finds in other cities where big business and big government meet. In the early 1990s, however, city planners latched on to the idea that a global city needed a business district where the world's most important firms could set up their China offices. Typically global firms have two headquarters in China, one in the city where they are most operational—often Shanghai—and another in Beijing from where they can deal with the Chinese government.

The downtown, Beijing's planners believed, ought to project all China is meant to be. The city cast aside much of what was dowdy and backward and built a district that has more than fulfilled the planners' ambitions. More than one hundred of the global Fortune 500 companies have a China headquarters or regional offices in the CBD.

The rise of the CBD near Ritan Park is one version of how the economic miracles of urban China happen. The central government poured in resources and incentives to deliver on China's promise to global companies. Beijing's local jurisdictions climbed on board so that the city could have a business district that would make it competitive with other cities in China. (Beijing competes fiercely with Shanghai.) Rich packages were offered for educated ethnic Chinese overseas—whether they were Chinese nationals or not—to come to the city and set up businesses. Local officials, who could profit politically and personally from development projects, tapped into the government's spigot of funds to build and build again. State-owned industrial companies tore down their plants and worker housing and replaced their old businesses with real estate speculation.[17] Today CBD sells the hyper-modern version of China exceedingly well. It teems with stylish, youthful Chinese office workers and a clique of international managers. The CBD is also rich with the chic, sometimes over-the-top amenities this vanguard demands.

Many of the buildings are designed by the world's leading architects from America, Europe, and Japan. Bradford Perkins, the founder of New York–based Perkins Eastman, one of the world's largest architecture firms, notes that for architects his age, sixty and over, China is an especially rewarding place to work and reinvent oneself. In a city such as Beijing, he says, he has clients who can dream up huge projects, and have them designed and built faster than it would take to do an environmental impact study in the United States. On the outskirts of Beijing there are newly built towns meant to house a million people, all built faster than it has taken New Yorkers to agree on a plan for the World Trade Center site.

Unlike many Western clients, Perkins says, Chinese clients prefer older architects for their experience and mature vision, even when it is creatively daring. Chinese professionals of a certain age, like its workers, are not regarded as up to snuff. "China is missing a whole generation of experienced, internationally trained architects our age," he notes. During the Cultural Revolution in the 1960s and 1970s, he says, few were trained, and those that were ended up building drab and functional government buildings.

Most of the buildings of the CBD house banks, financial firms, media companies, and other businesses, but others are luxury high-rise apartments. It is all built atop cleared land and an obliterated, outmoded past. Some of the CBD replaces Beijing's enormous, bleak Mao-era factories. The Chaoyang District was until the early 2000s the site of some of Beijing's biggest, dirtiest smokestack industries built on the Stalinist model of huge mass production. Market reform doomed the companies, even as the rising values of property in Beijing and the demand for a formal downtown made the land ideal for redevelopment. Once their armies of workers were let go, the idle buildings were razed.

What came down to make room for the new towers was the residential and economic infrastructure of the generation that now comes to spend their mornings in Ritan Park. The changes in Beijing, and China in general, made the old homes and old jobs of the older generation lose much of their value. When old factories in Beijing were razed, so too were the workers' housing units that were homes to much of the city's aging population.

Some of the older residents were eased out with promises of money and good apartments nearby. And like the beleaguered neighbors of the unyielding Nanjing woman in the lawn chair, others were treated more roughly, forced from their homes by local police or the goon squads dispatched by developers. Down-market housing complexes at the outskirts of the city are filled with idle, older Beijingers who have been consigned to apartments none would choose.

For Beijing to continue on its roll, it must promise a continuous supply of new and improved physical space and business infrastructure, and do its best to provide the world's best young workers for the world's best firms to hire. Thus does Beijing, the city and the national entity, drive and participate in the mass global age arbitrage that makes China a driver of globalization. It moves its old workers out of their homes and jobs, and makes way for the young. The recent remaking of the city has cleared between six hundred thousand and one million people from hundreds of thousands of old houses and apartment blocks.

More room will be needed. As China attracts hundreds of millions of young people out of its rural areas and smaller cities over the next forty years, other cities will grow, and new giant cities now in the works will mature into their own vast metropolises. But that will not take away from Beijing. The capital is adding about one million people a year, at which rate it will approach the size of metropolitan Tokyo by 2025.

Family Room

One of the miracles of modern Beijing is the recent expansion of the typical family's living space. In China overall, the average living space per person has widened threefold since 1980. For the newly prosperous in the country's powerhouse cities, it is far greater. Looking out at the Beijing sky shows how. The city, with 17 million people, is about four times as populous as it was in 1949, but it is also four times taller and wider. Verticalization and sprawl have allowed families who once lived with many generations in a single room to split up into their own, multiroomed apartments.

In a city with an enormous state bureaucracy, it is not surprising that many in Ritan Park have put in years of service to the Party, the military, or the central government. Or that they enjoy what in China are very good pensions. They may be better off even when compared to other fortunate urban pensioners. There is a good chance that when the city's housing began to get rearranged, a Beijinger with the right connections was offered rights to a Beijing house or apartment while the local property market was still heating up. Such a home, held long enough, could have radically changed the circumstances of an urban family. A home in the general vicinity of Ritan Park would be an especially rich stake in one of the greatest real estate booms in history. Geometric rises in real estate prices could have increased the value of living space more than a thousandfold. Leveraged correctly, the value of a home near Ritan Park could lead to the purchase of more homes, perhaps using some to earn rental income; others to speculatively "warehouse," or save until property values make them worth selling; and others as living quarters for their adult children.*

* The government still officially owns the land that Beijingers, and all Chinese, live on. When people "buy" homes, they take possession of long-term leases that can run up to one hundred years, but they do not get a deed to the land.

The fantastic real estate boom has given a large group of elderly (though, in China, still proportionally very small) a way to multiply their wealth that may never again be equaled in China. Even when property values fall back, when China goes through one of its bust periods, the reversals are never nearly enough to wipe out the gains made by those in the property game early enough. (Unless, of course, they are over-leveraged.) The superfueled property booms in Japan and Korea also created an older generation of property investors whose good timing has left a younger generation of people frustrated and resentful that they cannot enter the market. It also means that the later generation is less likely to marry young and more likely to linger in their parents' homes as they do in urbanized Japan and America. For the most part, Chinese families have not reached that stage yet, and the older winners in the property market have been acquiring homes for their children along the way. But that day is almost certainly coming, and may again radically change family living arrangements in China for urban families blessed by the property boom.

House Slaves

As China injects the miraculous market dynamic that transformed its eastern cities into other metropolises in the north, central, and western parts of the country, it will create millions more winners in the property market. That will bring problems of its own. The property boom so far has also spawned one of the world's largest gaps in wealth between haves and have-nots, and resurrected in China the landlord culture that the Communist revolution sought to overthrow. Talk to the people taking exercise in Ritan Park and some surprising patterns emerge. A high number of them have multiple homes as well as children and grandchildren who have been educated abroad and work in prestigious government posts or for multinational companies.

They are the winners, in a nation obsessed with the cost of housing in red-hot urban China. In 2010, a small, newly built apartment in Beijing cost about nine times a typical middle manager's salary, and more than the lifetime earnings of a common laborer. The issue of housing costs keeps millions glued to *Woju* (alternatively translated as *Narrow Dwellings* or *Snail House*), an uncharacteristically realistic television soap opera about the Guo sisters and their misadventures in the housing market. The older sister, Haiping, a married woman, craves a house outside a fictional city that is a lot like Shanghai. To save for a down payment, she and her husband live in a slum and eat instant ramen noodles.

When housing prices skyrocket, Haiping grows desperate.* Like China's growing numbers of white-collar "house slaves," she turns to a relative for help. Her younger sister, Haizao, steps in and insinuates herself into the affections of a corrupt official who lives high on bribes. *Woju* caused a storm of debate in the Chinese press and blogosphere, and around the dinner tables. It also struck a chord with local government broadcasters, who did not smile on the all-too-real portrayal of the corrupt and privileged wheeling and dealing of officials in the property market. Many pulled the series in midstream. Episodes continued to circulate on the Internet, where the show's following remained strong.

Perhaps one reason cases of intergenerational abuse are climbing in China's most prosperous cities is that the younger generation must rely on their parents to unlock their wealth if they are to have any hope of breaking into the housing market. Sixty percent of younger home buyers turn to their parents for help with the required down payment of 20 percent. If one doesn't have a parent who is already in the property market, that option is not open. Older parents with homes can find themselves under pressure—self-inflicted or otherwise—to cash out of them for homes for their children, and often find themselves moving to smaller quarters to facilitate their children's purchase.

---

* "[F]or the Chinese, worrying about house payments itself is becoming a health risk," reported CNN in January 2010. "A survey on the health of Chinese white-collar workers, released by the Chinese Medical Doctor Association, showed that buying property ranks as the top cause of pressure among 46 percent of the respondents, followed only by parents' health, difficulty in finding a spouse, and children's education." Reuters reports that in January 2010 property prices in seventy large Chinese cities spiked an average of 9.5 percent over the year before, the eighth consecutive year of steep increases. Seven big cities saw housing prices triple in 2009.

"It's normal," says Linsun Cheng, an economics historian at the University of Massachusetts, Dartmouth, and editor of the *Berkshire Encyclopedia of China*. "Many Chinese parents like to do that. Some, though, do not. Still, it is amazing how frugal older Chinese people can be. Even with very modest incomes they manage to save a lot. It is also amazing how many give their money to their children. They may see it as a kind of investment in themselves."

In a land where families depend on one another for social support, and where families are top heavy with older people and short on younger members, parents can feel that their sacrifice reinforces the family ties they will rely on as they age. Younger purchasers place themselves in the middle of a generational struggle for urban property in other ways, too. In a replay of what happened in Japan in the 1980s and 1990s, when Tokyo property peaked, Chinese banks now offer prospective buyers extra-long-term mortgages that can last a lifetime. That can place the burden of paying for a house on three or more generations within a family as older parents put up down payments, the buyers pay a mortgage for the first twenty years or more, and then their child assumes it after the buyer retires. Whether this will be a recipe for harmony or discord remains to be seen.

A Mass Delusion of Familial Happiness?

Outside Ritan Park, a woman in her midsixties scurries home after her morning constitutional. She says she is willing to talk on the run, but cannot pause. Nor does she offer her name. She has to get home before her son and daughter-in-law leave for work, in order to take over the care of her grandson. The boy is nearly five, she says, and she's in charge until the parents get home around eight at night.

After wandering the neighborhoods of Beijing and other Chinese cities talking to older people walking hand in hand with small children, or pushing strollers, a visitor finds it easy to get the idea that the role of caretaker has always been expected of the elderly, and that it aligns their lives with the traditional values of China. They love their grandchildren deeply and say they give them purpose. The role of Beijing's grandparents is evident every school day after-

SHOCK OF GRAY

noon around the time grade-school children are released by their teachers. All over the city, the sidewalks and parkways near the schools throng with men and women aged forty-five and up standing around, chatting with one another and looking for signs that their grandchildren will emerge. The youngest children dash to meet their grandparents, who seize their hands or hoist them onto a shoulder. The preteens mull around, talk to their friends, and, at the more posh schools, type this and that into their phones before their heads spring up to find their escorts.

Yet the hurrying woman does not look happy to leave the park, and when asked how she feels about her duties, she volunteers that the rosy picture offered by the grandparents is a kind of new mass delusion. Chinese people have a gift for making virtue out of necessity and grandparents today have to make the best of their situation. She says that in her case, she enjoyed herself once her children finally moved out of the house and she could spend more time with her friends and do activities she liked. But then her son and daughter-in-law had a child. They are busy professionals whose bosses expect them to put in long hours and to go out after work so they can talk about work some more.

The woman says that the rest of life stops for Chinese grandmothers once a baby comes along. "You lose about ten years," she says. "I don't see any of my old friends. They have grandchildren to take care of, too, and while they're at it, they are just lost. I moved to where my son lives, and they move to where they have to. Sometimes to different cities. We all get spread out all over the place. Then after the ten-year gap, you don't know who's going to be around, because you haven't seen them at all in the meantime." With that she waves good-bye and, walking even faster, huffs up the street.

Take My Hand as We Walk Home

If some grandparents are ornery about bowing out of their former routines to take on child-care duties, others regard the birth of a grandchild as their salvation. Julia Ling, a native Beijinger who once was the on-air host of an English language, drive-time radio talk show for the

328

government broadcast network, is a newlywed whose new career with a media start-up requires long hours and lots of travel around China. She is a key executive in the business and its prospects are strong, a fact that dims her prospects of having children in the next few years.

"My mother won't hear of how busy I am," she says, laughing, yet upset at the same time. "All she talks about is how I should get busy trying to have a baby. I say I don't want one, but you know, the baby wouldn't be for me, it would be for her. She says she has nothing to do, and wants to bring it up. She reminds me that she isn't getting any stronger, but that for now she has all the strength it takes to do whatever a child needs. I tell you, she won't keep quiet about it. We fight about it all the time. I think she's afraid that if I don't have a baby for her to take care of, I am going to forget about her, too; but if I do have one, then she will have me, my husband, and a grandchild to keep her from getting lonely when she really is old."

For many Chinese grandparents the motives to step in as a child-care provider are more complicated. Rural grandparents tend to their grandchildren while their adult children work in distant jobs. For poor Chinese farmers, the remittances from their working children to support the family on the farm may be the lion's share of their resources. Even a low wage in a factory can be three or four times the income of the average Chinese family farm, and any money sent home makes a big difference.

For the poor parents of the migrants who do establish themselves in the city, the chance to join their adult children and take over child-care duties may be an opportunity to reestablish themselves back into the system of family support. In the old-school version of the family bargain, intergenerational reciprocity—what parents could expect in exchange for being parents—was enough to coax children into watching over them in old age, especially when the older parents maintained economic control over the family assets. Now grandparents put in extra effort helping grandchildren, hoping they can chalk up a stronger claim to reciprocal treatment for themselves when they are old.

As Xiaomei Pei at Tsinghua University observes, "People always say that it is the traditional way in China for grandparents to take care of their grandchildren. That is a fantasy. Maybe in some cases it was true [we're primary caregivers], but for most families in China, at least until recently, it was always the mother's job to take care of her own children." And the mother's job to take care of the grand-mother, too.

Kicking the Older Generation, Hard

In her book *Private Life Under Socialism*,[18] UCLA anthropologist Yunxiang Yan traces fifty years of changes in intimate family rela-tions in Xiajia, a village in Heilongjiang Province, the northeastern region that has experienced an exceptionally high outpouring of young people to other parts of China. The book traces the fall of the "nuclearized family" over time. The story has its exalted and cruel elements. As families separated from the multigenerational arrange-ments to the forms pressed on them under Mao while the countryside was being collectivized, the younger men and women grew more in touch with their own and one another's emotions, but the change also left a vacuum in which the values of the family and ability to provide moral education and checks and balances broke down and allowed for heart-wrenching brutality and neglect by children as they ruthlessly worked strategies that extracted money from their usually quite poor parents "for the modernization of their own private lives."

Part of their cruel impulses grew from China's spirit of reform, guided by a perversion of Deng's often misunderstood dictum that "to get rich is glorious." Yan writes: "It is in that special historical context that villagers, along with their involvement in commodity production and the market, quickly embraced the values of . . . capi-talism characterized by global consumerism, which emphasized the 'I deserve . . . ' perspective and the legitimacy of personal desires." In her view, the almost maniacal push in China for the young genera-tion to attach their fortunes to what global capitalism could bring them did more damage to the traditional culture of China's rural families—which had survived the violent excesses and deprivations of Mao's rule (including a man-made famine that was the worst in world history)—than radical socialism ever did.

So far, she argues, there has been no effective way in China to counterbalance the egotism of the younger generation or its effects on their parents, especially among the rural communities she studied. What's more, the state abandoned public life, paid less attention to public order (except for the repression of dissent), and allowed nearly all the structures of village life to disintegrate. Local leaders often became the most predatory capitalists, exacting wealth from families before the children could get to it, and set the example for unbridled greed. The officials were under enormous pressure to push development, but for families who took from their own, the impulse was also to get a kind of promotion in status. That status took as its model the new mercenary ethos emblazoned by government information campaigns that lionized the wealthy and offered a constant barrage of new images from Hong Kong and the West of a material lifestyle all Chinese ought to aspire to. If some younger Chinese thought that kicking Mom and Dad down a peg was essential to getting ahead, so be it. The state was already kicking the older generation.

Against the picture Yan paints, it is no wonder that older Chinese parents look for any way they can to reaffirm their family ties and reassert their children's responsibilities. If the older family members get left back in the villages they must survive according to their own meager devices. The most shocking chapters in Yan's book are those that describe mistreatment of elderly parents, including the cruelty of local families that drove older fathers to their deaths, but did not drive the village to police bad behavior.

In the saddest cases, Yan describes how mistreatment and the overturning of the traditional family hierarchies led villagers to suicide. She tells, for instance, of the suicide of one older man who lived with a son and daughter-in-law who terrorized him. The older man tried hard to get along with them nonetheless. The couple refused to let the seventy-one-year-old man dine with them, and what food they did offer him was closer to a prison diet of scraps than the elaborate table they set out for themselves. Yan describes the dinner before the man's suicide as a rich affair put on for a visiting relative of the wife, with meat dishes, dumplings, and liquor. The father, who did not join the feast, asked for a portion of meat and dumplings, but the daughter rudely shooed him away.

"Then his son, who was already drunk, scolded him for being a shameless glutton," Yan writes. The villagers saw the son's drunken abuse as "the last straw in the old man's bitter life."

Despite this and several other cases that ended tragically for parents and children, life in Xiajia grew to revolve increasingly around the newly formed desires of a younger generation that flaunted, without consequence, its lack of filial values. "By the end of the 1990s," Yan observes, "the living conditions of some elderly parents worsened, and the family status of elders continued to decline. Elders trembled to speak of their fate, the middle-aged were worried about their immediate future, and young couples were confused by the storm of complaints from their parents and grandparents." No doubt, one of the worst fates for a person in China is to end up poor, old, and without family in a rural setting. Country villages often lack plumbing and running water, and a shortage of empathy in communities that stigmatize the disabled and the childless can leave the elderly helpless and isolated.

Rural poverty and the promise of urban lifestyles push millions of Chinese to leave their rural hometowns, though migration also offers a way out of the darker, more coercive demands of filial and matrimonial responsibility. Just as the breakdown of familial support contributes to China's excessively high suicide rates among the rural elderly, it has a similarly devastating effect on the young. While the elderly may feel they have no out once their family lives grow unbearable, younger Chinese can try to solve their family issues with their feet and relocate somewhere they can start fresh.

Send Money

Recent research on China's internal migrants suggests that, despite the formidable changes to their lives, they remain, by and large, committed to supporting their parents at home. Most of those with needy parents support them with money, and most work to stay in touch and provide emotional support as well. Chinese adult children are especially willing to send money home if they think that they will return someday to live and work.

There is yet another redemptive side of the story of the realigned

Chinese family, in which emotional ties within the family can remain surprisingly strong despite an onslaught of contemporary influences. In the spring of 2009, a group of ten executives from large British and North American companies made a fact-finding trip into the countryside of Jiangsu Province to acquaint themselves with the country outside of China's big cities. They spent one day observing a high school in Dongshan village, about an hour and a half away from Shanghai in one direction and two hours from Nanjing in the other. Chinese schools are ranked 1 to 5 according to their quality, and this school was ranked in the second highest tier. The English and math classes were impressive.

The hour at the end of the day was reserved for a question-and-answer period between the students and the executives. The students' favorite activities were visiting with their friends and helping out with school festivals. Some read, but said they would consider books only with happy endings. Most said they did not have time to do much more than study. Asked what they wanted to be when they grew up, many said they did not know.

One of the executives, a woman in her midforties who is the chief marketing officer for a large Canadian consumer products company, posed a question to the group. "If I gave you RMB 500 [about $74] to do anything you wanted with it, what would you do?"

At first, no one answered, but when prodded, one girl said that she would give it to her parents. Others weighed in and they all said the same.

The Canadian did not buy it. "No, I mean what if you could spend it on anything for yourself, something you've really wanted. What would it be?"

Again, the children said that they would give it to their parents. Then one boy leaned back in his chair, stroked his chin, and raised his hand. His radical idea? Save the money! There was some embarrassed laughter in the room. The other students eyed him. His neighbor slapped his arm. A girl at the end of the row suggested that he save the money so he could buy something for his parents later. There were teachers and the school principal in the room, so it is possible the students' answers were colored by what they thought would be in line with their instructors' moral standards.

Nevertheless, the saver stuck to his guns. He was going to save the money for something for himself later, he just did not yet know what. The others shook their heads.

"That's amazing, and it says a lot about you children in China," said the astonished Canadian executive. "I would have never said that when I was your age. I'd use the money to go buy shoes or jeans or to go out with my friends. What if I put a gun to your head and I said you have to spend this money on something fun for yourself or I will shoot you? What would you buy?"

The question met another long silence. The executive prodded them: "Have you girls seen any fashions in magazines that you might want?" Some nodded halfheartedly. "What magazines do you read?" They said they didn't have the money or the time for magazines. That sounded suspicious. Even in their school uniforms, the girls found ways to add fashionable touches to their looks. One girl turned to a boy next to her and said she knew what he would buy. He volunteered the answer. A basketball. But he'd give the leftover money to his parents.

High school children are not yet gripped by the housing madness. Nor are they on the marriage market yet. Or chasing urban lifestyles yet. They may grow more mercenary toward their parents. Then again, there seems to be a shift away from the worst behavior as families, adjusting as the first generation of parents that grew up under market reform, take stock and have their own children. As the state makes more noise about the pension reforms and about society's need to care for the elderly, it reverses, in part, the recent example the state has often set by willfully abandoning and victimizing its older citizens.

A Grandmother's Tale

Not far from Ritan Park stands one of Beijing's new forests of residential towers. Pink cement high-rise apartment buildings twenty stories tall have been dressed up with pitched roofs, turn-around driveways, and stiff-backed guards who watch over the complex with a forgetful seriousness that lets nearly all visitors pass but gives them a stern look as they do.

On a middle floor of one of the middle towers is the fifty-five-square-meter two-bedroom apartment of the Liu and Yan family.* Liu Yang is a thirty-six-year-old young executive with the China operations of a giant American business software company. His wife, Yan Jinteng, had a baby boy four months ago and has put her career on temporary hold. Liu Yang has invited his mother and father to live with them and take care of the baby, and the grandparents live in a small apartment in the same building. Liu Yang's mother is a sixty-six-year-old rosy-cheeked woman whose gray and white curly hair looks like a dandelion top.

The young parents took in the grandparents in part because they could use the help, but also because the grandparents had nowhere good to go. Liu Yang's mother, Yan Xingjun, has lived much of her life in a kind of industrial exile in revolutionary China. She has been waiting to tell her story and moves quickly to the couch to begin, even before name cards are traded, as is the custom, or tea put out. She does not tell her story very often, and even her son is unaware of some of its bitter chapters.

"I was born in Hunan Province," she starts. "My family was huge. We were a landlord family with property, and in our home there were forty family members. Some of the men went into the Nationalist Army during the war, but when the Chinese Communist Party took over they scattered all over the globe. Because some of my family was in the Kuomintang and fought the Communists, we suffered a lot in the first years of the People's Republic.

"Most of the men in the family were put in prison and my father was killed by the Communists. Some escaped to Taiwan, some went to Yunnan [in the southern extreme of China, near Vietnam and Laos]. In 1958, the year of the Great Leap Forward, I was sent to the city of Xining in Qinghai Province [northeast of Tibet]. It was a long way to go and I had to walk one whole day to the train station with my mother, whose feet had been bound and who could barely stand. We spent days on the train, sleeping on floors and in trucks.

"When we arrived, someone checked my health and three days later I was put to work in a carpet factory. My mother could not work because of her feet. I was given a bed in a dormitory that held

* No relation to Yunxiang Yan.

thirty workers to a room. There were two washbasins and we slept in shredded blankets. I retired from the factory in 1988 at age forty-five but worked another five years there. I earned my pension and they gave me a little extra money on top of that.

"I was young when I worked there, but I made friends with my roommates. I was so small when I lost my family, and I had only fragmented memories of any of them. I got married when I was twenty; then a few years later, the Cultural Revolution began. My mother and I were driven into the countryside and forced to leave the city because of our background. I would have had to leave my baby, but I just held on to it tight and appealed to the government. My mother and I were sent to the countryside for three months, but I was allowed to return after three months because a government edict declared people as young as me could not be guilty of their families' crimes and I went back to work in the factory and was reunited with my baby.

"But my husband, who was from a good [peasant] family background treated me like a beaten dog when I returned, so we separated. It was all politics. Because I had a bad family background, I was always forbidden to work on the huge carpets we made that had Mao Zedong's image on them. His nose might be five meters long on the carpet, but I couldn't even work on his nostril."

Yan Xingjun remarried in 1970 at the age of twenty-seven and had two more children. But she could not live together with just her family. "There were almost no traditional families at this time because apartments were assigned by your work unit, and they were smaller than even the smallest apartments today," she recalls. "My mother lived with me in the dormitory, and because of her feet she was in charge of my children. But she couldn't do it because of her feet, so she went back to her hometown. My children were then placed in the company nursery and I went to give milk every two hours."

In her first years at the factory, carpets were made by hand. Xining was an old textile center on the Silk Road. "Sometimes we were given only two or three hours to sleep in the dorms. The busiest time was around 1960 when the carpets we made were used to repay debts to the Soviet Union. Some of the carpets we made were enormous, and they took a lot of work at a time when the whole country had no food, and we had to keep working so hard. There was no vacation and for New Year's we received a gift of two steamed buns."

When the Gang of Four collapsed and the Cultural Revolution ended, she was promoted to quality inspector at the carpet factory. At the time of her retirement she earned RMB 160 a month, or about twenty dollars, and a little more than twice that in the five years she worked after retirement. "That seemed like a lot to me then. A chicken costs about RMB 5, so you get the idea. One day I wore nice new clothes to the factory and everyone wanted to know how much they cost. I remember saying I had spent RMB 80. I thought that was very expensive then."*

Before coming to Beijing the older couple lived again in Qinghai Province where they cared for a granddaughter whose parents were working hundreds of miles away in Chendu, the capital of Sichuan Province. When the granddaughter turned eleven and joined her parents, they moved to be with their son in Beijing.

"My granddaughter and I had a very close relationship," says Yan Xingjun tearfully. "I miss her more than I miss my daughter. I had three children that I left with my mother, so I was used to not being with them. When I was a mother I had to work so hard and I couldn't pay attention to them. But I love my granddaughter and grandson so much and I love spending time with him. Now I have become used to being with my family again, and I love big families. I don't know how to express it."

She cries and her daughter-in-law wraps an arm around her. They want her to know how loved she is. Her children feel strongly that the history and politics of modern China wronged the older woman by killing off her family members and then forcing a wedge between those who survived and came after.

In its latest incarnation, however, the modernization of China both separates and joins families. Market forces matched with new

* Chicken was expensive for Chinese workers during the Cultural Revolution and they rarely ate it. Yan Xingjun's pension today is RMB 1,000 a month, which means that her living expenses in Beijing are nearly all paid by her son and daughter-in-law. A whole chicken in a Beijing market today costs around RMB 20.

personal freedoms facilitates separation and reunion. Reunion, how-ever, is far easier, as are most things in modern China, for the small percentage of the population who are urbanites with money.

"My son kept encouraging me to move because he wanted me here when their baby was born and he knew it would take time to adjust to the city," says Yan Xingjun. "They even delayed having the baby, until we could come and they could afford a bigger apartment."

The daughter-in-law has a slightly different version of the story, one that echoes Julia Ling's battles with her mother. "Actually," she says good-naturedly, "my mother-in-law really pushed me to have a child, saying she wanted to take care of a baby while she was young enough to pitch in, and my father-in-law, who's four years older, was still strong enough to shop and do the cooking."

For the grandmother, being a grandparent fills an important void and gives her a connection she was denied. "I treat my children and grandchildren differently," she says. "With the grandchildren I only have the responsibility to love them. Educating them is the parents' responsibility."

In the Vegetable Market

Across the boulevard from Ritan Park, on a street full of European restaurants, cafés, and delicatessens that cater to the area's foreign-ers is a less glamorous, but no less alluring, old-style Chinese food market. Vegetable sellers stand in their stalls behind three-foot-tall mountains of greens. Butchers show off the hogs' heads and hocks they have to offer, while they chop away at another animal. There is a ham seller with delicious, dry-cured Jinhua hams from its name-sake city in Zhejiang Province south of Shanghai. The middle-aged seller says his hams are very popular with Europeans and that some Spanish and Italians have told him that the Chinese hams are some-times substituted for local ones because they are so much cheaper. He also says that the Italians and Spaniards learned to cure ham from the Chinese, just as they learned how to make spaghetti.

This local ham seller is among the saviors of the Chinese economy, the entrepreneurs and self-employed who ended the stranglehold of the state-owned firms, and allowed, usually involuntarily, the state-run sector to shed the burden of supporting workers for their whole lives. Since market reform began, individual Chinese have started up tens of millions of businesses. While the story of the rise of the Chinese private company is often told (including by me; in *China, Inc.*, I cited the establishment of 125 million private businesses between 1980 and 2005), the story of self-employed, older Chinese workers is less appreciated. Yet you see them in markets like the one outside of Ritan Park and in nearly every market in China.

You also see them as day laborers and contractors on the bottom rungs of the economy. Even as the senior exercisers work their way to the park, Beijing's legion of elderly trash haulers and recyclers are peddling, slowly and with all their might, their industrial-grade tricycles heaped with bales of cardboard, blimp-sized sacks of used pop bottles, flower deliveries, and housewares such as wash buckets, clothes hangers, paring knives, and windup toys.

About 45 percent of the Chinese workforce is in the informal sector, and the official retirement age in China pushes even those older workers who were never officially laid off into small-scale entrepreneurship and self-employment. Often their goal is to survive, but often, too, it is to solidify or reestablish their standing in their families. With the money they earn, these older men and women not only maintain their independence but help contribute to their grandchildren's education and welfare.

As the great wave of hundreds of millions of older Chinese men and women arrives, the relationship between generations will determine China's destiny.

CHAPTER 10

GENERATIONS AT THE TABLE

Estimated increase in the earth's population between now and the year 2055: more than 2 billion

Estimated number of people worldwide turning sixty-five every day in 2011: 126,000

In 2031: 216,000

Percent difference: 71

Percentage increase in daily births over the same period: 0.59

HERE'S A BOLD CLAIM: WHILE READING THIS BOOK YOUR chances of living a longer life have gone up. How so? It's because the more time you spend in the world, the more time the world gives you. For every hour we live, the average human life span increases between eleven and fifteen minutes. Every day sees the average life span grow another five hours. Your odds are better if you have avoided the obesity epidemic and live in a place that enjoys good health care, education, and freedom from war and terrible poverty. Also, you've tackled a complex topic and given your mind a workout that can help keep you cognitively fit, and so much the better if you've read while exercising on a treadmill. And if you enjoyed this book in a reading group, that's best, for you got the added benefit of sociability. A plate of Serrano ham and a good sherry for everyone would also give the discussion some added life, too.

Back to the Old Dinner Table

Let's recall the family's holiday table that we visited at the beginning of this book. We can go around the table again, this time not to count heads but to see how global aging is driven by the intimate decisions of families making the best of their lives.

In its earlier appearance, the largest group at the table was the young brothers, sisters, and cousins, who overflowed into "kids' tables" set up for them. At the main table sat a smaller collection of the children's parents, aunts, and uncles. The smallest group, the oldest generation that included grandparents, great-aunts, and great-uncles, and occasionally a great-grandparent, took up only a few chairs. My own family's crowded holiday tables were like this when I was a boy in the 1960s and 1970s, one of many children in the room.

Today, in aging places like those we've visited in this book, filling even one table can be hard. Grandparents still join the party. Relatives in middle age or older fill most of the occupied chairs. A few younger children, teens, and young adults sit off to one side. The chances that there are many cousins is slim, but the likelihood of stepbrothers and stepsisters is higher than before. More than half of the graying adults at the table today have either divorced or never wed. There is a strong likelihood some live alone. On the whole, the family is smaller and older than ever.

Decades of Love and Connection

One wonderful quality of families is that their members do not readily label one another as old. Families have a better sense of the continuity of life because they see one another over very long periods, often as long as sixty or seventy years. Such spans traverse all the great life events and create deep affinities. Families see how the parents are in the kids and how a kid lives on inside the adults. There are shared mythologies that provide younger members with the backstory on older generations. There is also the constant feed of new cultural information that bubbles up from the youngest members and keeps the older ones amused and somewhat up to date.

Maybe that is why family life and long, heartfelt friendships help people stay healthy and vital throughout their lives. And being with one's family allows one to have feelings for the younger generations. Even the oldest man in a wheelchair, the one who seems checked out all night, lifts his head and smiles when a certain younger woman walks into the room. Age has not claimed his mind entirely, and the family knows there's still a passionate, flirty soul somewhere inside.

Who are the happiest among the oldest people at the table? As we have seen, odds are the happiest are the ones who have maintained a thick network of family and friends. Who are the saddest? The ones who feel the most disconnected. Maybe pride, shyness, or lack of charisma has blocked them. Or perhaps it's a physical or mental illness that isolates them and frightens people off. Yet again, maybe they have outlived all their brothers and sisters and all their friends. They are a reminder that the battle against loneliness in late life never starts too early or runs too long.

In all probability, many of the seventy-, eighty-, and ninety-year-old grandparents at the table are not just passively living out their days but still doing things for their families. In the richer countries, they are still spending more money on their children and grandchildren than the younger generations are spending on them. That helps to keep the family glued together and gives the older relatives some skin in the younger people's game.

To stay engaged, the oldest generation needs to keep connecting with the youngest ones. A grandmother might suggest the grandkids visit them. To match dates, a granddaughter might pull out her iPhone, but Grandma has a customized phone made by a company named Jitterbug that sports a large-font display, large keys, and an earpiece designed to work with the latest digital hearing aids. A voice command in the mouthpiece fetches an operator hundreds of miles away who already has the grandmother's appointment book on a computer screen. With polite efficiency, the operator finds a date that will work for the visit with her granddaughter. It is a convenience that helps Grandma continue to thrive. The date may be for lunch, for the theater, or for an outdoorsy excursion.

Some of the grandparents may need more than attention from the younger generations, though. They may need money because they saved too little, spent down their savings on the care of a disabled spouse, had their pensions destroyed by the markets or cut by corporate management, or simply outlived their resources. Watching the younger family members eat and hear and walk with ease, the older ones may also contemplate how soon their inevitable frailties will require them to have extra care.

One of the older people at the table may have once been sharp, witty, and abundantly kind, but now he or she cannot figure out why dinner is taking place and only vaguely recognizes some of the family members. Life is a blessing, but because anyone over eighty-five has an even chance of suffering dementia, confronting a loved one whose mind has failed is a deeply frightening experience. In a time when medicine is more skilled at keeping bodies strong than at keeping minds able, demented loved ones can survive from one family gathering to another, leaving everyone else as sad witnesses to a long decline. We are at the dawn of an epidemic of elderly dementia, and the suffering of demented relatives, with their concomitant babbling, moaning, naked terror, and even violence can now dominate holidays the way the sound of children's play once did.

The Professional Caregiver

It costs money and lost wages to care for someone, and family caregivers often spend themselves into poverty to do so. No wonder a seat or two at the holiday dinner is reserved for a professional caregiver who can relieve, for a price, the family burden and help mediate between generations. Without them, the table would be missing some of its guests, or maybe even its host, the oldest person in the room. The caregivers are not family, but the family needs them, and, besides, when the occasion demands, family and caregivers alike say they are "just like family," which is why immigrant flows often follow the map of the aging world.[1]

Already rural areas all over the world, and high "sending countries" such as Ecuador and the Philippines, have seen how their homelands age due to out-migration by millions of young adult workers to places where they can serve the economic needs to an

343

aging world (and escape the aging dynamics of the places they are leaving). Over the next century, environmental stress may add another dimension to the movement of people. In July 2010, the U.S. National Academy of Sciences published a study by three Princeton scholars that described how agricultural failures due to climate change could lead to mass immigration from poorer countries to richer ones. A likely 10 percent reduction in crop yields on Mexican farms, for example, could compel up to 6.7 million more immigrants to try to make new lives in the United States, over and above those who would have come in any case. Those that come will likely be the usual younger group, leaving Mexico, which is already rapidly aging, an even older population to manage at home.[2]

When a caregiver takes a break from the big dinner, she heads to the den where the cable TV carries her soap operas from her home country and an Internet connection lets her video chat with her own children and parents. When she reemerges and takes a seat next to the wheelchair of her charge, out comes a box with the evening's doses of medicine and then the tactful suggestion that it is time for a trip to the bathroom.

The caregiver may be regarded as "just like family," but she has a family to support, too. That can put her at odds with the family at the table. Her generation of homegrown and immigrant caregivers is hitting the streets where they work and the corridors of power, demanding living wages. Nurses, nurse's aides, and untrained caregivers now comprise the developed world's most rapidly growing union movement, and in an aging world, labor organizers turn not to weakened assembly lines, schools, or city governments but to the growing numbers of low-wage, hardworking caregivers who fill nursing homes, hospital halls, and the private residences of people who need constant care. The new solidarity and bargaining power of caregivers may be hardest on families that need the care at a time when public budgets are in crisis and the generation of family members that pays for private care is strained by downsizing, outsourcing, and reduced public support. In 2015, when the baby boomers hit age sixty-five in big numbers, their parents will hit their high eighties in big numbers, too. That will work to the strength of the labor movement and be the bane of boomers and their parents.

A Hard Step to Take

When talk at the table moves to the tough decision of what next step to take with their loved one, family members—usually siblings and their spouses—are having a conversation that was once taboo but is now common. Even in China and the Philippines where people often say reflexively that they could never put a parent in "an old people's home," senior residences are springing up to accommodate the needs of families that are busy and far-flung. Like large corporations that move production abroad to save money, outsourcing senior care saves families money, and allows family members who stay behind to relinquish their caregiver roles and stick to their more lucrative jobs at home.

Technology can serve as an intermediate solution and it's increasingly likely to be discussed at the table. Enterprising families use webcams, intercoms, and Wi-Fi to monitor the movements of diminished older relatives.

The world's big technology companies have their own solutions. Intel and GE have multibillion-dollar projects to develop technology for the homes of dependent elderly. Philips's commitment to businesses that serve an aging population goes far beyond the home-monitoring service Lifeline, the Massachusetts firm that sees the market for its services grow as the population ages. Philips's other ventures that bet on an aging world include businesses that provide telemedicine that lets people have their vital signs watched from afar. Have a history of heart attacks, strokes, or arrhythmia? Philips and others offer real-time cardiac monitoring that follows you wherever you go. They also make defibrillators for the home, so that family members can snap heart attack victims back to life in ways that were once the sole province of paramedics and emergency room doctors. The company offers a line of advanced imaging equipment that is particularly good at detecting what ails older people and a special line of lighting for senior residences that helps people find their way when they leave their beds at night.

Philips and its competitors in the global home-health-care market benefit from an innovation boom aimed at commercializing technology suited to an aging population that craves independence at nearly any cost. Researchers at Concordia University in Pittsburgh have developed a suit of clothes lined with sensors that can link a family member or caregiver to sensors on a bedridden relative's body so that the body functions of the disabled person activate related sensations, called "mood memos," in the suit of the concerned person wearing the device. In effect, it creates a physical overlay of the sick person in the body of the well person. One sign of optimism for the growing market is the establishment of the Aging Technology Alliance, which despite its name is a Silicon Valley consortium of companies devoted to developing *new* technology for older people and their families.

The World Is Flatulent

Change is also coming to the way places for the aged are designed. At the annual convention of the American Association of Homes and Services for the Aging, health-care providers, equipment makers, architects, and home builders came together to create a house in which an impaired older person, living alone, could still host family gatherings. The kitchen had counters low enough to allow someone in a wheelchair to chop carrots. A pneumatic bottle opener helps pop open a bottle of wine, and the stove uses induction heating that can make a pot simmer but will never burn a hand that touches it. The floor is built to safely absorb a person's fall, and has sensors underneath to detect such an incident. With a push of a button, the kitchen cabinets over the counters descend slowly on hydraulic arms so that a can of tomato paste sitting at the back of the top shelf comes into easy reach. The bed can monitor every bodily function of sleeping ninety-year-olds, and even roll them over when they've been too still.

In the future, bathrooms will change, too. Toilets will sport stylish handrails, lift and drop on command, and even spray water in places that older people have a hard time reaching. And because the physical effects of age befoul the air, the toilet deodorizes its bowl, its user, and the room.

The Aging Workforce Meets
the Age of Forced Work

If there are a few people in their fifties and sixties sitting at the table, they are likely to be in good health and can count on at least another decade, or even two, of being in fine fiddle. Advertisements for communities, centers, and health clubs that promote active aging often use fit people in their fifties as their models. The women have nicely cropped gray hair and sleeveless blouses that show toned arms and streamlined curves. The men have hair, good teeth, and knit sweaters around their low-BMI frames. For the men at the table in their fifties, this ideal makes them excited, nervous, and envious. They may have as little a chance of looking like the advertisements of former swimsuit models as school-yard basketball players have of looking like LeBron James. Yet lifestyle changes now can still pay off in a better quality of life in the long run. Their medical budgets may be growing, but the money spent on care and prevention, on protecting their arteries, the excision of precancerous bits, and managing chronic diseases works so well that they perform ably at work, on the playing field, and in bed, too.

The sixty-year-olds don't feel markedly different physically from the fifty-year-olds, though their complaints build incrementally. If they worked physically taxing, repetitive jobs, they now have a hard time keeping up with younger people at work. Their bosses have been knocking on their doors with early retirement schemes for a few years now and they may finally be interested.

Finding a fun place to retire might sound good. Or perhaps a new, less physically demanding job or business, even if it pays less. Europeans, Americans, and east Asians have different but equally strong opinions about working past the typical retirement age. If schnitzel, bouillabaisse, or Yorkshire pudding is on the table, polls say that the overwhelming preference is to keep retirement ages where they are (as young as sixty but very slowly being legislated higher), and to stay retired once out the door. In the United States and east Asia, large numbers want to work longer, perhaps in new jobs, but the Asians want it most of all.

There is no global consensus on when retirement ought to begin, because there is no age that works equally well for everyone. Some people hit senior citizen status and possible retirement by reaching fifty (i.e., Chinese women in many jobs), or sixty (the French), or sixty-two (Greeks and early retirees in the United States), or sixty-five (Germans). In practice, as we have seen, retirements often start earlier, pushed by combinations of buyout packages and other income support that ends work for older employees. Add to that the fact that their work lives and financial futures are not nearly so certain as they once thought. Many jobs, even ones that once seemed solidly embedded in their local economy, have proved fleeting.

The Value of Age Discrimination

What to do? Can a world with more older people become an easier place for older people to work? Age arbitrage is now an essential strategy for businesses trying to compete in the global economy. If the companies that engineer the magic combination of younger workers and low wages win, management will continue to look for ways to jettison older, higher-wage workers. The fates of the people and businesses visited in the pages of this book suggest that places with proportionately bigger older populations suffer the most aggressive forms of age arbitrage. Whole industry sectors move out of these aging places to new locales that are well stocked with younger, eager workers. Even marginal differences matter. When the world's favorite young, low-cost locales of a generation ago (Taiwan, Hong Kong, Mexico, Central America, the Philippines) got a little older and a little more expensive, other places (China, Vietnam, India, Bangladesh) moved in and the former hot spots had to change their games. Some succeeded, others languished. Failing to consider how to discriminate against an aging local workforce is itself a management failure, because the rest of the productive world is genius at finding new ways to cut older people smaller parts of the economic pie.

If the holiday dinner is held near U.S. and European company towns where local workers were once "family," or Asian manufacturing centers formerly committed to "lifetime employment," a favorite topic that used to dominate discussion—how everyone is doing at work—is off the table. It might even be studiously avoided, so as to avoid arguments between new parents and the newly retired. The sorest points are how younger workers at the nearby company start at wages far below the former going rate, and that early retirees—whom the government helped ease out—get bigger monthly checks than young full-timers.

The perceived need in companies to shed older workers is a bind for everyone. If governments did not support jettisoned workers, the workers might still be cut.* Or, as in Japan, they might be kept on as younger workers get frozen out of jobs they could otherwise claim. Japan may be one of the best places in the world to grow old. But Japan's older people are also among the most vulnerable to want. One in five Japanese over age sixty-five lives in poverty. That reality helps explain why older Japanese people are so eager to stay in the workforce.

One way the collectivist cultures of many Asian and Mediterranean countries help their elderly is by allowing them to stay within long-standing social networks. Yet as University of Chicago psychologist John Cacioppo has observed, the people marginalized in collectivist cultures are even more prone to loneliness and despair. For older workers, the inner drive for a job, at any wage, and the chance to socialize, may also give employers license to pay older people less and reduce their status at work.**

The alternative for the older worker is isolation—which, as we've

* Without government support, noted Mark Haas of Duquesne University in Pittsburgh, a majority of workers in the industrialized world would be left poor. Prior to the advent of Social Security in the United States, poverty among the elderly was severe and people over sixty-five were poorer than any other age group. Today, the elderly fare as well as any group (poverty among children is the highest). In addition to the half of retired Americans who live on their Social Security payments, more than half of the households in Europe report they have nearly no money put aside. In France and Germany, government money accounts for nearly two-thirds of the after-tax income of older people; even small cuts in payments would push large numbers into the ranks of the poor.

** An easy way of knowing if a society is individualistic or collectivist, Cacioppo says, is by watching how people eat. If people don't mind often eating alone in restaurants, they are individualistic. If they feel the need to eat in groups and spend a lot of time passing plates of food, it's collectivist.

seen in the case of Japanese Big Junk and Soggy Leaves, can happen even at home with one's spouse. And increasingly for those who live alone. Everywhere in the aging world, but in Asia most of all, the number of solitary older people is climbing fast. Work can offer an escape from want, and also from emotional pain. In a world where families are shrinking, the lure of the workplace for older people may grow, and with it so may their willingness to accept a reduced wage, short hours, or menial work below their skill levels. There are alternatives. As the people in Sarasota know better than anyone, volunteer and social opportunities can substitute for a whole world of work, minus the money.

But there is another reality. Large numbers of people are unable to extend their careers. Upbeat literature promoting older workers often trucks out impressive statistics on the able and willing, but conveniently skirts the corollary figures on the less able and less willing. Although four in ten Americans over sixty-five say they are in excellent health, that leaves a large majority who say they are not. Health is probably the biggest impediment to full-time work. Multiple chronic diseases are common. Most are manageable enough to let people function well in most of their life activities. High blood pressure and a little arthritis won't keep a lawyer from his desk or a nurse from her station. But over time, the conditions compound. And when a slew of conditions do not conspire against an able person, they may conspire against a loved one who needs care. That is why flexible working conditions help older workers and why many mature adults cannot hold a job, even as they rate themselves as fully functional.

Social Insecurity

The adults in their later sixties at the table now meet nearly every legal and formal definition of old. If they live in a country where they are eligible for social security, now they get it. Their government's ability to pay it worries them. When they were young they took to the streets distrustful of governments run by old men and screamed to protest fat-cat capitalism and American imperialism. In France, Spain, Germany, middle America, and in some Asian capitals, the same group is back on the streets protesting, depending on the place, on measures again related to the welfare of their generation. Now the enemies are the welfare state and, again, global capitalism, which underwrites and overstretches the states. Signs and banners declare that older citizens are the unfair victims of state austerity plans. Their protests do not collide with those of the caregivers on the march, but their agendas do.

As the baby boomers move toward the last quarter of their lives, a demographic dénouement building for decades begins to play out. Its unfolding has been foretold in the population numbers for years, but the opening act transpired with force between 2007 and 2010. Boomers and their parents were the tragic heroes as the promises of a good society and a generous state collided with their own greed in the financial and housing markets unraveled in a series of spectacular collapses and near collapses. The sovereign debt crises in Europe, revolving political crises in Japan, the implosion of financial markets, the public debt of the United States, depressed housing markets nearly everywhere, and the rise of China as banker and broker to the world seemed at last to shake the world into the recognition of the magnitude and consequence of its aging demographic.

And yet China's new financial clout flows from its opposition to supporting its citizens in old age. Indeed, China's industrial policy seems built on a refusal by the state and industry to contribute meaningfully to the late-life needs of anyone (except for government workers), whether they are still working or not. The Chinese government says the country is still too poor to move to a more comprehensive social safety net, but it is the financial sacrifices of its people that are making China the financial juggernaut that more advanced welfare states turn to for billions of dollars in loans in their times of need. The other side of that same coin is that China attracts global companies looking to escape their obligations to aging workers at home. And then, when the financial footing of the countries that are losing their middle-class jobs gets undercut, the industrial state, namely China, that has best resisted pension regimes and other social benefits for its people ascends.

Lately, however, young Chinese workers have shown some signs that this system cannot stand and that they are unhappy with their lot in the world's age arbitrage schemes. In early 2010 discontent boiled up in a way seemingly orchestrated to show how China's young are enlisted to play off against older workers elsewhere. At Foxconn, a Taiwan-based electronics manufacturer that employs eight hundred thousand people, a series of ten suicides over six months rocked both the company and its global customers. Apple Computer, which employs Foxconn to make its products, came under attack because the popularity of its iPhones and iPads reportedly required workers to put in punishing stretches of overtime without commensurate increases in pay. The workers' despair over the long hours, the lack of benefits, and the low pay seemed reflected in the public sadness of the suicides. Not only did the deaths attract a predictable chorus against the exploitation of the workers, but also more widespread concern. Foxconn's woes were headline news, not just because some workers are treated harshly—that's old news— but also because the Foxconn story offered a perspective on the vast scale of sophisticated manufacturing that has been moved to places where workers' futures are so expendable. One of Foxconn's first reactions to the suicides was to suspend the only meaningful "pension plan" its line workers had, "the suicide pension" that paid families who sons or daughters killed themselves.

The Foxconn story also struck a chord because it came at a time of alarming rates of youth unemployment, general downward pressures on wages, and when workers with pensions and benefits were being pushed off the assembly lines and out of offices. And overall, the stories offered a stark look at a world where the fates of the young and old, near and far, are both bound together and also ruthlessly pitted against each other. Other factories in China, including a Honda plant, saw workers take the extraordinary step of going on strike, an exceedingly dangerous proposition in the authoritarian country of China; but perhaps less so when striking a Japanese company, which the Chinese government would be loathe to side with. At the insistence of the Chinese government, Honda had to up both pay and benefits. China, which had, in part, ridden to its position as the world's banker by providing the rest of the world's companies an escape from paying the higher wages and benefits of older workers at home, was now facing the nascent demands of workers at home clamoring for more income security in their own lives. One reason for the workers' anxiety may be that they see how poorly their parents were provided for in booming China. So far, no home-grown Chinese companies have come under a similar spotlight, though their practices can be far worse than those typical of large foreign companies. China is unlikely to let worker unrest spread far beyond a few foreign firms. That would threaten its newfound strength. We have entered an age when a state's economic power relates directly to how it chooses to provide for its population in old age, and China's frugality makes it stronger and stronger in relation to other countries where the costs of pensions and health care feed oceans of debt.

The reality of globalization and aging workforces hits directly at the idea of the bountiful state. Private pensions and flush public coffers seemed inviolable when countries had large, young workforces and their future competition from younger, larger, globalized competitors remained out of view. Globalization itself proved to be a mass, sophisticated form of age discrimination that undercut older workers, forced many states to support them as companies moved jobs, and reduced wages for those thrust out of the manufacturing economy. The wreckage of world financial markets may yet reverse and democratic governments may come to their senses and adjust state finances and retirement regimes to put promises in line with what they can realistically pay for. But when the price is paid, however, the family members in their fifties and sixties, and those younger, will bear the costs.

No matter how nations sort out their strained finances, the choice will have consequences that bear strongly on power relationships among nations. First, governments ruling over aging populations have two choices on how to spend their treasure. They can either provide for their aging population and triage their expenses on all else—defense, schools, infrastructure, etc.—or lower their commitments to provide for aging populations and then spend more on everything else. Europe is choosing the former, China the latter.

The long-term geopolitical scenarios are not easy to map out. In one school of thought, put forth by Richard Jackson and his colleagues at the Center for Strategic and International Studies, the aging of the world has a destabilizing influence on world affairs because it makes Japan, Europe, and the former Soviet states weak and strategically irrelevant, and thus ineffectual both as geopolitical rivals to the United States and as partners who might be needed to police poorer but much younger and more restless states. Europe and Japan, which have been "free-riders" alongside U.S. military spending, will, in this view, be forced by domestic politics to scrimp on defense even more. China will, Jackson believes, become too burdened by its aged population long before it can achieve great power status. The United States will have to find a way—and a way to pay—to police the world for the long run or give up the Pax Americana. That feeds into the dangers of failed states that have rejected globalization or been overlooked by it. The Cold War will be gone forever, yet the restless hordes will get more restless.

Mark Haas, of Duquesne University in Pittsburgh, lays out a slightly different scenario. In his view, the great costs of pensions and services that will be born by every industrialized country, including China, will offer the world a "Geriatric Peace," and the geopolitical ambitions of formerly bellicose states will fade as they age. In such a world, Haas believes, the ability of the United States to maintain (and disrupt) world order will be higher than ever. Haas also sees dangers from developing countries with large numbers of unemployed youth, especially men, and where religious and political ideologies foment radicalism. But he adds that those threats will tend to be local, since those dangerous places can only be so dangerous without allies that have war machines that match up to those of the United States.

The Future of Young People in an Old World

The complexities of global aging strain human comprehension. How can voters be asked to weigh measures that spare them the greed and uncertainty of the world financial system, which is arguably the most complex entity created by mankind? When experts with years of advanced training in multiple disciplines cannot come close to an agreement on what makes a workable system for an aging society, that fact seems like a good argument for socking more money away, and maybe for hiding at least a little gold under the floorboards. Or failing that, developing the intellectual capital of one's children, and one's self, to the hilt, so that the family possesses valuable, portable assets at all times.

The people in the aging world know as much. Education has replaced a big family as the world's preferred insurance for old age. If governments and the private sector creak under the weight of their commitments to provide social insurance, health care, and pensions, people are likely to have fewer children and to push even harder to educate them. Everywhere in the aging world there is hand-wringing over how to encourage parents to have more than one child. Even in China, where one child is the law, policy makers fret over how to reverse it. And yet it is hard to see how, in an urban world where people are forced to be their own insurance, the wheels of global aging could begin to turn the other way.

The Aging World: A Giant Feedback Loop

But there is yet another nearly inevitable but largely unseen scenario in a world that is committed to both supporting an aging population through welfare states and to skirting—through globalization strategies—the costs borne by the private sector. It is that the world will age far faster than even the most aggressive predictions offered by the world's governments and international organizations. Indeed, the world is now in a vast feedback loop in which the countries that now strike the world—and the military analysts that worry about them—as uneasily young, may in turn be counted among the fastest-aging places of all.

Let us again consider, in brief, the factors that change young societies into aging ones. Some lead to people living longer while others encourage them to have fewer children. To begin, there's literacy, preferably followed by enough years of education to allow people to read and follow instructions in a modern workplace. There's public health care for individuals. Moving a large segment of the population off farms, where their productivity is low, and into cities and factories, where their productivity is much higher, is a crucial stage, too. And then there are the powerful effects of allowing women to reach for better education and jobs.

As it turns out, the features of aging societies also look a lot like a checklist for globalization. Since the middle of the twentieth century, the countries that have most successfully grown from largely poor agrarian economies into formidable, modern, globally engaged industrial states have run through these steps. They did not run through them in order to age, of course. They did so because that was the recipe for meeting the needs of the rest of the world if they were to do business in a wider sphere and eventually compete on equal terms. If you want to sell manufactured goods to the U.S. or European market, you had better do your best to replicate the productive machinery of the U.S. and European economies. Make things better, or cheaper, but do so by besting the successful players at their own game. Reinvent your poor country, not their rich ones.

Japan was first. Japan wrote the postwar playbook. It grew to near superpower status by outmodernizing the modern world. But it took nearly half a century for the country to travel from being one of the youngest on earth to being one of the oldest. Then came a slew of others, including Korea, Taiwan, China, and Vietnam. Each adopted the same approach. Japanese competition pushed American companies to have their own global strategies to drive down costs and increase production. Foreign investment drove the early urbanization and industrialization of China, and China made a concerted effort to replicate the features of the Japanese and Western industrial economies on a scale that would match anything else in the world. Between Japan's postwar transformation and China's, the process sped up enormously. Every time the needle on the compass moved to the next spot that could offer young, low-cost industrial workers, the pace of the transition quickened, and so did the transition from young country to aging one. New shop-floor technologies that accelerated production were a part of the mix, as were improved air travel and telecommunications. But so, too, was the urgency of the aging world to move jobs and production to where young workers, by the tens of millions, could be used to replicate the labors of older workers at home and in the other aging, increasingly expensive places where they produced.

Now China is feeling the squeeze of a shrinking labor force and has one of the world's most rapidly aging populations. The pressures and promises of globalization have moved on to India, and the resulting effect there on aging has been one of the fastest yet. In the most recent census, India is now aging even faster than China. Many countries in Africa look like they are at the beginning of a development boom (often financed with Chinese investment). The continent is already faced with looming crisis as the numbers of elderly there grows geometrically, but if development and globalization seize upon Africa as it did east Asia, it may become the most rapidly aging place of all.

And so, as the aging world looks to the younger world for an economic safety valve, it puts in place the ever-gaining forces of global aging, with all its peril and promise.

Meanwhile, we must not succumb to the fear that our planet is in irreversible decay. It contains, after all, more of what we desire most—our own lifetimes. Few people want to live forever, but most of us want to live longer, and better. Given the spread of life-extending medicine, public health programs, and health-care literacy, many of us *will* live longer and better lives. Are we lucky then? If the answer is yes, then we must confront the paradox that is the Shock of Gray: the luckiest world is also the neediest one. And although the aging world is the sum of choices made by large populations, how we navigate the future of this world—how we love and care for ourselves and those we cherish—will also be an intensely personal matter.

One Last Story

Two years have passed since my now eighty-three-year-old mother saw penguins in Patagonia and danced giddily at her grandsons' Led Zeppelin tribute concert. For three years, she's lived alone in the suburban house my father designed and built for them in the 1980s. She still plants herbs and vegetables on one side of the yard and fills the other with jonquils and tulips. Inside, the upstairs room where my father kept his papers is rarely visited. A stain from a bottle of

India ink he spilled when he was weak still blackens his old desk. Lightbulbs need changing. The room holding the hot water heater flooded and nearly caused a fire.

The house is getting older, my mother says, and older houses need upkeep. She admits it is hard for her on her own. Her vision is failing and she no longer drives at night. "I feel more helpless," she admits.

But my father did build the house, and living in it keeps him near. My mother misses him. On his birthdays she asks her children to tell stories about him. Three years is not a long time, but the mood of the house and the neighborhood has changed. When my father died, she had lots of company from her nearby friends. They invited her over, and she had them to the house. They traded plantings, walked the nearby parks, and discussed their children. Out of that big group, now just one couple, friends for sixty years, is still nearby. The rest have left for predictable reasons: death, illness, the attraction of a warmer clime, or better care in a senior residence or with a child in another city.

Now my mom hears that the last nearby friends will move into a life care facility near their son in Colorado. "It makes me so sad," she says. She complains she doesn't know anyone close enough to the house for a small dinner party anymore.

My mom is resourceful, though. She recently bought a small apartment near the city center where she can walk to the plays, concerts, and movies she loves. One goal of the apartment was to be closer to her children and grandchildren. So far that is going according to plan. The Led Zeppelin–playing boys visit, as do her two granddaughters when they have breaks from college, though sometimes my mom has to chase them down. She has dinners for the family and she is close enough to join her children weekly in our homes.

But there's another need her move was meant to fill. The apartment was meant to lure my mother's older, widowed eighty-nine-year-old sister into the city so that they could go to the concerts together and have sleepovers. They bicker with each other a bit, but they could not be closer, these two elderly women who were girls together back in the 1940s.

That was the idea. But something happened: on a beautiful night last spring, over dinner in a street-side café, my aunt turned to my mother and asked her name. Shocked at first, my mother took my aunt's hand and told her that she was her sister. My aunt wondered aloud if it were true and asked my mother to share her maiden name. She did. My aunt nodded and asked my mother to write her name and number on a piece of paper so that they might get together for dinner some time.

In the next few days the flurry of activity that accompanies a person's unraveling began; calls to relatives and doctors, hurried arrangements with care facilities, and evaluations of finances, all while dealing with my aunt, who only recognized her family inter-mittently but sensed enough to know her life was changing fast. The clearest thing she said was that she wanted to go to bed to die.

My mother, a preternatural optimist who embraced the care of my father night and day for years, went to the big house and wept as none of us had seen her weep before. The weekend following the crisis with my aunt happened to be the college graduation of my daughter, an event my mother helped to make possible. When asked if she thought that we ought to cancel a party to celebrate, she insisted that was silly. When asked if she'd like to skip the party, she again said no, quite emphatically.

"I don't know if I'll dance with the kids at this one," she said, "but I might."

I was glad to hear that, and even more glad when I saw my mother dancing with my children. The time was precious, we all knew, for the years go by so fast.

ACKNOWLEDGMENTS

From the beginning, this book has been the beneficiary of the vast generosity of the people who are named within its pages and a very great number who are not. As I worked on the project I was often asked what I felt while writing a book about aging. My overriding feeling has been one of gratitude. The territory of *Shock of Gray* is womb to tomb and around the world, and the circle of people I have talked to on the topics herein is as unbounded as the circle I've traveled in while reporting it. My acknowledgments must begin with a universal thank-you to all who have heard me talk about this project since it began, and who generously shared their personal insights, intimate family stories, intimate bodily functions, and their hopes and fears. Thanks go also to the many who spoke frankly about the economics of their families, businesses, and communities. Some of the people I owe great thanks to are not mentioned in these acknowledgments because I thought it best to keep their confidences, or was asked to. I have no doubt I have left out people that I should have included and will regret not mentioning. The acknowledgments also skip over most of those mentioned in the body of *Shock of Gray*, either by their real names or pseudonyms, but that does not diminish my gratitude to them. This book, which offers my observations mixed with the insights granted to me by others, is, in the beginning and the end, my responsibility, so in addition to thanks I say none of its faults are owing to anyone who helped me. I am to blame for its shortcomings.

The idea for *Shock of Gray* grew out of discussions with my longtime friend, coach, collaborator, and editor, Colin Harrison, who has read nearly all my work, unpolished and otherwise, since he brought me into *Harper's Magazine* sometime in the last century before either of us imagined an aging world had anything to do with us. The subject of this book was decided on in conversations with Colin following *China, Inc.,* in which the discussion of the aging of China always stood out to both of us as a window to a far larger theme, perhaps one in which China's rise itself was, in many ways, a subset. He encouraged me to consider fleshing out the global implications of the change, and the result seemed too important, too compelling, and too interesting to resist. Throughout, Colin heard me out on germinating ideas and consistently energized the investigation with his curiosity, intellect, and verve. Thank you also to Susan Moldow, Nan Graham, Roz Lippel, Kelsey Smith, Paul O'Halloran, Kate Lloyd, and Katie Rizzo. Sloan Harris, who, back when he began representing me, said that he hoped to remain my agent until both our thoughts turned to retirement, has earned his wish, though not yet in the way he meant. Sloan has been an indispensable partner in this book, bringing his intelligence, professional and personal experience, and levelheaded counsel at every stage. Sloan does not just stick by his charges, he provides the glue that keeps body and soul together.

Jim Petersen, whom I have long counted on for his good judgment, laserlike ability to focus on what's important, and knack for synthesizing my writing for me, read every word of the manuscript in pieces as I wrote them, and suggested a slew of ways to expound on and add energy to the arguments, which I duly followed. I cannot overstate the importance of the long discussions in Hyde Park with Jonathan Zeitlin of the University of Amsterdam and Gary Herrigel of the University of Chicago. They helped me see how big the topic could be and, because Jonathan and Gary have such all-encompassing intellects, both gave me a basis on which to continue my reporting and a standard to shoot for.

Laura L. Carstensen, at Stanford University's new, but already outstanding, Center on Longevity, offered me the resources of the center just as I was getting my research under way, and granted me a way to jump-start the project by leveraging the center's network of scholars and supporters. Carstensen and her colleagues at the center, with their commitment to an interdisciplinary approach to aging that reaches well beyond social science and medicine, were particularly comprehending and supportive of the broad net of my research. Also at Stanford, Steve Goldband, who both championed my work and challenged my assumptions, helped me explore, often together with him, the deep resources of the university and Palo Alto in general. Adele Hayutin, the director of the center's Global Aging Program, introduced me to the trends in data unfolding in her research, and saved me embarrassment by offering skepticism at some grand, untested theories of mine that, with her in my head, I ultimately rejected. Carol Winograd opened my eyes to challenges in the practice of geriatric medicine and impressed on me the dangers of polypharmacy. Carol Dweck offered me a menu of tough questions to pursue in my research that informed me from beginning to end.

In each of the major geographic sections of this book I was blessed to have wonderful guides and mentors. (I will skip over those already mentioned in the text.) In Sarasota, I benefited from the friendship and advice of Kerry Kirschner, the city's former mayor who is now executive director at the Argus Foundation. Kerry went into high gear following our initial phone conversation, putting his considerable network at my disposal, and just as important, offered a long view of the community during my visits to the city. Tim Dutton and Kim Weaver at SCOPE were also enormously helpful. Their work to make Sarasota a national incubator for business and services for the elderly helped me see beyond the upscale service economy in the city. Also helpful was Dr. Bob Windom, who led me around to various care facilities in town. Dr. Kevin O'Neil, Art Mahoney, and Tom Oliver lent me their time and invaluable insights, too. George Spector, whose family runs what must be one of the finest communities of manufactured homes, kindly introduced me to the promise of that lifestyle and to active, caring residents who know how to get the most from their lives in Florida. Kathy Black of the University of South Florida, Sarasota, took time to explain peculiarities of the Florida service economy. Cheli and Bob Diamant and Harriette Bayer were my family away from home in Florida.

In Japan, my great friend and teacher Yoichi Kanamaru led me through city and country to show me the everyday implications of aging in his country. Kanamaru's cheer, optimism, and faith in human nature helped me see the resourcefulness of his countrymen as they deal with a world that, demographically, has turned upside down. His own company, Happy Elder, reflects his spirit with many projects designed to help older Japanese express their sentiments and tell their stories in ways that are creative and affirming. He made me feel that my journey in Japan was ours to share. Osamu "Sam" Senna, who translated *China, Inc.* into Japanese, also served, along with his insightful and generous wife, Reiko, as my host and cultural interpreter in Japan. Yukari Shinoda, my intrepid interpreter in Tokyo, led me into the world of her young adult friends in the theater, and never, or almost never, flinched as I asked her to help me delve into Japan's demimondes. I am also indebted to my friends Julia Adeney Thomas, associate professor of history at Notre Dame, for offering invaluable leads in Japan, and to David Leheny, professor of East Asian Studies at Princeton, for offering perspective on the divides among generations in Japan. I am grateful to the group of farmers—nearly all of them named Takahashi—in the beautiful Kuromori village, outside Hokuto City, for the day-long welcome and programs they arranged for me to get a glimpse at their endangered lifestyle. Gregory A. Boyko, then president of Hartford Financial Services Group in Japan, offered a sophisticated, data-driven view of financial life for Japan's retirees, and his own considerable wisdom on the mind-set of Japanese adults who learned from experience that speculation with retirement savings is a fool's game. Greg's love for the country and his commitment to the future of his clients struck me as an ideal template for the global financial services industry. Rick Moody at AARP encouraged me to go to Japan for that organization's international conference on aging in Asia, out of which grew many valuable leads. Rick also proved a great teacher, source, and sounding board back in the United States.

In Spain, I was lucky to have the always cheerful and inventive Diego Salazar at my side as reporter and interpreter while in Madrid and Guadalajara. In Barcelona, the astounding Daniel Sherr, who can translate, in any direction, in eight languages, took me to places where he needed, at one time or another, to use every one of them. While in Spain, a series of scholars, activists, and officials lent me time and expertise to understand their country. I am particularly indebted to Juan Díez-Nicolás of the World Values Survey; José Ignacio Fernández Martínez, general director of Senior Citizens of the Madrid Community; Margarita Delgado of the Spanish Council for Scientific Research; and Rosa Morena Roldan of the UGT labor union.

In Rockford, my research began with a generous invitation from Janyce Brennan Fadden, the indefatigable president of the Rockford Area Economic Development Council. Janyce, together with Tonya Lamia, Mark Podemski, Eric Voyles, and Carrie Zethmayr, let me ask every question I wanted and always found people and places that would deliver the answers. Their love for the community, all its treasures and warts, made me see the creative flow in a city that knows booms and busts all too well. My research in Rockford also depended on the kind contributions of Darcy Bucholz, executive director of the Boone and Winnebago Counties Workforce Investment Board; Father Burt Absalon and Jovie Reyes, who introduced me to Rockford's remarkable Filipino community; and Christine Villanueva, who helped bring added perspective to the interviews. Also thanks to Lucy Rivas of OSF Saint Anthony Medical Center, Allan Bojsen at Danfoss Drives, and Carmen Jordan. I am indebted to the Elling family for offering me a look at how church life in Rockford sustains the social life of the city's aging population.

In China, I was helped immeasurably by a crackerjack crew of translators, researchers, and interpreters. Many of them came through the help of my great friends Toni Piëch, Li Gong, and Isabel Cho, who were also patient enough to listen to how a foreign writer hoped to capture the demographic realities of modern China through the stories of families. In Beijing, Yuan Shang, then a student at Tsinghua University in Beijing, helped me through the first round of research by working a fruitful combination of grassroots and institutional sources. She was followed in Beijing by Zaoli Zhang, another terrific Tsinghua student who went on to graduate work at the University of Michigan. Both Yuan and Zaoli had an uncanny ability to put people at ease so that they could communicate the humor and pathos in their stories. My research in Nanjing was aided immeasurably by Jan Kiely at the Hopkins-Nanjing Center for Chinese and American Studies at Nanjing University. Jan, now at the Chinese University of Hong Kong, allowed me a place to stay; access to the best, most open research library in China; and a passport to the considerable expertise at the singular Hopkins-Nanjing Center and at Nanjing University. I was fortunate enough at the center to have several sessions with geographer Alana Boland of the University of Toronto, whose wide-ranging knowledge touched on nearly every aspect of my research and who helped me lay out the trail of my inquiry, both through the city of Nanjing and through the academic literature. The journey through Nanjing and environs was made possible by the help of Yuquiong Wang, a graduate student at the center who served as researcher and interpreter, and whose experience in the business world offered a valuable vantage point that helped in our interviews. In Shanghai, for this book, as for *China, Inc.*, the Shanghai Academy of Social Sciences provided a deep bench of experts and other support for the research, all arranged by one of the nicest, busiest, and unflappable people in Shanghai, Li Yihai, the director of the academy's International Programs Office.

No group thinks about the daily desires and needs of the older population, from active to infirm, more thoroughly than the talented and thoughtful architects and designers at Perkins Eastman. In Beijing, Chicago, Pittsburgh, and Cambridge, Massachusetts, Brad Perkins, Dan Cinelli, and David Hoglund gave me lessons in thinking as they do and introduced me to the extraordinary living spaces they create. I owe thanks, too, to Lori Miller at Perkins Eastman, who helped me see how the global view of architects can change one's everyday vision of an aging world. Also on the housing front, I owe thanks to Sarah Mashburn at the American Association of Homes and Services for the Aging (AAHSA) for connecting me to that organization's events and network of service providers.

I could not have completed the project without much help from people in my home base, Chicago. Adam Hubble helped with research on memory, and, coincidentally, performed the Herculean task of setting up a record system that proved over and over again to be a lifesaver. Jim Rank ordered my office and my thoughts and kept straight a gargantuan file system as only someone with mastery of the material could. Jim's good humor and work ethic were contagious, too. Jim's late father, Hugh Rank, offered smart, cheerful, and brave observations from the front, offering the point of view of a man science and nature told to give up but who never gave in. I miss Hugh, though he is a model for lifelong engagement, despite the odds, that will live on. Jeff Markos worked hard to keep me from veering from *The Chicago Manual of Style*. The insatiably curious Ricardo Rivera helped me plumb Spanish-language material and conduct interviews, and he provided valuable research and editorial assistance. Jim Burton and Carrie Fung, lawyers in the office of the Cook County Public Guardian, with the support of Robert Harris, who is the public guardian, made extraordinary efforts to show me a world of abandonment and abuse that may have otherwise remained unseen. They also showed me how good guys do good. Jonathan Perman of the Evanston Chamber of Commerce helped me understand the needs and strategies of communities that work hard to retain their best, most valuable young workers.

During a research trip to the United Kingdom, I was graciously greeted by Ian Philp, then in his former role as the U.K.'s national director for Older People in the Department of Health, and by Baroness Sally Greengross and Doctors Chris and Mata Foote, all of whom tutored me in the welfare of the aged in that nation and walked me through just how different the systems for senior citizens are on opposite sides of the Atlantic. Sir John Grimley Evans received me in Oxford at Green College, where he provided a recent history of geriatric medicine in the United Kingdom (in which he has been a central player) and insights into the puzzling divide in scholarship on aging, which can pit those with a medical point of view against those who distrust it. In London, Hodson and Luda Thornber graciously hosted me and lent me the use of their marvelous flat.

To explore the status of aging rural states in the United States, I made two trips to North Dakota. The first was the result of an invitation from Sheryl Wilkerson at Ygomi LLC. Traveling the state with Sheryl and Chris Daly of Verety LLC offered a look at how the most remote places can forge a place in the global service economy. On a subsequent visit to the state, I had the benefit of help and hospitality from the terrific crew at the North Dakota Trade Office, especially from its chief, Susan Geib, and with significant contributions from Larry White and Jeff Zent.

Acknowledgments

I must also thank friends and family who helped and listened to me during a time when I turned nearly every conversation to discussions of themes in *Shock of Gray*. I stopped being surprised at how impressively deep their knowledge of my topics proved to be, or at how their insights could propel me along. An incomplete list of helpful friends includes Brian and Jan Hieggelke, Alan Thomas, Dan Buettner, Alex Benes, Gioia Diliberto, Jeffrey Frankel, Richard Miller, Shelagh Lester-Smith, Mike Timperley, Irene Sherr, Amy Briggs, Lisa Kaplan, Kevin Lawler, Michael Cen, Tony Cardoza, Carrie Goldberg, David Epstein, and Gay Young Cho. Jonah Breslau helped with key research into the effects of metabolic syndrome on young people. My thanks also go to Linda Diamond Shapiro, Melissa Salter, Robb Mandelbaum, Jonathan Black, and John Koten, who offered thoughtful suggestions on the manuscript.

Acknowledgments often end with the group that means the most to authors, their family. I follow that form, though in my thanks my family deserves the top spot. In a book that is largely about family, mine has not just been a great support but an interactive test group for ideas. My mother, Elaine Fishman, proved unsurprisingly inspirational but surprisingly frank in her assessment of her older cohort. My sisters, Nancy Fishman and Jeanne Fishman, looked for interesting subjects for me to interview. My identical twin brother, Zack Fishman, worked to keep me cheerful while providing a cloned version of myself to observe. My children, Elly and Adam, both of them good writers and editors, took excited interest in the topic and the reporting of the book. They propped me up when I needed intervention and stayed a comfortable distance when that was prudent, too. My wife, Sara Stern, reviewed my ideas before they hit the page and reviewed my writing after. She clipped items from the news, rounded up experts, and reminded me every time I headed for the liquor cabinet or refrigerator between meals, and when I became stuck in my chair too long, that I was writing myself into the scariest parts of the book. She lovingly saw the writing of *Shock of Gray* as an education for both of us in how to be there for each other, fully engaged, as we face the private and public changes coming as we age. I can think of nothing for which I can be more grateful.

NOTES

INTRODUCTION: GRAY NEW WORLD

1. National Institute on Aging, U.S. National Institutes of Health, "Exploring the Role of Cancer Centers for Integrating Aging and Cancer Research," http://www.nia.nih.gov/ResearchInformation/Conferences AndMeetings/WorkshopReport/Figure4.htm. Also see National Institute on Aging, National Institutes of Health, U.S. Department of Health and Human Services, and U.S. Department of State, "Why Population Aging Matters: A Global Perspective," p. 3, http://www.nia.nih.gov/NR/rdonlyres/9E91407E-CFE8-4903-9875-D5AA75BD1D50/0/WPAM_final pdftorose3_9.pdf.
2. Panel on a Research Agenda and New Data for an Aging World, Committee on Population, and Committee on National Statistics Division of Behavioral and Social Sciences and Education National Research Council, Commission on Behavioral and Social Sciences and Education (CBASSE), "Preparing for an Aging World: The Case for Cross-National Research," National Academy Press, Washington, DC, 2001, p. 33, http://www.nap.edu/openbook .php?record_id=10120&page=R1.
3. Interview with S. Jay Olshansky, April 23, 2009.

CHAPTER 1:
GREETINGS FROM FLORIDA, GOD'S WAITING ROOM

1. Maine Development Foundation for the Maine Economic Growth Council, "Measures of Growth in Focus, 2008," p. 9, http://www.mdf.org/publications/Measures-of-Growth-in-Focus-2008/117/.
2. Robert Friedland, Katherine Mack, Susan Mathieu, and Laura Summer, "Measuring the Years: State Aging Trends & Indicators," Data Book, Center on an Aging Society, Health Policy Institute, Georgetown University for the National Governors Association Center for Best Practices, Aging Initiative,

State Policies for a Changing America, August 2004, http://www.nga.org/por-tal/site/nga/menuitem.9123e83a1f6786440ddcbeeb501010a0/?vgnextoid=83601d8692cc2010VgnVCM1000001a01010aRCRD.

3. "Aging: The Possibilities," community report, SCOPE, Sarasota, 2009, p. 8.

4. Interview with Jeff LaHurd. Also see Jeff LaHurd, *Sarasota, A Tropical History* (Charleston, S.C.: History Press, 2006). Jeff LaHurd, who heads the History Center in Sarasota, has written several books on his hometown. Even when others cite local lore, they often have gleaned it from LaHurd's volumes, which are recommended often. Jeff was also kind enough to spend time filling me with many stories and facts.

5. Oliver Sacks, *Musicophilia: Tales of Music and the Brain*, (New York: Random House, 2007), 249–250, 382.

6. Michael McDonough, "Selling Sarasota: Architecture and Propaganda in a 1920s Boom Town," *Journal of Decorative and Propaganda Arts* 23 (1998): 21.

7. Roscoe Burton, introduction to *Boom in Paradise*, by T. H. Weigel and Alfred H. King (New York, 1932), xi (quoted in McDonough, "Selling Sarasota," 11–31).

8. Jeffrey LaHurd interview, September 5, 2009.

9. McDonough, "Selling Sarasota," 17–23.

10. Philip Zimbardo and John Boyd, *The Time Paradox* (New York: Free Press, 2008), 240.

11. Caroline Oliver, *Retirement Migration, Paradoxes of Aging* (New York: Routledge, 2008), 11.

12. Nancy Morrow-Howell, "Civic Service Across the Life Course, Generations," *Journal of the American Society on Aging*, San Francisco (Winter 2006–07): 37–42.

13. John A. Krout, "'Active' Aging: Good for Elders?," *Aging Today*, American Society on Aging, San Francisco (March–April 2008): 7, 9.

14. "A Tale of Two Older Americas: Community Opportunities and Challenges," AdvantAge Initiative, Center for Home Care Policy and Research, Visiting Nurse Service of New York, 2003, http://www.vnsny.org/advantage/resources.html#report.

15. Age Wave and Harris Interactive, "Retirement at the Tipping Point: The Year That Changed Everything," 2009, www.agewave.com/Retirement TippingPoint.pdf.

16. Mike Vizvary, "Top Doctors," *Sarasota*, June 2006, http://www.sarasota magazine.com/Articles/Sarasota-Magazine/2006/06/Top-Doctors.asp.

17. Sarasota County Public Hospital District, Financial Statements and Supplemental Information, September 30, 2008 and 2007, http://www.docstoc.com/docs/3953617/SARASOTA-COUNTY-PUBLIC-HOSPITAL-DISTRICT-Financial-Statements-and-Supplemental-Information.

NOTES

CHAPTER 2:
A BRIEF HISTORY OF LIVING MUCH LONGER

1. Guy Brown, *The Living End: The Future of Death, Aging and Immortality* (Hampshire, U.K.: Palgrave Macmillan, 2007).
2. McNeill's work is cited in Bruce A. Carnes and S. Jay Olshansky, *The Quest for Immortality* (New York: W. W. Norton, 2003), 83, 87.
3. Linda Maria Gigante, "Death and Disease in Ancient Rome," address before the Innominate Society of Louisville, May 9, 2000, http://www.innominate society.com/Articles/Death%20and%20Disease%20in%20Ancient%20Rome .htm.
4. Brown, *The Living End*, 28.
5. David Boyd Haycock, *Mortal Coil* (New Haven, Conn.: Yale University Press, 2008), 9.
6. Ibid., 30.
7. I am indebted to Keith Montgomery, geographer and geologist at the University of Wisconsin, Marathon County, for his clear explanation of the compounding of factors that have led to longer life spans. See http://www .marathon.uwc.edu/geography/Demotrans/demtran.htm.
8. "Teens and Sex: The Role of Popular TV," Henry Kaiser Family Foundation, Menlo Park, California, July 2001.
9. "Global Age-Friendly Cities: A Guide," World Health Organization, Geneva, 2007.
10. European Union, "State of European Cities Report," May 2007, http:// nl.sitestat.com/eukn/s?themes.urban_policy.state-european-cities_3358 .external&ns_type=clickout&ns_url=http://ec.europa.eu/regional_policy/ sources/docgener/studies/pdf/urban/stateofcities_2007.pdf.
11. David Galea Vlahov and Nicholas Sandro Freudenberg, "The Urban Health 'Advantage,'" *Journal of Urban Health, Bulletin of the New York Academy of Medicine* 82, no. 1 (2005): 1.
12. "The Challenge of Slums: Global Report on Human Settlements 2003," United Nations Human Settlements Programme, p. 74.
13. Ibid., 2.
14. Wang Zhenghua, "Malnutrition Hits 30 Percent of Poverty Stricken Children," *China Daily*, October 8, 2005, p. 2.
15. Anthony Kuhn, "Nutrition Program Boosts Poor Students in China," NPR Weekend Edition, May 31, 2009, http://www.npr.org/templates/story/story .php?storyId=104753329.
16. Galea Vlahov and Sandro Freudenberg, "The Urban Health 'Advantage,'" 3–4.
17. Zachary Zimmer, Toshiko Kaneda, and Laura Spess, "An Examination of Urban Versus Rural Mortality in China Using Community and Individual Data," *Journals of Gerontology Series B: Psychological Sciences and Social*

Sciences 62:S349-S357 (2007), http://psychsoc.gerontologyjournals.org/cgi/
content/full/62/5/S349.

18. Clive Thompson, "Why New Yorkers Last Longer," *New York*, August 13, 2007.
19. Carnes and Olshansky, *The Quest for Immortality*, 83, 87.
20. Ibid., 87.

CHAPTER 3:
SEÑOR MOMENT: SPAIN'S DISCOVERY OF AGE

1. J. M. Lamet and E. Valdehita, "Inmobiliarias, inversores y bancos ya acumu-
   lan más de 3 millones de pisos," Expansion.com, September 9, 2009, http://
   www.expansion.com/2009/09/15/economia-politica/1253049638.html?a
   =2219269347c984063561f999b6e7e134&t=1253080789.
2. Mario Izquierdo, Juan F. Jimena, and Juan A. Rojas, "On the Aggregate
   Effects of Immigration in Spain," *Documentos de Trabajo,* no. 0714, Banco
   de España, Eurosistema, 2007, p. 7.
3. Trinidad Vicente, "Latin American Immigrant to Spain, Evolution and Legal
   Status of Latin American Immigrants in Spain (1999–2009)," Network
   Migration Migrative Citizenship Education, www.migrationeducation.org
   /48.1.html?&rid=162&cHash=96b3134cdb; and Tom Worden, "Spain
   Sees Sixfold Increase in Immigrants Over Decade," *Guardian,* February 8,
   2007, http://www.guardian.co.uk/world/2010/feb/-8/spain-sixfold-increase-
   immigrants.
4. Fabien Zamora, "Spaniards Return to Farm Work as Unemployment Soars,"
   AFP, March 3, 2009.
5. Population Reference Bureau, http://www.prb.org/Datafinder/Geography/
   Summary.aspx?region=221&region_type=2.
6. Xavier Medina, *Food Culture in Spain* (Kindle edition), Greenwood, 2005.
   Medina is senior researcher in the Department of Mediterranean Cultures at
   the European Institute of the Mediterranean in Barcelona, and general editor
   of the journal *Anthropology of Food*.
7. OECD, "The World at a Glance 2009," 19–44.
8. Antonia Trichopoulou, "Modified Mediterranean Diet and Survival:
   EPIC-Elderly Prospective Cohort Study," *BMJ*, doi:10.1136/bmj
   .38415.644155.8F, April 8, 2005.
9. BMJ Group, "Eat Yourself Happy? Mediterranean Diet Link to Less Depression," *Guardian*, October 6, 2009, http://www.guardian.co.uk/lifeandstyle/
   besttreatments/2009/oct/06/eat-yourself-happy-mediterranean-diet-link-to-
   less-depression.
10. Angelo Aquista and Laurie Anne Vendermolen, "The Mediterranean Pre-
    scription," Ascent Group, 2006, p. 7.

11. Ibid.

12. M. Ruiz-Canela López, et al., "Cured Ham and the Incidence of Cardio-vascular Events, Arterial Hypertension or Weight Gain," *Medicina clínica* (Barcelona), October 5, 2009.

13. C. N. Lopez, et al., "Costs of Mediterranean and Western Dietary Patterns in a Spanish Cohort and their Relationship with Prospective Weight Change," *Journal of Epidemiology and Community Health* (November 2009 issue, published online in September 2009), http://jech.bmj.com/cgi/content/abstract/63/11/920?maxtoshow=&HITS=10&hits=10&RESULTFORMAT=&fulltext=Mediterranean+diet&searchid=1&FIRSTINDEX=0&sortspec=relevance&resourcetype=HWCIT.

14. E. L. García, et al., "Social Network and Health-Related Quality of Life in Older Adults: A Population-Based Study in Spain," *Quality of Life Research: An International Journal of Quality of Life Aspects of Treatment, Care and Rehabilitation* (Netherlands, March 2005): 511–520.

15. Merry Pool and Jelena Kopanja, "Reverse Migration: Ecuador Lures Immigrants Back Home from U.S. and Spain," Feet in 2 Worlds, New School, New York City, September 2009, http://feetin2worlds.wordpress.com/2009/09/04/reverse-migration-ecuador-lures-immigrants-back-home-from-u-s-and-spain/; and Priscila Guillan, "Live Wires: Latin Americans Living in Spain Drive a Big Business in Sending Money Home," *Entrepreneur*, July 2006, http://www.entrepreneur.com/tradejournals/article/150956129.html.

16. Panel on a Research Agenda and New Data for an Aging World, Committee on Population, and Committee on National Statistics Division of Behavioral and Social Sciences and Education National Research Council, Commission on Behavioral and Social Sciences and Education (CBASSE), "Preparing for an Aging World: The Case for Cross-National Research," National Academy Press, Washington, DC, 2001, p. 33, http://www.nap.edu/openbook.php?record_id=10120&page=R1.

17. Benedict Moran, "U.S. Ecuador: Luring Migrants Home an Uphill Battle," Interpress Service, October 27, 2009, http://ipsnorthamerica.net/news.php?idnews=2627.

18. J. D. Mujica and R. G. Talavera, "Domestic Service and the Labour Market in Spain: A Gender Perspective on Migration," *Migration and Ethnic Themes (Migracijske i etničke teme)* 12 (2006): 96, http://hrcak.srce.hr/file/8133.

19. "Spain Ends Search for Immigrants," BBC News, July 21, 2007, http://news.bbc.co.uk/2/hi/europe/6910049.stm.

20. Jan Mansvelt Beck, "The Place of Language and the Language of Place in the Basque Country," Proceedings of the 4th International Symposium on Bilingualism (Somerville, Mass.: Cascadilla Press, 2005), http://www.lingref.com/isb/4/115ISB4.PDF.

21. Angeles Escrivá, "Peruvian Families Between Peru and Spain," paper deliv-

ered to 2003 meeting of the Latin American Studies Association, Dallas, March 27–29, 2003, lasa.international.pitt.edu/Lasa2003/EscrivaAngeles .pdf. Escrivá addresses the issue of migrants' willingness to return in the context of Spain's community of migrants from Peru.

22. Vicente Pinilla, María-Isabel Ayuda, and Luis-Antonio Sáez, "Rural Depopulation and the Migration Turnaround in Mediterranean Western Europe: A Case Study of Aragon," *Journal of Rural and Community Development* 3, no. 1 (2008), http://www.jrcd.ca/viewarticle.php?id=107.

23. Claudine Attias-Donfut and Francois-Charles Wolff, "Families, Aging and Social Policy: Intergenerational Solidarity in European Welfare States" (Chiara Saraceno, editor) (Cheltenham, U.K.: Edward Elgar Publishing Limited, 2008), 260.

24. Euroresidentes, "News from Spain: Spaniards Don't Want to Work After 60," January 15, 2008, http://www.euroresidentes.com/Blogs/2008/01/ retirement-in-spain.html.

25. OECD Labour Force Statistics by Age and Sex, 2006, stats.oecd.org/wbos/ default.aspx.

26. Agar Brugiavini, "Early Retirement in Europe," *European Review* 9, no. 4 (2001): 501.

27. Willi Leibfritz, "Retiring Later Makes Sense," *OECD Observer*, no. 234, October 2002, http://www.oecdobserver.org/news/fullstory.php/aid/824/ Retiring_later_makes_sense.html.

28. Steve Doughty, "Our Elderly Worse Off Than Romania's: British Pensioners Among the Poorest in Europe," *Daily Mail*, July 26, 2009, http://www .dailymail.co.uk/news/article-1202378/Our-elderly-worse-Romanias-British- pensioners-poorest-Europe.html.

29. Margarita Delgado, Gerardo Meil, and Francisco Zamora López, "Spain: Short on Children and Short on Family Policies," *Demographic Research* 19, article 27: 1059–104, http://www.demographic-research.org/volumes/ vol19/27/. Also, interview with Margarita Delgado, Madrid, February 11, 2008.

30. Jesús María Gómez García and Margarita Rico González, "Rural Development, Population Aging and Gender in Spain: The Case of Rural Women in the Autonomous Community of Castilla y León," ERSA conference papers, no. ersa04p379, European Regional Science Association, Vienna, 2004, http:// www-sre.wu-wien.ac.at/ersa/ersaconfs/ersa04/PDF/379.pdf. The data is drawn from Castilla-León (which borders Sigüenza's region of Castilla–La Mancha).

31. Interview with Margarita Delgado.

32. García and González, "Rural Development."

33. A good summary of the Ministry's White Paper and the history leading up to the Personal Autonomy and Dependent Care Law passed in 2007 can be found at the Eurofound website, http://www.eurofound.europa.eu/areas/ labourmarket/tackling/cases/es001.htm.

34. Xavier Bosch, "Spain Faces Massive Decline in Population," *BMJ*, April 1, 2000, p. 891, http://www.ncbi.nlm.nih.gov/pmc/articles/PMC 1117826/320(7239).

CHAPTER 4:
HOW WE (REALLY) DO (CONTINUOUSLY) AGE

1. Steven Austad, *Why We Age: What Science Is Discovering About the Body's Journey Through Life* (Hoboken, N.J.: Wiley, 1999), 126–127. Austad's book is an excellent overview of the modern theories on aging, concluding with his description of the Free Radical Hypothesis of Aging. My understanding of the science of aging, such as it is, owes much to Austad's clear and entertaining explication.
2. Stephen T. Sinatra, James C. Roberts, and Martin Zucker, *Reverse Heart Disease Now* (Hoboken, N.J.: Wiley, 2008), 44.
3. "Occasional Memory Loss Tied to Lower Brain Volumes," *Science Daily*, October 7, 2008, http://www.sciencedaily.com/releases/2008/10/081006180515.htm.
4. U.S. National Institutes of Health, National Institute on Aging, Conference Report, "Exploring the Role of Cancer Centers for Integrating Aging and Cancer Research," August 6, 2009, http://www.nia.nih.gov/Research Information/ConferencesAndMeetings/WorkshopReport/Introduction. htm. The quoted materials constitute the NIA's report's summary of NCI data.
5. Selected sources for this list:

National Institute on Aging, http://www.nia.nih.gov/.
Mayo Clinic, http://www.mayoclinic.com/health/aging/IIA00040.
Mark H. Beers, editor in chief, *Merck Manual of Health and Aging* (Whitehouse Station, N.J.: Merck Research Laboratories, 2004).
Leonard Hayflick, *How We Change with Age* (New York: Ballantine Books, 1994).
Sue V. Saxon and Mary Jean Etten, *Physical Change and Aging*, third ed. (New York: Tiresias Press, 1994).
Janet Horn and Robin Miller, *The Smart Woman's Guide to Midlife & Beyond* (Oakland, Calif.: New Harbinger Publications, 2008).
Waneen W. Spirduso, Karen L. Francis, and Pricilla G. MacRae, *Physical Dimensions of Aging*, second ed. (Champaign, Ill.: Human Kinetics, 2005).
"Five Ages of the Brain," *New Scientist*, April 4, 2009.
"Generations," *Journal of the American Society on Aging*, Special Issue on Falls and Fall-Related Injuries, Winter 2002–2003.

Albert Lee, "Aging Populations: A Rising Challenge in the Treatment of Osteoarthritis," *Hong Kong Medical Diary, Drug Review* 10, no. 10 (October 2005).

National Collaborating Centre for Chronic Conditions (UK), "Osteoarthritis, National Clinical Guideline for Care and Management in Adults," Royal College of Physicians, London, 2008.

Shlomo Stern, Solomon Behar, and Shmuel Gottleib, "Aging and Diseases of the Heart, Circulation," *Journal of the American Heart Association,* Dallas, TX (2003), 108:e99-e101, http://circ.ahajournals.org/cgi/content/full/108/14/e99.

6. Wray Herbert, "The Aging of Loneliness," Association for Psychological Science (previously the American Psychological Society), August 9, 2007, http://www.psychologicalscience.org/onlyhuman/2007/08/aging-of-loneliness.cfm.

7. Robert S. Wilson, Kristin R. Krueger, Steven E. Arnold, Julie A. Schneider, Jeremiah F. Kelly, Lisa L. Barnes, Yuxiao Tang, and David A. Bennett, "Loneliness and Risk of Alzheimer Disease," *Archives of General Psychiatry* 64, no. 2 (February 2007): 234–240, http://archpsyc.ama-assn.org/cgi/content/full/64/2/234.

8. Dean Ornish, "Love Is Real Medicine," *Newsweek*, October 3, 2005, http://www.newsweek.com/id/50926. And "Loneliness: A Molecule?," *Science Today at the University of California,* September 24, 2007, http://www.ucop.edu/sciencetoday/article/16508.

CHAPTER 5:
JAPAN, LAND OF THE MISSING SON

1. Akihiko Matsutani, *Shrinking Population Economics, Lessons from Japan,* trans. by Brian Miller (Tokyo: International House of Japan, Inc., 2006), xiii.

2. Mari Yamaguchi, "Japan's Rising Elderly Rates Stoke Worries About Pensions," Associated Press, May 24, 2008, http://www.redorbit.com/news/business/1401014/japans_rising_elderly_rates_stoke_worries_about_pensions/#.

3. Nohiro Ogawa, Robert D. Retherford, Rikiya Matsukura, "Demographics of the Japanese Family, Entering Uncharted Territory," *The Changing Japanese Family,* edited by Marcus Rebick and Ayumi Takenaka (New York: Routledge, 2006), 23.

4. Abdel R. Omran, "The Epidemiologic Transition: A Theory of the Epidemiology of Population Change," *Milbank Memorial Fund Quarterly* 49, no. 4 (2005): part 1, 1971, 509–38. See http://www.milbank.org/8304.html for the link to the article.

5. Ogawa et al., 22.
6. Ibid., 31.
7. *Kyodo News*, "Centenarians in Japan Soon to Exceed 30,000 for First Time," Japan Times Online, September 15, 2007, http://www.msnbc.msn .com/id/9324619/.
8. "Number of Japanese Living Past 100 Growing," Associated Press, September 13, 2005, http://www.msnbc.msn.com/id/9324619/.
9. Matsutani, *Shrinking Population Economics,* 8.
10. U.S. Census Bureau, "Projections by Age, Sex, Race and Hispanic Origin" (2004), www.census.gov/ipc/www/usinterimproj/.
11. Tokyo Municipal Government website, http://www.metro.tokyo.jp/ ENGLISH/PROFILE/overview03.htm.
12. Population of Japan in 2000, Statistics Bureau Ministry of Internal Affairs and Communications, http://www.stat.go.jp/english/data/kokusei/2000/final/ hyodai.htm#21.
13. Marcus Rebick and Ayumi Takenaka, *The Changing Japanese Family* (New York: Routledge, 2006), 3.
14. Misa Izuhara, "Changing Families and Policy Responses to an Aging Japanese Society," in Rebick and Takenaka, *Changing Japanese Family,* 165.
15. Ibid., 164.
16. Nick Clark, "Education in Japan," *World Education News and Reviews* 18, no. 3 (May/June 2005).
17. Gender Equality Bureau, Cabinet Office, Japan, http://www.gender.go.jp/ english_contents/women2004/statistics/s02.html. In 1980, 12.3 percent of female high school graduates in Japan went on to higher education compared to 39.3 percent of the males. In 1985, the numbers were 13.7 percent and 38.6 percent, respectively. In 2003, 34.4 percent of female high school graduates continued on, compared to 47.8 percent of the males.
18. Brian Shih, "Japan's Colleges Ease Entrance Exams," NPR *Weekend Edition*, May 21, 2005, http://www.npr.org/templates/story/story .php?storyId=4661500; and Tak Kumakura, "Japanese Schools on the Hunt for Students," *International Herald Tribune*, October 10, 2006, http:// www.iht.com/articles/2006/10/10/bloomberg/sxstudents.php; and David Cyranoski and I-han Chou, "Winds of Change Blow Away the Cobwebs on Campus," *Nature*, no. 429 (May 13, 2004): 210–214; and Bryan Walsh, "Economics 101," *Time*, July 4, 2005, http://www.time.com/time/magazine/ article/0,9171,501050711-1079524,00.html.
19. Naoki Ikegami, "Tokyo: A Pathbreaker in Longterm Care?," Chapter 19 in *Growing Older in World Cities, New York, London, Paris and Tokyo*, eds. Victor G. Rodwin and Michael K. Gusmano (Nashville: Vanderbilt University Press, 2006), 301.
20. Rebick and Takenaka, *Changing Japanese Family*, 8.
21. Joe Chen, Yun Jeong Choi, and Yasuyuki Sawada, "How Is Suicide Differ-

ent in Japan," Center for International Research on the Japanese Economy, Faculty of Economics, University of Tokyo, November 2007, www.mfj.gr.jp/web/lunch_seminar/documents/20080226–Sawada.pdf.

22. Yoshitomo Takahashi, Hideto Hirasawa, Keiko Koyama, Osamu Asakawa, Matazo Kido, Hiroshi Onose, Masahiko Udagawa, Yoshihiro Ishikawa, and Masato Uno, "Suicide and Aging in Japan: An Examination of Treated Elderly Suicide Attempters," *International Psychogeriatrics* 7 (1995): 239–251.

23. J. Sean Curin, "Suicide Also Rises in the Land of Rising Sun," *Asia Times*, July 28, 2004, http://www.atimes.com/atimes/Japan/FG28Dh01.html.

24. Izuhara, "Changing Families and Policy," 165; and Nicholas Kristof, "Once Prized, Japan's Elderly Feel Abandoned and Fearful," *New York Times*, August 4, 1997, http://query.nytimes.com/gst/fullpage.html?res=9F00E6D C133DF937A3575BC0A961958260; Justin McCurry, "Japan's Age-Old Problem," *Guardian*, April 17, 2007, http://www.guardian.co.uk/world/2007/apr/17/japan.justinmccurry. McCurry describes how the apartments became de facto senior residences and dangerous places for single older men, who ended up living in squalor and often turned up dead. The group enlisted local newspaper delivery services as a kind of deathwatch, urging deliverymen to alert the association when papers piled up. "Tokiwadaira has become a cheap place for old people who live alone. They move here when they retire and find it difficult to make friends. In many cases they're dead within a few years," said the head of a newly formed residents' association. "Go into their homes after [retired men] die and you can see straight away that most can't cook, clean, or do laundry. They don't even throw out their rubbish. They have no idea how to look after themselves."

25. "Declining Birth Rates Raising Concerns in Asia," *East-West Center News*, April 10, 2004, http://www.eastwestcenter.org/news-center/east-west-wire/declining-birth-rates-raising-concerns-in-asia/.

26. http://www.taisei-ind.jp/index.html.

27. Matsutani, *Shrinking Population Economics*, 4.

28. In mid-2008, the Nikkei Stock Average Index, the indicator of choice in the Japanese stock market, was about 30 percent lower than it had been at the market's peak in the late 1980s.

29. Marcus Rebick, *The Japanese Employment System: Adapting to a New Economic Environment* (Oxford, U.K.: Oxford University Press, 2005), 129–131.

30. Ibid., 125. Rebick cites OECD figures from 2003.

31. Roger Pulvers, "Forsake Not the Elderly, for They Bear a Great Bounty," *Japan Times*, August 12, 2007, http://search.japantimes.co.jp/cgi-bin/fl20070812rp.html.

32. Suvendrini Kakuchi, "Labour-Japan: Old Is Gold as Workforce Shrinks," Interpress Service New Agency, February 26, 2008, http://ipsnews.net/news.asp?idnews=36721.

33. David Alwinkle/Arudou Debito's website (http://www.debito.org/) details his decision to seek Japanese citizenship. Debito is married to a Japanese woman with whom he has two children. A specialist in immigration law for foreigners in Japan, he is also author of *Handbook for Newcomers, Migrants and Immigrants*.
34. Sharon Noguchi, "Hard Work, Furtive Living: Illegal Immigrants in Japan," *YaleGlobal*, March 2, 2006, http://yaleglobal.yale.edu/article.print?id=7067.
35. Katsuyuki Kawai (then Parliamentary Secretary of Foreign Affairs), speech at General Assembly of the Parliamentary Confederation of the Americas, Iguacu, Brazil, May 9, 2005, http://www.mofa.go.jp/region/latin/brazil/speech0505.html.
36. Jun Hongo, "Cabinet Interview, New Justice Minister: Hatoyama a Hawk on Death Penalty, Illegal Immigrants," *Japan Times*, September 4, 2007, http://search.japantimes.co.jp/cgi-bin/nn20070904a5.html.
37. Arudou Debito, "Treatment of Japan's International Residents, Problems and Solutions for a 21st Century Japan," 2007, http://www.debito.org/handout.html.
38. Martin Fackler, "Japan Faces Engineering Shortage," *International Herald Tribune*, May 18, 2008, http://www.iht.com/articles/2008/05/16/business/engineers.php.
39. Konica Minolta Annual CSR Report, 2007, 30–32.

CHAPTER 6:
CHEATING DEATH, ONE MOLECULE AT A TIME

1. Liz Szabo, "Aging Well Starts in Womb, as Mom's Choices Affect Whole Life," *USA Today*, June 30, 2009.
2. See Anders Forsdahl, "Commentary: Childhood Deprivation and Adult Mortality," *International Journal of Epidemiology* 31 (2002): 308, http://ije.oxfordjournals.org/cgi/content/full/31/2/308.
3. The account of the research on seasonality and the links of early childhood conditions to late life health is mainly drawn from Gabriele Doblhammer's thorough and engaging book tracing the history of research into the topic, *The Late Life Legacy of Very Early Life* (Berlin: Springer-Verlag, 2004).
4. Interviews with Tom Rando. Also see "Young Blood Revives Aging Muscles, Stanford Researchers Find," news release from the Stanford School of Medicine, February 16, 2005, http://med.stanford.edu/news_releases/2005/february/rando.htm.
5. Anthony Barnett and Helena Smith, "Cruel Cost of the Human Egg Trade," *Guardian*, April 30, 2006, http://www.guardian.co.uk/uk/2006/apr/30/health.healthandwellbeing.

6. Coco Ballantyne, "A Cut Above the Rest?: Wrinkle Treatment Uses Babies' Foreskins," *Scientific American,* February 12, 2009, http://www.scientific american.com/article.cfm?id=a-cut-above-the-rest-wrin.

7. "Ovarian Transplantation Restores Fertility to Old Mice and Also Lengthens Their Lives," *e! Science News,* June 29, 2010, http://esciencenews.com/ articles/2010/06/29/ovarian.transplantation.restores.fertility.old.mice.and .also.lengthens.their.lives. Also see Ian Sample, "Ovary Transplants Could Extend Women's Lifespan, Mice Study Suggests," *Guardian,* June 29, 2010, http://www.guardian.co.uk/science/2010/jun/29/ovary-transplants-women-lifespan-mice.

8. http://eyeborgproject.com.

CHAPTER 7:
THE TWISTING FATES OF THE
SCREW CAPITAL: ROCKFORD, ILLINOIS

1. Edna Bonacich and Juan David De Lara, "Economic Crisis and the Logistics Industry: Financial Insecurity for Warehouse Workers in the Inland Empire," *Change to Win,* February 18, 2009, www.warehouseworkers united.org/.../20090218-WarehouseWorkersPaper.pdf.

2. Monique Morrissey and Emily Garr, "Working the Graveyard Shift: Why Raising the Social Security Retirement Age Is Not the Answer," Economic Policy Institute, Briefing Paper #232, May 5, 2009, p. 13, http://www.epi .org/publications/entry/bp232/.

3. Steven Greenhouse, "65 and Up and Looking for Work," *New York Times,* October 24, 2009, http://www.nytimes.com/2009/10/24/business/ economy/24older.html.

4. Ruth Helman, et al., "The 2009 Retirement Confidence Survey: Economy Drives Confidence to Record Lows; Many Looking to Work Longer," Employee Benefit Research Institute, Issue Brief #328, April 2009, http:// www.google.com/url?sa=t&source=web&ct=res&cd=1&ved=0CAYQFjA A&url=http%3A%2F%2Fwww.ebri.org%2Fpublications%2Fib%2Findex. cfm%3Ffa%3Dibdisp%26content_id%3D4226&ei=npBPS7GPGJ HwNP6NwfwM&usg=AFQjCNHOVGouDtQKeo3EbDO7Vymy_ BzMXg&sig2=ynxa_N_3L6tnKKp6o_DpkA.

5. Kelly Evans and Sarah Needleman, "For Older Workers, a Reluctant Retirement," *Wall Street Journal,* December 8, 2009.

6. "Caregiving in the U.S.: Executive Summary," National Alliance for Caregiving and AARP, November 2009, http://assets.aarp.org/rgcenter/il/ caregiving_09_es.pdf.

7. Evans and Needleman, "For Older Workers, a Reluctant Retirement."

8. Sean F. Driscoll, "Tough Road to Adulthood for Jobless Teens," *Rock-*

ford Register Star, November 28, 2009, http://www.rrstar.com/archive/x1792915814/Tough-road-to-adulthood-for-jobless-teens.

9. V. Dion Haynes, "Blacks Hit Hard by Economy's Punch," *Washington Post*, November 24, 2009, http://www.washingtonpost.com/wp-dyn/content/article/2009/11/23/AR2009112304092.html.

10. Driscoll, "Tough Road to Adulthood for Jobless Teens."

11. Ibid.

12. Ruth Longoria Kingsland, "Recession Causing More Young Adults to Move Home," *Peoria Journal Star*, January 3, 2010, http://www.pjstar.com/news/x1444028591/Recession-causing-more-young-adults-to-move-home.

13. "Opportunity Returns," Northern Stateline Region, State of Illinois, October 2003, http://opportunityreturns.com/regional_plans/NorthernStateline_Regional_Plan.pdf (accessed in November 2009).

14. Richard Florida, *Who's Your City? How the Creative Economy Is Making Where to Live the Most Important Decision of Your Life* (New York: Basic Books, 2008).

15. Interview with Michelle Miller-Adams. Also see Michelle Miller-Adams, *The Power of a Promise: Education and Economic Renewal in Kalamazoo* (Kalamazoo, Mich.: W.E. Upjohn Institute and Grand Valley State University, 2009).

16. Sharon Stangenes, "On the Level: Single-Story Living Growing in Popularity Among Over-55 Home Buyers," *Chicago Tribune*, January 26, 2007.

17. William H. Frey, "Mapping the Growth of Older America: Seniors and Boomers in the Early 21st Century," *Living Cities Census Series* (Washington, DC, Metropolitan Policy Program, Brookings Institution, May 2007).

18. Glen P. Kenny, Jane E. Yardley, Lucie Martineau, and Ollie Jay, "Physical Work Capacity in Older Adults: Implications for the Aging Worker," *American Journal of Industrial Medicine* 51, no. 8 (2008): 610–625.

19. Leora Friedberg, "The Impact of Technological Change on Older Workers: Evidence from Data on Computer Use," *Industrial and Labor Relations Review* 56, no. 3 (April 2003), 511–529, http://www.jstor.org/pss/3590922.

20. Kevin Neuman, "Quit Your Job and Get Healthier? The Effect of Retirement on Health," *Journal of Labor Research* 29, no. 2 (June 2008): 177–201, http://www.springerlink.com/content/dg6271q10j775604/?p=af9593b10747465fa91981ef739996c0&pi=4.

21. Abdul Ali, et al., "What Entrepreneurs Are Up To," *Global Entrepreneurship Monitor*, 2008 National Entrepreneurial Assessment for the United States of America, Executive Report, Babson College and Baruch College (2009), p. 16, https://docs.google.com/viewer?url=http://www3.babson.edu/ESHIP/research-publications/upload/GEM_2008_US_Executive_Report.pdf.

22. Hughes M. Helm, Judith C. Hays, Elizabeth P. Flint, Harold G. Koenig, and Dan G. Blazer, "Does Private Religious Activity Prolong Survival? A

Six-Year Follow-up Study of 3,851 Older Adults," *Journals of Gerontology: Series A: Biological Sciences and Medical Sciences* 55, no. 7 (2000): M400–M405, http://biomedgerontology.oxfordjournals.org/content/55/7/M400.full.

23. AARP International, "Who Is Raising the World's Children? Grandparent Caregivers: Economic, Social and Legal Implications," April 4, 2008, remarks made by Amy Goyer at a panel discussion hosted by AARP International and the Aspen Institute Council of Women World Leaders on grandparent caregivers on March 11, 2008, at AARP headquarters in Washington, DC, http://www.aarpinternational.org/resourcelibrary/resource library_show.htm?doc_id=676636.

CHAPTER 8:
VULNERABLE, CHERISHED, FRAIL, KIND, BOTHERSOME, SWEET, EXPENSIVE, WISE, LONELY, AND IRRELEVANT: HOW DO WE SEE THE ELDERLY?

1. E. Arias, L. R. Curtin, R. Wei, and R. N. Anderson. United States Decennial Life Tables for 1999–2001, United States Life Tables. *National Vital Statistics Reports* 57, no. 1 (2008), National Center for Health Statistics, Hyattsville, MD, http://www.cdc.gov/nchs/products/pubs/pubd/lftbls/decenn/1999–2001.htm.

2. Charles Duhigg, "Shielding Money Clashes with Elders' Free Will," *New York Times*, December 25, 2007, http://www.nytimes.com/2007/12/24/business/24golden.html?fta=y.

3. Matthew G. Rhodes, "Age Estimation of Faces: A Review," *Applied Cognitive Psychology* 23 (2009):1–12, Wiley InterScience.

4. X. Geng, Z. H. Zhou, Y. Zhang, G. Li, and H. Dai, "Learning from Facial Aging Patterns for Automatic Age Estimation, Pattern Analysis and Machine Intelligence," *IEEE Transactions* 29, no. 12 (December 2007): 2234–40.

5. David J. Schneider, *The Psychology of Stereotyping*, Kindle edition (New York: Guilford Press, 2003), Locations, 224–228.

6. Ibid., 234–37.

7. Ibid., 175–178.

8. See Thomas M. Hess, Joey T. Hinson, and Elizabeth A. Hodges, "Moderators of and Mechanisms Underlying Stereotype Threat Effects on Older Adults' Memory Performance," *Experimental Aging Research*, North Carolina State University, April 1, 2009. Hess was interviewed about the paper by the News Office at North Carolina State University. For the press release see "Think Memory Worsens with Age? Then Yours Probably Will," April 22, 2009, http://news.ncsu.edu/news/2009/04/wmshessmemory.php.

9. Becca R. Levy, Martin D. Slade, and Thomas M. Gill, "Hearing Decline

Predicted by Elders' Stereotypes," *Journals of Gerontology: Series B: Psychological Sciences and Social Sciences* 61 (2006): P82–P87, http://psychsoc.gerontologyjournals.org/cgi/content/full/61/2/P82.

10. Levy allows for the possibility that other factors may help the elders in other cultures better preserve their hearing. One of the cultures where the elderly were revered is the Easter Islands, where there is little of the industrial din and pollution that Americans hear in the background their whole lives.

11. Amy J. C. Cuddy, Michael I. Norton, and Susan T. Fiske, "This Old Stereotype: The Pervasiveness and Persistence of the Elderly Stereotype," *Journal of Social Issues* 61, no. 2 (2005): 267–285.

12. Jeff Greenberg, Jeff Schimel, and Andy Martens, *Ageism: Denying the Face of the Future*, in *Ageism: Stereotyping and Prejudice Against Older Persons*, edited by Nelson, Todd (Cambridge, Mass.: MIT Press 2004), 27.

13. Robert Butler and Anti-Taskforce at the Longevity Center, "Ageism in America," 2006, http://www.ilcusa.org/pages/publications/ageism-sleep/ageism-in-america.php.

14. http://www.cnpea.ca/ageism.htm.

15. Writing in the February 9, 2009, issue of *The Nation*, William Greider argues that "Governing elites in Washington and Wall Street have devised a fiendishly clever 'grand bargain' . . . in the name of 'fiscal responsibility.' The government, they argue, having spent billions on bailing out the banks, can recover its costs by looting the Social Security system." Greider goes on to summarize the public campaign of billionaire investor Peter Peterson to create "fiscal reforms" to fill a purported $53 trillion hole in America's finances that is widening largely as a result of entitlement programs that serve the elderly. Greider argues that the proposals would "essentially dismantle Social Security" in order to benefit business. "The ugliest ploy in their campaign," Greider writes, "is the effort to provoke conflict between the generations."

16. Alice Wignall, "Keeping Body and Soul in Tune," *Guardian*, August 26, 2008, http://www.guardian.co.uk/lifeandstyle/2008/aug/26/healthandwellbeing.fitness. This article examines how singers perceive the effects on them. See S. M. Clift and G. Hancox, "The Perceived Benefits of Singing: Findings from Preliminary Surveys of a University College Choral Society," *Journal of the Royal Society for the Promotion of Health* 121, no. 4 (2001): 248–256.

CHAPTER 9:
CHINA: WILL IT GROW OLD BEFORE IT GROWS RICH?

1. Robert Fogel, "$123,000.000.000,000, China's Estimated Economy by the Year 2040. Be Warned," *Foreign Policy* (January/February 2010): 70–75.

2. Dadush, Uri, Stancil, Bennett, The G20 in 2050, International Economic Bulletin, November 2009, Carnegie Endowment for International Peace, Washington, DC, http://www.carnegieendowment.org/publications/index.cfm?fa=view&id=24195.

3. Zhao Chunzhe, "China's Elderly Population Reaches 167M," *China Daily*, January 29, 2010, http://www.chinadaily.com.cn/china/2010-01/29/content_9399043.htm.

4. David Pierson, "China's Elderly Will Overwhelm the Nation," *Los Angeles Times*, July 6, 2009, http://articles.latimes.com/2009/jul/06/business/fi-china-old6.

5. Howard French, "China Scrambles for Stability as Its Workforce Ages," *New York Times*, March 22, 2007, http://www.nytimes.com/2007/03/22/world/asia/22china.html.

6. Richard Jackson, Keisuke Nakashima, and Neil Howe, "China's Long March to Retirement Reform, The Graying of the Middle Kingdom Revisited," Center for Strategic and International Studies, April 22, 2009, p. 2.

7. Nicholas Eberstadt, "Growing Old the Hard Way: China, Russia, India," *Policy Review*, Hoover Institution, April/May 2006, http://www.hoover.org/publications/policyreview/2912391.html.

8. David E. Bloom, David Canning, Günther Fink, and Jocelyn E. Finlay, "Fertility, Female Labor Force Participation, and the Demographic Dividend," NBER Working Paper no. 13583, November 2007, http://www.nber.org/papers/w13583.

9. Tyrene White, *China's Longest Campaign: Birth Planning in the People's Republic*, 1949–2005 (Ithaca, N.Y.: Cornell University Press, 2006).

10. Jiang Jingxiong, Urban Rosenqvist, Wang Huishan, Ted Greiner, Lian Guangli, and Anna Sarkadi, "Influence of Grandparents on Eating Behaviors of Young Children in Chinese Three-Generation Families, *Appetite* 48, no. 3 (May 2007), http://www.sciencedirect.com/science?_ob=ArticleURL&_udi=B6WB2-4MJJBV8-1&_user=10&_coverDate=05%2F31%2F2007&_rdoc=1&_fmt=high&_orig=search&_sort=d&_docanchor=&view=c&_searchStrId=1211153990&_rerunOrigin=google&_acct=C000050221&_version=1&_urlVersion=0&_userid=10&md5=9d481b1fc9df41ee57c85fb98b8a9cd3.

11. AFP, "Caring for Mum, Dad Key to Career in China," Z News, April 9, 2007, http://www.zeenews.com/news364788.html.

12. AP Worldstream, "China Punishing Children Who Neglect Elderly Parents in Bid to Promote Filial Piety," January 11, 2006, http://www.accessmylibrary.com/article-1G1–76133898/caring-elderly-parents-polling.html.

13. Dalian News, "Lonely Couple Offer Grown Children 'Salary' for Visits," April 8, 2007, http://chinadigitaltimes.net/2007/09/lonely-couple-offer-grown-children-salary-for-visits-dalian-news/.

14. Qinwen Xu and Farooq Pasha, "The People's Republic of China, Sta-

tistical Profile," Sloan Center on Aging and Work at Boston College, November 2008, http://agingandwork.bc.edu/documents/CP05_Workforce_China_2008–11–13.pdf.

15. Yu Xie and Haiyan Zhu, "Do Sons or Daughters Give More Money to Parents in Urban China?" National Council on Family Relations, University of Michigan, *Journal of Marriage and Family* 71 no. 1 (2009): 175, http://dx.doi.org/10.1111/j.1741-3737.2008.00588.x.

16. Melinda Liu, "China's Empty Nest: An Aging Population Is Transforming the Family," *Newsweek*, March 10, 2008, http://www.newsweek.com/id/117840.

17. Interview with Yehua Dennis Wei, professor in the Department of Geography and Institute of Public Affairs, University of Utah, February 4, 2010. Also see Danlin Yu, "Wei's State Policy and Globalization of Beijing: Emerging Themes," *Habitat International* 30 (2006): 377–395.

18. Yunxiang Yan, *Private Life Under Socialism: Love, Intimacy, and Family Change in a Chinese Village, 1949–1999* (Stanford, Calif.: Stanford University Press, 2003).

CHAPTER 10:
GENERATIONS AT THE TABLE

1. Shuaizhang Feng, Alan B. Krueger, and Michael Oppenheimer, "Linkages Among Climate Change, Crop Yields and Mexico-U.S. Cross-Border Migration," Proceedings of the National Academy of Sciences, 2010, http://www.pnas.org/content/early/2010/07/16/1002632107#aff-1.

2. Lisa Eckenwiler, "Long-term Care and Migrant Health Workers: Considering Responsibilities," *George Mason University Global Studies Review*, March 2010, http://www.globality-gmu.net/archives/2040.

INDEX

INDEX

ABOUT THE AUTHOR

Ted C. Fishman's previous book is the international bestseller *China, Inc.: How the Rise of the Next Superpower Challenges America and the World*. Fishman's essays and reports have appeared in many of the world's most prominent journals, including *The New York Times Magazine, USA Today, National Geographic, Esquire, Money, Harper's Magazine, Inc., GQ, The Sunday Times* (London), and *Chicago Magazine*. He appears frequently on major broadcast networks, and his commentaries have been featured on Public Radio International's *Marketplace* and *This American Life*. A former floor trader and member of the Chicago Mercantile Exchange, he ran his own trading firm until 1992. He has been a visiting scholar at the Stanford Center on Longevity and a faculty director and lecturer with programs for global executives through Dartmouth's Tuck School of Business. As a speaker, he addresses audiences worldwide.

Ted Fishman has lived and worked in Japan and Indonesia. He is a graduate of Princeton University and currently lives in Chicago.